More Praise for Paul Loeb and *The Impossible Will Take a Little While*

"An anthology of some of the most powerful voices of our time." —*Boston Globe*

"Stop worrying, stop feeling sorry for humanity and read '*The Impossible Will Take a Little While*.'" —*Chicago Tribune*

"A powerful classroom resource that will help inspire your students to act." —American Association of Colleges and Universities

"Loeb has been doing wonderfully patient work, exploring the American conscience from the inside. I regard him as something of a national treasure." —Susan Sontag

"A must read." —*Teaching Tolerance*

"Hopeful, inspiring, and motivating. . . . May be required reading for us all." —*Sierra Club* magazine

"A book of essays meant to inspire people." —*Christian Science Monitor*

"A magnificent anthology celebrates hope, guts, and the power of taking action. . . . Loeb has compiled for us the words of 49 of the most gifted and heroic men and women of our time, 49 testimonials to stamina and compassion in the face of seemingly insurmountable odds, 49 reasons to keep hope alive in this time of frustration and fear." —*The Oprah Magazine* [Lead Review]

"An extremely important effort." —John Kenneth Galbraith

"This inspiring collection is such a song of hope in these difficult times." —Bonnie Raitt

"Inspirational . . . I pick and choose and savor my way through it." —*Phi Beta Kappa Key Reporter*

"Stunning insights . . . educational and inspirational." —*Seattle Times*

"A wonderful book, with some extraordinary folks contributing. It reminds us that darkness always comes before the dawn." —Reg Weaver, president, National Education Association

"For anyone worn down, *The Impossible Will Take a Little While* is a bracing double cappuccino!" —Barbara Ehrenreich

"The most important book I've worked on in my 36 years as an editor." —Chris Arden, *The Impossible*'s copy-editor

"A shot in the arm for all of us who feel withered by crisis and paralyzed with cynicism. . . . Every page sparkles with insight into how the most painful circumstances can drive us to our higher selves." —Aretha Williams, *San Antonio Express News*

"A compilation of essays, excerpts and exclamations from a wide range of people who have found hope despite all evidence to the contrary." —*Minneapolis Star Tribune*

"Moving essays and poems on how to maintain optimism in a post 9/11 world." —*Real Simple*

"Refreshingly empowering, healing, and amazingly inspirational. It touches the imagination, retrieves the faith, and is desperately needed by our country to provoke new hope and meaning. It is a glass half full for the cynic and the fearful, a compilation of vision for the complacent, and an antidote for the despondent—truly a must read for everyone." —*Steelabor*, United Steelworkers of America

"Reading this hymnbook of hope, one's heart cannot help but sing. I am moved and inspired by this magnificent book's rich stories and insights. They water the fragile, precious seed of hope, from which everything we love grows." —Vicki Robin, author, *Your Money or Your Life*

"This book embodies a new spirit of responsibility for the planet and those who inhabit it. We begin to sense what it might mean to treat the world as a sacred gift." —Bishop Thomas Gumbleton, former national president of Pax Christi

"An intelligent, impressive compendium of ideas and feelings that, if implemented, will lead to a far more civilized society." —Peter Matthiessen, author of *The Snow Leopard*

"Loeb's extensive personal interviews and traveling to campuses gives his work authenticity. The style of his writing makes his discoveries accessible." —Henry Louis Gates Jr., on Loeb's *Generation at the Crossroads*

"A powerful chorus of hope. Loeb introduces us to a community of heroic individuals who by their actions sustain themselves and can help inspire the rest of us. We gain courage knowing this community exists, acting at what Seamus Heaney calls the meeting point of hope and history, where what has happened is met by what we make of it." —Bill Meadows, president, Wilderness Society

"Paul Loeb is one of the finest spokespeople I know for a spiritually based citizen activism. A must read for people seeking to heal our country and the world." —Marianne Williamson

"Captures the way the fight for decency can change people and change circumstances, even when victory is still in the distance." —Rich Trumka, president, AFL-CIO

"A soul-stirring anthology which we guarantee will lift the spirits of anyone looking for reasons to carry on in the struggle to create a better world." —*The Lutheran*

"An impressive lineup. . . . [Explains] how and why to keep up the good fight—for whatever purpose—in the face of ridicule, violence, despair, bad odds, and/or unfavorable election results." —Madison, WI, *Capitol Times*

"A lot of smart people who have some influence on the course of history will read and admire you—and learn from you." —Kurt Vonnegut, to Paul Loeb

"Like few other chroniclers today, Paul Loeb uncannily captures the thoughts and hopes, inchoate though they be, of America. Loeb is a natural." —Studs Terkel

"A forceful testimonial to the unique power of hope." —Denis Hayes, founding coordinator, Earth Day

Loeb has brought together *The Impossible Will Take a While* with power and integrity. It is impossible to do justice to all the moving articles he has collected; one can only hope the collection will be widely used in schools and parishes across the country." —*The American Catholic*

"A book for the ravenous. Hope becomes a vision of a humane future that is already under way." —Robert Koehler, Tribune Media Services

"Everyone who believes in our humanity and the ideal of justice for all, but feels despair by the direction the world has taken will find their faith in our ability to serve the common good restored by Paul Loeb's symphony of powerful voices." —Charles Johnson, National Book Award winner, author of *Middle Passage*

THE IMPOSSIBLE WILL TAKE A LITTLE WHILE

Also by Paul Rogat Loeb

Soul of a Citizen
Living with Conviction in Challenging Times

Generation at the Crossroads
Apathy and Action on the American Campus

Hope in Hard Times
America's Peace Movement and the Reagan Era

Nuclear Culture
Living and Working in the World's Largest Atomic Complex

THE IMPOSSIBLE WILL TAKE A LITTLE WHILE

perseverance and hope in troubled times

edited by

PAUL ROGAT LOEB

BASIC BOOKS
A Member of the Perseus Books Group
New York

Published by Basic Books,
A Member of the Perseus Books Group

Books published by Basic Books are available at special discounts
for bulk purchases in the United States by corporations, institutions,
and other organizations. For more information, please contact
the Special Markets Department at the Perseus Books Group,
2300 Chestnut Street, Suite 200, Philadelphia, PA 19103,
or call (800) 810-4145, ext. 5000,
or e-mail special.markets@perseusbooks.com.

DESIGNED BY TRISH WILKINSON
Set in Goudy Oldstyle by Cynthia Young

Library of Congress Cataloging-in-Publication Data
The impossible will take a little while : perseverance and hope in troubled
times / edited by Paul Loeb.
pages cm
Includes bibliographical references and index.
ISBN 978-0-465–03173-3 (pbk.)—ISBN 978-0-465-03858-9 (e-book)
1. Social action. 2. Social change.
I. Loeb, Paul Rogat, 1952-editor of compilation.
HN65.I464 2014
303.4—dc23
2014005001

10 9 8 7 6 5 4

Contents

THREE: EVERYDAY GRACE

FOUR: REBELLIOUS IMAGINATION

FIVE: COURAGE IS CONTAGIOUS

SIX: THE GLOBAL STAGE

SEVEN: RADICAL DIGNITY

EIGHT: BEYOND HOPE

Introduction

I once heard Archbishop Desmond Tutu speak at a Los Angeles benefit for a South African project. He'd been fighting prostate cancer, was tired that evening, and had taken a nap before his talk. But when Tutu addressed the audience he became animated, expressing amazement that his native country, with its shameful history of racial oppression, had been chosen by God to provide the world with an unforgettable lesson in reconciliation and hope. Afterward, a few other people spoke, then a band from East L.A. took the stage and launched into an irresistibly rhythmic tune. People started moving to the music. Suddenly I noticed Tutu dancing away in the middle of the crowd. I'd never seen a Nobel Peace Prize winner, much less one with a potentially fatal illness, move with such joy and abandon. Tutu, I realized, knows how to have a good time. Indeed, it dawned on me that his ability to recognize and embrace life's pleasures helps him face its cruelties and disappointments, whether personal or political.

Few of us will ever match Tutu's achievements. But we'd do well to learn from someone who spent years challenging apartheid's brutal system of human degradation, has continued to speak out for justice since then, and yet remains lighthearted and free from bitterness. What allowed Tutu, Nelson Mandela, and untold numbers of unheralded South Africans to find the vision, strength, and courage to persist until apartheid finally crumbled? How did they manage to choose forgiveness over retribution while bringing to justice the administrators and executioners of that system? What similar strengths of spirit drove those who challenged entrenched racial segregation in the United States, or the dictatorships of Eastern Europe, Latin America, Egypt, and Tunisia? What now enables ordinary citizens to continue working to heal their communities and to strive for a more humane world, despite the perennial obstacles, the frequent setbacks?

We live in a time fraught with bad news. More than one in five children in America lives in poverty, and our country's economic inequality, the most extreme in the developed world, has grown to levels not seen in a hundred years. Our political system seems broken, captive to the greediest and most cynical. Almost every week brings an off-the-charts flood, drought, ice storm, hurricane, or forest fire, while scientists make clear that such events will continue to spiral out of control unless we address global climate change. Yet day-to-day demands of work, school, and family take so much of our attention that it's hard for us to engage such potentially overwhelming realities. Merely thinking about them is to flirt with despair.

And no one is immune, not even those whose occupations or passions directly involve helping others or bringing about constructive social change. For years, I've traveled throughout the country, lecturing to campus and community groups. Almost everywhere, I encounter people doing important work who nonetheless question whether their actions still matter, whether it's worthwhile to keep making the effort. I've heard this refrain from teachers struggling to help their students learn in crumbling inner-city classrooms; from nurses and doctors trying to deliver quality medical services while navigating bureaucratic mazes; from Chamber of Commerce members attempting to save small rural towns from going under; from eighteen-year-old students and eighty-year-old grandmothers.

Hope may actually be more beleaguered in the wake of a president who won the office in part by branding himself with it. Think of the once-omnipresent posters and stickers in which Obama's stylized portrait, as rendered by artist Shepard Fairey, appeared above the word *HOPE*. Too many of Obama's supporters expected him to live up to this iconic image; when his presidency didn't instantly transform American politics and key campaign promises remained unfulfilled, they retreated into demoralized withdrawal. We can debate how much the resulting spiral of disappointment was due to unrealistic expectations, Obama's shortcomings, the tenacity of his opponents, America's broken political structures, or the failure of Obama supporters to stay engaged following his initial election. But however we assess this particular president, the roller coaster of raised and dashed expectations has led many of us to conclude that political participation is a rigged and futile game.

Moments of doubt are inevitable, especially in a culture that embraces cynicism and mocks idealism as a fool's errand. But if we look at life through a historical lens, we find that the proverbial rock can be rolled, if not to the top of the mountain, then at least to successive plateaus. Indeed, simply pushing the rock in the right direction is cause for celebration. History also shows that even seemingly miraculous advances are in fact the result of many people taking small steps together over a long period of time. For every Desmond Tutu, there are thousands of anonymous men and women who have been equally principled, equally resolute in the same causes. Having over the years drawn inspiration from many of their stories, as well as from those of people whose names are more familiar, I created this book to invite readers to join a community of courageous souls stretching across the globe and extending backward and forward in time.

The writers assembled here have helped me maintain the belief that striving for a more humane world is worth the effort. Again and again, they've satisfied my hunger for hope and rescued me from despair. It's my wish that their example will similarly inspire you to take up the essential work of healing our communities, our nation, our planet—and to persist during a time when such involvement has never been needed more. Think of the following essays as a conversation in which some of the most eloquent, visionary, and provocative people of our age explore the historical, political, and spiritual frameworks that have shaped their lives. You may not agree with all the beliefs they espouse or the stands they take. But I hope their strength of conviction will inspire you.

The stories they tell embody the indomitable spirit expressed in the Billie Holiday lyric that inspired this book's title: "The difficult I'll do right now. The impossible will take a little while." Holiday confronted plenty of darkness, from the lynchings she sang about in "Strange Fruit" to her many personal demons. But her voice, still with us, rises above such circumstances, lifting our spirits. Aptly enough, the "impossible" quote emerged from a context that demanded the utmost perseverance and bravery; it was the motto of the World War II Army Corps of Engineers and Navy Seabees. Lyricist Carl Sigman wove the lines into a song after seeing them on the wall of his mess hall in North Africa. Imagination and courage feed each other.

Political and personal hopes are intertwined, of course. What keeps us committed to improving our communities and our country is akin to what gives us the strength to endure the challenges of our individual lives. So I've included pieces that straddle both worlds, such as Diane Ackerman's moving account of volunteering at a suicide prevention hotline, where she faced the daunting task of persuading people who'd given up on life that it was nonetheless worth holding on, and Mary Catherine Bateson's exploration of how the most powerful personal journeys rarely follow linear paths. But my primary focus is on what moves us beyond mere individual survival, beyond carving out a comfortable private existence, to broader, more enduring visions that can help us tackle common problems and keep on doing so regardless of the frustrations we may encounter.

An Orientation of the Heart

This isn't to say that the tasks before us are easy, or that success is guaranteed. But political hope isn't about certainty. It's about the sense that our actions can matter—even in circumstances where we could reasonably conclude that change is impossible. As Jim Wallis of the Christian social justice magazine *Sojourners* says, "Hope is believing in spite of the evidence, and then watching the evidence change."

Another way of expressing Wallis's sentiment is that hope is a way of looking at the world. Nowhere is this more apparent than in the stories of those, like Tutu and Mandela, who persist under the most dangerous conditions at times when even imagining aloud the possibility of change is deemed a crime or viewed as a type of madness. We can use their experience to fuel our own engagement, even if on a far more modest stage. In "We Are All Khaled Said," key Egyptian activist Wael Ghonim describes how he and his compatriots helped people realize they weren't alone in their outrage at President Hosni Mubarak's brutal thirty-year dictatorship, then inspired them to publicly challenge the regime. Similarly, former Czech president Václav Havel uses his country's experience to describe how a series of small, seemingly futile moral actions can bring down an empire. When the Czech rock band Plastic People of the Universe was outlawed and arrested because the authorities said their Frank Zappa–influenced music was "morbid" and had a "negative social impact," Havel organized a defense committee; that, in turn, evolved into the Charter 77 organization, which set the stage for Czechoslovakia's broader democracy movement. As Havel wrote three years before the Communist dictatorship fell, and thus before he could know the outcome of his actions, "Hope is not prognostication. It is an orientation of the spirit, an orientation of the heart."

How does a person come by such an orientation? The life of Rosa Parks offers a telling clue, provided that we look beyond the conventional renditions of her experience, which actually obscure how the human spirit can prevail in bleak times. We think, because we've been told the story again and again, that one day Parks stepped onto a bus in Montgomery, Alabama, and single-handedly and without apparent preparation inaugurated the civil rights movement by refusing to sit in the segregated section.

Such accounts, however well-meaning, belie a much more complex reality: that Parks had by that time been a civil rights activist for twelve years, was the secretary of the local chapter of the National Association for the Advancement of Colored People (NAACP), and acted not alone but in concert with and on behalf of others. The summer before her arrest, she'd taken a ten-day workshop and met with an older generation of civil rights activists at the Tennessee labor and civil rights center, Highlander Folk School, which is still going strong today. At the first NAACP meeting Parks attended, the focus was lynching, an "all-American" form of terrorism once so accepted in respectable circles that white gentlemen smoking cigars and ladies in their Sunday best posed for photos standing in front of black men being burned and hanged. (The pictures can be seen in all their horror at the National Civil Rights Museum, in Memphis.) Out of this bleak legacy and, more important, the years of struggle to overcome it, came the courage and determination of Parks and people like her—the community of like-minded souls I mentioned earlier.

Just as nothing cripples the will like isolation, nothing buoys the spirit and expands the horizon of what seems possible like the knowledge that others who faced equal or greater challenges in the past continued on nonetheless, to bequeath us a better world. Historian and theologian Vincent Harding imagines a river of social justice involvement that begins with the biblical prophets, goes forward into the future, and connects all who ever worked for change with all who ever will. In "The Progressive Story of America," Bill Moyers looks at a time a hundred years ago when wealthy interests appeared to have an iron grip on the country's political and economic life. Populists and progressives responded by speaking out on the injustices they saw, organizing and resisting until their voices could not be ignored. Against all odds, they redressed the balance between wealth and commonwealth and reclaimed America's democratic heritage in ways that could be a model for today.

Even in a seemingly futile moment or losing cause, one person may unknowingly inspire another, and that person yet a third, who could go on to change the world, or at least a small corner of it. Mandela called this process "the multiplication of courage." For example, those who first took a stand in Havel's Czechoslovakia inspired others who would later join them in overthrowing the regime, even though many of their initial efforts to bring democracy failed. Similarly, Rosa Parks's husband, Raymond, convinced her to attend her first NAACP meeting, the initial step on a path that brought her to that fateful day on the bus in Montgomery. But who got Raymond Parks involved? And why did that person take the trouble to do so? What experiences shaped their outlook, forged their convictions? The links in any chain of influence are too numerous, too complex to trace. But being aware that such chains exist, that we can choose to become part of them, and that they're essential for creating lasting change is one of the primary ways to sustain hope, especially when our individual actions may seem too insignificant to amount to anything.

Here's another example of unexpected ripple effects. In the early 1960s, my friend Lisa took two of her kids to a vigil in front of the White House to protest nuclear testing. The demonstration was small, a hundred women at most. Rain poured down. The women felt frustrated and powerless. A few years later, the movement against testing had grown dramatically, and Lisa attended a major march. Benjamin Spock, whose book on baby and child care had made him one of the most famous doctors in the world, addressed the gathering. He described how he'd come to take a stand, which, owing to his stature, had already influenced thousands. (Later, when he challenged the Vietnam War, he would influence far more.) Spock talked briefly about the risks of nuclear escalation and proliferation, then mentioned that when he was in DC a few years earlier he had seen a small group of women huddled with their kids. It was Lisa's demonstration. "If those women were out there in the rain," he said, "their cause must be really important." That's when he decided to join the movement.

Sometimes it's possible not only to achieve hoped-for goals but to do so with a greater impact than we might ever have anticipated. In 2004, I spent Election Day getting out the vote for my preferred candidates, as I do every year. Knocking on doors in a Seattle neighborhood, I spoke with three people who supported my candidate for governor but wouldn't have voted had I not contacted them: One forgot it was Election Day. Another didn't know if it was still okay to use an absentee ballot. The third needed a ride to the polls. My impact had nothing to do with eloquence or skill, and everything to do with simply showing up. After three recounts, my candidate won by 133 votes. If just a handful of the volunteers on my side had stayed home, or there'd been a few more on the other side, Washington State would have had a different governor—and significantly different laws and key appointments.

Four years later, that experience helped inspire me to found the Campus Election Engagement Project. Drawing on the most effective nonpartisan approaches from schools throughout the country, my colleagues and I help colleges and universities nationwide assist their students in registering to vote, educating themselves on issues and candidates, and showing up at the polls. I'd hoped the project would make a modest impact, but had no guarantees, and we encountered more than our share of obstacles and setbacks. Yet by 2012 we were working with 750 campuses, which together enrolled 5.5 million students—a far greater reach than I'd ever anticipated.

We live in a contradictory world. Dispiriting events coincide with progress for human dignity. But when change occurs, it's because people persist, whatever the nature of their causes. Only a short while ago, if you were gay, you were probably invisible and closeted, except for a handful of courageous activists who affirmed who they were despite major risks and costs. Who could have imagined then that Supreme Court justice Ruth Bader Ginsburg would conduct a gay marriage in Washington, DC, or that the IRS and the military would treat same-sex partners who'd married in states that permitted this as equal before the law? In "On Being Different," Dan Savage explores the powerful shift created by those who found the courage to publicly demand respect, then continued speaking out to inspire others.

Young immigration rights activists have told their stories as well. When Gaby Pacheco was seven, her family brought her illegally to the United States from Ecuador. She was the highest-ranked Junior ROTC student in her high school but couldn't join the Air Force because of her status. Enrolling in Miami/Dade Community College, she became student body president, then headed the statewide student government association. In January 2010, Gaby and three other students launched a four-month walk from Miami to DC that they called the Trail of DREAMs, putting their freedom on the line in support of a path to citizenship. That support grew as marchers, from other cities, joined them along the way. After initially resisting, President Obama issued an executive order halting all deportations of young women and men who were not legal residents but had grown up in this country and were in school, had graduated high school, or had served in the military. Gaby and her peers created what poet Audre Lorde calls "The Transformation of Silence." From a different political perspective, think about the Tea Party. At the time its activists began organizing, the Republican Party was in disarray, demoralized by the losses it incurred in 2006 and 2008. Tea Party members reached out through house parties, enlisting every network they could. They voiced their concerns at town halls and public meetings and held rallies in their hometowns, in state capitals, and in Washington, DC. And they organized to run candidates and get their supporters to the polls, in both primary and general elections. Whatever you might think of their stands (or those of any of the movements described in this book), their participation inarguably shifted American politics.

"The world gets worse. It also gets better," writes Rebecca Solnit in a wonderful essay called "Acts of Hope" (alas unavailable for this book, but accessible online under her name and that title). "And the future stays dark, in the sense that we cannot anticipate it." Change comes, Solnit argues in another essay, "Not by magic, but by the incremental effect of countless acts of courage, love, and commitment, the small drops that wear away stones and carve new landscapes, and sometimes by torrents of popular will that change the world suddenly."

But how do we find the strength to stay engaged on an issue like climate change, when we may not have the time to wait for the small drops to wear away the stones, or for the long arc of the moral universe to bend toward justice, to borrow the phrase that Martin Luther King adapted from abolitionist Theodore Parker? Within the past two years alone, we've seen the devastation of Hurricane Sandy; out-of-control wildfires in Texas, Colorado, New Mexico, and California (the latter threatening San Francisco's water supply); off-the-charts droughts, floods, and tornadoes throughout the Midwest and South; and what the National Weather Service called "biblical-level" floods in Colorado. And that's just in the United States.

Comparable weather-related catastrophes have devastated lives and communities in every country on earth. In 2012, Typhoon Bopha killed 2,000 people in the Philippines. Less than a year later, Typhoon Haiyan became the strongest tropical storm to make landfall in recorded human history. With 195-mile-an-hour winds and storm surges as high as trees, it forced more than 4 million people from their homes and killed over 6,000. In response, Philippine scientist and diplomat Naderev Sano held a protest fast at the UN Climate Summit. "To anyone who continues to deny the reality that is climate change," he said, "I dare you to get off your ivory tower and away from the comfort of your armchair. I dare you to go to the islands of the Pacific, the islands of the Caribbean and the islands of the Indian Ocean and see the impacts of rising sea levels; to the mountainous regions of the Himalayas and the Andes to see communities confronting glacial floods, to the Arctic where communities grapple with the fast-dwindling polar ice caps, to the large deltas of the Mekong, the Ganges, the Amazon, and the Nile where lives and livelihoods are drowned, to the hills of Central America that confront similar monstrous hurricanes, to the vast savannas of

Africa where climate change has likewise become a matter of life and death as food and water become scarce. Not to forget the massive hurricanes in the Gulf of Mexico and the eastern seaboard of North America. And if that is not enough, you may want to pay a visit to the Philippines right now." Sano concluded: "What my country is going through as a result of this extreme climate event is madness," asking participants to refuse "to accept a future where super-typhoons like Haiyan become a way of life."

So far, we've not acted to stop this madness, or not done nearly enough. Even when we recognize its importance, the very scale of the threat and the separation between the choices that fuel it and its escalating consequences have often produced just fatalistic resignation. Yet hopeful signs are emerging in this arena, too. As Mark Hertsgaard writes in "Kids, Trees, and Climate Change," solar and wind technologies are developing to the point where, as reported by institutions like Deutsche Bank and Bloomberg New Energy Finance, they're becoming sufficiently price-competitive to start displacing fossil fuels in the marketplace. Meanwhile, grassroots movements are making a difference. In "Reluctant Activists," psychologist Mary Pipher describes how helpless she felt when she learned that the Keystone XL pipeline, designed to carry Canadian tar sands oil, would pass through Nebraska, where she lives. Everyone assumed that the pipeline project, greased by more political money than the state had ever seen, was a done deal. Then Pipher took the radical action of hosting a potluck. The movement she and a handful of friends helped launch grew quickly to include students, small-town ministers and business owners, and Republican ranchers and farmers. It grew nationally, culminating in the arrest of more than a thousand people at the White House as a way of pressuring President Obama to veto the pipeline. Keystone has now been delayed at least three years. Because of this and similar efforts, Obama began speaking more forcefully about the perils of global climate change, and he supported his Environmental Protection Administration in setting strict emission limits on new coal plants that they could meet only through still-emerging carbon capture technology. In "Is There Hope on Climate Change?" David Roberts places his faith precisely in such unanticipated developments, even as the global scientific consensus grows ever more dire.

As the Nebraska Keystone activists learned, unexpected coalitions or allies can open up new possibilities. A few years ago I attended a conference of the Blue/Green Alliance, an organization founded by the Sierra Club and the United Steel Workers that works to ensure both decent jobs and environmental sustainability. (The alliance currently includes ten major unions and four large national environmental groups—a level of participation that in itself represents a victory for crossing expected boundaries.) The day after the conference, the same Washington hotel hosted the Conservative Political Action Conference (CPAC), and I stayed to interview participants about climate change. Sadly, most over forty years old doubted its reality. But among those younger, all but one of the twenty I approached considered it an issue that required urgent action. "Of course we need to deal with it," said a young woman who was reading a booklet titled "How to Dismantle Obamacare" and headed her college Young Republicans. When I told her about a Virginia Tech student whose campus sustainability coalition included the Virginia Tech Young Republicans, she said "That's awesome. That's how it should be. Conservatives should be leading on this." Recently, Georgia's Green Tea Coalition brought together the Tea Party Patriots and the Sierra Club, who together convinced the legislature to increase solar mandates for utility giant Georgia Power.

This Gorgeous World

Since we never know when one of our seemingly modest acts might help change history, or engage someone else who will play a key role, we'd do well to savor both the journey of engagement itself and the everyday grace that we can draw on along the way. In "The Small Work in the Great Work," the Reverend Victoria

Safford advises us to "plant ourselves at the gates of hope," even in situations that invite pessimism, because "with our lives we make our answers all the time, to this ravenous, beautiful, mutilated, gorgeous world." Though the habitability of the planet is threatened to an extent unprecedented in human history, the very richness of life can still renew our spirits, can still energize us. When I run on Seattle's many beaches, and wherever I go in my travels, I start out weighed down by the ills of the world and my personal obsessions. By a few miles in, the burden invariably lifts. I see the landscape with fresh eyes. I slow down, begin to take notice of my surroundings, and drink in its beauty. In "You Are Brilliant and the Earth Is Hiring," Paul Hawken talks about drawing hope from the majesty of the stars and the miraculous web of cells that constitutes our bodies. The community of conviction is part of and dependent on the entire community of life. And to that larger and vastly older community we can always return to find strength and sustenance.

I like to think that something akin to this realization is what motivated Tutu to dance so joyfully at the Los Angeles fundraising event. As the Polish poet Czesław Miłosz has written, "There are nothing but gifts on this poor, poor earth." Tutu, like other social and political activists who haven't forgotten the importance of enjoyment, passionately embraces the gifts placed before him. If it's a gift of music, he will dance. If a gift of food, he will eat. If the company of friends, he will converse, laugh, and share stories. Such are the small but necessary pleasures that enable him to look evil in the eye and be confident that the fight must be fought. For only someone who knows how good life can be is in a position to appreciate what's at stake when life is degraded or destroyed.

Even if the struggle outlives us, even if it's impossible to envision a time when it will end, conviction matters. Actions of conscience confirm the link between our fate and that of everyone and everything else on the planet, respecting and reinforcing the fundamental connections without which life itself is impossible. Whether we flourish or perish depends on how well we understand and act in accordance with this interdependence—the same interdependence that led King to conclude that "we are caught in an inescapable network of mutuality, tied in a single garment of destiny." In "From Hope to Hopelessness," Margaret Wheatley, author of *Turning to Each Other*, strips this notion to its essentials when she argues that only by renouncing the certainty that our actions will be effective can we persist through hard times. As long as we are connected to our fellow human beings, Wheatley says, we can draw strength precisely from feeling "groundless, hopeless, insecure, patient, clear. And together." I would add that this sense of connection should be extended to the nonhuman world—not only for its sake but also for ours.

As Solnit reminds us, "It's always too soon to go home. And it's always too soon to calculate effect. From the time the English Quakers first took on the issue of slavery, three quarters of a century passed before it was abolished in Europe and America. Few if any working on the issue at the beginning lived to see its conclusion, when what had once seemed impossible suddenly began to look, in retrospect, inevitable. And as the law of unintended consequences might lead you to expect, the abolition movement also sparked the first widespread women's rights movement, which took about the same amount of time to secure the right to vote for American women in 1920, has achieved far more in the subsequent years, and is by no means done. Activism is not a journey to the corner store; it is a plunge into the dark."

Plunging into the dark doesn't mean acting randomly, without direction. We want to be deliberate in what we do and say, asking how we can bring in new allies, involve key communities, and tell the stories that embody our issues powerfully enough to engage hearts and minds. But we also need the long-term perspective that can help us persist.

Humility may be another lesson taught by this gorgeous world's interdependence. Among other things, humility counsels restraint. It says that giving up on life and the living is a form of arrogance. In "Only Justice Can Stop a Curse," Alice Walker examines the politics of bitterness, the temptation to conclude that we're destined for extinction: "*Let the Earth marinate in poisons. Let the bombs cover the ground like rain. Let the heated atmosphere go mad.*" But Walker also remembers the acts of others that have given her cause to hope, then resolves that she will not be defeated by despair. What is this but a form of humility—and forgiveness? And everyone needs forgiveness—ourselves for not taking on every cause and winning every battle; and others, our neighbors and co-workers, relatives and friends; and especially those who disagree with our beliefs or accept the lies and misdirections so commonplace in our culture.

Nor should we forget that courage is contagious, that it overcomes the silence and fear that estrange people from one another. Examples of human courage and vision are transferrable. They can echo far beyond particular causes, countries, and historical times. Gandhi's inspirers included Russian novelist Leo Tolstoy and America's Henry David Thoreau. Key US civil rights leaders like Bayard Rustin and James Lawson traveled to India to learn from Gandhi's compatriots. The US civil rights movement inspired those challenging South African apartheid and the Eastern European Communist dictatorships. Key Arab Spring activists met with counterparts who had helped overturn apartheid and bring down Serbian dictator Slobodan Milosevic.

As participants in these movements remind us, we gain something profound when we stand up for our beliefs, just as part of us dies when we know that something is wrong but do nothing. We could call what we gain "radical dignity." We don't have to tackle every issue, but if we avoid them all, if we remain silent in the face of cruelty, injustice, and oppression, we sacrifice part of our soul. Indeed, when we keep on acting based on our conscience, we affirm our humanity—the core of who we are and what we hold in common with others.

A Community of Voices

You may wonder if the community of voices I've included in this book speaks to people representing all political perspectives, or only to those who happen to match my personal sentiments.

Certainly the individuals I've brought together share a passion for democracy and justice. That's why I admire them. And most are critical of a runaway global market that would reduce us all to our monetary worth. But their specific politics often can't be pigeonholed: How do you categorize those who challenged Communist dictatorships in Czechoslovakia, Poland, and Bulgaria? Or the long-entrenched dictatorships in Egypt and Tunisia? Their courage inspires me, yet many conservatives responded with equal hope to the overthrow of these repressive regimes. What of those working, whatever their political beliefs on other issues, to create a sustainable world for their grandchildren? Many of the issues these contributors take on, such as Diane Ackerman's work with the suicide hotline, are simply about trying to respond compassionately to our fellow human beings.

Even regarding major public issues, the voices in this book sometimes differ. In a brief but powerful vignette, "Fragile and Hidden," the late Catholic peace and justice activist Henri Nouwen wrote of the hope and wisdom he gained while caring for a man who could not walk or speak. He then asked us to speak for "unborn life, life on death row, the life of the severely handicapped, the life of the broken and the homeless." I'm staunchly pro-choice and will remain so. Nouwen was not. We were raised in different traditions, lived through different times, developed divergent views of the world. Yet Nouwen's essay gives me hope, which is why I included it. If you, as a reader, disagree with the views or actions of particular writers, including my own opinions, that's fine. In fact, I hope the conversation these voices create will model a process through which citizens can at times agree to disagree, even regarding highly consequential concerns, while still drawing inspiration for the larger task of taking on critically important issues.

Similarly, I hope that the voices in this book will help close a troubling divide between secular and religious readers. Those rooted in more secular humanist ethics at times recoil at religious language, even when it's used to explain actions that they'd normally find tremendously admirable. Those of strong religious persuasion can react in the opposite manner, trusting only moral action that's grounded in an explicitly faith-based perspective. To me, religious and secular perspectives on justice offer complementary ways of understanding our responsibility to our fellow human beings. So I've included people representing both moral frameworks, and those who meld the two. I hope you'll view the chorus of voices in the pages to follow as united in an overarching cause—forging a common vision of human courage and connectedness.

Since I first created this book, I've received thousands of e-mails attesting to the many ways its stories have given people the courage to act and keep on acting for a more just world, even in the most difficult times. I've now developed a new edition, helping the original writers update their essays to speak as strongly as possible to the present moment, and adding new pieces that I've found equally powerful. Whatever issues call you to act, I hope the resulting conversation will inspire you to join the community of those who work to create a better world. Because in pursuit of that aim, all are called to participate.

A Note to the Reader

This book combines original commissioned articles with excerpts from books and magazines. I've worked with the authors to edit and adapt existing pieces, at times reordering original sequences and combining them with new material. Since most of the pieces are adapted in some fashion, I've chosen not to use ellipses to indicate particular cuts or changes.

Classroom Use, Reading Groups, and Lectures

To my delight, *The Impossible Will Take a Little While* has found an extensive audience in college and high school classes. Educators throughout the country have assigned it in every conceivable discipline and from first-year common reading programs to graduate seminars. So I've posted online study questions that those teaching the book have found the most useful, along with descriptions of related community-service projects that they created. Readers have also found many of these same questions helpful for community reading groups. You can find them at

www.paulloeb.org/impossible-classroom.html.

For information on buying bulk discounted books for reading groups or any other use, see

www.paulloeb.org/buy.html.

Find information on my college and community lectures at

www.paulloeb.org/lectures.html.

Sign up for my e-mail newsletter or Facebook page and get a flier to pass the word at

www.paulloeb.org/subscribe.html.

Or click the relevant links at

www.theimpossible.org.

PART ONE

Seeds of the Possible

From THE CURE AT TROY

Seamus Heaney

Human beings suffer,
They torture one another,
They get hurt and get hard.
No poem or play or song
Can fully right a wrong
Inflicted and endured.

The innocent in gaols
Beat on their bars together.
A hunger-striker's father
Stands in the graveyard dumb.
The police widow in veils
Faints at the funeral home.

History says, Don't hope
On this side of the grave.
But then, once in a lifetime
The longed-for tidal wave
Of justice can rise up,
And hope and history rhyme.

So hope for a great sea-change
On the far side of revenge.
Believe that a further shore
Is reachable from here.
Believe in miracles
And cures and healing wells.

Call miracle self-healing:
The utter, self-revealing
Double-take of feeling.
If there's fire on the mountain
Or lightning and storm
And a god speaks from the sky

That means someone is hearing
The outcry and the birth-cry
Of new life at its term. . . .

Excerpted from Seamus Heaney, *The Cure at Troy: A Version of Sophocles' Philoctetes* (Noonday Press, 1991). Seamus Heaney's other books include *Beowulf: A New Verse Translation* (W. W. Norton, 2001), *Opened Ground: Selected Poems 1966–1996* (Farrar, Straus and Giroux, 1999), *Field Work* (Farrar, Straus and Giroux, 2009), and *Human Chain* (Farrar, Straus and Giroux, 2011).

A memoir about volunteering at a suicide hotline may seem like an odd choice to begin a book on political hope and persistence. But Diane Ackerman's "A Slender Thread" got me thinking about the thin, sometimes fading line that separates hope from despair in political and personal life. As Ackerman wrestles with the profound depression of one of her callers, she provides insight into the bleak moments we all face. Why do some people give up on life, on love, on a better day tomorrow, and others do not? Why does a person give up at a particular moment? The answers to these questions are complex and may always elude us. But Ackerman pinpoints two features of human experience essential to any meditation on that all-important line between hope and despair: the value of believing that we have options and the ability to savor the richness of the world. Indeed, the line becomes precariously thin precisely when people feel they have no choice and that the world is an unforgiving wasteland.

Please don't misunderstand. I'm not equating active citizens who lose faith, either temporarily or permanently, in their ability to make a difference in the world with those so despairing that they see no option but to take leave of the world altogether. Nor am I ignoring the many real occasions that seriously test one's faith, in any realm, public or private. Life can be cruel, capricious, and ugly. But it also brings an abundance of gifts, which we forget at our peril. Those who give up on life are abandoning the possibility that the world is a generous enough place to be worth their staying around.

As with the admittedly different situation of engaged citizens who burn out, those calling on Ackerman's help line wrestle with a sense of suffocation, of constriction, of spiritual exhaustion. This sense springs from a belief that all imaginable choices have been tried and found wanting. "Suicidal people have tunnel vision," writes Ackerman. "No other choice seems possible. A counselor's job is to put windows and doors in that tunnel." Whether the challenge is political or personal, effective remedies differ from individual to individual. But solutions always involve altering perspective, replacing tunnel vision with an expanded view that lets in more light and more possibilities—the oxygen upon which hope thrives.

For forty years, I've been reading Jonathan Kozol's books with admiration, even as they've troubled my soul. Kozol has made it his life's work to bear witness to the "savage inequalities" that divide the children of privilege from the children of poverty, a divide that continues to widen. A doctor's son, Kozol started out, fresh from Harvard, as a teacher in an inner-city Boston school, and there he discovered the dark side of the American dream. Ever since, he's been bringing the invisible to light, telling memorable and disturbing stories of children whose only idea of home is a welfare hotel, who are routinely exposed to brutality and addiction, who live with hunger and fear throughout much of their lives. One need only look at the schools to which we exile these kids, where toilets don't work, classes meet in hallways and stairwells, and pencils and paper are either scarce or absent, to realize that not only do we continue to leave an appalling number of children behind, we treat them as if they were disposable from the day they enter the public education system, as if they had no worthwhile future. We then do our best to make their projected failure a self-fulfilling prophecy.

Like Kozol, Marian Wright Edelman has spent her life challenging this malign neglect. She began, along with Alice Walker, as a Spelman College student of activist-historian Howard Zinn. Edelman became a civil rights activist and lawyer, then founded the Children's Defense Fund, which for more than forty years has fought for the right of all children to be treated with dignity and respect, and not just be used as fodder for political campaign slogans. Time and again, she's heard the callous rationalizations put forward by apologists for the many injustices done to children: They're not smart enough. They come from bad families. They don't try hard enough. All variations, of course, on the theme that the poor and the powerless deserve their fate, which is to say, the fate society arranges for them, intentionally or not. Edelman is also keenly aware that the cause she has championed all her life—the well-being of the only true innocents among us—will continue long after she's gone.

Yet neither Edelman nor Kozol has given up. Like all of us, they experience bleak moments. But they persevere. As they attest in their own ways, Edelman and Kozol continually find themselves renewed by the "outcry and the birth-cry" of hope, to use Seamus Heaney's phrase, embodied in the tenacious spirit of the children they fight for. From that, they draw inspiration and find the courage to resist anyone or anything that might harm those children. Kozol, for instance, wonders at "the almost inexplicable spiritual resilience" of the kids he's come to know in a desperately poor Bronx neighborhood, where violent death and dashed hopes are a constant backdrop. He takes heart from the care they give each other; from their imagination, especially when it defies the loss and sorrow that surrounds them; and from the constancy of parents, grandparents, and engaged community members who nurture them, day in and day out.

Similarly, Edelman draws strength from lives beginning to bloom, the "seeds of hope," as she puts it; they remind us that every child has the potential to be a Gandhi, a Martin Luther King, or a Harriet Tubman. She takes this idea further, connecting the potential in each child to the urgency of protecting all children, not only our own but those of our neighbors, our fellow Americans, and, indeed, people everywhere. If children are the embodiment of our faith in a common future, if their instinctive optimism and appetite for experience represent unqualified affirmations of life, then by neglecting or mistreating them we not only fail in our moral responsibility, we place that future at risk. We squander the seeds on which the garden of humanity depends. Being aware of that, Edelman suggests, can stiffen the resolve of individuals and inspire in them the fierce conviction that's needed to counter indifference to injustice, especially to children.

It's ironic—and encouraging—that, while rallying us to their defense, children should be capable of empowering us, of reminding us that the seemingly powerless have potential moral strength. And no issue looms over our children's future more than our ability to maintain a habitable planet, a habitability threatened most acutely by climate change. Paul Hawken began his public involvement in 1965 as the press coordinator for Martin Luther King's historic Selma-to-Montgomery march. He then turned a small Boston store into Erewon Trading Company, one of the largest natural foods wholesalers in America. Drawing from this success and others, Hawken then began working to help businesses radically diminish their environmental footprint, without sacrificing their financial bottom line. His book *The Ecology of Commerce* even inspired the founder of the world's largest modular carpet company, Interface Global, to pursue a goal of zero environmental impact. Interface now uses recycled or bio-based sources for half their raw materials (up from next to nothing, fifteen years before), has cut their greenhouse gas emissions nearly in half, and has diminished their landfill use by 80 percent, all while creating record profits for a billion-dollar-a-year company.

Readers began sending me Hawken's University of Portland commencement speech, "You Are Brilliant and the Earth Is Hiring," shortly after he gave it, and students began making it the centerpiece of alternative commencements. "If you look at the science about what is happening on earth and aren't pessimistic," Hawken says, "you don't understand the data. But if you meet the people who are working to restore this earth and the lives of the poor, and you aren't optimistic, you haven't got a pulse." It's an open question, Hawken acknowledges, whether we'll address the crises we face before it's too late. But it's also a question that will be answered by the choices we make every day of our lives.

The centerpiece of Hawken's talk is an Adrienne Rich poem that I'd originally included as a separate piece:

> *. . . My heart is moved by all I cannot save:*
> *so much has been destroyed*
>
> *I have to cast my lot with those*
> *who age after age, perversely,*
>
> *with no extraordinary power,*
> *reconstitute the world.*

That's the task that Hawken—and all whose voices weave through this book—urges us to take on.

As I explore in an earlier book, *Soul of a Citizen*, we don't have to be perfect saints or know every answer to every conceivable question to begin working for a more just world. We can be wounded or hesitant ourselves, sometimes profoundly so. I met Danusha Veronica Goska during an online forum on that book. She explores a variation on the theme of tackling seemingly overwhelming issues by contrasting "political paralysis" with her own predicament, dealing with a periodically immobilizing disease similar to multiple sclerosis, despite which she nonetheless continued to be engaged. After working in the Peace Corps and with Mother Teresa, Goska draws hope from ordinary human kindness, like that of strangers who gave her rides when she could not walk; by so doing, they redefined the world "from a place where nobody sees and nobody cares, into a place where compassion is a possibility and change something that can be hoped for." Hope and history may not always rhyme, to borrow another phrase from Heaney. But human generosity is a starting point toward bringing them together.

CHAPTER ONE

A Slender Thread

Diane Ackerman

I'm afraid of losing Louise. *Losing her.* A shorthand for an avalanche of hurt, the phrase sounds too casual, the equivalent of misplacing a set of keys or an umbrella. I suppose it's my fundamental belief in the uniqueness of people that makes me cherish how irreplaceable they are. Louise has many talents, a lively mind, a quirky and unusual point of view, and a generous heart. I don't want life to lose her. I don't want society to lose her. I don't want to lose her from the pageant of humankind.

We use only a voice and a set of ears, somehow tied to the heart and brain, but it feels like mountaineering with someone who has fallen, a dangling person whose hands you are gripping in your own. But if she truly wishes to die? We don't hear from her when she's not depressed. In stabler times, I don't think she would choose death. But I respect her right to choose, and I tell her so.

"Look, you can always kill yourself. That's one option tonight. Why don't we put that up on the shelf for a moment and talk about what some other options might be."

Because she feels bereft of them, I want her to have choices. Choice is a signature of our species. We choose to live, sometimes we choose our own death, but most of the time we make choices just to prove choice is possible. Above all else, we value the right to choose one's destiny. The very young and some lucky few may find their days opening one onto another like a set of ornate doors, but most people make an unconscious vow each morning to get through the day's stresses and labors intact, without becoming overwhelmed or wishing to escape into death. Everybody has thought about suicide, or knows somebody who committed suicide, and then felt "pushed another inch, and it could have been me." As Emile Zola once said, some mornings you first have to swallow your toad of disgust before you can get on with the day. We choose to live. But suicidal people have tunnel vision—no other choice seems possible. A counselor's job is to put windows and doors in that tunnel.

"Options?" She says the word as if it were too large for her mouth. It probably seems tragically impersonal for what she is feeling. "You mean like eating dinner?" she asks acidly.

"Have you had anything to eat today?"

A dry little laugh. "I bought some lamb chops but couldn't face cooking them. I don't want to eat something more nervous than I am." I laugh. Her delivery was perfect. She laughs again. It is barely more than a chuckle.

"Cold. . . . " She launches the word like a dark cloud, not attached to anything special, a nimbus of pure pain.

"How come so cold and lonely tonight?"

"I'm always lonely, lonelier than life," she says faintly; then rallying a little, she explains, "When I worked at Montessori, I used to meet people there, or when my kids were little, through their activities. Now I don't meet anyone. Not at work in that pathetic office. My job is horrible. Not hard, you know, just the same rain barrel full of soak every day, boring and lonely, but it's the only one I could find. There's nothing out there for a middle-aged woman, and the minute they learn I've been hospitalized, they're afraid to hire me, like I'm going to napalm their filing cabinets or Crazy Glue their customers' thumbs to the counter or something."

A thought she has obviously entertained in some detail.

"I understand. You hate your job, you don't make friends there, and it's hard to find a new one. Every workday must feel like a wasteland." "Oppressive," she corrects. Not too little of a good thing, too much of a bad.

"Oppressive. Maybe we can figure out some other work. . . . "

"It's hopeless. I've tried everywhere. There's nothing."

Before I can reply, she swerves to: "and I haven't had a date in years, haven't been laid since I don't know when. And then there are my kids. I mean, they're teens, and suddenly Mom's a drag. We fight all the time. About ridiculous things, small things. I don't even know what we're fighting about half the time. They don't want me to hug and kiss them anymore. I can understand that, but it hurts."

Breathless, she sounds like a child trying to tell a story faster than her tumbling words. I was rushing her. She wasn't finished with her lamentation. She still needs to be heard, so I sit quietly and listen, a borrowed heart.

"There's no point to my life. I'm not doing anything of value with it. No one would miss me. No one would care if I were gone. Well, that's not true, it might change how a couple of people feel—give my ex a few sleepless nights, send a message to my Neanderthal boss, make my kids feel sorry about how cruel they can be. . . . "

Magical thinking—the belief that suicide will change a relationship with someone. One of the warning signs. "I'm lonelier than life," she says again. She likes the phrase. "How do I get out of this?" she bleats. A primal cry, not a question. Then she says almost too low to hear, "I just want the pain to end. I only want to lose consciousness."

"What a heavy burden that must be. I can hear how low you're feeling, how meaningless life seems, how bleak things look. I'm so sorry you're suffering like this."

"Promise you won't send the police," she says, reading my mood.

"How about if I promise that I won't, and you promise not to give me reason to?" She doesn't answer.

"Too much?" I ask.

"Yeah," she says. Kindly, not critically. Her tone says: We are in this together. "I just don't want to be alone right now . . . in these last minutes." I think she said minutes.

"I'm worried about you," I say. "How about if I send someone over to be with you?" The tinkling of ice cubes against glass, and a small sip between sniffles. I didn't realize she was drinking. She doesn't sound drunk, but the alcohol won't help her mood and it might give her the wrong kind of courage.

"I'm not at home," she says. "Anyway, it's too late for that. I put my coat on, but I don't need to, do I, to be warm when I fly." She sounds wrung-out, exhausted, giving up. "At least it won't hurt much."

"Won't hurt much?"

"I took a bunch of Tylenol. . . . "

My heart starts to pound, and with a huge effort at control I ask: "How much Tylenol did you take?"

"I don't know," she whines, "a bunch, enough."

That's it. I can't stand the risk any longer. Every call with Louise has seemed this dire, a last call for help, and she has survived. But suppose tonight is the exception, suppose this is the last of last times? What is different tonight? I'm not sure. Then it dawns on me. Something small. I'm frightened by how often she has been using the word "only," a word tight as a noose. Without letting her hear, I notify the police to trace the call and accompany her to the hospital, where a doctor will give her yet another type of medication.

"I'll stay with you." Which problem to focus on? Which section of the tunnel to drill windows in? Her job? Her family problems? Maybe her sense of isolation. The outer one, I mean, the one that can be eased by friends and acquaintances. The inner one is another matter. So often loneliness comes from being out of touch with parts of oneself. We go searching for those parts in other people, but there's a difference between feeling separate from others and separate from oneself.

"You said no one would care if you died. But I would care."

"I bet you say that to all the callers," she says, mustering a touch of coyness.

"Not so. You and I have had some good talks over the past few months."

Leaning on the desk, I focus my eyes on the wood grain's many streaks and knots. If it had color, it would look like a Navajo blanket. Hard as I try to concentrate solely on hearing, sights keep trickling in. So does the fragrance of coffee brewing in the kitchen. The long vowels of the wind. The chatter of the Venetian blinds against a drafty window frame.

"Yes," she says, "you've been swell. You've been my only friend, well, not friends exactly, not to you, I mean I'm just one of . . . ."

"You'd be surprised how well you can get to know someone over the telephone. I bet you've gotten to know me a little, too, and the other counselors."

"Yes," she says, "I have actually. *You* always sound so calm and even. I envy how together you must be. My life is shooting out of my hands, and I wish I could have your . . . spirit level."

"I'm not always level. Believe me, my life has problems, too. It's easier to be calm when someone else is in trouble."

"Oh," she says, with a mixture of surprise and relief. "Anyway, you're a good person: patient, and kind, and strong. . . . "

"So are you. All those things."

"Strong? That's a good one. If you could see how weak I am. . . . " Her voice trails away.

"Amazingly strong." Be careful, I think, not to use the past tense. She might interpret that as an obituary. "Look how you've been fighting the torrents of depression—for years. That takes such courage. You've been working during that time, raising two kids, surviving the nightmare of an ugly divorce. Okay, you've lost jobs, but you've picked yourself up and found new jobs. You've even volunteered during the flood—filling sandbags and making sandwiches, I think you said once—and you've found the time and energy and heart to do volunteer work, and helped other people in trouble. You've been heroic. You're being strong tonight, calling us. Given how bad you're feeling, that takes real strength. I admire your courage."

"Admire?" she says, letting the word hover a long moment while she considers it. "You wouldn't want to live my life. It's only bad choices . . . except . . . " Sniffling.

"Death is always a possibility, but not the best."

Silence. I can feel her thinking it over.

"*Lonelier than life*, you said. Why don't we think of a few ways to help you solve that problem," I suggest. Broaden the perspective. The hardest job when someone is depressed.

"There aren't any."

"Sure there are." Off the top of my head, I list some ways for her to ease her loneliness—through classes, volunteer work, athletics, music, nature centers, city projects, and such. Not one appeals to her. I didn't think any would. Nonetheless, I ask her to consider the list and arrange it in order of preference, "even though we'll agree that you're too tired and fed up to do any of them and they all sound bad anyway." Despite her strong resistance to each item, she goes through the motions of ranking them, and that distracts her a little.

"Will you hold on?" she asks abruptly. "There's someone at the door."

Damn, the police. That was fast—she must be at home after all. Maybe I didn't need to send them. And she'll be angry, she'll feel lied to and betrayed. She does. I hear her screaming at me, at the telephone, at the world. She calls me a liar, and she's right. I lied to her. Not about what mattered, only about the trace, and only because her life is in danger, and only because I deduced that some part of her craves life or she wouldn't have called.

Maybe I could have calmed her and talked her round? Maybe someone else would have prevailed, someone who can do this slow tango of life and death with more grace and cunning. Suppose the hospital releases her right away and she heads straight for the gorge? Knowing and not knowing about callers, that's what gets to me. My chest feels rigid as a boat hull, my ribs tense. Taking a large breath and letting it out slowly, I press my open palms against my face, rub the eyebrows, then the cheekbones and jaw, and laugh. Not a ha-ha laugh, a small sardonic one, the kind we save for the ridiculous, as I catch myself slipping into a familiar trap. I did fine. I did the best I could. Maybe the best anyone could tonight.

My shoulders feel skewered, and a long grinding pain twitches down my right side. Rolling my head in slow circles, twisting my shoulders, stretching my arms, arching my spine, I realize that during the past two hours my back never touched the chair. The perfect recipe for backache. She'll hate me, hate me, I think, as I get up stiffly and go to the kitchen for tea. Yes, but she'll be *alive* to hate me. Until the next time, anyway, the next rock-bottom night when she longs to fly.

Helping Louise survive is always an ordeal. Tonight she sounded even more determined and death bound than usual. It was the right choice. I think. Maybe. On the write-up sheet, under "Caller," I write "Louise," put the letter "H" for "high" in the box marked "suicide risk," attach a yellow Lethality Assessment sheet, and add a few details of the call. Pressing my fingertips to my face, I push again on the brow bones, as if I could rearrange them, but they ache from a place I can't reach with my hands.

A few weeks later, a new postcard on the Crisis Center bulletin board catches my eye. On one side is a reproduction of the Edward Hopper painting *Nighthawks*, in which three lonely souls sit drinking coffee in an overlit diner. Turning the card over, I find a neat, even handwriting, in blue ink, addressed to the agency. *I'm writing to thank whoever the counselor was I spoke with. . . .* Notes to Suicide Prevention frequently begin that way. But when the large open loops and rounded *d*'s mention the day and hour, my thoughts quicken. That was *my* shift. My eyes slide to the signature. It's from Louise, who has signed her real name.

Sitting down on the couch, I read the card carefully, and learn that she went from the emergency room to a psychiatric hospital in Pennsylvania, where she spent three weeks "in palatial bedlam." When she returned to town, she met an acquaintance who volunteers for Displaced Homemakers; Louise discovered a genial group of people there, and even took a paying job at the agency. A month later, she's "finally in a good place," by which I know she means several terrains, including her job and her mood. I cross the fingers of both hands and tap the interlocked fingertips together. May this small placard be true; may she find peace. She blesses the soul who "took my life in her hands that night," thanks us all for our good work, is just writing "to let you know what happened—I bet you don't hear that very often." We don't.

Adapted from *A Slender Thread: Rediscovering Hope at the Heart of Crisis* (Vintage, 1998). Ackerman is also the author of *The Zookeeper's Wife: A War Story* (W. W. Norton, 2008) and *One Hundred Names for Love: A Memoir* (W. W. Norton, 2012).

CHAPTER TWO

Ordinary Resurrections

Jonathan Kozol

The weather remained snowless in New York during January. Martin Luther King Day fell, as always, on a Monday, even though his birthday was a day or two before. A teenage boy named Gabriel was stabbed in the heart three times that day across the street from St. Ann's Church, in the Mott Haven neighborhood of the South Bronx. He died in the operating room later that night. A friend of the murderer was murdered in retaliation in the same encounter.

"There are two large stains of blood on the cement where Gabriel was stabbed," said Mother Martha, the lawyer turned Episcopal minister who runs St. Ann's. Gabriel's cousin, a shy boy whose mother was in the hospital, made a point of bringing Mother Martha to see the shrine where people had left notes and photographs and flowers and a number of small candles on the sidewalk at the spot where Gabriel collapsed. He left a package of Rice Krispies treats for Gabriel because he said they were his favorite snack.

"Then it began to rain, so everything was moved inside the building so the notes and pictures wouldn't get all wet and so the candles wouldn't be extinguished by the rain."

The news became more hopeful at the start of February. A well-known dancer who'd heard about the children's program at the church had come to talk with Mother Martha and decided to begin a series of dance classes. "He did a trial class to see how it would go," she said. Eight-year-old Elio was in the group. "He was the star!"

"Was Pineapple there?" I asked about a plump, energetic nine-year-old who liked to take charge of other children and knew how to console their tears.

"Yes," she replied. "Most of them were." Pineapple, Mother Martha said, had gotten thinner in the past two months, but, according to Katrice, a neighborhood grandmother who runs the St. Ann's food pantry, she still did not look too much like the skinny fashion models she once viewed as her professional role models. "She dances *good!*" Katrice insisted when I asked. Thinking of Pineapple doing pirouettes, her arms above her head, her feet in sweat socks pointed high up on her toes, I felt a twinge of envy and regret that I had not been there.

The lighthearted messages were interrupted by disturbing ones during the weeks that followed. An innocent African immigrant was shot to death one night by the police in the South Bronx. His death before a fusillade of more than forty bullets from the guns of four policemen who had fired, almost point-blank, as he stood before the doorway of his home set off more than a month of protests leading to a civil disobedience campaign. A wide array of ordinary citizens and advocates and members of the clergy of diverse religious faiths, including Mother Martha, were arrested.

More painful to the children were some other deaths that took place in the streets and neighborhoods around St. Ann's, which Mother Martha called "the ordinary dyings," most of which get little notice from outside the area. Two boys were gunned down in a late-night killing just outside a store on St. Ann's Avenue a few steps from Ali's, where I'd been getting coffee for so many years. One of the boys died instantly. The other would survive, I later learned.

Miss Rosa had to speak about this killing to the children on the intercom at P.S. 30 prior to dismissing them because there was a rumor of a payback killing in the playground opposite the school. "This is Mama Rosa speaking," she began her message to the children, as she told me in her office when I got back to New York to visit her late in the afternoon a few days after the event. At times like these, she said, a principal has to attempt to draw on every bit of credibility she may have earned in children's eyes, speaking not as an official of the school but as a parent—or, in this case, a grandparent—which is not a way all principals can speak, because the children do not view them always with the confidence that they invest in her.

Later in the spring she had to speak to children in that role again when one of her first-graders was incinerated in a fire that swept through his home. The six-year-old, according to a child who was close to him, had gotten out but then ran back into the building in an effort to retrieve his teddy bear and was unable to escape a second time. Mother Martha wasn't sure the part about the teddy bear was right but seemed reluctant to discuss it when I asked. The story of the teddy bear, however, was repeated by some other children who had known the boy who died. The notion that he'd tried to save his bear and that the two of them, the boy and his bear, had been consumed together, may have softened the effects of grief and given the illusion of a purpose to the purposeless.

There were other tragedies in weeks to come. Three girls, all twelve-year-olds, were raped in a short period of time in the South Bronx, one on a roof, one in a hallway, and one underneath the stairs of an apartment building. A fourteen-year-old hanged herself at school and was discovered by a classmate in the toilet stall in which she somehow had attached the rope. A sixteen-year-old boy was shot and badly wounded by an officer near Morris Park. Another young man was shot in the face on St. Ann's Avenue, again on the same corner as Ali's.

But the story of the boy who died to save his bear, as children in the neighborhood insisted that he did, retained a special meaning for the children, and a sense of closeness—even, possibly, an element of moral glory—that the other tragedies did not.

"This was his chair," the child's teacher told me on my next trip to New York. It was during recess. She was sitting at one of the children's tables, grading papers in the quiet of the room before the kids came back. "For days after he died they wouldn't let another child sit here," she recalled. "If another child tried to take his place they'd say, 'This was *his* chair.'"

I've had conversations like this with schoolteachers in the past after a child in their class had died of illness, in an accident, or, as in this case, in a household fire. The recent presence of the child in the class, the place he sat, the things he used to say and do, the way he looked the last time he was there, are always recollected vividly and painfully by teachers, who may often suffer longer with these memories than children do.

"He was a sweet boy and was terribly attached to me," the teacher said. "He used to bring me pictures he had drawn for me."

From a folio of children's work she took a picture of a boy painted in blue and chalky white: a large round head, a round heart for a nose, two round blue eyes with long lashes, and two rudimentary arms. The background was a blue-black sky dotted by stars.

"Friday he was here. We had a party in the corridor that day. The children broke piñatas. He was excited, happy! With that happy face of his! 'Look!' he said. 'Look, teacher! I have candies!' He was absent Monday and he died on Monday night.

"He did go back into the building—to get *something*," she believed, but she did not know what it was. "One of the papers said they found his body in a closet. Another said that he was found behind a sofa. His sister said he thought his father was inside. He went 'to save his daddy.' Others say it was the bear. . . . "

She pulled another picture from the folio. "He did this for me just two weeks ago." It was a picture of a parrot with the red and green and yellow colors of the tropics. There was a note to her beneath the parrot's feet. "I love you, Mrs. Caraballo."

The children came upstairs from recess. The teacher stood behind the chair in which the child used to sit and watched the other children take their chairs. I went downstairs to visit with Mr. Bedrock, then to see Miss Rosa for a while. Throughout the afternoon, I couldn't get those long blue lashes from my mind.

"He was alive and now he's dead," said Tabitha, who told me that she knew the boy. She's in the third grade now. She knows the story of the teddy bear and does not like it when I seem to question whether it is accurate or not. Miss Rosa later spoke with me about the way the children build these small mythologies, and why they do, and why a grown-up shouldn't look too hard into these pieces of belief. Like Mother Martha, she resisted my attempts to clarify the "truth" about the boy and bear. I'm glad the children have these women to defend and honor the epiphanies they weave around the unacceptability of grief.

I go back to Mott Haven when I can, and when I know I need to. Every time I do, I feel renewed in spirit by the generosity and understanding of the children and the love and courage of the grown-ups at the church.

Katrice's swollen feet still seem to give her a good deal of pain, and now she has another worry on her mind because her doctor told her last week that he saw "something he didn't like" in looking at an X-ray of her breast. She has a cancer history, so a referral is in order. Miss Elsie has some problems with blood sugar—she's a diabetic—and she suffers from high blood pressure as well. Others in the older generation who come in to supervise the children at the afterschool program are suffering the usual infirmities of age.

Still, life abundant fills the church on weekday afternoons when children crash into the room at three o'clock with all the pent-up energy that children have when they're released from school. The younger ones still race into the older women's arms to bring them up-to-date on all the interesting news.

"Guess what, Katrice?"

"What is it, child?" she replies as she looks down upon a package of excitement that will not let go of her. "Katrice?" the child says again.

"Words to tell, and ears to hear," Katrice says rhythmically, not really to the child, more to me or to herself. Her fingers go to work at helping to unbutton buttons and unwrap the child from her winter coat, which is too heavy for this season. The child squirms beneath Katrice's hands. At last, her arms released from padded sleeves, she brings the coat across the room and reaches up to hang it on a hook.

Elio doesn't end up on the overturned blue milk box in the corner of the kitchen anymore. Other children take the space he used to occupy. Katrice still stands there by the child who's in isolation, with her disapproving looks and knowledgeable nods. She tells me that she still does not like leaving here at night. She always feels a sense of letdown when the final child has gone home, she says.

"Okay, that's it. I guess. . . ."

It sounds a little like Pineapple in her "mop-up" mode. The difference, though, is that there isn't the same feeling of finality. When Pineapple says, "That's it!" she doesn't say, "I guess. . . ." She wraps it up and leaves no room for anyone to open it again. Katrice, like almost anyone who's lived for more than fifty years, knows more about the unpredictables in life. The uncompletedness of most experience is part of what permits her, and compels her, to be tentative.

Katrice stands there in the kitchen doorway as the last one leaves, her arms folded so firmly. "You leaving now?"

"Not yet," I say.

"Okay," she says.

I step outside with her to say good-bye and watch her as she goes out to the street and heads up St. Ann's Avenue in the direction of her home. "No one runs from good," she told me once. Yet people do. Night comes, and we have other obligations.

At home, reminders of the children are on every side of me. The walls are covered with their writings and their pictures. In the place of honor is a present that Pineapple gave me several years ago, an imitation stained-glass window that she made from tissue paper, brightly colored with green paint and with a wash of light-blue ink. It's a landscape: grass and sky and one tremendous puffy-looking cloud that looks like an amoeba or a fish or a distended blimp that's losing air, and also, partly hidden by a hill, a jolly-looking thing with orange rays that look like dragons' teeth and is supposed to be the sun.

It's right here in my window so I get a chance to see it every morning when I come downstairs. It's a slight thing. I would guess she did it quickly. When I asked her recently if it was supposed to be a rising sun or setting sun, she seemed at first not to remember what I meant. "That old thing?" she finally said. "I gave that to you *years* ago!" She thought about it for a time, then said she wasn't sure what she intended. "You decide," she told me uselessly.

Friends who see it here cannot decide if it's supposed to be the end of day or the beginning. Either way, I think that orange thing with dragons' teeth is beautiful; and, at the risk of being sentimental about somebody whose sunny disposition brings a lot of joy into a world that has too many cloudy afternoons, I like to think it's rising.

Adapted from *Ordinary Resurrections: Children in the Years of Hope* (Perennial, 2001). Jonathan Kozol's other books include *Amazing Grace: Lives of Children and the Conscience of a Nation* (Perennial, 1996), *Death at an Early Age* (his first book, reissued in 1990 by New American Library), *Savage Inequalities* (Broadway Books, 2012), and *Fire in the Ashes: Twenty-Five Years Among the Poorest Children in America* (Broadway Books, 2013). For over fifty years he's been a tireless advocate for children like those of Mott Haven.

CHAPTER THREE

Standing Up for Children

Marian Wright Edelman

Dr. Benjamin Mays, president of Morehouse College and mentor to Dr. Martin Luther King, Jr., and thousands of other Black youths, including me, once said: "The tragedy of life doesn't lie in not reaching your goal. The tragedy lies in having no goal to reach. It isn't a calamity to die with dreams unfilled, but it is a calamity not to dream. It is not a disgrace not to reach the stars, but it is a disgrace to have no stars to reach for. Not failure, but low aim, is a sin."

It's time to do whatever it takes to make our nation treat our children right and to live up to its promise of fair opportunity. We must meet the needs of the whole child in the richest, most powerful nation on earth now. Children do not come in pieces. They live in families and communities. We have the money. We have the know-how. And we have the responsibility to ensure all children what we now provide for some children. God did not make two classes of children and will hold us accountable for every one of them.

Can our children become the healing agents of our national and world transformation and future spiritual and economic salvation? Edmond McDonald wrote that when God wants an important thing done in this world or a wrong righted, He goes about it in a very singular way. He doesn't release thunderbolts or stir up earthquakes. God simply has a tiny baby born, perhaps of a very humble home, perhaps of a very humble mother. And she puts it in the baby's mind, and then—God waits. The great events of this world are not battles and elections and earthquakes and thunderbolts. The great events are babies, for each child comes with the message that God is not yet discouraged with humanity, but is still expecting goodwill to become incarnate in each human life. And so God produced a Gandhi and a Mandela and a Harriet Tubman, an Eleanor Roosevelt and a Martin Luther King, Jr., and each of us to guide the earth towards peace rather than conflict.

I believe that protecting today's children—tomorrow's Mandelas and Mother Teresas and Aung San Suu Kyis—is the moral and common sense litmus test of our humanity in a world where millions of child lives are ravaged by the wars, neglect, abuse, and racial, ethnic, religious, and class divisions of adults.

Something is awry when the net worth of the world's 1,426 billionaires is nearly 10 times the combined yearly income of the 1.2 billion people living on less than $1.25 a day, and when the income gap between the top and bottom fifths of the world's population has more than doubled in the last generation. Something is awry when, in the United States, the 400 highest-earning taxpayers earned as much as the combined tax revenue of 20 states in 2009. The US is first among industrialized nations in defense expenditures, military exports, Gross Domestic Product, the number of millionaires and billionaires, and health care spending. But we're thirty-fourth in the percent of children living in poverty; thirty-fourth in teenage births; and thirty-first in preventing infant mortality. We're last in protecting our children against gun violence, and Sandy Hook was only one of many needless tragedies: since 1963, firearms have killed an estimated 166,500 children and teens in our homes, schools, and neighborhoods, more than the toll of all our combat deaths in the Vietnam, Afghanistan, and Iraq wars combined.

What legacies, principles, values, and deeds will we stand for and send to the future through our children, and to a world desperately hungering for moral leadership and community? Few human beings are blessed to experience the beginning of a new millennium. How will progress be measured over the next thousand years if we survive them? By the kill power and number of weapons of destruction we can produce and traffic at home and abroad, or by our willingness to shrink and destroy the prison of violence we've constructed in the name of peace and security? Will we be remembered by how many material things we can manufacture, advertise, sell, and consume, or by our rediscovery of more lasting, non-material measures of success—a new Dow Jones for the purpose and quality of life in our families, neighborhoods, cities, and national and world communities? Will we be remembered by how rapidly technology, corporate merger mania, and greed can render human beings obsolete, or by a better balance between corporate profits and corporate caring for children, families, communities, and the environment? Will we be remembered by how much a few at the top can get at the expense of the many at the bottom and in the middle, or by our struggle for a concept of enough for all? Will we be remembered by the glitz, style, and banality of too much of our culture, or by the substance of our efforts to rekindle an ethic of caring, community, and justice in a world driven too much by money, technology, and weaponry?

A thousand years from now, will America's dream be alive, be remembered, and be worth remembering? Is America's dream big enough for every fifth child who is poor, every seventh child who is Black, every fourth child who is Latino, and every twelfth child who is mentally or physically challenged? Is our world's dream big enough for all of the children God has sent as messengers of hope and life?

So many of the formidable threats that millions of poor children of all races, but especially Black children, face today are actually dangerous steps backwards: the cradle to prison pipeline that now places one in three Black boys (and one in six

Latino boys) born in 2001 at risk of imprisonment. Mass incarceration of people of color—especially Black males. Huge racial disparities in often harsh and arbitrary zero-tolerance school discipline policies that deny countless children essential education and push them into the criminal justice system. Massive attacks on voting rights with new requirements that particularly impact the poor, minority groups, the elderly, the disabled, and the young. Resegregating and substandard schools denying millions of poor Black and Latino children skills they will need in our increasingly competitive globalized economy. Each and all of these are siren calls for attentive action.

We are once again at a critical turning point for our children and nation. Despite all the harsh lessons of the past and all the lofty rhetoric about who we want and need to be as a 21st century multicultural nation in a multiracial and multicultural world, we're heading in the wrong direction. We need to correct course and challenge the economic and racial inequality that threatens the very idea of America.

What to do about priorities that bring good news to the rich and bad news to the poor, defy the prophets and the gospels, and mock American values of fair play and opportunity? How do we reorder these priorities for our children's and nation's sake?

Have a positive vision for our children and nation. It is not enough just to be against the dismantlement of (and cuts to) children's programs that still don't reach all children who are eligible or need them. We must demand what all children need. A lot of people say that's unrealistic. Yet their futures and our nation's future depend on it. Some say our nation cannot afford this. I say nonsense. The tax cutters and the war profiteers don't ever stop asking for or getting far more. Our nation does not have a money problem. We have a values and priorities problem. If we can find the billions of dollars needed to fight wars in Iraq and Afghanistan and give repeated irresponsible tax breaks targeted to corporations and the wealthy, we can find the money to educate and protect our children in their critical early years. We can't afford not to.

Believe we can save all of our children and then do it. We can transform our nation's priorities if we truly believe we can. Don't ever give up insisting that children be protected first whatever the political or economic weather. An anonymous sage whose words I keep above my kitchen sink wrote: "If you think you are beaten, you are. If you think that you dare not, you don't. If you'd like to win, but you think you can't, it's almost a cinch that you won't. If you think you'll lose, you're lost, for out in the world you'll find success begins with a person's will. Life's battles don't always go to the stronger or faster ones. But sooner or later the one who wins is the one who thinks she can. It's all in the state of mind."

Have faith and act without ceasing. There's a Biblical story about a judge who neither feared God nor had respect for people. In his city there was a widow who kept coming to him saying, "Grant me justice against my opponent." For a while he refused; but later he said to himself, "Though I have no fear of God and no respect for anyone, yet because this widow keeps bothering me, I will grant her justice, so that she may not wear me out by continuously coming." And the Lord said, "Listen to what the unjust judge says. And will not God grant justice to his chosen ones who cry to him day and night? Will he delay long in helping them? I tell you, he will quickly grant justice to them." (from Luke 18:1–7)

Like the powerless widow, we must wear down our powerful leaders through persistent witnesses all over America and the world, until they hear and do right by our children. We must call, write, visit, hold prayer vigils, take our leaders on Child Watches, make them see and feel the suffering of children. We must tie our children to community, state, and national budget and policy choices and tell those who represent us what they can and must do to help. And we must hold our leaders accountable with our votes for what they actually do. More people committed to children need to run for office and not forget about children when they win.

Don't be intimidated or silenced by budget experts or political spin-masters. Don't let anyone label us unrealistic or unpatriotic or say we're engaging in class warfare or are being partisan when we share the facts—the truth—about unjust national budget and policy priorities. Unless we reverse our course, lavish tax cuts for the wealthy, bloated military budgets, and subsidies and exemptions for massively profitable companies that need no public help, we will starve our national government of the resources needed to serve our vulnerable young, elderly, disabled, and sustain our public infrastructure for decades to come. You do not need to be able to debate the technicalities of budget and tax policy to know it's disingenuous to argue that we need to cut the deficit when we are giving away billions in tax breaks to corporations and the wealthiest Americans. You don't need a Ph.D. in Philosophy or Theology to know it's morally wrong and hypocritical for leaders to cut food assistance to poor children while increasing subsidies to wealthy farmers, or say that we need to cut the deficit for the sake of our grandchildren while leaving millions of children alive now behind in poverty, without health coverage, in crumbling schools and understaffed classrooms, and alone after school without supervision.

Be strong and courageous and leave the results to God. "Plant the seed of hope and caring and leave the garden to God," Henry David Thoreau wrote. Many dismissed him as a crank or a social deviant. But Leo Tolstoy read Thoreau's essay "Civil Disobedience"; Gandhi learned about it from Tolstoy; Dr. Martin Luther King, Jr., read Gandhi; and the Civil Rights Movement made history. Don't be afraid to be a voice in the wilderness for children and the poor. It's the moral and sensible thing to do.

Trust and serve God and recognize that every single one of us can make a difference. Let God use us, unworthy, weak, and inadequate as we are. God used a stutterer, Moses, as spokesperson to Pharaoh. God took a 100-year-old man, Abraham, to create a people so numerous as to cover the face of the earth. God used a boy with a slingshot to slay a giant who had paralyzed the king's army armed to the teeth with the best military weapons. God gave a young girl, Esther, courage to go ask the king to protect her people, saying if I die, I die. God heard aging and barren Hannah's ceaseless prayers for a child and gave her a son, Samuel, whom she rededicated to God. And God used five women—Moses' mother and sister, Pharaoh's daughter, and two midwives—to save a slave baby named Moses who liberated the Hebrew people. If these five very unlikely female social revolutionaries were God's instruments for transforming history, then let us believe we can be God's instruments to save our children today. If those of us who call ourselves Christians really believe God sent a poor baby to save the world and to challenge the unjust political order of his day, why are we silent today when so many poor babies are suffering?

Assign ourselves right now to be a voice for justice for children in these scary and turbulent times of greed and economic uncertainty and terrorism and war. Wendell Phillips, the abolitionist, fervently condemned slavery in the 1840s as a "moral outrage" when his cause seemed hopeless. A friend asked him after a speech, "Wendell, why are you so on fire?" Phillips replied: "I am on fire because I have mountains of ice before me to melt." John Woolman did not wait for Abraham Lincoln, the Civil War, or the Emancipation Proclamation to speak and act against slavery. He traveled by horseback to home after home of individual Quakers to discuss the incompatibility of slavery with Quaker principles and urged them to stop being slave owners. Harriet Tubman didn't wait for President Lincoln and the Civil War either. She ran away from slavery and returned again and again to deliver others from slavery to freedom. Just do the right thing for children—right now—whatever the risk.

Never give up. Making our nation and world fit for our children and grandchildren is a task for marathoners—not sprinters. It is a complex and long-term struggle that must be pursued with both urgency and persistence. The playwright Bertold Brecht said: "There are those who struggle for a day and they are good. There are those who struggle for a year and they are better. There are those who struggle all their lives. These are the indispensable ones." Be an indispensable one for our children's and world's sake.

Recognize and honor the sacredness of each and every child. One of the reasons I believe so many millions of children are left behind—in the United States and in our globalizing world—is that too many in power and of privilege distinguish between their own children and other people's children. Yet as Mahub Ul Haq, a creator of the World Human Development Index, once presciently reminded us, "abolishing poverty in the 21st century must become a collective responsibility since human life is not safe in the rich nations if human despair travels in poor nations. Let us recognize that consequences of global poverty travel across national frontiers without passport in the form of drugs, AIDS, pollution, and terrorism."

Children—all children—are the world. Children are hope and life. Children are our immortality. Children are the seeds and the molders of history and the transmitters of our values—good and bad. When are we going to wake up and open our hearts? When are we going to act to build a nation and world fit and safe for and worthy of our children and grandchildren? When is our moral reach going to match our military and economic reach in a world in desperate need of hope and peace and justice?

Organize, mobilize, and hold our leaders accountable. It's time for children's advocates and all people of conscience to wake up, ask hard questions, act boldly, and hold ourselves accountable for holding our leaders accountable for taking children out of harm's way. It's time to close the adult hypocrisy gap between word and deed for children. It's time to compete with those who would destroy, neglect, and lead our children astray. The soul snatchers have been busy at work turning family and child dreams into drugs and violence, greed and consumption. The corporate lobbyists and budget cutters have been relentless and swift in pursuing their special interests and turning child hopes into cold despair and grinding child futures into dust. Child advocates must get better and tougher at reclaiming our children's birthright of economic, social, and environmental well-being, setting aside personal and organizational egos for their greater good. We must seek and welcome new voices and make new alliances. If our nation and world are fit for children they are fit for everyone.

"A PRAYER TO THE GOD OF ALL CHILDREN"

O God of the children of Afghanistan, Pakistan, and India,
Of Israel, Iraq, and Iran, Jerusalem and Jericho
Of Korea, Burundi and Rwanda
Of South Africa, South Carolina, South Side Chicago,
and Sandy Hook
Help us to love and respect and act now to protect them all.

O God of Black, Brown and White children, of children of every hue,
Of children who are rich and poor and in between
Of children who speak English, Hmong, and Russian,
Spanish and Chinese, Hebrew and Arabic, languages we
cannot discern
Help us to love and respect and act now to protect them all.

O God of the child prodigy and child prostitute,
Of children of rapture and children of rape
Of runaway and thrown away children
without parent or place, friend or future
Help us to love and respect and act now to protect them all.

O God of children of destiny and despair,
Of children who are healthy and children in pain
Of children who ridicule, torment and taunt
Help us to love and respect and act now to protect them all.

O God of children of peace and children of war
Of those who die from violence in their communities, homes,
and schools,
Of children without hope and children with hope to spare
Of children who are loved and children who are unloved
They are all your children.
Help us to love and respect and act now to protect them all.

Marian Wright Edelman is the founder and president of the Children's Defense Fund (*www.childrensdefense.org*) and has been an advocate for justice for forty years. Her books include *The Measure of Our Success: A Letter to My Children and Yours* (Perennial, 1993), *Guide My Feet: Prayers and Meditations for Our Children* (Perennial, 2000), *Lanterns: A Memoir of Mentors* (Perennial, 2000), *I'm Your Child, God: Prayers for Our Children* (Hyperion, 2004), *I Can Make a Difference: A Treasury to Inspire Our Children* (Amistad, 2005), and *The Sea Is So Wide and My Boat Is So Small: Charting a Course for the Next Generation* (Hyperion, 2008).

CHAPTER FOUR

You Are Brilliant and the Earth Is Hiring

Paul Hawken

You are going to have to figure out what it means to be a human being on earth at a time when every living system is declining, and the rate of decline is accelerating. Kind of a mind-boggling situation . . . but not one peer-reviewed paper published in the last thirty years can refute that statement. Basically, civilization needs a new operating system, you are the programmers, and we need it within a few decades.

This planet came with a set of instructions, but we seem to have misplaced them. Important rules like don't poison the water, soil, or air, don't let the earth get overcrowded, and don't touch the thermostat have been broken. Buckminster Fuller said that spaceship earth was so ingeniously designed that no one has a clue that we are on one, flying through the universe at a million miles per hour, with no need for seatbelts, lots of room in coach, and really good food—but all that is changing.

There is invisible writing on the back of the diploma you will receive, and in case you didn't bring lemon juice to decode it, I can tell you what it says: You Are Brilliant and the Earth Is Hiring. The earth couldn't afford to send recruiters or limos to your school. It sent you rain, sunsets, ripe cherries, night blooming jasmine, and that unbelievably cute person you are dating. Take the hint. And here's the deal: Forget that this task of planet-saving is not possible in the time required. Don't be put off by people who know what is not possible. Do what needs to be done, and check to see if it was impossible only after you are done.

When asked if I am pessimistic or optimistic about the future, my answer is always the same: If you look at the science about what is happening on earth and aren't pessimistic, you don't understand the data. But if you meet the people who are working to restore this earth and the lives of the poor, and you aren't optimistic, you haven't got a pulse. What I see everywhere in the world are ordinary people willing to confront despair, power, and incalculable odds in order to restore some semblance of grace, justice, and beauty to this world. The poet Adrienne Rich wrote,

> *" . . . so much has been destroyed*
>
> *I have to cast my lot with those*
> *who age after age, perversely,*
>
> *with no extraordinary power,*
> *reconstitute the world."*

There could be no better description. Humanity is coalescing. It is reconstituting the world, and the action is taking place in schoolrooms, farms, jungles, villages, campuses, companies, refugee camps, deserts, fisheries, and slums.

You join a multitude of caring people. No one knows how many groups and organizations are working on the most salient issues of our day: climate change, poverty, deforestation, peace, water, hunger, conservation, human rights, and more. This is the largest movement the world has ever seen. Rather than control, it seeks connection. Rather than dominance, it strives to disperse concentrations of power. Like Mercy Corps, it works behind the scenes and gets the job done. Large as it is, no one knows the true size of this movement. It provides hope, support, and meaning to billions of people in the world. Its clout resides in idea, not in force. It is made up of teachers, children, peasants, businesspeople, rappers, organic farmers, nuns, artists, government workers, fisher folk, engineers, students, incorrigible writers, weeping Muslims, concerned mothers, poets, doctors without borders, grieving Christians, street musicians, and as the writer David James Duncan would say, the Creator, the One who loves us all in such a huge way.

There is a rabbinical teaching that says if the world is ending and the Messiah arrives, first plant a tree, and then see if the story is true. Inspiration is not garnered from the litanies of what may befall us; it resides in humanity's willingness to restore, redress, reform, rebuild, recover, re-imagine, and reconsider. "One day you finally knew what you had to do, and began, though the voices around you kept shouting their bad advice," is Mary Oliver's description of moving away from the profane toward a deep sense of connectedness to the living world.

Millions of people are working on behalf of strangers, even if the evening news is usually about the death of strangers. This kindness of strangers has religious, even mythic origins, and very specific eighteenth-century roots. Abolitionists were the first people to create a national and global movement to defend the rights of those they did not know. Until that time, no group had filed a grievance except on behalf of itself. The mostly British founders of this movement were largely unknown—Granville Clark, Thomas Clarkson, Josiah Wedgwood—and their goal was ridiculous on the face of it: at that time three out of four people in the world were enslaved. Enslaving each other was what human beings had done for ages. And the abolitionist movement was greeted with incredulity. Conservative spokesmen ridiculed the abolitionists as liberals, progressives, do-gooders, meddlers, and activists. They were told they would ruin the economy and drive England into poverty. But for the first time in history a group of people organized themselves to help people they would never know, from whom they would never receive direct or indirect benefit. And today tens of millions of people do this every day. It is called the world of non-profits, civil society, schools, social entrepreneurship, non-governmental organizations, and companies who place social and environmental justice at the top of their strategic goals. The scope and scale of this effort is unparalleled in history.

The living world is not "out there" somewhere, but in your heart. What do we know about life? In the words of biologist Janine Benyus, life creates the conditions that are conducive to life. I can think of no better motto for a future economy. We have tens of thousands of abandoned homes without people and tens of thousands of abandoned people without homes. We have failed bankers advising failed regulators on how to save failed assets. We are the only species on the planet without full employment. Brilliant. We have an economy that tells us that it is cheaper to destroy earth in real time rather than renew, restore, and sustain it. You can print money to bail out a bank but you can't print life to bail out a planet. At present we are stealing the future, selling it in the present, and calling it gross domestic product. We can just as easily have an economy that is based on healing the future instead of stealing it. We can either create assets for the future or take the assets of the future. One is called restoration and the other exploitation. And whenever we exploit the earth we exploit people and cause untold suffering. Working for the earth is not a way to get rich, it is a way to be rich.

The first living cell came into being nearly 40 million centuries ago, and its direct descendants are in all of our bloodstreams. Literally you are breathing molecules this very second that were inhaled by Moses, Mother Teresa, and Bono. We are vastly interconnected. Our fates are inseparable. We are here because the dream of every cell is to become two cells. And dreams come true. In each of you are one quadrillion cells, 90 percent of which are not human cells. Your body is a community, and without those other microorganisms you would perish in hours. Each human cell has 400 billion molecules conducting millions of processes between trillions of atoms. The total cellular activity in one human body is staggering: one septillion actions at any one moment, a one with twenty-four zeros after it. In a millisecond, our body has undergone ten times more processes than there are stars in the universe, which is exactly what Charles Darwin foretold when he said science would discover that each living creature was a "little universe, formed of a host of self-propagating organisms, inconceivably minute and as numerous as the stars of heaven."

So I have two questions for you all: First, can you feel your body? Stop for a moment. Feel your body. One septillion activities going on simultaneously, and your body does this so well you are free to ignore it, and wonder instead when this speech will end. You can feel it. It is called life. This is who you are. Second question: who is in charge of your body? Who is managing those molecules? Hopefully not a political party. Life is creating the conditions that are conducive to life inside you, just as in all of nature. Our innate nature is to create the conditions that are conducive to life. What I want you to imagine is that collectively humanity is evincing a deep innate wisdom in coming together to heal the wounds and insults of the past.

Ralph Waldo Emerson once asked what we would do if the stars only came out once every thousand years. No one would sleep that night, of course. The world would create new religions overnight. We would be ecstatic, delirious, made rapturous by the glory of God. Instead, the stars come out every night and we watch television.

This extraordinary time when we are globally aware of each other and the multiple dangers that threaten civilization has never happened, not in a thousand years, not in ten thousand years. Each of us is as complex and beautiful as all the stars in the universe. We have done great things and we have gone way off course in terms of honoring creation. You are graduating to the most amazing, stupefying challenge ever bequested to any generation. The generations before you failed. They didn't stay up all night. They got distracted and lost sight of the fact that life is a miracle every moment of your existence. Nature beckons you to be on her side. You couldn't ask for a better boss.

The most unrealistic person in the world is the cynic, not the dreamer. Hope only makes sense when it doesn't make sense to be hopeful. This is your century. Take it and run as if your life depends on it.

Paul Hawken gave this Commencement Address at the University of Portland in 2009. He worked with Martin Luther King, Jr., in Selma, Alabama; founded leading natural-foods wholesaler Erewhon and the Smith & Hawken garden supply company; and currently heads a thin-panel solar company. His books include *The Ecology of Commerce* (HarperCollins, 1993) and *Blessed Unrest* (Viking, 2007). *Carbon, The Business of Life* will be published in 2014.

Adrienne Rich's poem is excerpted from "Natural Resources," in *The Fact of a Doorframe: Selected Poems 1950–2001* by Adrienne Rich (W. W. Norton, 2002).

CHAPTER FIVE

Political Paralysis

Danusha Veronica Goska

It was September 1998, in Bloomington, Indiana. As part of the conference on Spirituality and Ecology: No Separation, a group of concerned citizens was gathered in the basement of St. Paul Catholic Center. They were thinking and talking about living their ideals. Some had planted trees in Africa. Some described ways that they honor the indigenous spirit of a place, and their own ancestors. Elderly nuns and young feminists recounted their part in women's struggle. One frustrated woman voiced the nagging worry of many. "I want to do something, but what can I do? I'm just one person, an average person. I can't have an impact. I live with the despair of my own powerlessness. I can't bring myself to do anything. The world is so screwed up, and I have so little power. I feel so *paralyzed*."

I practically exploded.

Years before I had been stricken by a debilitating illness. Perilymph fistula's symptoms are like those of multiple sclerosis. On some days I was functional. On others, and I could never predict when these days would strike, I was literally, not metaphorically, paralyzed. I couldn't leave the house; I could barely stand up. I had moved to Bloomington for grad school. I knew no one in town. I couldn't get health care because I hadn't enough money, and the Social Security administration, against the advice of its own physician and vocational advisors, denied my claim.

That's why I imitated Mount Vesuvius when the conference participant claimed that just one person, one average person, can't do anything significant to make the world a better place; that the only logical option was passivity, surrender, and despair.

I raised my hand and spoke. "I have an illness that causes intermittent bouts of paralysis," I explained. "And that paralysis has taught me something. It has taught me that my protestations of my own powerlessness are bogus. Yes, some days I can't move or see. But you know what? Some days I can move. Some days I can see. And the difference between being able to walk across the room and not being able to walk across the room is epic.

"I commute to campus by foot along a railroad track. In spring, I come across turtles who have gotten stuck. The track is littered with the hollowing shells of turtles that couldn't escape the rails. So, I bend over, and I pick up the still living trapped turtles that I do find. I carry them to a wooded area and let them go. For those turtles, that much power that I have is enough.

"I'm just like those turtles. When I have been sick and housebound for days, I wish someone—anyone—would talk to me. To hear a human voice say my name; to be touched: that would mean the world to me.

"One day an attack hit me while I was walking home from campus. It was a snowy day. There was snow on the ground, and more snow was falling from the sky. I struggled with each step; wobbled and wove across the road. I must have looked like a drunk. One of my neighbors, whom I had never met, stopped and asked if I was okay. He drove me home.

"He didn't hand me the thousands of dollars I needed for surgery. He didn't take me in and empty my puke bucket. He just gave me one ride, one day. I am still grateful to him and touched by his gesture. I'd lived in the neighborhood for years, and so far he has been the only one to stop. The problem is not that we have so little power. The problem is that we don't use the power that we have."

Why do we deny that power? Why do we not honor what we can do?

Part of the reason is that "virtue" is often defined as the ultimate commodity, something exclusive, like a Porsche or a perfect figure, that only the rich and famous have access to. "Virtue" is defined as so outside of normal human experience or ability that you'd think, if you were doing it right, you'd know, because camera crews and an awards committee would appear on your lawn.

Thus the defining of virtue is surrendered to a Madison Avenue mentality. I remember when the Dalai Lama came to Bloomington in 1999. The words "virtue" and "celebrity" were confused until they became synonymous. The Dalai Lama's visit was the most glamorous event Bloomington had seen in years. Suddenly even our barbershop scuttlebutt featured more movie stars than an article from *People* magazine. "Did you see Steven Segal on Kirkwood Avenue? Richard Gere gets in tomorrow." Virtue becomes something farther and farther out of the reach of the common person.

I was once a Peace Corps volunteer. I also volunteered for the Sisters of Charity, the order begun by Mother Teresa. When people learn of these things, they sometimes act impressed. I am understood to be a virtuous person.

I did go far away, and I did wear a foreign costume. But I don't know that I was virtuous. I tried to be, but I was an immature, inadequately trained girl in foreign countries with obscenely unjust regimes and little to no avenues for progress. My impact was limited.

To put myself through college, I worked as a nurse's aide. I earned minimum wage. I wore a pink polyester uniform and I dealt with the elderly and the dying, ignored people who went years without seeing a loved one, who died alone. When I speak of this job, I never impress anyone. I am not understood to be a virtuous person. Rather, I am understood to be working class.

I loved this difficult, low-paid work not out of any masochistic sense of personal elevation through suffering. I loved it because I physically and emotionally touched people every day, all day long; I made them comfortable; I made them laugh; I challenged them; they rose to meet the challenges. In return, patients shared with me the most precious commodity in the universe: their humanity.

This essay is not a protest against selfishness, which, well done, can be a beautiful thing. There is nothing I envy, and appreciate, so much as a life led with genuinely unconscious, uncomplicated self-absorption. It's a sort of karmic performance art. Isn't that quality why some people so love observing cats? And I do not begrudge my fellow travelers' enthusiasm for glamour; there's nothing I like more. The right dress worn by the right starlet on Oscar night probably does as much to feed the soul as a perfect haiku.

Rather, I'm protesting the fallacy that to be virtuous, one must be on TV, one must be off to a meeting on how to be a better person, or one must have just come from a meeting on how to be a better person, but one can pass up every opportunity to actually *be* a better person.

It's sad how sometimes "virtue celebrities" intimidate us with their virtue résumés. We think, "Gee, I'll never travel to Malaysia and close a sweatshop; I'm not brave enough (or organized or articulate enough) to champion a cause. I have to go to work every day, and I just don't have the time or the gifts to be a virtuous person."

I go to a food bank every two weeks to get my food. I have no car. I can't carry two weeks worth of food the three miles back to my house. Every week, I get a ride home from other food bank patrons. These folks don't pause for a second to sigh, "Oh, problems are so big, I'm so powerless; will it really help anything if I give you this ride?" They don't look around to make sure someone is watching. They just, invisibly, do the right thing. I get rides in old, old cars. In one car I could see the road beneath whiz past under broken-down flooring; in another,

I shared space with a large, lapping dog. I once got a ride from a man who told me he'd just gotten out of jail. Another time, my chauffeur's tattoos ran up and down his naked chest and back. When I was sick, I went from agency to agency, begging people with glamorous titles and impressive virtue résumés for help. Most did nothing.

The *Lamed Vov Tzaddikim* are the thirty-six hidden saints of Jewish folklore. Unlettered and insignificant, they work at humble trades and pass unnoticed. Because of these anonymous saints, the world continues to exist. Without their insignificant, unnoticed virtue—Poof!—God loses divine patience, and the world goes up in smoke.

Sometimes we convince ourselves that the "unnoticed" gestures of "insignificant" people mean nothing. It's not enough to recycle our soda cans; we must Stop Global Warming Now. Since we can't Stop Global Warming Now, we may as well not recycle our soda cans. It's not enough to be our best selves; we have to be Gandhi. And yet when we study the biographies of our heroes, we learn that they spent years in preparation doing tiny, decent things before one historical moment propelled them to center stage.

Moments, as if animate, use the prepared to tilt empires. Ironically, saints we worship today, heroes we admire, were often ridiculed, tortured, or, most punishingly, ignored in their own lifetimes. St. John of the Cross gave the world the spiritual classic, *The Dark Night of the Soul*. It was inspired by his own experience of being imprisoned by the members of his own religious order. Before Solidarity, Lech Walesa, the Nobel Peace Prize winner who helped bring down communism, was a nonentity; a blue-collar worker in an oft-ridiculed Eastern European backwater. He was always active; one moment changed this small man's otherwise small-time, invisible activism into the kind of wedge that can topple a giant. Now, that moment past, Walesa has returned to relative obscurity.

—

Besides the pressure of virtue as an unattainable status reserved for the elect, there may be another reason why people don't live their own ideals. It may be that many who do not live what they believe have been stunted. They've been told many times: "What you feel does not matter; what you believe is ridiculous; what you envision is worthless; just sit back and obey the priest, the preacher, the teacher, the cop, the mob, the man in charge, or your own fear." When the still, small voice whispers to them that they ought to visit an elderly neighbor, or write a letter to the editor, or pull a few strings and let the indigent patient in to see the doctor, even though the red tape says they cannot, they tell the still, small voice "Stifle yourself!"

Such self-numbed people may see themselves as perpetual victims. "I have nothing!" they insist. "I have no power! I can't do anything! I have nothing to give! Everybody picks on me!" These are the folks who begrudge so much as a smile to their neighbors. Even as they live in houses, drive cars, enjoy health, they see themselves as naked, starving, homeless, penniless wretches waiting to be rescued by whomever is in charge. Their sense of victimization does not allow them to see that *they* are in charge—of their own choices.

While working or traveling in Africa, Asia, and Eastern Europe, I occasionally met people who really did have next to nothing, but who stunned me with their insistence on the abundance of their own humanity. One afternoon, as I trekked to my teaching post in the Himalayas, a monsoon storm turned day into night and a landslide wiped out my trail. I got terribly lost; coming to a strange village, exhausted, I sat on the porch of a peasant home. Inside, the family was eating roasted cow-corn kernels for dinner. Roasted cow-corn kernels were to be their entire dinner; there was nothing else on their menu.

A man inside saw that a human form was sitting on his porch. He couldn't have seen that I was American, or anything else, for that matter. It was dark night by then, in a village without electricity. In any case, I was wearing a sari. He whispered to his wife, "Someone is sitting on our porch. We have to cook rice." Rice is the highest-status food in that economy. And, by "rice," they meant, for them, an elaborate meal consisting of rice, lentils, and vegetables.

This feeling of being seen, this conviction that every act one performs matters to a supremely consequential audience, can come from a belief in God. Psalm 139 articulates how thoroughly and consequentially *witnessed* the theist feels.

> *O Lord, You have searched me*
> *and You know me.*
> *You know when I sit and when I rise;*
> *You perceive my thoughts from afar.*
> *. . . Before a word is on my tongue*
> *You know it completely, O Lord.*
> *Where can I go from Your Spirit?*
> *Where can I flee from Your presence?*
> *If I go up to the heavens, You are there;*
> *if I make my bed in the depths, You are there.*

The very marrow of the believer's bones is impregnated with the conviction that everything he does is avidly witnessed by God, and that everything he does matters to God. Whether or not one's fellow incarnate beings see is secondary.

Non-theists, including atheists, can also have this feeling that one is witnessed, that everything one does matters. Not just a personalized God sees and tallies human action. Disembodied forces that can never be tampered with also weigh our deeds. For some, karma plays witness. You may be able to fool your fellow humans, but, ultimately, you can't cheat karma.

In many cultures, there is a disembodied force that demands that every action be ethical: honor. "*Bog, Honor, Ojczyzna,*" or "God, Honor, Country," is the Polish national motto. My stays in Poland introduced me to otherwise empty-handed activists who faced off against Nazis, Communists, and now, capitalism, with relentless personal power. "Burnout" and "apathy" were not in their vocabulary. Even when serving time in prisons that appeared on no map, they felt visible. Honor recorded their every deed, and ensured that it mattered.

I suspect that we all have our three-in-the-morning moments, when all of life seems one no-exit film noir, where any effort is pointless, where any hope seems to be born only to be dashed, like a fallen nestling on a summer sidewalk. When I have those moments, if I do nothing else, I remind myself: the ride in the snow; the volunteers at the food bank; the Nepali peasants who fed me. Activists like the Pole Wladyslaw Bartoszewski who, decades before he would earn any fame, got out of Auschwitz only to go on to even more resistance against the Nazis, and then the Soviets. Invisible, silent people who, day by day, choice by choice, unseen by me, unknown to me, force me to witness myself, invite me to keep making my own best choices, and keep me living my ideals.

In 2000, Indiana State Senate aid Rick Gudal arranged for Dr. Richard Miyamoto to perform a pro bono surgery that ended Danusha Veronica Goska's perilymph fistula symptoms. Today, Dr. Goska is adjunct professor at William Paterson University and, like so many adjuncts nowadays, is eagerly seeking a full-time teaching job. Please feel free to contact her for job inquiries. She is the author of *Bieganski: The Brute Polak Stereotype in Polish-Jewish Relations and American Popular Culture* (Academic Studies Press), which won the 2010 Halecki Award for Outstanding Book on the Polish Experience in America. Her novel *Save Send Delete* (Roundfire Books) tells the true story of her yearlong debate about God, and love affair, with a celebrity atheist she saw on TV, and Julie Davis named it one of the year's ten-best books. You can reach Dr. Goska at *dgoska@yahoo.com*.

PART TWO

Dark Before the Dawn

From SEPTEMBER 1, 1939

W. H. Auden

. . . All I have is a voice
To undo the folded lie,
The romantic lie in the brain
Of the sensual man-in-the-street
And the lie of Authority
Whose buildings grope the sky:
There is no such thing as the State
And no one exists alone;
Hunger allows no choice
To the citizen or the police;
We must love one another or die. . . .

Excerpted from "September 1, 1939," in *Collected Poems* by W. H. Auden (Random House, 1940).

One of the ideas that runs throughout this collection and unites an unruly array of nationalities, sensibilities, interests, and historical situations is that living with conviction is of value in itself, regardless of the outcome. Simply keeping the "affirming flame" alive is a victory. But when doing so under conditions in which implacable night reigns, and surrounded by forces aiming to extinguish the human spirit, we can at times transform scattered, sputtering flames into beacons of promise whose light reaches across the globe. There are many wonderful stories of people who have persisted, one step at a time and shoulder to shoulder with others, until they have achieved important victories. But those who make us believe that anything is possible, and fire our imagination over the long haul, are often the ones who have survived the bleakest of circumstances themselves. They have every reason to despair, but don't, so may have the most to teach us, not only about how to hold true to our beliefs but about how persistence, vision, and courage can bring about seemingly impossible social change.

"We forget," wrote historian Howard Zinn, "how often in this century we have been astonished by the sudden crumbling of institutions, by extraordinary changes in people's thoughts, by unexpected eruptions of rebellion against tyrannies, by the quick collapse of systems of power that seemed invincible." I've long admired Zinn's resiliency and life-affirming challenges to injustice. His essay, "The Optimism of Uncertainty," celebrates these qualities in others. Zinn took the long view of history, calling attention to the moments when courage and constancy unexpectedly prevail, and the unpredictable nature of human affairs works in favor of freedom and fairness. Even while documenting the worst instances of arrogance, greed, and cruelty, Zinn never lost faith in what the human spirit can accomplish.

It's tempting, when following recent news, to take for granted the recent success of the gay rights movement and to deem it almost inevitable that the US military would not only permit gay service members to marry but guarantee their spouses full standard rights. Or that the IRS would issue its own "equal before law" ruling once the Supreme Court had weighed in. Or that the Social Security administration would do the same. Yet until fairly recently, gay marriage had been unthinkable. Forty years ago, as Dan Savage writes in "On Being Different," to be gay usually meant to be closeted. The alternative was too painful. In an essay Savage quotes from that time, "What It Means to Be a Homosexual," noted writer Merle Miller describes how a long-time friend he came out to explained, while planning a visit, "'I've always leveled with you, Merle, and I'm going to now. I've changed my mind about bringing [his sixteen-year-old son]. I'm sure you understand.'" Miller shouldn't take it personally, his friend said. He just didn't want to risk his son being corrupted.

If you were gay back then, you were most likely living in the shadows. To step out into the light risked condemnation, job loss, separation from relatives and friends, even physical attack. Yet gay activists known and unknown spoke out, organized, and persisted, because, as Savage writes, they were standing up for their own dignity against the lies that defamed them. As a result of their courage, and that of others they inspired, Savage and his husband can now take two straight teenage friends of their straight adopted son D.J. along on a Hawaiian vacation, without anyone thinking it exceptional. Indeed, the parents of the kids were delighted, caring only that they trusted Dan and his husband to ensure "that their sons would be eating decent meals, brushing their teeth twice a day, and getting to bed at a reasonable hour." That respect is still far from universally granted for those perceived as gay: After a fifteen-year-old bullied by classmates killed himself in Greensburg, Indiana, Savage founded the It Gets Better Project so that people could post encouraging and supportive video stories. Young GLBT kids could log in from wherever they lived, from small rural towns to big cities, thereby overcoming the isolation that can make being different impossible to bear. Fifty million people have now watched the videos, with those posting testimonials for the site ranging from President Obama to major-league baseball teams. The response attests to a hard-won cultural shift.

Appropriately, Savage's essay came to me through my friend Karen Maeda Allman, a staffer at Seattle's Elliott Bay Bookstore who recently took advantage of Washington State's new gay marriage law to formalize her own fifteen-year union. Karen's father was white and her mother Japanese. Their 1957 marriage would have been illegal due to interracial marriage bans in half the states in the country, and would have been illegal in California just nine years before. The ability of both Karen and Dan to marry those they love is the fruit of precisely the kinds of unheralded acts of courageous optimism that Howard Zinn described.

Successful citizen movements also, as Zinn explored, embody persistence. Nelson Mandela and Václav Havel embodied this persistence in situations where all doors seem closed and all possibilities precluded. In "The Dark Years," Mandela writes of his Robben Island imprisonment and how he and his fellow prisoners maintained their quest for justice, even when told they would die in captivity. With no apparent reason to believe they'd ever be released, Mandela and his compatriots devised small ways to resist, "making a way out of no way," to use a phrase of sociologist Joseph Scott. They smuggled messages and newspaper headlines cell-to-cell on scraps of toilet paper, sang or whistled freedom songs to raise their morale, and kept their dignity until even some of the guards began to show them respect. For a staggering twenty-seven years, Mandela kept alive the flame of hope that he embodied. Even more remarkable, by the time he was released he had, as he describes it, also escaped the narrow compass of hatred by recognizing that those who had put him in prison needed to be liberated as well.

Prophetically, Václav Havel wrote "An Orientation of the Heart," three years before the 1989 "Velvet Revolution" brought down Czechoslovakia's Communist dictatorship. Havel and his ragtag community of writers, musicians, and political activists are living examples of how seemingly futile actions on the part of ordinary and otherwise flawed human beings can bring about powerful results. When we stand up for what we believe, Havel makes clear, we may not create the immediate results we hope for: countering the marginalization of an ethnic, religious, or sexual minority, reforming a dictatorship, reining in runaway economic greed. But our actions may nevertheless yield unforeseen but equally desirable results. Critics mocked Havel and the early human rights initiatives in which he and others participated—in particular, a petition to free jailed dissidents. Those who circulated the petitions were labeled "exhibitionistic," their motives dismissed as nothing more than an attempt "to draw attention to themselves." Dissenters everywhere—including the United States—habitually receive the same treatment. This suggests that the fraternity of the cynical and contemptuous, like the fellowship of the activists they dismiss, transcends political systems and historical circumstances.

Indeed, in one sense, Havel and the other petitioners failed completely. Their initial efforts didn't free a single political prisoner. But their campaign was worthwhile, in fact essential, in a more significant sense, though its results were less visible and dramatic, at least insofar as those of us watching from afar were concerned. Upon release, the Czech dissidents said that the mere fact that others had taken up their cause had sustained them during their incarceration: another example of Mandela's multiplication of courage. Soon after, Havel himself was imprisoned for four years, and many of his compatriots also were jailed. Yet their once seemingly hopeless actions helped build a movement that eventually toppled the regime.

Was this exhibitionism? I'd call it a defiant exercise of freedom, but with a beat you can dance to—provided, of course, by the Plastic People of the Universe, the band the Czech authorities considered so much of a threat to the existing order that they'd tried to jail them.

The essence of the story bears repeating: When, in 1986, Havel described the growing cracks in the seemingly rock-solid wall of oppressive rule, he had no way of knowing that the Czech dictatorship would fall in three years. Indeed, he had almost every reason to believe otherwise. Yet he stubbornly surveyed the cracks: the dissenting voices, the underground publishing ventures, and the theater groups that didn't exist a few years earlier; the so-called Jazz Section, an officially sanctioned cultural organization, now suddenly sponsoring rebellious music; the meeting places, such as churches and cafés, where people began to imagine "a world very different from the one that breathes on us from the newspapers, from TV and the Prague radio." To the outside world, President Gustav Husák and his administration seemed firmly entrenched, a model of Soviet-style social discipline. Government officials refused even to negotiate with the dissidents, much less acknowledge the alternative vision that Havel came to represent. Yet Havel, and that vision, eventually triumphed.

Václav Havel, we should remember, did not always star on the main stage of history. When the authorities banned his plays, he worked in a brewery. He drank and smoked too much, agonized over betrayals and failures, longed to do better. He considered himself anything but a moral giant. Remember that. Remember, too, that working alongside Havel, as well as Mandela, were vast numbers of anonymous people. We can be sure that the commitment of these unheralded heroes provided the greatest inspiration for the leaders whose names we all know.

As I'll continue to explore in this book, there's no challenge larger than climate change. If we fail to address it and end up with a world of perpetual disaster, all the other advances for human dignity become jeopardized. So when we do put even potential brakes on the expansion of the most damaging fossil fuel sources, it's a significant source of hope. I've known psychologist Mary Pipher for twenty-four years, since before she wrote *Reviving Ophelia*, her landmark book on adolescent girls. Along with millions of others who read her words, I've appreciated her extraordinarily wise and reflective voice. *The Shelter of Each Other* looked at how American families can resist an all-consuming culture, where everything is for sale. And I've given *Another Country*, her book on aging, to more friends than any other I can think of. But Pipher hasn't been primarily a political activist. She'd attend occasional peace demonstrations, and publicly returned a major American Psychological Association award as a protest against her profession's involvement in Guantanamo and other sites that conducted torture. But that was a more personal statement, though it triggered a broader conversation. She didn't view herself an organizer.

So it was inspiring to read *The Green Boat*, Pipher's book on overcoming climate-change denial, in which she talked about feeling increasingly bleak about the present and future disasters we were creating, then learned that the Keystone XL pipeline would be running through her home state of Nebraska, carrying Canadian tar sand extracts that were much worse in their climate impact than even conventional fuels. As described in "Reluctant Activists," she felt helpless before the massive financial and political clout of the pipeline company, TransCanada. The national and local consensus was that the pipeline was simply a done deal, greased by more money than Nebraska's local political officials had ever seen. So, not knowing what else to do, she took the exceedingly radical step of holding a potluck with a handful of friends to talk about how to respond. They talked, shared good food, reminded themselves that they weren't alone. Their next meeting brought in more people, and they began reaching out to ranchers, Republican farmers, college students, urban progressives, small-town business owners, and refugees from countries where oil companies called the shots. A longtime farmer and rancher who was also a staunch political conservative became a key spokesperson. He described how his parents had fought to hold on to the family land during the Great Depression, and how this Canadian company was trying to bully him out of it for private greed. The local resistance of

Pipher and others soon spread nationwide, to the point where over a thousand people got arrested at the White House to pressure President Obama to deny the necessary authorization. As I write, the future of the pipeline is uncertain. But Pipher and the pipeline opponents have delayed it for more than three years from its initial timeline. Obama's Environmental Protection Agency has taken the nearly unprecedented step of challenging the State Department for its flawed initial review. And judging from recent comments, Obama may end up vetoing the pipeline entirely. It's a perfect example of how we can start with a situation that looks wholly unwinnable, jump in, learn as we go, reach out to unlikely allies—and eventually have a shot at actually prevailing.

History, as Havel says, is ours for the making. We never know where our actions will lead.

CHAPTER SIX

The Optimism of Uncertainty

Howard Zinn

In this awful world where the efforts of caring people often pale in comparison to what is done by those who have power, how do I manage to stay involved and seemingly happy?

Some quick lessons: Don't let "those who have power" intimidate you. No matter how much power they have, they cannot prevent you from living your life, thinking independently, speaking your mind.

Find people to be with who share your values and commitments, and who also have a sense of humor.

Understand that the major media will not tell you of all the acts of resistance taking place every day in the society—the strikes, protests, individual acts of courage in the face of authority. Look around (and you will certainly find it) for the evidence of these unreported acts. And for the little you find, extrapolate from that and assume there must be a thousand times as much as you've found.

Note that throughout history people have felt powerless before authority, but that at certain times these powerless people, by organizing, acting, risking, persisting, have created enough power to change the world around them, even if a little. That is the history of the labor movement, the women's movement, the anti–Vietnam War movement, the disabled persons' movement, the gay and lesbian movement, the movement of black people in the South.

Remember that those who have power and seem invulnerable are in fact quite vulnerable. Their power depends on the obedience of others, and when those others begin withholding that obedience, begin defying authority, that power at the top turns out to be very fragile. Generals become powerless when their soldiers refuse to fight, industrialists become powerless when their workers leave their jobs or occupy the factories.

When we forget the fragility of that power at the top we become astounded when it crumbles in the face of rebellion. We have had many such surprises in our time, both in the United States and in other countries.

Don't look for a moment of total triumph. See engagement as an ongoing struggle, with victories and defeats, but in the long run slow progress. So you need patience and persistence. Understand that even when you don't "win," there is fun and fulfillment in the fact that you have been involved, with other good people, in something worthwhile. You need hope.

Is an optimist necessarily a blithe, slightly sappy whistler in the dark of our time? I am totally confident not that the world will get better, but that only confidence can prevent people from giving up the game before all the cards have been played. The metaphor is deliberate; life is a gamble. Not to play is to foreclose any chance of winning. To play, to act, is to create at least a possibility of changing the world.

What leaps out from the history of the past hundred years is its utter unpredictability. This confounds us, because we are talking about exactly the period when human beings became so ingenious technologically that they could plan and predict the exact time of someone landing on the moon, or walk down the street talking to someone halfway around the Earth.

Who foresaw that, on that day in Montgomery, Alabama, in 1955, when Rosa Parks refused to move from the front of the bus, this would lead to a mass protest of black working people, and a chain of events that would shake the nation, startle the world, and transform the South?

Let's go back to the turn of the century. A revolution to overthrow the tsar of Russia, in that most sluggish of semi-feudal empires, not only startled the most advanced imperial powers, but took Lenin himself by surprise and sent him rushing by train to Petrograd. Given the Russian Revolution, who could have predicted Stalin's deformation of it, or Khrushchev's astounding exposure of Stalin, or Gorbachev's succession of surprises?

Who would have predicted the bizarre shifts of World War II—the Nazi-Soviet pact (those embarrassing photos of von Ribbentrop and Molotov shaking hands), and the German army rolling through Russia, apparently invincible, causing colossal casualties, being turned back at the gates of Leningrad, on the western edge of Moscow, in the streets of Stalingrad, followed by the defeat of the German army, with Hitler huddled in his Berlin bunker, waiting to die?

And then the post-war world, taking a shape no one could have drawn in advance: the Chinese Communist revolution, which Stalin himself had given little chance. And then the break with the Soviet Union, the tumultuous and violent Cultural Revolution, and then another turnabout, with post–Mao China renouncing its most fervently held ideas and institutions, making overtures to the West, cuddling up to capitalist enterprise, perplexing everyone.

No one foresaw the disintegration of the old Western empires happening so quickly after the war, or the odd array of societies that would be created in the newly independent nations, from the benign village socialism of Nyerere's Tanzania to the madness of Idi Amin's adjacent Uganda.

Spain became an astonishment. A million died in the civil war, which ended in victory for the Fascist Franco, backed by Hitler and Mussolini. I recall a veteran of the Abraham Lincoln Brigade telling me that he could not imagine Spanish Fascism being overthrown without another bloody war. But after Franco was gone, a parliamentary democracy came into being, open to Socialists, Communists, anarchists, everyone.

In other places too, deeply entrenched dictatorships seemed suddenly to disintegrate—in Portugal, Argentina, the Philippines, Iran.

The end of World War II left two superpowers with their respective spheres of influence and control, vying for military and political power. The United States and the Soviet Union soon each had enough thermonuclear bombs to devastate the Earth several times over. The international scene was dominated by their rivalry, and it was supposed that all affairs, in every nation, were affected by their looming presence.

Yet the most striking fact about these superpowers was that, despite their size, their wealth, their overwhelming accumulation of nuclear weapons, they were unable to control events, even in those parts of the world considered to be their respective spheres of influence.

The failure of the Soviet Union to have its way in Afghanistan, its decision to withdraw after almost a decade of ugly intervention, was the most striking evidence that even the possession of thermonuclear weapons does not guarantee domination over a determined population.

The United States has faced the same reality. It could send an army into Korea but could not win, and was forced to sign a compromise peace. It waged a full-scale war in Indochina, conducted the most brutal bombardment of a tiny peninsula in world history, and yet was forced to withdraw. And in Latin America, after a long history of US military intervention having its way again and again, this superpower, with all its wealth and weapons, found itself frustrated. It was unable to prevent a revolution in Cuba, and the Latin American dictatorships that the United States supported from Chile to Argentina to El Salvador have fallen. In the headlines every day we see other instances of the failure of the presumably powerful over the presumably powerless, as in Brazil, where a grassroots movement of workers and the poor elected a new president pledged to fight destructive corporate power.

Looking at this catalog of huge surprises, it's clear that the struggle for justice should never be abandoned because of the apparent overwhelming power of those who have the guns and the money and who seem invincible in their determination to hold on to it. That apparent power has, again and again, proved vulnerable to human qualities less measurable than bombs and dollars: moral fervor, determination, unity, organization, sacrifice, wit, ingenuity, courage, patience—whether by blacks in Alabama and South Africa, peasants in El Salvador, Nicaragua, and Vietnam, or workers and intellectuals in Poland, Hungary, and the Soviet Union itself. No cold calculation of the balance of power need deter people who are persuaded that their cause is just.

I have tried hard to match my friends in their pessimism about the world (is it just my friends?), but I keep encountering people who, in spite of all the evidence of terrible things happening everywhere, give me hope. Especially young people, in whom the future rests. I think of my students. Not just the women of Spelman College, who leapt over a hundred years of national disgrace to become part of the civil rights movement. Not just the fellow in Alice Walker's poem "Once," who acted out the spirit of a new generation:

It is true—
I've always loved
the daring
    ones
Like the black young
man
Who tried
to crash
All barriers
at once,
    wanted to
swim
At a white
beach (in Alabama)
Nude.

I think also of my students at Boston University and people all over the country who, anguished about the war in Vietnam, resisted in some way, facing police clubs and arrests. And brave high school students like Mary Beth Tinker and her classmates in Des Moines, Iowa, who insisted on wearing black armbands to protest the war and, when suspended from school, took their case to the Supreme Court and won.

Of course, some would say, that was the Sixties. But throughout the period since, despite widespread head-shaking over the "apathy" of successive student generations, an impressive number of students continued to act.

I think of the determined little group at Boston University who, emulating groups at a hundred other schools, set up a "shantytown" on campus to represent apartheid in South Africa. The police tore it down, but the students refused to move and were arrested.

In South Africa, shortly before, I had visited Crossroads, a real shantytown outside of Cape Town, where thousands of blacks occupied places that looked like chicken coops, or were jammed together in huge tents, sleeping in shifts, six hundred of them sharing one faucet of running water. I was impressed that young Americans who had not seen that with their own eyes, had only read or seen photos, would be so moved to step out of their comfortable lives and act.

We have recently seen students all over the country campaigning for a living wage for campus employees, and against global sweatshops and pre-emptive wars. Beyond those activists, there is a much larger population of students who have no contact with any movement, yet have deep feelings about injustice.

Since I've stopped teaching, I've spent much of my time responding to invitations to speak. What I've discovered is heartening. In whatever town, large or small, in whatever state of the Union, there is always a cluster of men and women who care about the sick, the hungry, the victims of racism, the casualties of war, and who are doing something, however small, in the hope that the world will change.

Wherever I go—whether San Diego, Philadelphia, or Dallas; Ada, Oklahoma, or Shreveport, Louisiana; Presque Isle, Maine, or Manhattan, Kansas—I find such people. And beyond the handful of activists there seem to be hundreds, thousands more who are open to unorthodox ideas.

But they tend not to know of each other's existence, and so, while they persist, they do so with the desperate patience of Sisyphus endlessly pushing that boulder up the mountain. I try to tell each group that it is not alone, and that the very people who are disheartened by the absence of a national movement are themselves proof of the potential for such a movement. I suppose I'm trying to persuade myself as well as them.

Arriving at Morehead State University in rural eastern Kentucky, in the midst of the 2003 Iraq War, I found the lecture room crowded with fifteen hundred students (out of a total enrollment of six thousand). I spoke against the war and received an overwhelming reception. Earlier, when I'd been picked up at the airport by a group of faculty peace activists, one of them had brought their fourteen-year-old daughter, who'd defied her high school principal by wearing an anti-war T-shirt to school. I have found such people in all parts of the country, more and more, as evidence that the truth makes its way slowly but surely.

It is this change in consciousness that encourages me. Granted, racial hatred and sex discrimination are still with us, war and violence still poison our culture, we have a large underclass of poor, desperate people, and there is a hard core of the population content with the way things are, afraid of change.

But if we see only that, we have lost historical perspective, and then it is as if we were born yesterday and we know only the depressing stories in this morning's newspapers, this evening's television reports.

Consider the remarkable transformation, in just a few decades, in people's consciousness of racism, in the bold presence of women demanding their rightful place, in a growing public awareness that gays are not curiosities but sensate human beings, in the long-term growing skepticism about military intervention despite brief surges of military madness.

It is that long-term change that I think we must see if we are not to lose hope. Pessimism becomes a self-fulfilling prophecy; it reproduces itself by crippling our willingness to act.

There is a tendency to think that what we see in the present moment will continue. We forget how often in this century we have been astonished by the sudden crumbling of institutions, by extraordinary changes in people's thoughts, by unexpected eruptions of rebellion against tyrannies, by the quick collapse of systems of power that seemed invincible.

The bad things that happen are repetitions of bad things that have always happened—war, racism, maltreatment of women, religious and nationalist fanaticism, starvation. The good things that happen are unexpected. Unexpected, and yet explainable by certain truths that spring at us from time to time, but which we tend to forget.

Political power, however formidable, is more fragile than we think. (Note how nervous are those who hold it.)

Ordinary people can be intimidated for a time, can be fooled for a time, but they have a down-deep common sense, and sooner or later they find a way to challenge the power that oppresses them.

People are not naturally violent or cruel or greedy, although they can be made so. Human beings everywhere want the same things: They are moved by the sight of abandoned children, homeless families, the casualties of war; they long for peace, for friendship and affection across lines of race and nationality.

One semester, when I was teaching, I learned that there were several classical musicians signed up in my course. For the last class of the semester I stood aside while they sat in chairs up front and played a Mozart quartet. Not a customary finale to a class in political theory, but I wanted the class to understand that politics is pointless if it does nothing to enhance the beauty of our lives. Political discussion can sour you. We needed some music.

Revolutionary change does not come as one cataclysmic moment (beware of such moments!) but as an endless succession of surprises, moving zigzag toward a more decent society.

We don't have to engage in grand, heroic actions to participate in the process of change. Small acts, when multiplied by millions of people, can transform the world.

To be hopeful in bad times is not just foolishly romantic. It is based on the fact that human history is a history not only of cruelty, but also of compassion, sacrifice, courage, kindness. What we choose to emphasize in this complex history will determine our lives. If we see only the worst, it destroys our capacity to do something. If we remember those times and places—and there are so many—where people have behaved magnificently, this gives us the energy to act, and at least the possibility of sending this spinning top of a world in a different direction. And if we do act, in however small a way, we don't have to wait for some grand utopian future. The future is an infinite succession of presents, and to live now as we think human beings should live, in defiance of all that is bad around us, is itself a marvelous victory.

Howard Zinn's books include *A People's History of the United States* (Harper Perennial, 2005), *The Power of Nonviolence: Writings by Advocates of Peace* (Beacon Press, 2002), *You Can't Be Neutral on a Moving Train* (Beacon Press, 1994), *Howard Zinn on History* (Seven Stories Press, 2000), and *The Zinn Reader* (Seven Stories Press, 2009). This essay is adapted in part from essays in *You Can't Be Neutral* and *Howard Zinn on History*, and from an essay of Zinn's on *www.zmag.org*.

CHAPTER SEVEN

On Being Different

Dan Savage

Terry found a vacation rental for us in Hawaii.

The house was just steps from the beach—a very important detail for my husband—and it had six bedrooms. That's not the kind of vacation home we can typically afford, but there had been a last-minute cancellation, some other family had forfeited a large deposit, and my husband, ever the bargain hunter, snagged us a deal. Six bedrooms! We invited two other couples, both gay, to join us. They were thrilled. Our then thirteen-year-old son invited two of his friends, both straight, to join his boring gay dads and their boring gay friends at the beach for two weeks. Their parents were thrilled.

It was on that beach in the summer of 2011 that I read Merle Miller's essay "What It Means to Be a Homosexual" exactly forty years after it first appeared in *The New York Times Magazine*. Miller was a famous public intellectual; he was a war correspondent during the Second World War, a novelist and a historian after. He went on to be an editor at *Harper's* and *Time* magazine. Miller came out in "What It Means to Be a Homosexual," which was published later that year in book form as *On Being Different*.

As my son and his friends roughhoused in the surf with Terry and the spryer halves of the two couples who joined us, I was sitting on the beach reading this passage:

> The fear of it simply will not go away, though. A man who was once a friend, maybe my best friend, the survivor of five marriages, the father of nine, not too long ago told me that his eldest son was coming to my house on Saturday: "Now, please try not to make a pass at him."
>
> He laughed. I guess he meant it as a joke; I didn't ask.
>
> And a man I've known, been acquainted with, let's say, for twenty-five years, called from the city on a Friday afternoon before getting on the train to come up to my place for the weekend. He said, "I've always leveled with you, Merle, and I'm going to now. I've changed my mind about bringing _______ [his sixteen-year-old son]. I'm sure you understand."
>
> I said that, no, I didn't understand. Perhaps he could explain it to me.
>
> He said, "_______ is only an impressionable kid, and while I've known you and know you wouldn't, but suppose you had some friends in, and . . . "

D.J. came out to his boring gay dads as straight when he was eleven; both of the teenage boys he invited to Hawaii with us were straight. And the parents of D.J.'s friends? They were straight.

And they understood.

Which is why they didn't hesitate to say yes. The parents of D.J.'s friends knew they could trust us and our friends—two gay men they knew, four other gay men they'd never met—alone with their sons. (They also knew that their sons would be eating decent meals, brushing their teeth twice a day, and getting to bed at a reasonable hour—Terry and I have a reputation among D.J.'s friends and their parents for being joy-killing, rule-enforcing hard-asses.)

What worried Miller's friends—the "it" that his friends and acquaintances feared—was seduction. Gay men, given access to young boys, would "seduce" them into the gay lifestyle. My parents used to believe that. Among the questions I got when I came out to my family was whether an older gay man had ever seduced me.

I have known quite a few homosexuals, and I have listened to a great many accounts of how they got that way or think they got that way. I have never heard anybody say that he (or she) got to be a homosexual because of seduction.

I have known quite a few heterosexual parents since Terry and I adopted D.J. nearly a decade and a half ago. Despite the fact that more same-sex couples are adopting today than ever before, Parentlandia remains overwhelmingly straight. And not once in all the time since we became parents has a straight parent expressed the slightest anxiety about his or her son or daughter spending time with D.J., or with us, or with our gay and lesbian friends, despite the best efforts of anti-gay "Christian" conservatives to prop up the old bigotries and fears.

Have I mentioned that one of D.J.'s dads is a notorious sex-advice columnist, a recovering drag queen, and a political bomb thrower?

It has gotten better. Not perfect.

Better.

Billy Lucas was a fifteen-year-old kid growing up in Greensburg, Indiana. Lucas wasn't openly gay—he may not have been gay at all—but he was perceived to be gay by his peers and relentlessly bullied. Classmates told him to kill himself; they told him he didn't deserve to live; they told him that God hated him. School administrators, according to a lawsuit filed by Lucas's family, witnessed the abuse and did nothing to stop it. Some may have participated in the bullying of Lucas.

On Thursday, September 9, 2010, Lucas hanged himself in his grandmother's barn. His mother found his body.

Lucas's death moved Terry and me to start the It Gets Better Project. The idea was simple: There were LGBT kids out there who couldn't picture futures with enough joy in them to compensate for the pain they were in now. We wanted to reach those bullied and isolated lesbian, gay, bisexual, and transgender youth. We wanted to talk to them about the future, about their futures, and offer them encouragement. We were particularly interested in reaching LGBT kids growing up in places like Greensburg, Indiana, and other parts of the country where there aren't support groups for queer kids or Gay-Straight Alliances in the schools. We particularly wanted to reach gay, lesbian, bi, and trans kids with parents who would never allow their kids to attend an LGBT youth support group.

"You got to give 'em hope," Harvey Milk said. By sharing our stories, and encouraging other LGBT adults to do the same, we wanted to give LGBT kids hope.

Four weeks after we posted the first video to YouTube, the president of the United States uploaded his own It Gets Better video. (It took Ronald Reagan seven years to even say the word AIDS—it has gotten better.) More than fifty thousand videos have been posted as of this writing, they have been viewed more than fifty million times, and we have heard from thousands of LGBT kids who have been helped by the project.

The It Gets Better Project has generated a lot of goodwill and raised awareness about the challenges faced by LGBT youth. But the project was motivated by anger. Kids were being brutalized and bullied—sometimes bullied to death—for being queer. And not just by their peers: The LGBT kids who most needed to hear from us were the ones whose own parents were least likely to approve. LGBT kids are four times likelier to attempt suicide; LGBT kids whose families are hostile—LGBT kids who are being bullied by their own parents—are at eight times greater risk for suicide.

When we uploaded that first video, it was with a sense of defiance. We were going to talk to these LGBT kids whether their parents wanted us to or not. We were going to talk to them whether their preachers wanted us to or not. We were going to talk to them whether their teachers wanted us to or not. These kids were being told that LGBT people were sick, sinful, and unhappy, and we were going to expose the lies and call out the liars—even if the liars were their own parents.

Anger motivated us to start the It Gets Better Project, just as anger motivated Miller to write his groundbreaking essay. Gay people were coming out and demanding their rights in the wake of the Stonewall Riots, which prompted an explosion of commentary, much of it as bigoted, misinformed, and vile as the insults that Billy Lucas had to face every day. Miller, in an explosive coming-out scene, announced to two colleagues that he was "sick and tired of hearing such goddamn demeaning, degrading bullshit about me and my friends."

That exchange—that anger—led Miller to write "What It Means to Be a Homosexual" and to come out in the most public possible way. The social change we've witnessed over the last forty years was never a given. Change began when people like Merle Miller decided that they had finally had enough. Change began when LGBT people began to stand up for themselves and their friends.

> I am sick and tired of hearing such goddamn demeaning, degrading bullshit about me and my friends.

In that single sentence Miller captured the anger that has motivated LGBT activists from the Mattachine Society to the Stonewall Riots to ACT UP to the It Gets Better Project. Every LGBT rights activist I've ever met is someone who grew sick and tired of hearing such goddamn demeaning, degrading bullshit about themselves and their friends and decided to speak up and fight back.

That's what the LGBT movement is at its core: people standing up for themselves and their friends and their lovers and people with HIV and bullied LGBT kids. The LGBT movement is still facing down the liars and pushing back against the degrading bullshit. Gay people of Miller's generation knew that gay life, as described by the shrinks and the religious bigots, looked nothing like gay life as they lived it. Miller, in anger, came to the defense of himself and his friends and helped to change the world. Today, in anger, we come to the defense of LGBT kids, gay kids growing up in parts of the country where goddamn demeaning, degrading bullshit is being screamed in their faces.

And we are sick and tired of it.

I'm often asked if I wish there had been an It Gets Better Project when I was a gay kid growing up on the north side of Chicago.

There was.

It wasn't on YouTube, which didn't exist when I was a kid, or on television, which didn't acknowledge the existence of gay people when I was a kid, and the president of the United States certainly wasn't a part of it. Courageous gay activists existed. The Stonewall Riots happened in 1969, and people like Harry Hay, Frank Kameny, and Del Martin had been organizing and speaking out for years before then. But I didn't know about them.

So here's what the It Gets Better Project looked like for me in 1976: I was with my mom and dad and brothers and sister at Water Tower Place, a shopping mall near downtown Chicago. We were going to the movies—*Logan's Run*—and in front of us in line were two young gay men. They were holding hands. I was eleven years old. I was old enough to be aware, painfully so, of being different than other boys. My mother glared at the gay men in line, shook her head, and said, "They're weird," to my father, and put a protective hand on my shoulder and pulled me closer to her. She didn't reach for my brothers or my sister. Just me.

While my parents could only see dangerous perverts—it was the only thing their upbringing allowed them to see—I saw a future. I'd always known that I was different and now I knew how. I was different like them; they were different like me; I was going to be like them when I grew up. And they didn't look unhappy. They looked happy and free. They looked like they were in love.

Just by being out, just by being themselves, by taking each other's hands in public, those guys in that line at Water Tower Place gave me hope.

"Somewhere in Des Moines or San Antonio there is a young gay person who all of a sudden realizes that she or he is gay," Harvey Milk said in 1978 in his famous "hope" speech. "And that child has several options: staying in the closet; suicide. And then one day that child might open a paper that says 'Homosexual elected in San Francisco' and there are two new options: the option is to go to California, or stay in San Antonio and fight."

I was one of those kids that Harvey Milk was talking about when he gave that speech. I was thirteen years old in 1977, when Milk was elected to the San Francisco Board of Supervisors after three previous runs for office, and I only knew a few things about being gay at that time: My parents thought gay people were sick, my peers thought gay people were disgusting, and that woman who sold orange juice on the television thought gay people were pedophiles. I briefly contemplated suicide as a teenager, not because I was particularly depressed or unhappy, but because I wanted to protect my parents. I was a good kid, a well-behaved mama's boy, and I had concluded that my mother and father would rather have a dead kid than a gay one.

But hearing about Milk's election reinforced the message those two men waiting in line at Water Tower Place had unwittingly sent me a year and a half earlier. There was a place for me in this world. I had options other than staying in the closet or committing suicide.

"I know that you cannot live on hope alone," Milk said, "but without it, life is not worth living. And you, and you, and you have got to give 'em hope."

Hope can save lives—hope has saved lives—but we can do better than hope. By pushing back against the goddamn demeaning, degrading bullshit that is still being hurled at us and others, by defeating it once and for all, we can deliver change.

> [The] closets are far from emptied. There are more in hiding than out of hiding. That has been my experience anyway.

I don't think that's the case today; not in the West, at any rate. Our closets aren't empty, of course, but the closet is the exception now, no longer the rule. (And the closet cases—the Wests and Haggards and Craigs and Rekers—are ridiculous figures, not tragic ones.)

In 1971, when he was fifty and just coming out publicly, Miller was awed by the strength, self-possession, and impatience of gay men and lesbians who were coming out in their early twenties. Just over ten years later—in 1982—I would come out to my family when I was still in high school. I recently heard from the father of a thirteen-year-old boy. His son, a middle school student, had just come out and his father wanted advice on parenting a gay kid. He didn't want to fail his son.

We've gone from a world where Merle Miller couldn't come out until middle age—the world he describes in *On Being Different*—to a world where thirteen-year-old boys are coming out to their families and all their dads want to know is how they can best support their gay sons.

It has gotten better. Not perfect. Better.

But you can't know how far you've come if you don't know where you started. Adult gay men and lesbians don't raise the next generation of gays and lesbians; our history isn't passed from parent to child. That's why it's critically important for gay men and lesbians, for bisexual and transgender people, to learn their history.

Straight people with LGBT family members, friends, and co-workers should know the history of the LGBT rights movement too. All straight people should know the story of the gay liberation movement, because it is also the story of straight liberation. The LGBT rights movement liberated straight people from their prejudices and their fears; it helped straight people rebuild relationships with the lesbian, gay, bisexual, and transgender family members and friends that their prejudices had estranged them from.

People like Merle Miller and, yes, those guys in line for *Logan's Run*, came out because they were sick and tired of what LGBT people were subjected to. And by coming out at a time when it was so much more dangerous, personally and professionally, Miller helped to remake the world. Miller and all the gay men and lesbians who came out in the 1950s, '60s, and '70s—men and women who came out in big ways (by writing cover stories for *The New York Times Magazine*) and small (by taking their lover's hand in line at a movie theater)—made the world a better, safer place for all the gay, lesbian, bisexual, and trans men and women who would come after them. They made it a better, safer place for me. They made it possible for thirteen-year-old gay boys to come out to their fathers.

They made it better.

I'm roughly the same age now that Miller was when he wrote his groundbreaking essay. I'm creeping up on fifty. Like Miller, I have a mild case of writer's block; I've worked as a writer and an editor, and like Miller, I'm "an infrequent visitor to gay bars and was never comfortable in them." (I feel about gay bars the way many American Jews feel about Israel: happy to have a homeland, don't want to live there.)

Writing in 1971—when homosexuality was still a crime in forty-eight states—Miller observed, "I think social attitudes will change, are changing, quickly too."

When I finally came out in 1982, telling my Catholic parents I was gay didn't just mean telling them I was like those guys at the movies my mother wanted to protect me from. It meant I would never marry and I would never have children. I would certainly never be trusted alone with someone else's child.

But there I was, just four short decades after Miller wrote *On Being Different*, just three short decades after I sat down with my mother and forced the words "I'm gay" out of my mouth. There I was, sitting on the beach next to my husband, while our teenage son dove through waves. with his friends, two boys who were entrusted to our care by their straight parents.

"In the battle between reality and fundamentalism of all varieties reality always wins—if it is given the freedom to breathe and we show the courage necessary to accept it," author and political commentator Andrew Sullivan writes in response to reading Miller's essay. "Even then it takes time. But when a truth has been suppressed by a massive lie for centuries, its eventual emergence is almost a miracle."

That day on the beach, reading Miller's essay and recalling what coming out meant when Miller did it and what it meant when I did, it did feel like a miracle.

Thank you, Mr. Miller, for telling your story; thank you for your anger; thank you and all the others who fought back against the demeaning, degrading bullshit. We couldn't have made it to that beach without you.

Dan Savage is the author of *American Savage* (Dutton, 2013), from which this essay was taken. An earlier version appeared as the Foreword to *On Being Different* by Merle Miller (Penguin Classics, 2012). Savage is also a nationally syndicated sex-advice columnist and the editor of *It Gets Better* (Penguin, 2012).

CHAPTER EIGHT

The Dark Years

Nelson Mandela

The challenge for every prisoner, particularly every political prisoner, is how to survive prison intact, how to emerge from prison undiminished, how to conserve and even replenish one's beliefs. The first task in accomplishing that is learning exactly what one must do to survive. To that end, one must know the enemy's purpose before adopting a strategy to undermine it. Prison is designed to break one's spirit and destroy one's resolve. To do this, the authorities attempt to exploit every weakness, demolish every initiative, negate all signs of individuality—all with the idea of stamping out that spark that makes each of us human and each of us who we are.

Our survival depended on understanding what the authorities were attempting to do to us, and sharing that understanding with each other. It would be very hard if not impossible for one man alone to resist. I do not know that I could have done it had I been alone. But the authorities' greatest mistake was keeping us together, for together our determination was reinforced. We supported each other and gained strength from each other. Whatever we knew, whatever we learned, we shared, and by sharing we multiplied whatever courage we had individually. That is not to say that we were all alike in our responses to the hardships we suffered. Men have different capacities and react differently to stress. But the stronger ones raised up the weaker ones, and both became stronger in the process. Ultimately, we had to create our own lives in prison. In a way that even the authorities acknowledged, order in prison was preserved not by the warders but by ourselves.

Prison and the authorities conspire to rob each man of his dignity. In and of itself, that ensured that I would survive, for any man or institution that tries to rob me of my dignity will lose because I will not part with it at any price or under any pressure. I never seriously considered the possibility that I would not emerge from prison one day. I never thought that a life sentence truly meant life and that I would die behind bars. Perhaps I was denying this prospect because it was too unpleasant to contemplate. But I always knew that someday I would once again feel the grass under my feet and walk in the sunshine as a free man.

I am fundamentally an optimist. Whether that comes from nature or nurture, I cannot say. Part of being optimistic is keeping one's head pointed toward the sun, one's feet moving forward. There were many dark moments when my faith in humanity was sorely tested, but I would not and could not give myself up to despair. That way lay defeat and death.

Our first June and July were the bleakest months on Robben Island. Winter was in the air, and the rains were just beginning. It never seemed to go above forty degrees Fahrenheit. Even in the sun, I shivered in my light khaki shirt. It was then that I first understood the cliché of feeling the cold in one's bones. At noon we would break for lunch. That first week all we were given was soup, which stank horribly. In the afternoon, we were permitted to exercise for half an hour under strict supervision. We walked briskly around the courtyard in single file.

On one of our first days pounding rocks, the authorities placed an enormous bucket in the courtyard and announced that it had to be half full by the end of the week. We worked hard and succeeded. The following week, the warder in charge announced that we must now fill the bucket three-quarters of the way. We worked with great diligence and succeeded. The next week we were ordered to fill the bucket to the top. We knew we could not tolerate this much longer, but said nothing.

We even managed to fill the bucket all the way, but the warders had provoked us. In stolen whispers we resolved on a policy: no quotas. The next week we initiated our first go-slow strike on the island: We would work at less than half the speed we had before to protest the excessive and unfair demands. The guards immediately saw this and threatened us, but we would not increase our pace, and we continued this go-slow strategy for as long as we worked in the courtyard.

Robben Island had changed since I had been there for a fortnight's stay in 1962. There were few prisoners then; the place seemed more like an experiment than a full-fledged prison. Two years later, Robben Island was without question the harshest, most iron-fisted outpost in the South African penal system. It was a hardship station not only for the prisoners but for the prison staff. Gone were the Coloured warders who had supplied cigarettes and sympathy. The warders were white and overwhelmingly Afrikaans-speaking, and they demanded a master-servant relationship. They ordered us to call them "baas," which we refused. The racial divide on Robben Island was absolute: there were no black warders, and no white prisoners.

Moving from one prison to another always requires a period of adjustment. But journeying to Robben Island was like going to another country. Its isolation made it not simply another prison, but a world of its own, far removed from the one we had come from. The high spirits with which we left Pretoria had been snuffed out by its stern atmosphere; we were face-to-face with the realization that our life would be unredeemably grim. In Pretoria, we felt connected to our supporters and our families; on the island, we felt cut off, and indeed we were. We had the consolation of being with each other, but that was the only consolation. My dismay was quickly replaced by a sense that a new and different fight had begun.

From the first day, I had protested about being forced to wear short trousers. I demanded to see the head of the prison and made a list of complaints. The warders ignored my protests, but by the end of the second week, I found a pair of old khaki trousers unceremoniously dumped on the floor of my cell. No pin-striped three-piece suit has ever pleased me as much. But before putting them on I checked to see if my comrades had been issued trousers as well.

They had not, and I told the warder to take the trousers back. I insisted that all African prisoners must have long trousers. The warder grumbled, "Mandela, you say you want long pants and then you don't want them when we give them to you." The warder balked at touching trousers worn by a black man, and finally the commanding officer himself came to my cell to pick them up. "Very well, Mandela," he said, "you are going to have the same clothing as everyone else." I replied that if he was willing to give me long trousers, why couldn't everyone else have them? He did not have an answer.

Shortly after we started working at the quarry, we were joined in Section B by a number of other prominent political prisoners. To counterbalance the effect of these new political allies, the authorities also put a handful of common-law prisoners in our section. These men were hardened criminals, convicted of murder, rape, and armed robbery. They were members of the island's notorious criminal gangs, either the Big Fives or the Twenty-Eights, which terrorized other prisoners. They were brawny and surly, and their faces bore the scars of the knife fights that were common among gang members. Their role was to act as agents provocateurs, and they would attempt to push us around, take our food, and inhibit any political discussions we tried to have.

The gang members worked in their own clique apart from us at the quarry. One day, they began singing what sounded like a work song. In fact, it was a famous work song with their own adapted lyrics: "Benifunani eRivonia?" which means "What did you want at Rivonia?" The next line was something like "Did you think that you would become the government?" They sang exuberantly and with a mocking tone. They had obviously been encouraged by the warders, who were hoping that the song would provoke us.

Although the more hotheaded among us wanted to confront them, instead we decided to fight fire with fire. We had far more and better singers among us than they had, and we huddled together and planned our response. Within a few minutes, we were all singing the song "Stimela," a rousing anthem about a train making its way down from Southern Rhodesia. "Stimela" is not a political song, but in the context it became one, for the implication was that the train contained guerrillas coming down to fight the South African army.

For a number of weeks our two groups sang as we worked, adding songs and changing lyrics. Our repertoire increased, and we were soon singing overt political songs, such as "Amajoni," a song about guerrilla soldiers, the title of which was a corruption of the English slang word for soldier, Johnny; and "Tshotsholoza," a song that compares the struggle to the motion of an oncoming train. (If you say the title over and over, it mimics the sound of the train.) We sang a song about the Freedom Charter, and another about the Transkei, whose lyrics said, "There are two roads, one road is the Matanzima road, and one road is the Mandela road, which one will you take?"

The singing made the work lighter. A few of the fellows had extraordinary voices, and I often felt like putting my pick down and simply listening. The gang members were no competition for us; they soon became quiet while we continued singing. But one of the warders was fluent in Xhosa and understood the content of our songs, and we were soon ordered to stop singing. (Whistling was also banned.) From that day on we worked in silence.

I saw the gang members not as rivals but as raw material to be converted. There was a nonpolitical prisoner among us, nicknamed Joe My Baby, who later joined the ANC [African National Congress] and proved invaluable in helping us smuggle material in and out of prison.

Newspapers were more valuable to political prisoners than gold or diamonds, more hungered for than food or tobacco; they were the most precious contraband on Robben Island. News was the intellectual raw material of the struggle. We were not allowed any news at all, and we craved it. Walter Sisulu, even more than myself, seemed bereft without news. The authorities attempted to impose a complete blackout; they did not want us to learn anything that might raise our morale or reassure us that people on the outside were still thinking about us.

We regarded it as our duty to keep ourselves current on the politics of the country, and we fought long and hard for the right to have newspapers. Over the years, we devised many ways of obtaining them, but back then we were not so adept. One of the advantages of going to the quarry was that warders' sandwiches were wrapped in newspaper and they would often discard these newsprint wrappers in the trash, where we secretly retrieved them. We would distract the warders' attention, pluck the papers out of the garbage, and slide them into our shirts.

One of the most reliable ways to acquire papers was through bribery, and this was the only area where I tolerated what were often unethical means of obtaining information. The warders always seemed to be short of money, and their poverty was our opportunity.

When we did get hold of a paper, it was far too risky to pass around. Possession of a newspaper was a serious charge. Instead, one person would read the paper, usually Kathy [Ahmed Kathrada] or, later, Mac Maharaj. Kathy was in charge of communications, and he had thought of ingenious ways for us to pass information. Kathy would go through the paper and make cuttings of relevant stories, which were then secretly distributed to the rest of us. Each of us would write out a summary of the story we were given; these summaries were then passed among us, and later smuggled to the general section. When the authorities were particularly vigilant, Kathy or Mac would write out his summary of the news and then destroy the paper, usually by tearing it into small pieces and placing it in his ballie [iron pail used as a toilet], which the warders never inspected.

Another technique was to write in tiny, coded script on toilet paper. The paper was so small and easily hidden that this became a popular way of smuggling out messages. When the authorities discovered a number of these communications, they took the extraordinary measure of rationing toilet paper. Govan was then ailing and not going to the quarry, and he was given the task of counting out eight squares of toilet paper for each prisoner per day.

The most important person in any prisoner's life is not the minister of justice, not the commissioner of prisons, not even the head of prison, but the warder in one's section. If you are cold and want an extra blanket, you might petition the minister of justice, but you will get no response. If you go to the commissioner of prisons, he will say, "Sorry, it is against regulations." The head of prison will say, "If I give you an extra blanket, I must give one to everyone." But if you approach the warder in your corridor, and you are on good terms with him, he will simply go to the stockroom and fetch a blanket.

I always tried to be decent to the warders in my section; hostility was self-defeating. There was no point in having a permanent enemy among the warders. It was ANC policy to try to educate all people, even our enemies: we believed that all men, even prison service warders, were capable of change, and we did our utmost to try to sway them.

In general, we treated the warders as they treated us. If a man was considerate, we were considerate in return. Not all of our warders were ogres. We noticed right from the start that there were some among them who believed in fairness. Yet, being friendly with warders was not an easy proposition, for they generally found the idea of being courteous to a black man abhorrent. Because it was useful to have warders who were well disposed toward us, I often asked certain men to make overtures to selected warders. No one liked to take on such a job.

We had one warder who seemed particularly hostile to us. This was troublesome, for at the quarry we would hold discussions among ourselves, and a warder who did not permit us to talk was a great hindrance. I asked a certain comrade to befriend this fellow so that he would not interrupt our talks. The warder was quite crude, but he soon began to relax a bit around this one prisoner. One day, the warder asked this comrade for his jacket so that he could lay it on the grass and sit on it. Even though I knew it went against the comrade's grain, I nodded to him to do it.

A few days later, we were having our lunch under the shed when this warder wandered over. The warder had an extra sandwich, and he threw it on the grass near us and said, "Here." That was his way of showing friendship.

This presented us with a dilemma. On the one hand, he was treating us as animals to whom he could toss a bit of slop, and I felt it would undermine our dignity to take the sandwich. On the other hand, we were hungry, and to reject the gesture altogether would humiliate the warder we were trying to befriend. I could see that the comrade who had befriended the warder wanted the sandwich, and I nodded for him to take it.

The strategy worked, for this warder became less wary around us. He even began to ask questions about the ANC. By definition, if a man worked for the prison service he was probably brainwashed by the government's propaganda. He would have believed that we were terrorists and Communists who wanted to drive the white man into the sea. But as we quietly explained to him our non-racialism, our desire for equal rights, and our plans for the redistribution of wealth, he scratched his head and said, "It makes more bloody sense than the Nats [Nationalists]."

It was during those long and lonely years that my hunger for the freedom of my own people became a hunger for the freedom of all people, white and black. I knew as well as I knew anything that the oppressor must be liberated just as surely as the oppressed. A man who takes away another man's freedom is a prisoner of hatred; he is locked behind the bars of prejudice and narrow-mindedness. I am not truly free if I am taking away someone else's freedom, just as surely as I am not free when my freedom is taken from me. The oppressed and the oppressor alike are robbed of their humanity.

When I walked out of prison, that was my mission, to liberate the oppressed and the oppressor both. Some say that has now been achieved. But I know that that is not the case. The truth is that we are not yet free; we have merely achieved the freedom to be free, the right not to be oppressed. We have not taken the final step of our journey, but the first step on a longer and even more difficult road. For to be free is not merely to cast off one's chains, but to live in a way that respects and enhances the freedom of others. The true test of our devotion to freedom is just beginning.

I have walked that long road to freedom. I have tried not to falter; I have made missteps along the way. But I have discovered the secret that after climbing a great hill, one only finds that there are many more hills to climb. I have taken a moment here to rest, to steal a view of the glorious vista that surrounds me, to look back on the distance I have come. But I can rest only for a moment, for with freedom come responsibilities, and I dare not linger, for my long walk is not yet ended.

Adapted from *Long Walk to Freedom* (Back Bay Books, 1995). Nelson Mandela is former president of South Africa and also the author of *Conversations with Myself* (Picador, 2011).

CHAPTER NINE

An Orientation of the Heart

Václav Havel

The kind of hope I often think about (especially in situations that are particularly hopeless, such as prison) I understand above all as a state of mind, not a state of the world. Either we have hope within us or we don't; it is a dimension of the soul; it's not essentially dependent on some particular observation of the world or estimate of the situation. Hope is not prognostication. It is an orientation of the spirit, an orientation of the heart; it transcends the world that is immediately experienced, and is anchored somewhere beyond its horizons.

Hope, in this deep and powerful sense, is not the same as joy that things are going well, or willingness to invest in enterprises that are obviously headed for early success, but, rather, an ability to work for something because it is good, not just because it stands a chance to succeed. The more unpropitious the situation in which we demonstrate hope, the deeper that hope is. Hope is definitely not the same thing as optimism. It is not the conviction that something will turn out well, but the certainty that something makes sense, regardless of how it turns out. In short, I think that the deepest and most important form of hope, the only one that can keep us above water and urge us to good works, and the only true source of the breathtaking dimension of the human spirit and its efforts, is something we get, as it were, from "elsewhere." It is also this hope, above all, which gives us the strength to live and continually to try new things, even in conditions that seem as hopeless as ours do, here and now.

I leave it to those more qualified to decide what can be expected "from above"—that is, from what is happening in the sphere of power. I have never fixed my hopes there; I've always been more interested in what was happening "below," in what could be expected from "below," what could be won there, and what defended. All power is power over someone, and it always somehow responds, usually unwittingly rather than deliberately, to the state of mind and the behavior of those it rules over. One can always find in the behavior of power a reflection of what is going on "below." No one can govern in a vacuum. The exercise of power is determined by thousands of interactions between the world of the powerful and that of the powerless, all the more so because these worlds are never divided by a sharp line: Everyone has a small part of himself in both.

Having said that, if I try to look without bias at what is going on "below," I must say that here too I find a slow, imperceptible, yet undoubtedly hopeful movement. If we compare how society behaves now, how it expresses itself, what it dares to do—or, rather, what a significant minority dares to do—with how it was in the early Seventies, those differences must be obvious. People seem to be recovering gradually, walking straighter, taking a renewed interest in things they had so energetically denied themselves before. New islands of self-awareness and self-liberation are appearing, and the connections between them, which were once so brutally disrupted, are multiplying. A new generation, not traumatized by the shock of the Soviet occupation, is maturing: For them, the invasion of 1968 is history. Something is happening in the social awareness, though it is still an undercurrent as yet, rather than something visible.

And all of this brings subtle pressure to bear on the powers that govern society. I'm not thinking now of the obvious pressure of public criticism coming from dissidents, but of the invisible kinds of pressure brought on by this general state of mind and its various forms of expression, to which power unintentionally adapts, even in the act of opposing it.

One is made aware of these things with special clarity when one returns from prison and experiences the sharp contrast between the situation as he had fixed it in his mind before his arrest, and the new situation at the moment of his return. I have observed this in my own case, and others have had the same experience. Again and again, we were astonished at all the new things that were going on, the greater risks people were taking, how much more freely they were behaving, how much greater and less hidden was their hunger for truth, for a truthful word, for genuine values.

Just take for example the unstoppable development of independent culture: Ten years ago there were no *samizdat* periodicals, and the idea of starting one would have been considered suicidal; today there are dozens of them, and people who were, until recently, famous for their caution are now contributing to them. Think of all the new *samizdat* books and publishing ventures; think of how many anonymous and improbable people are copying them out and distributing them; think of all the attention this is enjoying with the public! It bears no comparison whatever with the early Seventies.

But, then, think of all the new things in the sphere of public or permissible culture, or, rather, on its margins, in that vital gray belt or gray zone between official and independent cultures, where these spheres, which until very recently were so sharply divided, are now beginning to mix and mingle. If you were to find yourself at a concert of some young singer and songwriter or a nonconformist band, or in the audience of one of those new small theatres that are springing up everywhere, you would feel that the young people you see there live in their own world, a world very different from the one that breathes on us from the newspapers, from TV, and the Prague radio.

It's not just that there now exists, as there did not ten years ago, an instrument—in Charter 77—for constantly monitoring power. Or take the rapid awakening and spread of religious feeling among young people. This is not an accidental phenomenon; it is an inevitable one: The endless, unchanging wasteland of the herd life in a socialist consumer society, its intellectual and spiritual vacuity, its moral sterility, necessarily causes young people to turn their attentions somewhere further and higher; it compels them to ask questions about the meaning of life, to look for a more meaningful system of values and standards, to seek, among the diffuse and fragmented world of frenzied consumerism (where goods are hard to come by), for a point that will hold firm—all this awakens in them a longing for a genuine moral "vanishing point," for something purer and more authentic. These people simply long to step outside the general automatic operations of society and rediscover their natural world and discover hope for this world.

Or take VONS [an acronym for the Committee for the Defense of the Unjustly Persecuted]. A few of us were arrested and sent to prison for working in this "anti-state center." When that happened, VONS did not cave in; others immediately filled in and continued the work. We didn't cave in either; we served our sentences, and VONS is here to this day, working energetically on, and apparently no one thinks anymore of prosecuting it for what it does.

To outside observers, these changes may seem insignificant. "Where are your ten-million-strong trade unions?" they may ask. "Where are your members of parliament? Why does the prime minister not negotiate with you? Why is the government not considering your proposals and acting on them?" But for someone from here who is not completely indifferent, these are far from insignificant changes; they are the main promise of the future, since such a person has long ago learned not to expect it from anywhere else.

I can't resist a question of my own. Isn't the reward of all those small but hopeful signs of movement this deep, inner hope that is not dependent on prognoses, and which was the primordial point of departure in this unequal struggle? Would so many of those small hopes have "come out" if there had not been this great hope "within," this hope without which it is impossible to live in dignity and meaning, much less find the will for the "hopeless enterprise" which stands at the beginning of most good things?

[At another point in his book, Havel describes a petition that he and other Czechoslovak writers circulated to free a group of people imprisoned for their dissent, the first large writers' petition since the Soviet tanks rolled in and crushed the brief hopes of the 1968 "Prague Spring." The petition was politically mild, appealing to President Gustav Husák's generosity, and asking him to include the prisoners in the Christmas amnesty. Yet critics said it would do nothing to free those in jail, and might actually make things worse for them—and that those who circulated it were just trying to draw attention to themselves. If the petitioners really wanted to help, the critics said, they could quietly raise money for the prisoners' families. In the novel *The Unbearable Lightness of Being*, Milan Kundera was particularly caustic, using the voice of his character Dr. Tomás to mock both the petition and those who circulated it. Yet, as Havel explains, even seemingly futile actions can have unanticipated results.]

At the time, writers had not yet been sharply divided into those who were banned and those who were permitted to publish, and it wasn't clear yet which of them would sign the petition and which would not. In fact, some signed it who today are considered official writers. But it was the first significant act of solidarity in the Husák era, and therefore was something quite new.

The powers that be were very hostile to the petition, and several of those who signed immediately withdrew their signatures as soon as this hostility became clear. All those who did not sign or who withdrew their signatures argued in ways similar to Tomás in Kundera's novel. They said they couldn't help anyone this way, that it would only annoy the government, that those who had already been banned were being exhibitionistic, and, worse, that through this petition, they were trying to drag those who still had their heads above water down into their own abyss by misusing their charity. Naturally the president did not grant an amnesty, and so some signatories went on languishing in prison, while the beauty of our characters was thus presumably illuminated. It would seem, therefore, that history proved our critics to be correct.

But was that really the case? I would say not. When the prisoners began to come back after their years in prison, they all said that the petition had given them a great deal of satisfaction. Because of it, they felt that their stay in prison had a meaning: It helped renew the broken solidarity. They knew, better than those of us who were outside, that the petition's significance transcended the question of whether or not they would be released—because they knew that they would not be released. But knowing that people knew about them, that someone was on their side and did not hesitate to support them publicly, even in a period of general apathy and resignation: This was of irreplaceable value. If for no other reason, that petition was important because of such feelings. (From my own experience, I know that news of people outside expressing their solidarity with him helps a person survive in prison.)

But the petition had a far deeper significance as well: It marked the beginning of a process in which people's civic backbones began to straighten again. This was a forerunner of Charter 77 and of everything the Charter now does, and the process has had undeniable results. Since that time, there have been hundreds of petitions, and although the government has reacted to none of them, it has had to respond to the changed situation which this endless flow of demands ultimately created. These results are indirect, modest, and long-range. But they exist.

Here's one example: In the early Seventies, prisoners were given long sentences for nothing, and almost no one, either at home or abroad, paid any attention, which was why the government could get away with such sentences. Today, after fifteen years of ant-like work that often seemed quixotic, and regardless of the continuing suspicion that the petitioners were merely exhibitionists who wished to illuminate "the entire misery of the world" and the glory of their own characters, all that has changed. Now all the authorities have to do is lock someone up for forty-eight hours for political reasons and newspapers all over the world write about it. In other words, international interest has been aroused, and the government has to take this interest into account. It can't get away with the sort of thing it used to get away with. It can no longer expect that no one will see what it is doing, or that no one will dare criticize it. It must—though it may not want to—reckon with the phenomenon of its own shame.

This, of course, has wider consequences. Today far more is possible. Think of this: Hundreds of people today are doing things that not a single one of them would have dared to do at the beginning of the Seventies. We are now living in a truly new and different situation. This is not because the government has become more tolerant; it has simply had to get used to the new situation. It has had to yield to continuing pressure from below, which means pressure from all those apparently suicidal or exhibitionistic civic acts.

People who are used to seeing society only "from above" tend to be impatient. They want to see immediate results.

Anything that does not produce immediate results seems foolish. They don't have a lot of sympathy for acts which can only be evaluated years after they take place, which are motivated by moral factors, and which therefore run the risk of never accomplishing anything.

Unfortunately, we live in conditions where improvement is often achieved by actions that risk remaining forever in the memory of humanity in the form that the petition in Kundera's novel took: an exhibitionistic act of desperate people. History is not something that takes place "elsewhere"; it takes place here; we all contribute to making it.

Adapted from *Disturbing the Peace* (Alfred A. Knopf, 1990, original Czech publication in 1986), translated by Paul Wilson. Václav Havel was the former president of the Czech Republic. His most recent political book was *To the Castle and Back* (Vintage, 2008).

CHAPTER TEN

Reluctant Activists

Mary Pipher

My journey began in the cataclysmic spring of 2010. The earth was experiencing its warmest decade, its warmest year, and the warmest April, May, and June on record. Pakistan hit its record high (129 degrees), as did Sudan (121 degrees) and Saudi Arabia and Iraq (both 126 degrees). For the first time in human memory, lightning ignited fires in the peat bogs of Russia and these fires spread to the wheat fields farther south. As doctors from Moscow rode to the rescue of heat and smoke victims, they fainted in their un-air-conditioned ambulances.

All over the world, crops withered and workers dropped from heat exhaustion. Livestock died from heat and rare frogs in the Amazon rain forests disappeared. Our planet and all living beings seemed to be gasping for breath. In Nebraska, after weeks of "hundred-year" rains, much of my state was declared a flood disaster area. In July, the heat index in Lincoln reached 115 degrees for several days in a row. That same month I read Bill McKibben's *Eaarth*, in which he argues that the earth as we used to know it already has vanished due to climate change. Without immediate action, he writes, our familiar ways of life will disappear, not in our grandchildren's adulthoods, but in the lifetimes of middle-aged people alive today.

None of my reading about the environment had quite prepared me for this. I couldn't stop reading McKibben's book, though I hated what I was learning. When I finished it, I felt shell-shocked. For a few days, all I could feel was despair. Everything seemed so hopeless and so over. I teared up when I looked at flowers or listened to the flickers and kingbirds that nested near our home. When I picked raspberries with my grandchildren, I felt my heart breaking two ways at once—for the children's beauty and for their vulnerability.

I thought about all the care we lavish on these children. We make sure they eat healthy foods and brush their teeth with safe toothpastes. We examine and treat every little bug bite or scratch. We spend hours reading them books and teaching them everything from how to make guacamole to how to find, cut, and polish rocks. And yet, we—all the grandparents in the world, including myself—haven't worked hard enough to secure for them a future with clean air and water and diverse, healthy ecosystems. What is wrong with us? Where have our hearts and minds been?

That summer, when I listened to friends talking about mundane details of life, I wanted to shout at them, "Wake up! Our old future is gone. Matters are urgent. We have to do something—now."

However, after years of being a therapist and a mother, I have learned that shouting "Wake up" doesn't work. In fact, that was one of my most dispiriting realizations. I wanted desperately to preserve the world I loved, but I didn't even know how to share this fact with my closest friends.

I also realized that I wasn't doing enough. I was recycling waste and using metal water bottles. I shopped at the local farmers' market and I drank shade-grown coffee. By current standards, I was being a responsible citizen. But I still felt inadequate and guilty. My efforts were in no way commensurate with the gravity of the situation. I knew I had to find a way out of my state of mind. I couldn't survive with all that awareness every minute of my day. I wanted to be happy again, to be able to laugh, and to snuggle with my grandchildren without worrying about whether they'd spend their teenage years defending a meager supply of potable water with old shotguns. I wanted hope. But I couldn't forget or ignore what I now understood.

What pulled me out of my despair was the desire to get to work. I didn't know what I was going to do, I felt unqualified for virtually everything involving the environment, but I knew I had to do something. It was unclear how much my action would benefit the world, but I knew it would help me. Action has always been my healing tonic.

That fall, I read in the newspaper that the corporation TransCanada planned to build a two-thousand-mile pipeline across North America. The Keystone XL pipeline was slated to travel from Alberta to the Gulf of Mexico, across Nebraska's Sandhills. It would carry a load of crude oil, extracted from tar sands, across the Ogallala Aquifer and most of the major river systems west of the Mississippi. I had trouble breathing as I struggled to absorb this information. As I realized some of the effects, I once again spiraled downward.

The intensity of my emotions around the pipeline required me, a reluctant activist, to become more involved. I invited my friend Brad, a soft-spoken organic gardener, and my friend Marian, from nearby Spring Creek Prairie, to my house to discuss what we could do to stop TransCanada from shipping tar sands sludge through our state.

We met over soup and artisan sourdough. I wanted the event to be more like a party than a meeting. I assumed that my friends were like me—too busy already and tired at the end of a workday. They would only return if they were relaxed and having fun. We shared what little we knew about the pipeline and talked about people in our community who might be interested in joining our cause. We agreed that for our next meeting, in a week, we would invite anyone we knew who might want to jump on board. Eight people came to that meeting.

After introducing ourselves to each other, we began to compare notes. Jane was the director of a political nonprofit called Bold Nebraska. A commanding, articulate woman, she'd been talking in the kitchens of ranchers and farmers along the proposed route, and told us that TransCanada had been bullying them into selling easements. One rancher told her that the land in the Sandhills could not recover from the digging of an oil pipeline. His grandfather had plowed a furrow to stop a prairie fire a hundred years ago. Since then, every generation of his family had tried unsuccessfully to restore the land.

Ken was a tall, skinny, tired-looking lobbyist for the Nebraska Sierra Club. Duane directed the Nebraska Wildlife Federation. They told us how TransCanada was working with state officials, lobbyists, the press, and public relations people to get support for the pipeline. Ken said, "I've never seen money washing around the halls of the capitol the way I have this year."

At this point in the discussion, we were all feeling a bit overwhelmed and starting to know too much. Despite the fact that several of us were looking at our feet and could no longer speak, Tim jumped in with more bad news. He made the connection between tar sands development and rising CO_2 levels, between our local struggles and a much larger climate catastrophe. As renowned climate scientist James Hansen has written, the tar sands "contain twice the amount of carbon dioxide emitted by global oil use in our entire history." Because of that and because they're so energy intensive to extract, Hansen believes that if they're fully exploited it's "game over for the planet."

TransCanada had assured Nebraskans that the XL pipeline would be safe. But none of us was born yesterday. Ken recalled that in the 1980s, just before the Chernobyl nuclear plant exploded and spewed radioactive materials around the globe, the Soviets had reported that it would be safe for at least a thousand years.

We had all come into the meeting feeling isolated, hopeless, and disempowered. But despite the grim content of our discussion, as the night went on, we became increasingly hopeful. This seems counterintuitive, but I think I know why it happened. That night, we weren't just complaining and bemoaning our situation, we were planning ways to understand and prepare for the coming storm. And we had shipmates.

All of us were progressives who had worked for lost causes all of our lives. None of us ever seemed to vote for a candidate who won. We didn't think we'd win this battle, either. We had no money, organization, or public support. But we were not just going to lie down and surrender.

We called ourselves a coalition and decided that our first action would be a rally in January 2011 on the steps of our state capitol in Lincoln. We hugged each other good-bye under the stars. Afterward, while rinsing the dishes clean, I realized I was humming. That was something I hadn't done in a long time.

Our group met every other week. Over chili or pesto pizzas, we charted our course. Every meeting, we heard more reports about what was happening with the pipeline. And every meeting, we planned a new series of actions that we would immediately undertake. We tried all the ordinary ways citizens influence their representatives: we requested meetings, made calls, and wrote letters. However, we were shut out of any high-level political discussions. Everything important was happening behind the scenes and only TransCanada had access. Ken and Jane, who were spending a lot of time at the capitol, were continually frustrated by the closed-door meetings, secret agreements, and influence peddling they were seeing. TransCanada had rented land from county commissioners along the pipeline's route in case the company wanted to store equipment. It was sending charming lobbyists and PR people to work with lawmakers. Later we'd find out that the company had bought up almost all of the airtime on television and radio, newspaper space, and public relations firms in the state, just to make sure that even if our side had money to get our message out, we would have little access to vehicles of communication. Ken reported that although he had been working within our state's political system for years, he'd never seen anything this corrupt.

I realized that in spite of my lifelong education in civic affairs, there was still a part of me that was idealistic about government and believed that it functioned the way I was taught in high school. That idealism died as we talked about politics and the pipeline. When I thought about how rigged the game was, I was beyond anger; I was too disappointed to be angry.

Our only hope was grassroots organizing of our citizens. At this stage, Nebraskans didn't know much about what was happening. TransCanada's ads peppered the state. In most of the counties in the state, "environmentalist" was a dirty word. However, as our coalition discussed strategies, we realized our battles were not ideological, but rather they were about local control of resources and public health. In fact, as Jane had discovered, our first allies were the landowners who were threatened with eminent domain and the people who depended on clean water and soil to make their livings—farmers, livestock producers, and dairymen.

Our first organized protest was a rally on the steps of the state capitol in January. We didn't know what to expect, but over a hundred people arrived, most in their twenties or sixties. People wore puffy coats and gloves, and many carried handmade signs with heartfelt statements. I recognized many of the attendees, but was struck by the number of newcomers.

Dressed in cowboy boots and jeans, Jane led the rally. Her two young daughters distributed buttons and bumper stickers as she spoke. She was spirited, passionate, and pregnant, which was a dramatic reminder of the generations to come. We waved signs and banners and began by singing the National Anthem. As we shivered under a statue of Abraham Lincoln, we listened to ranchers, lawyers, grandmothers, and scientists explain why the pipeline was a bad idea. The crowd applauded and whooped in agreement.

Afterward, shivering coalition members gave interviews to the local media and passed around sign-up sheets so that we could all stay connected. Many people walked directly into the capitol to find their state senators and ask their positions on the pipeline. I drove home chilled and hungry. And elated. One of our speakers, Randy Thompson, may be the most unlikely activist I have ever met. He was a middle-aged farmer and rancher and the former operator of an auction house, or what Nebraskans call a "sale barn." He had never been politically involved and liked to spend his time playing golf, drinking coffee with his neighbors, and enjoying his family. A political conservative, Randy looked like John Wayne and dressed in jeans, western shirts, and a cowboy hat and boots. He was a compelling symbol for Nebraskans.

Even though he would never call himself an environmentalist, when TransCanada threatened him with taking his land through eminent domain, Randy was outraged. "TransCanada's corporate lawyers tried to bully me," he said at our initial rally. "They had no respect. They treated the land my parents worked so hard to keep in the family like it was a bunch of dirt." Randy grew up in a house with hungry people who struggled to keep their farm. That day he told the crowd, "When I thought of my parents and all that they had suffered to hold on to this land, I decided to fight."

Like Big Red football in Nebraska, Randy was able to attract progressives and conservatives, urban and rural citizens, and university academics and farmers. At one event he said, "All my friends warned me about radicals. But I have not met any yet. I just keep meeting more people like me who want to protect our water and our way of life."

Jane suggested we call our campaign "I Stand with Randy," and Bold Nebraska purchased life-size cutouts of Randy for major events and for public places. In the cutouts, Randy was saying, "We will not be bullied."

Our group's emotions rose and fell like ocean waves. To our dismay and frustration, the legislature was doing nothing to regulate pipelines or protect us. But we were excited to make connections with many national groups. Bill McKibben's 350.org decided to make stopping the pipeline its first priority. The Sierra Club and other environmental groups joined in. At our local meetings we were laughing more. We learned to always pair information with action suggestions. People seemed to be able to "afford to" listen when the conversation ended with something specific they could do. We tailored suggestions to our listeners. Some people were willing to rearrange their lives to fight for the cause. Others, for many good reasons, were only able to do small actions.

Because all of us were inured to failure, success was a little discombobulating. We were accustomed to being marginalized. But now we were riding on a powerful current much bigger than we were. Citizens all over the state were united against our common enemies: our unresponsive state government and the big bully TransCanada. Suddenly, urban progressives were drinking coffee in the kitchens of ranchers. Republican farmers were attending strategy meetings at the headquarters of Bold Nebraska. Refugees were working side by side with college students and small-town business owners. Ken was invited to remote places that historically would have tarred and feathered anyone from the Sierra Club, addressing community centers filled with people who, much to his astonishment, were on his side.

Over the next months, TransCanada became a topic in city cafés, bars, Rotary Clubs, auction barns, and church basements. Many newspapers in our state provided their readers with tutorials on land, water, and energy issues. At our first Big Red football game of the season, eighty-five thousand fans booed when a TransCanada ad flashed on the jumbo screen in the stadium. The next day the University of Nebraska's chancellor announced that TransCanada would no longer be allowed to advertise at university events.

Bowing to popular pressure and looking toward his next election, our Republican governor, Dave Heineman, wrote a letter asking President Obama to reroute the pipeline so it wouldn't go through the Sandhills and over the Ogallala aquifer. Members of our coalition knew Heineman was playing a political game. He wrote this letter to pass the buck to President Obama. When the White House supported TransCanada's decisions about a route, which he fully expected the president would do, Governor Heineman could blame Obama for not protecting us.

But because this had become a national movement, Obama was also feeling pressure from ordinary citizens, over a thousand of whom were arrested at the White House asking him to deny the pipeline permit. Much to our governor's surprise, Obama responded to his letter by delaying the pipeline process and calling for more environmental reviews. In January 2012, Obama denied an initial permit to TransCanada, the first and only international pipeline permit ever denied by the US government. Obama cited our Republican governor in his decision.

This wasn't the end of the fight, but something transformative was happening, something none of us had even dared to imagine. At our meetings, we looked wide-eyed at each other. One of our most common questions was, "Can you believe this?" Our coalition was allowing us to turn our individual anger, fear, and sorrow into something better and stronger. We had begun as a small group of people in my living room and ended up as a force to be reckoned with. As I write, I don't know what will finally happen with the tar sands, but I do know what has happened to me. I do this work because acting as if I have hope gives me hope. The process of trying to make things better is the healthiest way I have of responding to the world around me.

Adapted from *The Green Boat: Reviving Ourselves in a Capsized Culture* (Riverhead Books, 2013). Pipher's other books include *Reviving Ophelia* (Riverhead Books, 2005), *Another Country* (Riverhead Books, 2000), *The Shelter of Each Other* (Riverhead Books, 2008), *Writing to Change the World* (Riverhead Books, 2007), and *Letters to a Young Therapist* (Basic Books, 2005).

PART THREE

Everyday Grace

THE PEACE OF WILD THINGS

Wendell Berry

When despair for the world grows in me
and I wake in the night at the least sound
in fear of what my life and my children's lives may be,
I go and lie down where the wood drake
rests in his beauty on the water, and the great heron feeds.
I come into the peace of wild things
who do not tax their lives with forethought
of grief. I come into the presence of still water.
And I feel above me the day-blind stars
waiting with their light. For a time
I rest in the grace of the world, and am free.

From *New Collected Poems* (Counterpoint Press, 2013). Wendell Berry's other books include *A Place in Time* (Counterpoint Press, 2013) and *The Unsettling of America* (Sierra Club Books, 1996).

So much of our interaction with the world is shaped by our perspective, the point of view by which we interpret experience. The second section of this book explored the big picture: world historical change furthered by the rarest and most visionary of leaders—and by ordinary individuals finding the courage to act. Their determination, strength, and persistence give us ample cause for hope, particularly when we remember how much the odds seemed stacked against them.

But the very magnitude of these successes may tempt us to dismiss their actions and to wonder how their examples could apply to the more modest stages on which most of us practice our efforts at change. One lesson, suggested in the Desmond Tutu story with which I began this book, is the power of drawing inspiration from more humble sources, like the richness and beauty of everyday experience. The more we draw on these gifts, what prophetic Kentucky farmer and poet Wendell Berry calls "the grace of the world," the more strength we'll have to continue working for change.

Savoring these gifts becomes more important than ever in a time when, as novelist Barbara Kingsolver observes, the "wells of kindness seem everywhere to be running dry." We are all subject to such depletion, including those for whom social activism is second nature. The overwhelming scale of global environmental crises, America's deepening economic divides (and the pressures they bring to our lives), and the ongoing toll of violence and war all can easily overtake our ability to respond. We're deluged with images and information, appeals, and action alerts from every conceivable medium. After a while, what's wrong in the world monopolizes our attention. What's right, what warrants celebration, falls from view. At that point, we risk flying a banner of service to humanity while becoming mostly ambassadors of doom.

In "Mountain Music," Scott Russell Sanders describes how his seventeen-year-old son accused him of exactly this during a hiking trip. "Your view of things is totally dark," the boy complained. "It bums me out. You make me feel the planet's dying and people are to blame and nothing can be done about it. There's no room for hope." While Sanders is delighting in a wilderness hike, his son feels overwhelmed by messages of impending ecological disaster that Sanders has repeated to him too often. Of course, as anyone with teenage children will recognize, the son might instead have chosen to complain that Sanders had squeezed the toothpaste from the middle instead of the end of the tube. But it's a poignant moment that forces Sanders to reassess his outlook on life.

How do we make our children aware of injustice without implying that the world is irredeemably corrupt? We certainly don't want to mask our feelings. Being moved by the pain of others and by the damage done to the natural world is the foundation of conscience, of a sense of responsibility to something beyond ourselves. Conveying that to our children is an essential parental duty. But as Sanders painfully learned, exposing kids—or anyone we wish to reach—to a relentless barrage of negativity can be counterproductive. I remember a student who'd taken a course on the nuclear arms race during its mid-1980s height. "Before I began," she said, "I was worried. Now I feel totally bleak." Actually, Sanders is lucky. His son's rebellion is a form of affirmation. He didn't just retreat into cynicism but, rather, left "room for hope." He wanted to leave the earth, like their campsite, a better place than he found it.

It is no simple task to demonstrate to our children, or to others, that we believe the gamble of engagement is worth the cost and that there's ample reason to remain hopeful no matter how troubling the world can be. To do it well, we need to take time to replenish whatever the wellsprings are that nurture our soul. Kingsolver offers a clue to how to do this when she says that "God is in the details, the completely unnecessary miracles sometimes tossed up as stars to guide us." Be alert, in other words, to moments of everyday grace, especially opportunities to savor our connections to the community of life, because therein lies our sustenance.

In "The Sukkah of Shalom," Rabbi Arthur Waskow argues that vulnerability is central to such experiences. Reflecting on the attacks of September 11, 2001, Waskow uses the Jewish Sukkot shelter, constructed of leaves and branches, as a metaphor for our times, when the weapons and material goods in which our culture places its trust will not necessarily protect us. The more we acknowledge this vulnerability, Waskow insists, the more we nurture our common human bond.

We also draw hope from moments of human generosity. September 11 brought forth many of those moments, but also fear and mistrust. In "Gate A-4," poet Naomi Shihab Nye remembers her hesitation a half dozen years later, at the height of the Iraq War, when an announcement came over an airport loudspeaker. "If anyone in the vicinity of Gate A-4 understands any Arabic," the voice said, "please come to the gate immediately." "Well, one pauses these days," she remembers. But then she stepped up to translate for an elderly Palestinian woman, who was lying on the floor, crying because her flight was late. Slowly and patiently Nye drew the woman out of her isolation and fear. She helped her call relatives to tell them about the delay, and others just to talk. Soon several more travelers joined them, creating an unexpected communion around homemade *mamool* cookies. What brings humans together can be stronger than what divides us.

Catholic theologian Henri Nouwen takes the paradox of drawing strength from vulnerability still further. In "Fragile and

Hidden," he describes a Canadian community, L'Arche, where mentally handicapped people live with their assistants, and where he resided for twelve years. Nouwen writes memorably about a man in his care who can neither walk nor speak, and never will, a man who nevertheless is a constant source of inspiration because his every breath says yes to life. In her book *A Natural History of the Senses*, Diane Ackerman describes Helen Keller: "Blind, deaf, mute, Helen Keller's remaining senses were so finely attuned that when she put her hands on the radio to enjoy music, she could tell the difference between the cornets and the strings." Keller was an activist as well, a feminist and a socialist, and an early crusader for the rights of the disabled, though we rarely hear about those aspects of her life. She was also, Ackerman says, a great sensualist, writing at length about "life's aromas, tastes, touches, feelings, which she explored with the voluptuousness of a courtesan."

In "Getting Our Gaze Back," Rose Marie Berger makes a similar point in reference to the natural world. "We have more in common with flowers than microchips," she reminds us, and therefore need to find oases of respite amid the pervasive distractions of contemporary existence. Berger isn't advocating a retreat to cloistered Martha Stewart land, where every nail is perfectly manicured and a bath full of rose petals always awaits (though for many of us there's nothing like a long soak to soothe our spirits). Instead, she speaks eloquently of the need to pause regularly to renew ourselves, precisely so that we can serve as a creative force in the larger public sphere.

Berger's comments remind me of the time Howard Zinn invited four musicians to play a Mozart quartet in front of his class, because, as he wrote, "Political discussion can sour you. We needed some music." In other words, it was time to broaden his students' perspective, to remind them that the world is a place where beauty and grace exist alongside sordidness and violence—and that it is on behalf of expanding the domain of the former that we denounce and resist the latter. All genuine efforts to heal our society or the environment are at root acts of love, acts of caring as well as condemning. The following lines from Ellen Bass's poem "Pray for Peace" convey this idea vividly:

Making love, of course, is already a prayer.
Skin and open mouths worshipping that skin,
the fragile case we are poured into,
each caress a season of peace . . .
With each breath in, take in the faith of those
who have believed when belief seemed foolish,
who persevered. With each breath out, cherish.

Breathing in and breathing out. Trading caresses. Pay attention and it soon becomes clear that nature is essentially rhythmical. Why should it be any different for human beings? And why shouldn't we let our spirits be buoyed by the knowledge that winter is always followed by spring? In "There Is a Season," the Quaker writer and educator Parker Palmer compares nature's seasons to those of our personal and political lives, showing how seeds sown in seemingly barren ground can bring unexpected fruits.

Palmer didn't compose the piece specifically for citizen-activists. "I wrote it for myself and anyone else who wants to live as deeply as possible into every season of our everyday lives," he told me. "But since I believe that the activism we most need is not a specialized activity, but an outflow of everyday living, I hope that this essay will speak to activists of that stripe—to all who work to speak truth to power in a world of great deceit, all who work to live as healers in a world of great suffering."

I saw the impact of Palmer's words on one of my heroes, a St. Louis evangelical minister whose homeless empowerment project provides community-run housing, a farm where participants can raise organic vegetables and tilapia, and a television channel on one of the major commercial frequencies, all run by people who'd once lived on the streets. The TV station's prime staple was older entertainment reruns, but also included the minister's own interview show, *The Poor Have Suffered Enough*. The minister lived extremely simply, barely more comfortably than the people his project housed, which had caused his wife of many years to eventually leave, exhausted by this Spartan existence. We all make our own decisions about the level of material comfort we need while working for social change, but the minister said Palmer's piece helped get him through, with its focus on the lessons we can learn from hard times and its faith that even the most difficult seasons will yield to better days, brighter prospects.

CHAPTER ELEVEN

Gate A-4

Naomi Shihab Nye

Wandering around the Albuquerque Airport Terminal, after learning my flight had been delayed four hours, I heard an announcement: "If anyone in the vicinity of Gate A-4 understands any Arabic, please come to the gate immediately."

Well—one pauses these days. Gate A-4 was my own gate. I went there.

An older woman in full traditional Palestinian embroidered dress, just like my grandma wore, was crumpled to the floor, wailing. "Help," said the flight agent. "Talk to her. What is her problem? We told her the flight was going to be late and she did this."

I stooped to put my arm around the woman and spoke haltingly. "Shu-dow-a, shu-bid-uck, habibti? Stani schway, min fadlick, shu-bit-se-wee?" The minute she heard any words she knew, however poorly used, she stopped crying. She thought the flight had been cancelled entirely. She needed to be in El Paso for major medical treatment the next day. I said, "No, we're fine, you'll get there, just late, who is picking you up? Let's call him."

We called her son, I spoke with him in English. I told him I would stay with his mother till we got on the plane. She talked to him. Then we called her other sons just for the fun of it. Then we called my dad and he and she spoke for a while in

Arabic and found out of course they had ten shared friends. Then I thought just for the heck of it why not call some Palestinian poets I know and let them chat with her? This all took up two hours.

She was laughing a lot by then. Telling about her life, patting my knee, answering questions. She had pulled a sack of homemade *mamool* cookies—little powdered sugar crumbly mounds stuffed with dates and nuts—from her bag and was offering them to all the women at the gate. To my amazement, not a single traveler declined one. It was like a sacrament. The traveler from Argentina, the mom from California, the lovely woman from Laredo—we were all covered with the same powdered sugar. And smiling. There is no better cookie.

Then the airline broke out free apple juice and two little girls from our flight ran around serving it and they were covered with powdered sugar too. And I noticed my new best friend—by now we were holding hands—had a potted plant poking out of her bag, some medicinal thing, with green furry leaves. Such an old country traveling tradition. Always carry a plant. Always stay rooted to somewhere.

And I looked around that gate of late and weary ones and thought, This is the world I want to live in. The shared world. Not a single person in that gate—once the crying of confusion stopped—seemed apprehensive about any other person. They took the cookies. I wanted to hug all those other women too.

This can still happen anywhere. Not everything is lost.

From *Honeybee* (Greenwillow Books, 2008). Naomi Shihab Nye's most recent books are *Transfer* (poems) and *There Is No Long Distance Now* (very short stories). She has worked as a visiting writer all her adult life and lives in old-downtown San Antonio, Texas, with her husband, photographer Michael Nye, a block from the lovely little river.

CHAPTER TWELVE

Mountain Music

Scott Russell Sanders

On a June morning high in the Rocky Mountains of Colorado, snowy peaks rose before me like the promise of a world without grief. A creek brimful of meltwater roiled along to my left, and to my right an aspen grove shimmered with freshly minted leaves. Bluebirds kept darting in and out of holes in the aspen trunks. Butterflies flickered beside every puddle.

With all of that to look at, I gazed instead at my son's broad back as he stalked away from me up the trail. Sweat had darkened his gray T-shirt in patches the color of bruises. His shoulders were stiff with anger that would weight his tongue and keep his face turned from me for hours. Anger also made him quicken his stride, gear after gear, until I could no longer keep up. I had forty-nine years on my legs and heart and lungs, while Jesse had only seventeen on his. My left foot ached from old bone breaks and my right knee creaked from recent surgery. Used to breathing among the low muggy hills of Indiana, I was gasping up here in the alpine air, a mile and a half above sea level. Jesse would not stop, would not even slow down unless I asked; and I was in no mood to ask. So I slumped against a boulder beside the trail and let him rush on ahead.

The day, our first full one in Rocky Mountain National Park, had started out well. I woke at first light, soothed by the roar of a river foaming along one edge of the campground, and

I looked out from our tent to find half a dozen elk, all cows and calves, grazing so close by that I could see the gleam of their teeth. Just beyond the elk, a pair of ground squirrels loafed at the lip of their burrow, noses twitching.

Up to that point, and for several hours more, the day was equally unblemished. Jesse slept on while I sipped coffee and studied maps and soaked in the early light. We made our plans over breakfast without squabbling. I felt buoyant as we hiked along Cow Creek toward the waterfall. We talked easily the whole way, joking and teasing, more like good friends than like father and son. Yet even as we sat at the base of the falls, our shoulders touching, the mist of Bridal Veil cooling our skin, we remained father and son, locked in a struggle that I could only partly understand.

For the previous year or so, no matter how long our spells of serenity, Jesse and I had kept falling into quarrels, like victims of malaria breaking out in fever. We might be talking about soccer or supper, about the car keys or the news, and suddenly our voices would begin to clash like swords. I had proposed this trip to the mountains in hopes of discovering the source of that strife. Of course I knew that teenage sons and their fathers always fight, yet I sensed there was a deeper grievance between us, beyond the usual vexations. Jesse was troubled by more than a desire to run his own life, and I was troubled by more than the pain of letting him go.

The peace between us held until we turned back from the waterfall and began discussing where to camp the following night. Jesse wanted to push on up to Thunder Lake, nearly 11,000 feet, and pitch our tent on snow. I wanted to stop a thousand feet lower and sleep on dry dirt.

"We're not equipped for snow," I told him.

"Sure we are. Why do you think I bought a new sleeping bag? Why did I call ahead to reserve snowshoes?"

I suggested that we could hike up from a lower campsite and snowshoe to his heart's content. He loosed a snort of disgust. "I can't believe you're wimping out on me, Dad."

"I'm just being sensible."

"You're wimping out. I came here to see the backcountry, and all you want to do is poke around the foothills."

"This isn't wild enough for you?" I waved my arms at the view. "What do you need, avalanches and grizzlies?"

Just then, as we rounded a bend, an elderly couple came shuffling toward us, hunched over walking sticks, white hair jutting from beneath their straw hats. They were followed by three toddling children, each one rigged out with tiny backpack and canteen. Jesse and I stood aside to let them pass, returning nods to their cheery hellos.

When they had trooped by, Jesse muttered, "We're in the wilds, huh, Dad? That's why the trail's full of grandparents and kids." Then he quickened his pace until the damp blond curls that dangled below his billed cap were slapping against his neck.

"Is this how it's going to be?" I called after him. "You're going to spoil the trip because I won't agree to camp on snow?"

He glared around at me. "You're the one who's spoiling it, you and your hang-ups. You always ruin everything." With that, he swung his face away and lengthened his stride and rushed on ahead.

The rocks that give these mountains their name are ancient, nearly a third as old as the Earth, but the Rockies themselves are new, having been lifted up only 6 or 7 million years ago, and they were utterly new to me, for I had never seen them before except from airplanes. I had been yearning toward them since I was Jesse's age, had been learning about their natural and human history, the surge of stone and gouge of glaciers, the wandering of hunters and wolves. Drawn to these mountains from the rumpled quilt of fields and forests in the hill country of the Ohio Valley, I was primed for splendor. And yet, now that I was here, I felt blinkered and numb.

My quarrel with Jesse changed nothing about the Rockies, but changed everything in my experience of the place. What had seemed glorious and vibrant to me when we set out that morning now seemed bleak and bare. It was as though anger had drilled a hole in the world and leached the color away.

I was still simmering when I caught up with Jesse at the trailhead, where he was leaning against our rented car, arms crossed over his chest, head sunk forward in a sullen pose I knew too well, eyes hidden beneath the frayed bill of his cap. Having to wait for me to unlock the car no doubt reminded him of another gripe: I had the only set of keys. Because he was too young to be covered by the rental insurance, I would not let him drive. He had fumed about my decision, interpreting it as proof that I mistrusted him, still thought of him as a child. That earlier scuffle had petered out with him grumbling, "Stupid, stupid. I knew this would happen. Why did I come out here? Why?"

We drove. In the depths of Big Thompson Canyon, where the road swerved along a frothy river between sheer rock face and spindly guardrail, I could bear the silence no longer. "So what are my hang-ups?" I demanded. "How do I ruin everything?"

"You don't want to know," he said.

"I want to know. What is it about me that grates on you?"

I do not pretend to recall the exact words we hurled at one another after my challenge, but I remember the tone and thrust of them, and here is how they have stayed with me:

"You wouldn't understand," he said.

"Try me."

He cut a look at me, shrugged, then stared back through the windshield. "You're just so out of touch."

"With what?"

"With my whole world. You hate everything that's fun. You hate television and movies and video games. You hate my music."

"I like some of your music. I just don't like it loud."

"You hate advertising," he said quickly, rolling now. "You hate billboards, lotteries, developers, logging companies, and big corporations. You hate snowmobiles and jet-skis. You hate malls and fashions and cars."

"You're still on my case because I won't buy a Jeep?" I said, harking back to another old argument.

"Forget Jeeps. You look at any car, and all you think is pollution, traffic, roadside crap. You say fast food's poisoning our bodies and TV's poisoning our minds. You think the Internet is just another scam for selling stuff. You think business is a conspiracy to rape the Earth."

"None of that bothers you?"

"Of course it does. But that's the world. That's where we've got to live. It's not going to go away just because you don't approve. What's the good of spitting on it?"

"I don't spit on it. I grieve over it."

He was still for a moment, then resumed quietly. "What's the good of grieving if you can't change anything?"

"Who says you can't change anything?"

"You do. Maybe not with your mouth, but with your eyes." Jesse rubbed his own eyes, and the words came out muffled through his cupped palms. "Your view of things is totally dark. It bums me out. You make me feel the planet's dying, and people are to blame, and nothing can be done about it. There's no room for hope. Maybe you can get along without hope, but I can't. I've got a lot of living still to do. I have to believe there's a way we can get out of this mess. Otherwise, what's the point? Why study, why work, why do anything if it's all going to hell?"

That sounded unfair to me, a caricature of my views, and I thought of many sharp replies; yet there was too much truth and too much hurt in what he said for me to fire back an answer. Had I really deprived my son of hope? Was this the deeper grievance—the source of our strife—that I had passed on to him, so young, my anguish over the world? Was this what lurked between us, driving us apart, the demon called despair?

"You're right," I finally told him. "Life's meaningless without hope. But I think you're wrong to say I've given up."

"It seems that way to me. As if you think we're doomed."

"No, buddy, I don't think we're doomed. It's just that nearly everything I care about is under assault."

"See, that's what I mean. You're so worried about the fate of the Earth, you can't enjoy anything. We come to these mountains, and you bring the shadows with you. You've got me seeing nothing but darkness."

Stunned by the force of his words, I could not speak. If my gloom cast a shadow over the creation for my son, then I had failed him. What remedy could there be for such a betrayal?

Through all the shouting and then talking and then painful hush, our car hugged the swerving road, yet I cannot remember steering. I cannot remember even seeing the stony canyon, the white mane of the Big Thompson whipping along beside us, the oncoming traffic. Somehow we survived our sashay with the river and cruised into a zone of burger joints and car-care emporiums and trinket shops. I realized how often, how relentlessly, I had groused about just this sort of commercial dreck, and how futile my complaints must have seemed to Jesse.

He was caught between a chorus of voices telling him that the universe was made for us, that the Earth is an inexhaustible warehouse, that consumption is the goal of life, that money is the road to delight—and the stubborn voice of his father saying none of this is so. If his father was right, then most of what humans babble every day—in ads and editorials, in sitcoms and song lyrics, in thrillers and market reports and teenage gab—is a monstrous lie. Far more likely that his father was wrong, deluded, perhaps even mad.

It is an old habit of mine, the watching and weighing of my son's experience. Since his birth, I have enveloped him in a cloud of thought. How's he doing? I wonder. Is he hungry? Hurting? Tired? Is he grumpy or glad? Like so many other exchanges between parent and child, this concern flows mainly one way; Jesse does not surround me with thought. On the contrary, with each passing year he pays less and less attention to me, except when he needs something, and then he bristles at being reminded of his dependence. That's natural, mostly, although teenage scorn for parents also gets a boost from popular culture. My own father had to die before I thought seriously about what he might have needed or wanted or suffered. If Jesse has children of his own one day, no doubt he will brood on them as I have brooded on him for these seventeen years. Meanwhile, his growing up requires him to break free of my concern; I accept that, yet I cannot turn off my fathering mind.

Before leaving for Colorado, I had imagined that he would be able to meet the Rockies with clear eyes, with the freshness of his green age. So long as he was in my company, however, he would see the land through the weather of my moods. And if despair had so darkened my vision that I was casting a shadow over Jesse's world—even here among these magnificent mountains and tumultuous rivers—then I would have to change. I would have to learn to see differently. Since I could not forget the wounds to people and planet, could not unlearn the dismal numbers—of pollution and population and poverty—that foretold catastrophe, I would have to look harder for antidotes, for medicines, for sources of hope.

Scott Russell Sanders is the author of twenty-four books, including *Staying Put* (Beacon Press, 1994); *The Force of Spirit* (Beacon Press, 2001); *Hunting for Hope* (Beacon Press, 1999), from which this essay was adapted; *A Conservationist Manifesto* (Indiana University Press 2009); and *Earth Works* (Indiana University Press, 2012). He is a retired professor of English at Indiana University.

CHAPTER THIRTEEN

The Sukkah of Shalom

Rabbi Arthur Waskow

In 2001, just a few weeks after the 9/11 attacks, the Jewish community celebrated the harvest festival of Sukkot. Many did so by building a *sukkah*—a fragile hut with a leafy roof, the most vulnerable of houses. Vulnerable in time, since it lasts for only a week each year. Vulnerable in space, since its roof must be not only leafy but leaky enough to let in the starlight and gusts of wind and rain.

In our evening prayers throughout the year, just as we prepare to lie down in vulnerable sleep, we plead with God, "Spread over us Your sukkah of shalom—of peace and safety."

Why does the prayer plead for a sukkah of shalom rather than a temple or fortress or palace of shalom, which would surely be more safe and more secure?

Precisely because the sukkah is so vulnerable.

For much of our lives we try to achieve peace and safety by building with steel and concrete and toughness:

Pyramids

Air raid shelters

Pentagons

World Trade Centers

But the sukkah reminds us: We are in truth all vulnerable. If as the prophet Dylan sang, "A hard rain's gonna fall," it will fall on all of us. And on 9/11/01, the ancient truth came home: We all live in a sukkah. Even the widest oceans, the mightiest buildings, the wealthiest balance sheets, the most powerful weapons did not shield us.

There are only wispy walls and leaky roofs between us. The planet is in fact one interwoven web of life. The command to love my neighbor as I do myself is not an admonition to be nice: It is a statement of truth like the law of gravity. However much and in whatever way I love my neighbor, that will turn out to be the way I love myself. If I pour contempt upon my neighbor, hatred will recoil upon me.

Only a world where all communities feel vulnerable, and therefore connected to all other communities, can prevent such acts of rage and mass murder.

The sukkah not only invites our bodies to become physically vulnerable, but also invites our minds to become vulnerable to new ideas. To live in the sukkah for a week, as Jewish tradition teaches, would be to leave behind not only the rigid walls and towers of our cities, but also our rigidified ideas, our assumptions, our habits, our accustomed lives.

Indeed, the tradition teaches that Sukkot is the festival on which we open ourselves to what is foreign to us. We pray especially that prosperity and peace pervade all nations, not only the Jewish people. Sukkot is the festival when we invite holy guests into the sukkah—"guests" precisely because they are our higher selves, our unaccustomed selves.

By leaving our houses, we create the time and space to reflect upon our lives. To "reflect" is to look in the mirror at our "reflections." Indeed, for a moment in 2001 many Americans did pause to ask themselves the question, "Why did those attackers hate us? Did we do anything to bring such hate upon us?"

But the government of the United States moved at once to change that question into, "Why did those attackers dare to hate us?" And it immediately gave the answer, "Because we are free and they hate freedom."

Can we imagine a president addressing Congress to say:

> For forty days your government will take no action except to gather evidence of who perpetrated this mass murder. We urge all Americans to gather in *sukkot*—in all the places where we might explore the open weave of half-walled space between us and the rest of the world, between humanity and the rest of the planetary web of life. We urge us all to reflect.
>
> We invite not only those who from a distance have studied Islam but those Americans and others who themselves are Muslims, to talk with the rest of us in these *sukkot* (the plural of *sukkah*).
>
> We invite those who have lived in the despairing slums and rain-ravaged huts of the world, who have studied alongside the humiliated, angry citizens of the future in the crippled nations that make up half the world, to talk with the rest of us in these *sukkot*. To reflect with us.

We can imagine it, but in 2001 we could not expect it from the government of the United States. For we have built a culture that has as little space for the sukkah of reflection, of hospitality to new, uncomfortable ideas, as it does for the sukkah of vulnerability and physical discomfort.

So we got what was most to be expected: not a call to reflect. Not a call to pursue the criminals through new forms of international and transnational law. Not a call to understand and address the underlying grievances that turned a few to terrorism and many more to rage against American power.

Instead, from the government of the United States a call to war. Not merely a war, but a "Crusade"—the word that beyond all others was most likely to arouse suspicion, fear, and rage in the Muslim world. War and Crusade—the archetypal reverse of self-reflection. The opposite of looking inward. The impulse not only to look outward but to smash whatever is out there.

And in the year and a half that followed the 9/11 attacks, the US government launched not just one war but two. In each, all it cared about was smashing a repressive government that did not obey American dictates (repressive governments that did obey were not attacked) and establishing its control over resources or strategic territory that it wanted.

Our leaders responded to our vulnerability by trying harder to make ourselves invulnerable. But in a vulnerable world, this takes more and more ferocity, more and more coercion, more and more violence—at home as well as abroad.

What would it mean to recognize that we all live in vulnerable sukkot? Here are a few examples:

Could we teach all our children the Torah, the Prophets, the Song of Songs, the Talmud, the New Testament, the Quran, the Upanishads, the teachings of the Buddha and of King and Gandhi, as treasuries of wisdom—and sometimes of great danger—that are as crucial to the world as Plato and Darwin and Einstein?

Could we learn to see the dangers in "our own" as well as in "the other" teachings, and learn to strengthen those elements in all traditions that call for nonviolence, not bloody Crusades and jihads and holy wars for holy lands?

Instead of only mouthing wishes, could we insist on doing deeds: strengthening the International Criminal Court and expanding its jurisdiction to cases of international terrorism? Creating peace between a secure Israel and a viable Palestine? Sharing abundance between the Starving World and the Obese World? Sharing disarmament among nations with suicide bombers and those (like our own) with hundreds or thousands of weapons of mass destruction? Learning to breathe easy and use far less of the fuels that so quickly become a cause for war—instead of choking and scorching the planet with greenhouse gases of mass desolation?

Not every demand of the poor and disempowered is legitimate simply because it is an expression of pain. But can we open the ears of our hearts to ask: Have we ourselves had a hand in creating the pain? Can we act to lighten it?

Can we create for ourselves a sukkah in time, a sukkah of reflection and renewal, as well as recognizing the sukkah of vulnerable space in which we actually live?

Could we in every year use the days that surround 9/11 to gather for reflection, for self-examination? Could we gather in a mood of Awe rather than fear, to mourn what tears the world apart and learn what weaves the world together?

The choice we face is broader than politics, deeper than charity. It is whether we see the world chiefly as property to be controlled, defined by walls and fences that must be built ever higher, ever thicker, ever tougher; or made up chiefly of an open weave of compassion and connection, open sukkah next to open sukkah.

Whatever we build where the tall Twin Towers once stood, America and the world will be living in a leafy, leaky, shaky sukkah. Hope comes from raising that simple truth to visibility. We must spread over all of us the sukkah of shalom.

Rabbi Arthur Waskow is director of the Shalom Center (*www.theshalomcenter.org*) and author of *A Time for Every Purpose Under Heaven: The Jewish Life-Spiral as a Spiritual Path* (with Phyllis Berman; Farrar, Straus and Giroux, 2002), *Seasons of Our Joy: A Modern Guide to the Jewish Holidays* (Jewish Publication Society, 2012), *Godwrestling, Round 2* (Jewish Lights Publishing, 1998), and other books of spiritual search and struggle toward peace, justice, and healing the Earth. Part of this essay appeared in *From the Ashes: A Spiritual Response to the Attack on America*, compiled by the editors of Beliefnet (Rodale Press, 2002).

CHAPTER FOURTEEN

Getting Our Gaze Back

Rose Marie Berger

My office window faces east. Our unfriendly neighbor planted a peach tree in the tiny green space between her building and ours. My window frames the tree and the bright yellow spikes of winter cabbage gone to flower. Someone has dangled a plastic great horned owl from the telephone wires. I stare out. Two houses down, during the Iraq war, a blue-and-white banner hung from the second-floor porch. It said "Kalamazoo for Peace." Michigan is far from our inner-city, working-poor, Washington, D.C., neighborhood. Swallowtails, cabbage whites, skippers, and orange sulphurs follow scent trails to the tiny patches of flowers blooming furiously in the middle of the city. The window's iron security bars cast vertical shadows across my computer screen in the morning.

I've noticed about myself recently that I stare out the window and daydream when I'm desperate. The unrelenting beam of information aimed at me via the computer screen too often occupies my eyes. The mind silts up with details, images, pleas for help, advertisements, and thousands of worthy campaigns for social change. "Life shouldn't be this hard," I think.

Eventually, nothing can float freely in the stream of my consciousness; everything is stuck. After some time staring at my mind-mud, I turn to the window. I watch butterflies and wonder about color variations on peaches.

"Daydreaming," says artificial intelligence researcher Erik Mueller, "is spontaneously recalling or imagining personal or vicarious experiences in the past or future." He argues that it improves efficiency, assists creativity, and regulates emotions. The odd thing is that Mueller is studying human daydreaming to teach computers how to do it.

I find this interesting because computers were developed primarily to process information. What flows through the Internet—to websites, smart phones, to e-mail—is an explosion of semi-random details from wider and wider sources. The human brain, however, is not made to process data. It works by matching patterns. Our minds create order out of chaos by discerning patterns and then using those patterns in unique ways. It's our secret of survival. Is one reason I look out my window while thinking "life shouldn't be this hard" because the saturation of data forces my brain to work against itself? Is daydreaming a dose of self-medication in a data-processed world? We are not computers, not machines. We have more in common with flowers than microchips.

Bernard of Clairvaux, a Benedictine monk, wrote in 1149 about the necessity of resting the mind in God. It is this kind of meditation, he says, that "replaces confusion with order, checks the inclination to lose oneself in uncertainty, gathers together that which is dispersed, penetrates into that which is hidden, discovers what is true and distinguishes it from that which merely appears as such."

By mid-afternoon the view outside my window is deep in shade. Pigeons and doves are settled in alongside the owl. The butterflies are absent—perhaps moved on to warmer microclimes. The dark green leaves are still. A rusty bedspring leans against the fence and trash from the alley dumpster is caught in the fence. I give over my intellect, my tired eyes, and some part of my soul to the cool of the afternoon. I rest.

Isn't this kind of holy daydreaming an essential quality of Sabbath? I learn humility from a tree that flowers, fruits, and multiplies whether I sleep or am awake. I am awed by butterflies that can trace the scent of sweetness without extensive computer-generated data and global positioning satellites. I look out my window through the security bars. My mouth waters in anticipation of summer peaches.

Rose Marie Berger is associate editor of *Sojourners* magazine (*www.sojo.net*), where this article first appeared.

CHAPTER FIFTEEN

Fragile and Hidden

Henri Nouwen

Because life is very small, you can never see it happening. Have you ever seen a tree actually grow? Can you see a child grow? Growth is too gentle, too tender. Life is basically hidden. It is small and begs for constant care and protection. If you are committed to always saying yes to life, you are going to have to become a person who chooses it when it is hidden.

I have a case in point from my own life. I live in a community with handicapped adults. Just after I moved in they asked me if I would be willing to take care of Adam. Adam cannot speak. Adam cannot walk. Adam is what some people might call "a vegetable." "Would you be willing to wash Adam?" they asked. "Would you be willing to dress him and give him breakfast?"

As I began to take care of Adam, I slowly discovered what life is about. Adam began to teach me about the smallness of living. As I bathed this twenty-five-year-old man, washed his face, combed his hair, fed him, and dressed him, I began to realize what an incredible gift life is. Adam spoke to me in a language I didn't know he could speak. He told me how hidden, vulnerable, and deep life is. Being with him gave me a sense of being closely in touch with living. After a while I felt an enormous desire to leave my office and my books and to be with Adam, because he would tell me what life was about.

I began to realize that every time people say yes to life in whatever form—the unborn life, life on death row, the life of the severely handicapped, the life of the broken and the homeless—they start to give hope to each other. I had never experienced hope so concretely until I began to wash Adam. Adam strengthened my hope. It wasn't optimism. Adam is never going to get better. But he offers hope. This hope can form a very strong bond among people who are willing to go where life is fragile and hidden.

From *The Road to Peace: Writings on Peace and Justice*, edited by John Dear (Orbis Books, 1998). The late Catholic theologian Henri Nouwen tells the story of Adam in more detail in *Adam: God's Beloved* (Orbis Books, 1997). Another of his books is *Life of the Beloved: Spiritual Living in a Secular World* (Crossroad Publishing Company, 2002). See *www.henrinouwen.org*.

CHAPTER SIXTEEN

There Is a Season

Parker Palmer

Here is a story for activists about Thomas Merton—the late Trappist monk, social critic, spiritual visionary, and writer—whose books continue to have an important impact on movements for peace and racial justice.

In the early 1960s, Merton, who lived in a hermitage on the grounds of a monastery out in the Kentucky woods, published a book titled *Seeds of Destruction*. In it he dissected the deep-rooted and persistent racism of American society, and prophesied a racial conflagration soon to come. For this he was taken to task in a book review written by a well-known white liberal urban activist, who said, in effect, "How dare this hermit, who has copped-out on society by retreating to the woods, tell those of us who are hard at work on the front lines that we will not prevail!"

A decade later, after Merton's prophecy of "the fire next time" had come to pass, the reviewer apologized to Merton in print. Merton, he acknowledged, had seen and spoken more truth from his perch out in the forest than most activists of those times had seen and spoken from the city streets. Sometimes we get a deeper look into the world's heart—and our own—when we stand not on the shifting sands of society and ego but on the bedrock realities of the natural, and spiritual, world.

In my own life as a citizen-activist, involved as I have been for forty years with educational reform, racial justice, peace, and community-building, I know how easy it is to lose perspective. One day I get swept away on an updraft of hope—often tainted by an illusion of my own prowess—that things are getting better and better. The next day I get swept under by a tidal wave of despair—often driven by some blow to my own ego—as the mindless or intentional cruelty of the powers and principalities overwhelms me and everything I care about. If I stay trapped too long in this kind of whiplash, I grow weary of it and start looking for escape, not engagement.

That is not the way I want my life to be. I want to see things steady and see them whole—see both the world and myself that way—so I can stay engaged with the struggle. As I have tried to do so, I have found that it helps to stay attuned to the rhythms of the natural world, with its endless cycle of birthing, dying, being reborn, and dying to live once again. Through all her ups and downs, Mother Nature is in this for the long haul: I want to be like her!

I do not mean that we must learn to embrace the death of innocents in the political world the way we must learn to embrace the death that comes with the cycles of nature. There is a big difference between state-sponsored or state-condoned killing and the dying that happens in an ecosystem when winter descends. I mean that—if we want to hang in there as citizen-activists—we must learn to "winter through" inwardly, spiritually, letting our inevitable failures become the seedbed for another cycle of planting new life, not the muck and mire of withdrawal and terminal defeat.

Metaphors are more than literary devices: Most of us use metaphors, albeit unconsciously, to name our experience of life. But these personal metaphors do much more than describe reality as we know it. Animated by the imagination, one of the most vital powers we possess, our metaphors often become reality, transmuting themselves from language into the living of our lives.

I know people who say, "Life is like a game of chance—some win, some lose." But that metaphor can create a fatalism about losing or an obsession with beating the odds. I know other people who say, "Life is like a battlefield—you get the enemy, or the enemy gets you." But that metaphor can result in enemies around every corner and a constant sense of siege. We do well to choose our metaphors wisely.

"Seasons" is a wise metaphor for the movement of life, I think. It suggests that life is neither a battlefield nor a game of chance but something infinitely richer, more promising, more real. The notion that our lives are like the eternal cycle of the seasons does not deny the struggle or the joy, the loss or the gain, the darkness or the light, but encourages us to embrace it all—and to find in all of it opportunities for growth.

If we lived close to nature in an agricultural society, the seasons as metaphor and fact would continually frame our lives. But the master metaphor of our era does not come from agriculture—it comes from manufacturing. We do not believe that we "grow" our lives—we believe that we "make" them. Just listen to how we use the word in everyday speech: we make time, make friends, make meaning, make money, make a living, make love.

If we accept the notion that our lives are dependent on an inexorable cycle of seasons, on a play of powers that we can conspire with but never control, we run headlong into a culture that insists, against all evidence, that we can make whatever kind of life we want, whenever we want it. Deeper still, we run headlong into our own egos, which want desperately to believe that we are always in charge.

Transformation is difficult, so it is good to know that there is comfort as well as challenge in the metaphor of life as a cycle of seasons. Illumined by that image, we see that we are not alone in the universe. We are participants in a vast communion of being, and if we open ourselves to its guidance, we can learn anew how to live in this great and gracious community of truth. We can, and we must—if we want our sciences to be humane, our institutions to be sustaining, our healings to be deep, our lives to be true.

AUTUMN

Autumn is a season of great beauty, but it is also a season of decline: The days grow shorter, the light is suffused, and summer's abundance decays toward winter's death. Faced with this inevitable winter, what does nature do in autumn? She scatters the seeds that will bring new growth in the spring—and she scatters them with amazing abandon.

In my own experience of autumn, I am rarely aware that seeds are being planted. Instead, my mind is on the fact that the green growth of summer is browning and beginning to die. My delight in the autumn colors is always tinged with melancholy, a sense of impending loss that is only heightened by the beauty all around. I am drawn down by the prospect of death more than I am lifted by the hope of new life.

But as I explore autumn's paradox of dying and seeding, I feel the power of metaphor. In the autumnal events of my own experience, I am easily fixated on surface appearances—on the decline of meaning, the decay of relationships, the death of a vocation. And yet, if I look more deeply, I may see the myriad possibilities being planted to bear fruit in some season yet to come.

In retrospect, I can see in my own life what I could not see at the time—how the job I lost helped me find work I needed to do, how the "road closed" sign turned me toward terrain I needed to travel, how losses that felt irredeemable forced me to discern meanings I needed to know. On the surface it seemed that life was lessening, but silently and lavishly the seeds of new life were always being sown.

In a paradox, opposites do not negate each other—they cohere in mysterious unity at the heart of reality. Deeper still, they need each other for health, as my body needs to breathe in as well as breathe out. But in a culture that prefers the ease of either/or thinking to the complexities of paradox, we have a hard time holding opposites together. We want light without darkness, the glories of spring and summer without the demands of autumn and winter, and the Faustian bargains we make fail to sustain our lives.

When we so fear the dark that we demand light around the clock, there can be only one result: artificial light that is glaring and graceless and, beyond its borders, a darkness that grows ever more terrifying as we try to hold it off. Split off from each other, neither darkness nor light is fit for human habitation. But if we allow the paradox of darkness and light to be, the two will conspire to bring wholeness and health to every living thing.

Winter

Winter where I live in the upper Midwest is a demanding season—and not everyone appreciates the discipline. It is a season when death's victory can seem supreme: few creatures stir, plants do not visibly grow, and nature feels like our enemy. And yet the rigors of winter, like the diminishments of autumn, are accompanied by amazing gifts.

One gift is beauty, different from the beauty of autumn but somehow lovelier still: I am not sure that any sight or sound on Earth is as exquisite as the hushed descent of a sky full of snow. Another gift is the reminder that times of dormancy and deep rest are essential to all living things.

But, for me, winter has an even greater gift to give. It comes when the sky is clear, the sun brilliant, the trees bare, and first snow yet to come. It is the gift of utter clarity. In winter, one can walk into woods that had been opaque with summer growth only a few months earlier and see the trees clearly, singly and together, and see the ground they are rooted in.

A few years ago, my father died. He was more than a good man, and the months following his death were a long, hard winter for me. But in the midst of that ice and loss, I came into a certain clarity that I lacked when he was alive. I saw something that had been concealed when the luxuriance of his love surrounded me—saw how I had relied on him to help me cushion life's harsher blows. When he could no longer do that, my first thought was, "Now I must do it for myself." But as time went on, I saw a deeper truth: It never was my father absorbing those blows but a larger and deeper grace that he taught me to rely upon.

When my father was alive, I confused the teaching with the teacher. My teacher is gone now, but the grace is still there—and my clarity about that fact has allowed his teaching to take deeper root in me. Winter clears the landscape, however brutally, giving us a chance to see ourselves and each other more clearly, to see the very ground of our being.

In the upper Midwest, newcomers often receive a classic piece of wintertime advice: "The winters will drive you crazy until you learn to get out into them." Here, people spend good money on warm clothing so they can get outdoors and avoid the "cabin fever" that comes from huddling fearfully by the fire during the long frozen months.

SPRING

Before spring becomes beautiful, it is plug ugly, nothing but mud and muck. I have walked in the early spring through fields that will suck your boots off, a world so wet and woeful it makes you yearn for the return of ice. But in that muddy mess, the conditions for rebirth are being created.

Though spring begins slowly and tentatively, it grows with a tenacity that never fails to touch me. The smallest and most tender shoots insist upon having their way, coming up through ground that looked, only a few weeks earlier, as if it would never grow anything again. The crocuses and snowdrops do not bloom for long. But their mere appearance, however brief, is always a harbinger of hope, and from those small beginnings, hope grows at a geometric rate. The days get longer, the winds get warmer, and the world grows green again.

In my own life, as my winters segue into spring, I not only find it hard to cope with mud but hard to credit the small harbingers of larger life to come, hard to hope until the outcome is secure. Spring teaches me to look more carefully for the green stems of possibility: for the intuitive hunch that may turn into a larger insight, for the glance or touch that may thaw a frozen relationship, for the stranger's act of kindness that makes the world seem hospitable again.

Late spring is potlatch time in the natural world, a great giveaway of blooming beyond all necessity and reason—done, it would appear, for no reason other than the sheer joy of it. The gift of life, which seemed to be withdrawn in winter, has been given once again, and nature, rather than hoarding it, gives it all away. There is another paradox here, known in all the wisdom traditions: If you receive a gift, you keep it alive not by clinging to it but by passing it along.

From autumn's profligate seedings to the great spring giveaway, nature teaches a steady lesson: If we want to save our lives, we cannot cling to them but must spend them with abandon. When we are obsessed with bottom lines and productivity, with efficiency of time and motion, with the rational relation of means and ends, with projecting reasonable goals and making a beeline toward them, it seems unlikely that our work will ever bear full fruit, unlikely that we will ever know the fullness of spring in our lives.

Summer

Where I live, summer's keynote is abundance. The forests fill with undergrowth, the trees with fruit, the meadows with wildflowers and grasses, the fields with wheat and corn, the gardens with zucchini, and the yards with weeds. In contrast to the sensationalism of spring, summer is a steady state of plenty, a green and amber muchness that feeds us on more levels than we know.

Nature does not always produce abundance, of course. There are summers when flood or drought destroy the crops and threaten the lives and livelihood of those who work the fields. But nature normally takes us through a reliable cycle of scarcity and abundance in which times of deprivation foreshadow an eventual return to the abundant fields.

This fact of nature is in sharp contrast to a human nature that seems to regard perpetual scarcity as the law of life. Daily I am astonished at how readily I believe that something I need is in short supply. If I hoard possessions, it is because I believe that there are not enough to go around. If I struggle with others over power, it is because I believe that power is limited. If I become jealous in relationships, it is because I believe that when you get too much love I will be shortchanged.

The irony, often tragic, is that by embracing the scarcity assumption, we create the very scarcities we fear. If I hoard material goods, others will have too little and I will never have enough. If I fight my way up the ladder of power, others will be defeated and I will never feel secure. If I get jealous of someone I love, I am likely to drive that person away. If I cling to the words I have written as if they were the last of their kind, the pool of new possibilities will surely go dry. We create scarcity by fearfully accepting it as law, and by competing with others for resources as if we were stranded on the Sahara at the last oasis.

In the human world, abundance does not happen automatically. It is created when we have the sense to choose community, to come together to celebrate and share our common store. Whether the "scarce resource" is money or love or power or words, the true law of life is that we generate more of whatever seems scarce by trusting its supply and passing it around. Authentic abundance does not lie in secured stockpiles of food or cash or influence or affection, but in belonging to a community where we can give those goods to others who need them—and receive them from others when we are in need.

Here is a summertime truth: Abundance is a communal act, the joint creation of an incredibly complex ecology in which each part functions on behalf of the whole and, in return, is sustained by the whole. Community not only creates abundance—community is abundance. If we could learn that equation from the world of nature, the human world might be transformed.

Part of this essay appeared in *Let Your Life Speak: Listening for the Voice of Vocation* (Jossey-Bass, 1999). Parker Palmer's other books include *The Courage to Teach* (Jossey-Bass, 1997), *The Active Life* (Jossey-Bass, 1999), *A Hidden Wholeness: The Journey Toward an Undivided Life* (Jossey-Bass, 2009), and *Healing the Heart of Democracy* (Jossey-Bass, 2011).

PART FOUR

Rebellious Imagination

CELEBRATION OF THE HUMAN VOICE

Eduardo Galeano

Their hands were tied or handcuffed, yet their fingers danced, flew, drew words. The prisoners were hooded, but leaning back, they could see a bit, just a bit, down below. Although it was forbidden to speak, they spoke with their hands. Pinio Ungerfeld taught me the finger alphabet, which he had learned in prison without a teacher:

"*Some of us had bad handwriting,*" he told me. "*Others were masters of calligraphy.*"

The Uruguayan dictatorship wanted everyone to stand alone, everyone to be no one: In prisons and barracks, and throughout the country, communication was a crime.

Some prisoners spent more than ten years buried in solitary cells the size of coffins, hearing nothing but clanging bars or footsteps in the corridors. Férnandez Huidobro and Mauricio Rosencof, thus condemned, survived because they could talk to each other by tapping on the wall. In that way they told of dreams and memories, fallings in and out of love; they discussed, embraced, fought; they shared beliefs and beauties, doubts and guilts, and those questions that have no answer.

When it is genuine, when it is born of the need to speak, no one can stop the human voice. When denied a mouth, it speaks with the hands or the eyes, or the pores, or anything at all. Because every single one of us has something to say to the others, something that deserves to be celebrated or forgiven by others.

From *The Book of Embraces* (W. W. Norton, 1992), translated by Cedric Belfrage with Mark Schafer. Galeano's other books include the *Memory of Fire* trilogy: *Genesis*, *Faces & Masks*, and *Century of the Wind* (all W. W. Norton, 1998); *Mirrors* (Nation Books, 2010); and *Children of the Days* (Nation Books, 2013). Galeano started out as an excellent radical journalist, writing in conventional prose: He wrote a classic but straightforward book on the plunder of Guatemala by US corporations. Then, he became touched by some incandescent spark and began forging a poetic vision of amazing richness.

From LAST NIGHT AS I WAS SLEEPING

Antonio Machado
Translated by Robert Bly

Last night as I was sleeping,
I dreamt—marvelous error!—
that a spring was breaking
out in my heart.
I said: Along which secret aqueduct,
Oh water, are you coming to me,
water of a new life
that I have never drunk?

Last night as I was sleeping,
I dreamt—marvelous error!—
that I had a beehive
here inside my heart.
And the golden bees
were making white combs
and sweet honey
from my old failures. . . .

Excerpted from "Last Night As I Was Sleeping," in *Times Alone: Selected Poems of Antonio Machado*, translated and edited by Robert Bly (Wesleyan University Press, 1983).

The thing with feathers. Those are the words Emily Dickinson used to forge an image of hope and suggest a kinship with uplift, lightness of being, the ability of the human spirit to overcome its burdens and soar. Hope is what gives us flight—in short, freedom, or at least an abiding hunger for it. As we've seen, we can draw inspiration from moments of everyday grace, "tossed up as stars to guide us," whether they involve other human beings or the natural world. But sometimes the best way to enlarge our perspective is to rise above the "reality" that's been orchestrated for us and, too often, against us. Beware in particular of the admonition "There's no alternative." Rarely is that true. Telling a story of prisoners of conscience who refused to be defeated by solitary confinement, Eduardo Galeano declares that "no one can stop the human voice." Do you hear the faint rustling of wings in that assertion? That's the sound of imagination unfettered, emboldened—defying complacency, expedience, resignation, fear, fatalism, anything that threatens to constrain the human spirit.

Imagination, in this sense, is a form of generosity: It creates an expansive vision of what's possible and helps us recognize the fundamental bonds that exist between us. It frees us from what may be a bleak present to give us a glimpse of futures that our more rational minds may deem impossible to achieve. Antonio Machado's poem embodies this generous outlook. He dreams of a spring breaking out in his heart, bringing "water of a new life that I have never drunk," and golden bees "making sweet honey from my old failures." In "Childhood and Poetry," Pablo Neruda recalls when another boy passed a toy sheep to him through a fence hole. He couldn't see the stranger. Nor had he asked for the gift. The experience not only fueled Neruda's extraordinary poetry but reinforced his belief that justice and reciprocity can prevail. "To feel the affection that comes from those whom we do not know," he writes, " . . . widens out the boundaries of our being, and unites all living things."

In "To Love the Marigold," Susan Griffin writes of imagination taking wing as surrealist poet Robert Desnos reads palms and saves lives in a World War II concentration camp. Griffin also examines the work of artist Tina Modotti, Edward Weston's lover and model, who became a world-renowned photographer. Griffin attempts to answer the question, Can imagination save us? She is careful to distinguish between what might be called the capitulatory version of imagination, through which we shield ourselves from pain and disappointment by taking refuge in a private fantasy world, and the rebellious version that Modotti and Desnos advocated and practiced. This bolder form of flight gives us the fortitude to grasp the world as it is, including in its most horrific moments, while at the same time reconfiguring it. "What was obscure comes forward," Griffin explains. "Lies are revealed, memory shaken, new delineations drawn over the old maps: It is from this new way of seeing the present that hope for the future emerges." Capitulatory imagination seeks escape from responsibility. Rebellious imagination embraces it, enlarges it, celebrates it. It lets us view the world with fresh eyes. Sometimes, it makes possible an unlikely transformation by restoring us to a new kind of innocence, one in which experience, no matter how dismal, is subsumed within a larger, more luminous vision: the gleam in the eye of those who have every reason to weep.

The unity of living things that Neruda fortuitously discovered as a boy and Modotti's solidarity with the Mexican radicals she photographed further demonstrate the alchemy of community, a theme throughout this book. In isolation, imagination can breed obsession and estrangement. Shared imagination, by contrast, leads outward, to other people and new possibilities. It is more likely to encourage engagement. When veterans of the most difficult campaigns, such as the civil rights struggles of the 1960s, describe what sustained them during the constant threats of violence and terror, they say, "It was the people," because they could not have persisted on their own. Former Student Nonviolent Coordinating Committee (SNCC) chairman Congressman John Lewis adds his voice to this chorus in "Walking with the Wind." He describes the shared formative experience that kept him going through the bleakest of times, and still does: his holding hands with other children and moving from corner to corner of a tiny house to prevent it from blowing off its foundation during a storm. The gesture was nothing less than an act of communal faith that no single individual could have accomplished alone; indeed, few if any in the group would have believed it possible. What a perfect parable for those of us who wish to stand firm against the political storms of our time, and even change the climate that produces them.

In a similar testament to the power of community, I remember reading how the Ku Klux Klan once surrounded a black church where a nighttime civil rights meeting was being held. When the activists within started singing, their life-affirming voices rolling forth into the dark and mounting a full-throated challenge to the politics of hate, the Klan members silently dispersed. Shared song lifted people's spirits, connected them to something larger than themselves, and transformed the space around the singers and performers to create a soaring, swelling resonance the power of which even hostile outsiders recognized. Music is shared more covertly in Toni Mirosevich's "Rough Translation," a vignette that highlights parallels between resistance to the Soviet dictatorship and the jazz musician's "deviation from the score." For Mirosevich and the Russian immigrant whose story she tells, John Coltrane was a call to freedom on smuggled-in cassettes.

Creative resistance, lampooning, and playfulness unite the last four contributors to this section: Walter Wink, Vern Huffman, Sherman Alexie, and Tony Kushner. Jesus and the legendary community organizer Saul Alinsky are rarely mentioned together, but in "Jesus and Alinsky," theologian Wink considers them fellow travelers and offers a staggeringly imaginative (and influential) rereading of key New Testament stories. Wink turns the tables on the notion of "turn the other cheek," arguing that Jesus counseled neither resignation nor passivity. Instead, turning the other cheek was part of a comprehensive strategy that employed ridicule and irony in an attempt to force the Roman occupiers to recognize the Jews as equals, not as slaves. By nonviolently unmasking corruption, deceit, and oppression, Wink argues, even those most dispossessed gain a measure of self-respect before which few autocratic regimes can long stand.

Instances of creative resistance abound, as do people whose compelling brand of resistance is characterized by mischievous audacity, but we rarely hear about them. Consider the so-called Cha Cha Cha, a nonviolent uprising that helped free Zambia from British rule. Vern Huffman describes a revealing example of the movement's approach: assembling a crowd of very large and naked women to greet the British administrator when he arrived at the airport, singing songs of greeting. Another example of inspired resistance is Charlotte, North Carolina's Latin America Coalition, whose members dressed as clowns to respond to a 2012 Nazi and Ku Klux Klan rally, answering chants of White Power with their own White Flour (while tossing flour in the air) and Wife Power. Or consider the students at various Occupy protests who called attention to the burden of student debt by wearing graduation robes and linking themselves to massive papier-mâché balls and chains with "$1 trillion" written on them.

Humor and creativity are also needed to renew our own spirits, as some of the most renowned social justice activists of our time remind us. One might assume that such a profoundly spiritual and engaged individual as the Dalai Lama would be the picture of solemnity, the world's incalculable ills etched on his grave countenance. He, like Desmond Tutu, has witnessed the ugliest realities of our time: conquest, murder, torture, the systematic degradation of human lives. Yet the Dalai Lama is an inveterate jokester and teaser, as joyous as Tutu. During a Seattle visit, he gave my mayor a scarf. "It's made in China," he said, with a watchful smile. The mayor stepped back as if he'd been offered a poisonous snake. "Just kidding," the Dalai Lama added. Everyone laughed and relaxed, still slightly in awe, but of a playful human being, not a stern, unapproachable saint.

Sometimes only untamed irreverence can heal our bodies or souls. Or as comedian Louis C.K. has put it, "Everything that's difficult you should be able to laugh about." That's why I've included "Do Not Go Gentle," by Sherman Alexie, the author of *The Lone Ranger and Tonto Fistfight in Heaven* and *The Absolutely True Diary of a Part-Time Indian*. Alexie's story doesn't directly address political change, though America's unhealed wounds are visible throughout this tale of grief, despair, and deliverance. Alexie draws on his own experience: He and his wife spent the initial weeks of their first child's life at the neonatal intensive care unit of a Seattle hospital while their son hovered between life and death. His riveting tale—with its wild generosity, wicked sexual humor, and abundant imagination—gives me hope in a way that transcends parties and platforms.

Playwright Tony Kushner is wild at heart, too. He also knows well the power of humor to liberate. And he recognizes that if we don't do battle with human destructiveness in all its disguises, and do so together, evil really will, as he has said in another context, waltz into our living room eating pretzels and seduce us all into distracted complacency. "Despair is a lie we are telling ourselves," Kushner says. But imagination unbound can overcome it.

CHAPTER SEVENTEEN

Childhood and Poetry

Pablo Neruda,
Translated by Robert Bly

One time, investigating in the backyard of our house in Temuco the tiny objects and minuscule beings of my world, I came upon a hole in one of the boards of the fence. I looked through the hole and saw a landscape like that behind our house, uncared for, and wild. I moved back a few steps, because I sensed vaguely that something was about to happen. All of a sudden a hand appeared—a tiny hand of a boy about my own age. By the time I came close again, the hand was gone, and in its place there was a marvelous white sheep.

The sheep's wool was faded. Its wheels had escaped. All of this only made it more authentic. I had never seen such a wonderful sheep. I looked back through the hole, but the boy had disappeared. I went into the house and brought out a treasure of my own: a pinecone, opened, full of odor and resin, which I adored. I set it down in the same spot and went off with the sheep.

I never saw either the hand or the boy again. And I have never again seen a sheep like that either. The toy I lost finally in a fire. But even now, [at] almost fifty years old, whenever I pass a toyshop, I look furtively into the window, but it's no use. They don't make sheep like that anymore.

I have been a lucky man. To feel the intimacy of brothers is a marvelous thing in life. To feel the love of people whom we love is a fire that feeds our life. But to feel the affection that comes from those whom we do not know, from those unknown to us, who are watching over our sleep and solitude, over our dangers and our weaknesses—that is something still greater and more beautiful because it widens out the boundaries of our being, and unites all living things.

That exchange brought home to me for the first time a precious idea: that all of humanity is somehow together. That experience came to me again much later; this time it stood out strikingly against a background of trouble and persecution.

It won't surprise you then that I attempted to give something resiny, earthlike, and fragrant in exchange for human brotherhood. Just as I once left the pinecone by the fence, I have since left my words on the door of so many people who were unknown to me, people in prison, or hunted, or alone.

That is the great lesson I learned in my childhood, in the backyard of a lonely house. Maybe it was nothing but a game two boys played who didn't know each other and wanted to pass to the other some good things of life. Yet maybe this small and mysterious exchange of gifts remained inside me also, deep and indestructible, giving my poetry light.

From *Neruda and Vallejo*, translated and edited by Robert Bly (Beacon Press, 1971). Chilean poet Pablo Neruda won the Nobel Prize in Literature in 1971.

CHAPTER EIGHTEEN

To Love the Marigold

Susan Griffin

A few years ago, while visiting Paris, I went to see a small exhibit of photographs taken by Tina Modotti in the Twenties and Thirties in Mexico. Upstairs in the gallery, the harried mood of the rue de Rennes rapidly peeled away. I was startled by the beauty of the images Modotti made and the impact of her life story. In one photograph, a line of Mexican men, mostly workers or peasants, stand staring at the camera. They have assembled at the headquarters of the Communist Party in Mexico. One of them is holding a flag taken from the United States Army by the first Sandinistas in Nicaragua. The moment is a victory and you can see this in the men's faces. But the camera's eye also catches a tender quality of innocence and hope, an expression one so seldom sees any longer even on the faces of any but the youngest children.

One might say that life is so difficult now, or that there has been so much violence that innocence is no longer possible. But this explanation is too easy. The lives of the men in this photograph were undoubtedly very difficult and violence was palpably present—another series of newspaper photographs in this show depicts Tina Modotti as she is questioned by police just after her lover, a militant organizer, was assassinated. She was with him on the street when he was shot. He died in her arms.

Saturated with the beauty and sorrow of these images, my mood changes again as I descend the stairs. I join a line that is flanked by police who check everyone's bags. Throughout the summer a number of bombs have exploded in public places in Paris. The randomness of this violence is as much a part of modern life as the lone skyscraper of Montparnasse, which towers over me as I step out onto the street, reminding me once more that this is a different age than the one Modotti recorded.

Outwardly the most obvious change is technological. Like surrounding armies, steel and glass structures can be seen at the edge of this old city of Paris. Efficiency with its faster cars and airplanes, television, computers and e-mail, defines modern life here. Yet strangely, in this brave new world with its promise of every possible sensation and comfort, one feels diminished. The unapproachable immensity of the skyscraper in front of me, blotting out the immensity of the sky, appears now as an icon of an anonymous power, in whose shadow I feel powerless.

Among those who would seek or want social change, despair is endemic now. A lack of hope that is tied to many kinds of powerlessness. Repeating patterns of suffering. Burgeoning philosophies of fear and hatred. Not to speak of the failure of dreams. Where once there were societies that served as models for a better future, grand plans, utopias, now there is distrust and dissatisfaction with any form of politics, a sense of powerlessness edging into nihilism.

Yet Modotti's beautiful images still speak in me. The eye of her camera is so fresh. A bunch of roses, encountered, almost as if caressed, come alive as if never before in the frame of her camera. And it's the same with a typewriter or a crowd standing under umbrellas in the rain, her vision original, allowing one to see the familiar again in a fuller dimension. Even in her photograph of the Mexican Communist Party, one sees a layer of existence beneath theory; a desire for a better life and for justice that is radiantly evident among those she photographed. Perhaps it's precisely now, as old systems of meaning perish, that new meanings can be revealed.

In these years after the end of the Cold War, a time of the failure of old paradigms and systems of thought, perhaps hope lies less in the direction of grand theories than in the capacity to see, to look past old theories that may obscure understanding and even promise. To assume what the Buddhists call beginner's mind. And to see what exists freshly and without prejudice clears the path for seeing what might exist in the future, or what is possible.

Even in the grimmest of circumstances, a shift in perspective can create startling change. I am thinking of a story I heard a few years ago from my friend Odette, a writer and a survivor of the Holocaust. Along with many others who crowd the bed of a large truck, she tells me, the surrealist poet Robert Desnos is being taken away from the barracks of the concentration camp where he has been held prisoner. As the truck leaves the barracks, the mood is somber; everyone knows the truck is headed for the gas chambers. And when the truck arrives no one can speak at all; even the guards fall silent. But this silence is soon interrupted by an energetic man who jumps into the line and grabs one of the condemned. Improbable as it is, Odette told me, Desnos reads the man's palm.

Oh, he says, I see you have a very long lifeline. And you are going to have three children. He is exuberant. And his excitement is contagious. First one man, then another, offers up his hand, and the prediction is for longevity, more children, abundant joy.

As Desnos reads more palms, not only does the mood of the prisoners change but that of the guards too. How can one explain it? Perhaps the element of surprise has planted a shadow of doubt in their minds. If they told themselves these deaths were inevitable, this no longer seems inarguable. They are in any case so disoriented by this sudden change of mood among those they are about to kill that they are unable to go through with the executions. So all the men, along with Desnos, are packed back onto the truck and taken back to the barracks. Desnos has saved his own life and the lives of others by using his imagination.

Because I am seized by the same despair as my contemporaries, for several days this story poses a question in my mind. Can the imagination save us? Robert Desnos was famous for his belief in the imagination. He believed it could transform society. And what a wild leap this was, at the mouth of the gas chambers, to imagine a long life! In his mind he simply stepped outside the world as it was created by the SS.

In the interest of realism, this story must be accompanied by another. Desnos did not survive the camps. He died of typhus a few days after the liberation. His death was one among millions, men, women, and children who died despite countless creative acts of survival and the deepest longings to live.

In considering what is possible for the future one must be careful not to slide into denial. Imagination can so easily be trapped by the wish to escape painful facts and unbearable conclusions. The New Age idea that one can wish oneself out of any circumstance, disease, or bad fortune is not only sadly disrespectful toward suffering, it is also, in the end, dangerous if escape replaces awareness.

But there are other dangers. What is called "realism" can lead to a kind of paralysis of action and a state of mind that has relinquished desire altogether. Especially now, when the political terrain seems so unnavigable, the impulse is toward cynicism. For months before the World Conference of Women met in Beijing, an informal debate circulated among women in the United States. Alongside the serious questions of China's violations of human rights, another question was posed. Why should we meet at all? What good will it do?

What is required now is balance. In the paucity of clear promise, one must somehow walk a tightrope, stepping lightly on a thin line drawn between cynicism and escape, planting the feet with awareness but preserving all the while enough playfulness to meet fear. For those who went to the conference in Beijing, though, something momentous occurred. In the creation of a different arena, defined in different ways by women from all over the world, another possible world began to exist, if even temporarily, and this has nurtured desire and imagination.

One might say that human societies have two boundaries. One boundary is drawn by the requirements of the natural world and the other by the collective imagination. The dominant philosophies of Western societies have pitted imagination against nature. The effects of this dualism upon nature are devastatingly clear. But the effects on the human imagination are also terrible. Dividing the mind from the body, sensuality, and experience creates small and tortured thought from which frenetic, soulless, and destructive societies have been born.

In the harsh world of the concentration camp, whose regime was designed to crush both body and spirit, how was it possible for Desnos to keep the larger possibilities of life alive in his mind? I find the thread of an answer in the lines of one of his poems:

Having said having done
What pleases me
I go right I go left
And I love the marigold.

It is ironic that a society that has dreamt of mastering nature would create a feeling of such terrible powerlessness for the great majority. Though for at least the last two hundred years, technology itself has been the source of a hope for freedom and equality—new machines that would free us all from labor, chemicals that will conquer disease, methods of agriculture that would feed everyone—and now the latest hope, that computer networking will somehow magically create a more democratic public arena. But what I see now, standing in this brave new world, is that this technological mandate has become more deterministic in our minds than any law of nature. In this light, progress assumes a demonic aspect, like an engine that cannot be stopped but must bear down on whoever or whatever is in its path.

Such a moment does not require less but rather more imagination. For to imagine is not simply to see what does not yet exist or what one wants to exist. It is also a profound act of creativity to see what is. To see, for instance, that the freedom of public discourse is being circumscribed by corporate power requires an imaginative leap.

At the same time, the act of seeing changes those who see. This is perhaps most clear with self-perception. By my perceptions of who I am or what I feel, not only do I re-create my idea of who I am but I also change myself. Perception is not simply a reflection of reality but a powerful element of reality. Anyone who meditates has had this experience: Observing the activities of the mind changes the mind until, bit by bit, observation creates great changes in the soul. And the effect is the same when the act of perception is collective. A change in public perception will change the public. This is why acts of imagination are so important.

Like artistic and literary movements, social movements are driven by imagination. I am not speaking here only of the songs and poems and paintings that have always been part of movements for political and social change, but of the movements themselves, their political ideas and forms of protest. Every important social movement reconfigures the world in the imagination. What was obscure comes forward, lies are revealed, memory shaken, new delineations drawn over the old maps: It is from this new way of seeing the present that hope for the future emerges.

What remains with me from Modotti's images is not just a portrait of dreams that failed but of dreams that are still alive and of aspiration itself, that learning of the soul that never ceases. No one can stop us from imagining another kind of future, one which departs from the terrible cataclysm of violent conflict, of hateful divisions, poverty, and suffering. Let us begin to imagine the worlds we would like to inhabit, the long lives we will share, and the many futures in our hands.

This essay originally appeared in the now-defunct *Whole Earth Review* and then in *Utne Reader*. Susan Griffin's books include *The Book of the Courtesans* (Broadway Books, 2002), *The Eros of Everyday Life* (Anchor, 1996), *Woman and Nature* (Sierra Club Books, 2000), *A Chorus of Stones* (Anchor, 1993), and *Wrestling with the Angel of Democracy* (Trumpeter, 2009).

CHAPTER NINETEEN

Walking with the Wind

John Lewis

This little story has nothing to do with a national stage, or historic figures, or monumental events. It's a simple story, a true story, about a group of young children, a wood-frame house, and a windstorm.

The children were my cousins—about a dozen of them, all told—along with three siblings. And me. I was four years old at the time, too young to understand there was a war going on over in Europe and out in the Pacific as well. The grown-ups called it a world war, but I had no idea what that meant. The only world I knew was the one I stepped out into each morning, a place of thick pine forests and white cotton fields and red clay roads winding around my family's house in our little corner of Pike County, Alabama.

We had just moved that spring onto some land my father had bought, the first land anyone in his family had ever owned—110 acres of cotton and corn and peanut fields, along with an old but sturdy three-bedroom house, a large house for that part of the county, the biggest place for miles around. It had a well in the front yard, and pecan trees out back, and muscadine grapevines growing wild in the woods all around us—*our* woods.

My father bought the property from a local white businessman who lived in the nearby town of Troy. The total payment was $300. Cash. That was every penny my father had to his name, money he had earned the way almost everyone we knew made what money they could in those days—by tenant farming. My father was a sharecropper, planting, raising, and picking the same crops that had been grown in that soil for hundreds of years by tribes like the Choctaws and the Chickasaws and the Creeks, Native Americans who were working this land long before the place was called Alabama, long before black or white men were anywhere to be seen in those parts.

Almost every neighbor we had in those woods was a sharecropper, and most of them were our relatives. Nearly every adult I knew was an aunt or an uncle, every child my first or second cousin. That included my Uncle Rabbit and Aunt Seneva and their children, who lived about a half mile or so up the road from us.

On this particular afternoon—it was a Saturday, I'm almost certain—about fifteen of us children were outside my Aunt Seneva's house, playing in her dirt yard. The sky began clouding over, the wind started picking up, lightning flashed far off in the distance, and suddenly I wasn't thinking about playing anymore; I was terrified. I had already seen what lightning could do. I'd seen fields catch on fire after a hit to a haystack. I'd watched trees actually explode when a bolt of lightning struck them, the sap inside rising to an instant boil, the trunk swelling until it burst its bark. The sight of those strips of pine bark snaking through the air like ribbons was both fascinating and horrifying.

Lightning terrified me, and so did thunder. My mother used to gather us around her whenever we heard thunder and she'd tell us to hush, be still now, because God was doing his work. That was what thunder was, my mother said. It was the sound of God doing his work.

But my mother wasn't with us on this particular afternoon. Aunt Seneva was the only adult around, and as the sky blackened and the wind grew stronger, she herded us all inside. Her house was not the biggest place around, and it seemed even smaller with so many children squeezed inside. Small and surprisingly quiet. All of the shouting and laughter that had been going on earlier, outside, had stopped. The wind was howling now, and the house was starting to shake. We were scared. Even Aunt Seneva was scared.

And then it got worse. Now the house was beginning to sway. The wood plank flooring beneath us began to bend. And then, a corner of the room started lifting up.

I couldn't believe what I was seeing. None of us could. This storm was actually pulling the house toward the sky. With us inside it. That was when Aunt Seneva told us to clasp hands. Line up and hold hands, she said, and we did as we were told. Then she had us walk as a group toward the corner of the room that was rising. From the kitchen to the front of the house we walked, the wind screaming outside, sheets of rain beating on the tin roof. Then we walked back in the other direction, as another end of the house began to lift.

And so it went, back and forth, fifteen children walking with the wind, holding that trembling house down with the weight of our small bodies.

More than half a century has passed since that day, and it has struck me more than once over those many years that our society is not unlike the children in that house, rocked again and again by the winds of one storm or another, the walls around us seeming at times as if they might fly apart.

It seemed that way in the 1960s, at the height of the civil rights movement, when America itself felt as if it might burst at the seams—so much tension, so many storms. But the people of conscience never left the house. They never ran away. They stayed, they came together and they did the best they could, clasping hands and moving toward the corner of the house that was the weakest.

And then another corner would lift, and we would go there.

And eventually, inevitably, the storm would settle, and the house would still stand.

But we knew another storm would come, and we would have to do it all over again. And we did. And we still do, all of us. You and I. Children holding hands, walking with the wind. That is America to me—not just the movement for civil rights but the endless struggle to respond with decency, dignity, and a sense of brotherhood to all the challenges that face us as a nation, as a whole.

That is the story, in essence, of my life, of the path to which I've been committed since I turned from a boy to a man, and to which I remain committed today. It is a path that extends beyond the issue of race alone, and beyond class as well. And gender. And age. And every other distinction that tends to separate us as human beings rather than bring us together.

That path involves nothing less than the pursuit of the most precious and pure concept I have that has guided me like a beacon ever since, a concept called the Beloved Community. That concept ushered me into the heart of the most meaningful and monumental movement of this past American century. We need it to steer us all where we deserve to go in the next.

Adapted from *Walking with the Wind: A Memoir of the Movement* (Harcourt Brace, 1998). The son of Alabama sharecroppers, John Lewis participated in the 1961 Freedom Rides, chaired the Student Nonviolent Coordinating Committee (SNCC), helped coordinate Mississippi's "Freedom Summer," and now represents Georgia's Fifth District in Congress. He is also the author of *Across That Bridge* (Hyperion, 2012) and co-author of a graphic novel on the civil rights movement, *March: Book One* (Top Shelf Productions, 2013).

CHAPTER TWENTY

Rough Translation

Toni Mirosevich

Here she is not afraid. Of the neighbor with a glass turned over and placed against the wall, a small strain of jazz overheard. Enough proof to call the authorities. (Definition of authorities in Russia: anyone other than you.) Imagine it. Louis Armstrong as ticket to the hoosegow. If feet tap to the music, feet tramp down the hall.

(Her father, who is unhappy here, calls every day. When talking of home he says the same phrase over and over again: "I was always afraid, and I was happy.")

"We always whispered," she yells over the Coltrane I have on to make her feel at ease. Between cuts a quick silence opens. She brings her voice down low, draws her lips tight, small. Still wary. "Do you know anyone who would want to go back? Anyone?"

I put on Brubeck. She tells me how music was smuggled in, the risk taken. Sailors, in from the Black Sea, slipped tapes from pocket to pocket while the crew unloaded cargo (each move closely watched, each box counted, once, twice). Late at night, somewhere in Odessa, they would find a lab. With X-ray film, a grooving needle, an amplifier, somehow a rough copy was made. The scratchy horn of Miles on *Kind of Blue*. Ella's scat. The world of improvisation. Deviation from the score.

When she's finished the tale, I say, "Where there's a will . . . ": some platitude, a way to buy time. Only to have this surface later:

Why did we believe it was different with them—not in their fiber to resist, to improvise? As if the glum faces seen on the nightly news were unable, unwilling, to carry a tune?

Before the evening is over we go through all of *Take Five*, all of *A Love Supreme*. Each time I reach for the volume knob she laughs. I crank it up and up and up till the floor shakes. The neighbor next door pounds back with her broom handle, one-two, one-two, perfect syncopation.

When she leaves I go straight to bed, pull the covers up over my head to keep the chill away. What will I ever have to compare, what can come close? Then, in the next beat, one slim memory surfaces like a stray riff: nights spent under cover, my mother's soft footfall by the door, the small pink transistor held to the ear, the precious, precious sound.

Toni Mirosevich teaches writing at San Francisco State University and is the author of *The Rooms We Make Our Own* (Firebrand Books, 1996), from which this essay is excerpted; *Pink Harvest* (Mid List Press, 2007); and *The Takeaway Bin* (Spuyten Duyvil, 2010).

CHAPTER TWENTY-ONE

Jesus and Alinsky

Walter Wink

You have heard that it was said, "An eye for an eye and a tooth for a tooth." But I say to you, Do not resist one who is evil. But if anyone strikes you on the right cheek, turn to him the other also; and if anyone would sue you and take your coat, let him have your cloak as well; and if anyone forces you to go one mile, go with him two miles. (Attributed to Jesus in Matthew 5:38–41, Revised Standard Version.)

Many who have committed their lives to working for change and justice in the world simply dismiss Jesus's teachings about nonviolence as impractical idealism. And with good reason. "Turn the other cheek" suggests the passive, Christian doormat quality that has made so many Christians cowardly and complicit in the face of injustice. "Resist not evil" seems to break the back of all opposition to evil and counsel submission. "Going the second mile" has become a platitude meaning nothing more than "extend yourself." Rather than fostering structural change, such attitudes encourage collaboration with the oppressor.

Jesus never behaved in such ways. Whatever the source of the misunderstanding, it is neither Jesus nor his teaching, which, when given a fair hearing in its original social context, is arguably one of the most revolutionary political statements ever uttered.

When the court translators working in the hire of King James chose to translate *antistenai* as "resist not evil," they were doing something more than rendering Greek into English. They were translating nonviolent resistance into docility. The Greek word means more than simply to "stand against" or "resist." It means to resist violently, to revolt or rebel, to engage in an insurrection. Jesus did not tell his oppressed hearers not to resist evil. His entire ministry is at odds with such a preposterous idea. He is, rather, warning against responding to evil in kind by letting the oppressor set the terms of our opposition.

A proper translation of Jesus's teaching would then be, "Do not retaliate against violence with violence." Jesus was no less committed to opposing evil than the anti-Roman resistance fighters like Barabbas. The only difference was over the means to be used.

There are three general responses to evil: (1) violent opposition, (2) passivity, and (3) the third way of militant nonviolence articulated by Jesus. Human evolution has conditioned us for only the first two of these responses: fight or flight.

Fight had been the cry of Galileans who had abortively rebelled against Rome only two decades before Jesus spoke. Jesus and many of his hearers would have seen some of the two thousand of their countrymen crucified by the Romans along the roadsides. They would have known some of the inhabitants of Sepphoris (a mere three miles north of Nazareth) who had been sold into slavery for aiding the insurrectionists' assault on the arsenal there. Some also would live to experience the horrors of the war against Rome in 66–70 C.E., one of the ghastliest in history. If the option of fighting had no appeal to them, their only alternative was flight: passivity, submission, or, at best, a passive-aggressive recalcitrance in obeying commands. For them no third way existed.

Now we are in a better position to see why King James's servants translated *antistenai* as "resist not." The king would not want people concluding they had any recourse against his or any other sovereign's unjust policies. Jesus commands us, according to these king's men, to resist not. Jesus appears to say that submission to monarchial absolutism is the will of God. Most modern translations have meekly followed the King James path.

Neither of the invidious alternatives of flight or fight is what Jesus is proposing. Jesus abhors both passivity and violence as responses to evil. His is a third alternative not even touched by these options. The *Scholars Version* translates *antistenai* brilliantly: "Don't react violently against someone who is evil."

Jesus clarifies his meaning by three brief examples. "If anyone strikes you on the right cheek, turn to him the other also." Why the right cheek? How does one strike another on the right cheek anyway? Try it. A blow by the right fist in that right-handed world would land on the left cheek of the opponent. To strike the right cheek with the fist would require using the left hand, but in that society the left hand was used only for unclean tasks. As the *Dead Sea Scrolls* specify, even to gesture with the left hand at Qumran carried the penalty of ten days penance. The only way one could strike the right cheek with the right hand would be with the back of the hand.

What we are dealing with here is unmistakably an insult, not a fistfight. The intention is not to injure but to humiliate, to put someone in his or her place. One normally did not strike a peer in this way, and if one did the fine was exorbitant (4 *zuz* was the fine for a blow to a peer with a fist, 400 *zuz* for backhanding him; but to an underling, no penalty whatever). A backhand slap was the normal way of admonishing inferiors. Masters backhanded slaves; husbands, wives; parents, children; men, women; Romans, Jews.

We have here a set of unequal relations, in each of which retaliation would be suicidal. The only normal response would be cowering submission. It is important to ask who Jesus's audience is. In every case, Jesus's listeners are not those who strike, initiate lawsuits, or impose forced labor. Rather, Jesus is speaking to their victims, people who have been subjected to these very indignities. They have been forced to stifle their inner outrage at the dehumanizing treatment meted out to them by the hierarchical system of caste and class, race and gender, age and status, and by the guardians of imperial occupation.

Why then does Jesus counsel these already humiliated people to turn the other cheek? Because this action robs the oppressor of the power to humiliate them. The person who turns the other cheek is saying, in effect, "Try again. Your first blow failed to achieve its intended effect. I deny you the power to humiliate me. I am a human being just like you. Your status (gender, race, age, wealth) does not alter that. You cannot demean me."

Such a response would create enormous difficulties for the striker. Purely logistically, how can he now hit the other cheek? He cannot backhand it with his right hand. If he hits with a fist, he makes himself an equal, acknowledging the other as a peer. But the whole point of the back of the hand is to reinforce the caste system and its institutionalized inequality.

The second example Jesus gives is set in a court of law. Someone is being sued for his outer garment. Who would do that and under what circumstances? Only the poorest of the poor would have nothing but an outer garment to give as collateral for a loan. Jewish law strictly required its return every evening at sunset, for that was all the poor had in which to sleep. The situation Jesus alludes to is one with which his hearers would have been too familiar: The poor debtor has sunk ever deeper into poverty, the debt cannot be repaid, and his creditor has hauled him into court to wring out repayment.

Indebtedness was the most serious social problem in first-century Palestine. Jesus's parables are full of debtors struggling to salvage their lives. It is in this context that Jesus speaks. His hearers are the poor ("if anyone would sue you"). They share a rankling hatred for a system that subjects them to humiliation by stripping them of their lands, their goods, finally even their outer garments.

Why then does Jesus counsel them to give over their inner garment as well? This would mean stripping off all their clothing and marching out of court stark naked! Put yourself in the debtor's place; imagine the chuckles this saying must have evoked. There stands the creditor, beet-red with embarrassment, your outer garment in one hand, your underwear in the other. You have suddenly turned the tables on him. You had no hope of winning the trial; the law was entirely in his favor. But you have refused to be humiliated. At the same time you have registered a stunning protest against a system that spawns such debt. You have said, in effect, "You want my robe? Here, take everything! Now you've got all I have except my body. Is that what you'll take next?"

Nakedness was taboo in Judaism. Shame fell not on the naked party but the person viewing or causing one's nakedness (Genesis 9:20–27). By stripping you have brought the creditor under the same prohibition that led to the curse of Canaan. As you parade into the street, your friends and neighbors, startled, aghast, inquire what happened. You explain. They join your growing procession, which now resembles a victory parade. The entire system by which debtors are oppressed has been publicly unmasked. The creditor is revealed to be not a "respectable" moneylender but a party in the reduction of an entire social class to landlessness and destitution. This unmasking is not simply punitive, however; it offers the creditor a chance to see, perhaps for the first time in his life, what his practices cause—and to repent.

Jesus in effect is sponsoring clowning. In so doing he shows himself to be thoroughly Jewish. A later saying of the Talmud runs, "If your neighbor calls you an ass, put a saddle on your back."

The Powers That Be literally stand on their dignity. Nothing takes away their potency faster than deft lampooning. By refusing to be awed by their power, the powerless are emboldened to seize the initiative, even where structural change is not possible. This message, far from being a counsel of perfection unattainable in this life, is a practical, strategic measure for empowering the oppressed. It provides a hint of how to take on the entire system in a way that unmasks its essential cruelty and to burlesque its pretensions to justice, law, and order.

Jesus's third example, the one about going the second mile, is drawn from the enlightened practice of limiting the amount of forced labor that Roman soldiers could levy on subject peoples. A soldier could impress a civilian to carry his pack one mile only; to force the civilian to go farther carried with it severe penalties under military law. In this way Rome tried to limit the anger of the occupied people and still keep its armies on the move. Nevertheless, this levy was a bitter reminder to the Jews that they were a subject people even in the Promised Land.

To this proud but subjugated people Jesus does not counsel revolt. One does not "befriend" the soldier, draw him aside, and drive a knife into his ribs. Jesus was keenly aware of the futility of armed revolt against Roman imperial might. He minced no words about it, though it must have cost him support from the revolutionary factions.

But why walk the second mile? Is this not to rebound to the opposite extreme: aiding and abetting the enemy? Not at all. The question here, as in the two previous instances, is how the oppressed can recover the initiative, how they can assert their human dignity in a situation that cannot for the time being be changed. The rules are Caesar's but not how one responds to the rules. The response is God's, and Caesar has no power over that.

Imagine then the soldier's surprise when, at the next mile marker, he reluctantly reaches to assume his pack (sixty-five to eighty-five pounds in full gear). You say, "Oh no, let me carry it another mile." Normally he has to coerce your kinsmen to carry his pack; now you do it cheerfully and will not stop! Is this a provocation? Are you insulting his strength? Being kind? Trying to get him disciplined for seeming to make you go farther than you should? Are you planning to file a complaint? To create trouble?

From a situation of servile impressment, you have once more seized the initiative. You have taken back the power of choice. The soldier is thrown off balance by being deprived of the predictability of your response. Imagine the hilarious situation of a Roman infantryman pleading with a Jew, "Aw, come on, please give me back my pack!" The humor of this scene may escape those who picture it through sanctimonious eyes. It could scarcely, however, have been lost on Jesus's hearers, who must have delighted in the prospect of thus discomfiting their oppressors.

Some readers may object to the idea of discomfiting the soldier or embarrassing the creditor. But can people engaged in oppressive acts repent unless made uncomfortable with their actions? There is, admittedly, the danger of using nonviolence as a tactic of revenge and humiliation. There is also, at the opposite extreme, an equal danger of sentimentality and softness that confuses the uncompromising love of Jesus with being nice. Loving confrontation can free both the oppressed from docility and the oppressor from sin.

Even if nonviolent action does not immediately change the heart of the oppressor, it does affect those committed to it. As Martin Luther King, Jr., attested, it gives them new self-respect and calls on strength and courage they did not know they had. To those with power, Jesus's advice to the powerless may seem paltry. But to those whose lifelong pattern has been to cringe, bow, and scrape before their masters, to those who have internalized their role as inferiors, this small step is momentous.

JESUS'S THIRD WAY

- Seize the moral initiative.
- Find a creative alternative to violence.
- Assert your own humanity and dignity as a person.
- Meet force with ridicule or humor.
- Break the cycle of humiliation.
- Refuse to submit or to accept the inferior position.
- Expose the injustice of the system.
- Take control of the power dynamic.
- Shame the oppressor into repentance.
- Stand your ground.
- Force the Powers into decisions for which they are not prepared.
- Recognize your own power.
- Be willing to suffer rather than retaliate.
- Force the oppressor to see you in a new light.
- Deprive the oppressor of a situation where force is effective.
- Be willing to undergo the penalty of breaking unjust laws.

It is too bad Jesus did not provide fifteen or twenty more examples since we do not tend toward this new response naturally. Some examples from political history might help engrave it more deeply in our minds:

In Alagamar, Brazil, a group of peasants organized a long-term struggle to preserve their lands against attempts at illegal expropriation by national and international firms (with the connivance of local politicians and the military). Some of the peasants were arrested and jailed in town. Their companions decided they were all equally responsible. Hundreds marched to town. They filled the house of the judge, demanding to be jailed with those who had been arrested. The judge was finally obliged to send them all home, including the prisoners.

During the Vietnam War, one woman claimed seventy-nine dependents on her United States income tax, all Vietnamese orphans, so she owed no tax. They were not legal dependents, of course, so were disallowed. No, she insisted, these children have been orphaned by indiscriminate United States bombing; we are responsible for their lives. She forced the Internal Revenue Service to take her to court. That gave her a larger forum for making her case. She used the system against itself to unmask the moral indefensibility of what the system was doing. Of course she "lost" the case, but she made her point.

During World War II, when Nazi authorities in occupied Denmark promulgated an order that all Jews had to wear yellow armbands with the Star of David, the king made it a point to attend a celebration in the Copenhagen synagogue. He and most of the population of Copenhagen donned yellow armbands as well. His stand was affirmed by the Bishop of Sjaelland and other Lutheran clergy. The Nazis eventually had to rescind the order.

It is important to repeat such stories to extend our imaginations for creative nonviolence. Since it is not a natural response, we need to be schooled in it. We need models, and we need to rehearse nonviolence in our daily lives if we ever hope to resort to it in crises.

Maybe it would help to juxtapose Jesus's teachings with legendary community organizer Saul Alinsky's principles for nonviolent community action (in his book, *Rules for Radicals*) to gain a clearer sense of their practicality and pertinence to the struggles of our time. Among the rules Alinsky developed in his attempts to organize American workers and minority communities are these:

(1) Power is not only what you have but what your enemy thinks you have.
(2) Never go outside the experience of your people.
(3) Wherever possible go outside the experience of the enemy.

Jesus, like Alinsky, recommended using your experience of being belittled, insulted, or dispossessed in such a way as to seize the initiative from the oppressor, who finds reactions like going the second mile, stripping naked, or turning the other cheek totally outside his experience. This forces him or her to take your power seriously and perhaps even to recognize your humanity.

Alinsky offers other suggestions. Again we see the parallels:

(4) Make your enemies live up to their own book of rules.
(5) Ridicule is your most potent weapon.
(6) A good tactic is one that your people enjoy.
(7) A tactic that drags on too long becomes a drag.

The debtor in Jesus's example turned the law against his creditor by obeying it, following the letter of the law, but throwing in his underwear as well. The creditor's greed is exposed by his own ruthlessness, and this happens quickly and in a way that could only regale the debtor's sympathizers, just as Alinsky suggests. This puts all other such creditors on notice and arms all other debtors with a new sense of possibilities.

Alinsky's list continues:

(8) Keep the pressure on.
(9) The threat is usually more terrifying than the thing itself.
(10) The major premise for tactics is the development of operations that will maintain a constant pressure on the opposition.

Jesus, in his three brief examples, does not lay out the basis of a sustained movement, but his ministry as a whole is a model of long-term social struggle that maintains a constant pressure. Mark depicts Jesus's movements as a blitzkrieg. His teaching poses immediate and continuing threats to the authorities. The good he brings is misperceived as evil, his following is overestimated, his militancy is misread as sedition, and his proclamation of the coming Reign of God is mistaken as a manifesto for military revolution.

Disavowing violence, Jesus wades into the hostility of Jerusalem openhanded, setting simple truth against force. Terrified by the threat of this man and his following, the authorities resort to their ultimate deterrent, death, only to discover it impotent and themselves unmasked. The cross, hideous and macabre, becomes the symbol of liberation. The movement that should have died becomes a world religion.

Alinsky offers three last suggestions:

(11) If you push a negative hard and deep enough it will break through to its counterside.
(12) The price of a successful attack is a constructive alternative.
(13) Pick the target, freeze it, personalize it, polarize it.

Alinsky delighted in using the most vicious behavior of his opponents—burglaries of movement headquarters, attempted blackmail, and failed assassinations—to destroy their public credibility. Here were elected officials, respected corporations, and trusted police, engaging in patent illegalities to maintain privilege.

In the same way, Jesus suggests amplifying an injustice (turning the other cheek, removing your undergarment, going the second mile) to expose the fundamental wrongness of legalized oppression. The law is "compassionate" in requiring that the debtor's cloak be returned at sunset, yes; but Judaism in its most lucid moments knew that the whole system of usury and indebtedness was itself the root of injustice and should never have been condoned (Exodus 22:25). The restriction of enforced labor to carrying the soldier's pack a single mile was a great advance over unlimited impressment, but occupation troops had no right to be on Jewish soil in the first place.

Jesus was not content merely to empower the powerless, however. Here his teachings fundamentally transcend Alinsky's. Jesus did not advocate nonviolence merely as a technique for outwitting the enemy but as a just means of opposing the enemy in such a way as to hold open the possibility of the enemy's becoming just as well.

To Alinsky's list I would like to add another "rule" of my own: Never adopt a strategy you would not want your opponents to use against you. I would not object to my opponents using nonviolent direct actions against me, since such a move would require them to be committed to suffer and even die rather than resort to violence against me. It would mean they would have to honor my humanity, believe God can transform me, and treat me with dignity and respect.

Today we can draw on the cumulative historical experience of nonviolent social struggle. But the spirit, the thrust, the surge for creative transformation that is the ultimate principle of the universe—this is the same one we see incarnated in Jesus. Freed from literalistic legalism, his teaching reads like a practical manual for empowering the powerless to seize the initiative even in situations impervious to change.

To risk confronting the Powers with such clown-like vulnerability, to affirm at the same time our own humanity and that of those we oppose, to dare to draw the sting of evil by absorbing it—such behavior is unlikely to attract the faint of heart. But to people dispirited by the enormity of the injustices that crush us and the intractability of those in positions of power, Jesus's words beam hope across the centuries. We need not be afraid. We can assert our human dignity. We can lay claim to the creative possibilities that are still ours, burlesque the injustice of unfair laws, and force evil out of hiding from behind the façade of legitimacy.

The late Walter Wink's books include *Jesus and Nonviolence: A Third Way* (Fortress Press, 2003), *Engaging the Powers* (Fortress Press, 1992), *The Powers That Be* (Harmony, 2010), and *The Bible in Human Transformation* (Fortress Press, 2010). Printed with the permission of Walter Wink.

CHAPTER TWENTY-TWO

Stories from the Cha Cha Cha

Vern Huffman

Simon Kapwepwe didn't approve of the racist law in Rhodesia requiring black Africans to do all their shopping through the windows of stores. Never allowed to step inside, they were to present their money at the window and have goods passed out through the window. Simon devised a way to challenge the law, saving enough money to buy a car. He went to the window of the Land Rover dealer and waved his cash at a salesman. He pointed out the vehicle he wanted and asked them to pass it through the window, as the law required. The salesman offered to bring the vehicle to the gate, but Simon was adamant that the law be followed. A crowd gathered and, in the ensuing fracas, Simon went in and got his car, driving it out through the window and bringing down the entire wall. This was the beginning of the nonviolent uprising known as the Cha Cha Cha.

In Northern Rhodesia, which would become Zambia, the rebels were organized but not armed. Though many were followers of the teachings of Mahatma Gandhi, there were episodes of stone throwing and destruction of government property. But the key element was noncooperation with the colonial infrastructure. The people of this region had survived for a thousand years without the colonists and were not interested in buying into a system that did not respect them. And the colonists were not prepared to face living in Africa without the support of native inhabitants.

After several months of this insurrection, the British chose a new administrator for the colony. With his stiff upper lip and strong sense of discipline, this man would soon whip those unruly natives into line! But Julia Chikamonenga organized a welcome party at the Lusaka airport. She gathered together the biggest women she could find to explain her plan. When the new administrator stepped from his plane, he looked across a sea of huge Zambian women, all naked, singing songs of greeting. When he got his mouth closed, he stepped back onto the airplane and ordered the pilot to return him to London.

Within weeks, Zambia was an independent nation, and Simon Kapwepwe later became its vice president.

Vern Huffman is an artist and peace activist who works for Boeing Commercial Aviation in Everett, Washington. His wife, Majori Funka, was a member of the Zambian National Dance Troupe and taught at the University of Zambia.

CHAPTER TWENTY-THREE

Do Not Go Gentle

Sherman Alexie

My wife and I didn't know Mr. Grief in person until our baby boy got his face stuck between his mattress and crib and suffocated himself blue. He died three times that day, Mr. Grief squeezing his lungs tight, but the muscular doctors and nurses battled that suffocating monster man and brought our boy back to life three times. He was our little blue baby Jesus.

I'm lying. Our baby wasn't Jesus. Our baby was alive only a little bit. Mostly he was dead and slept his way through a coma. In Children's Hospital, our baby was hooked up to a million dollars' worth of machines that breathed, pissed, and pooped for him. I bet you could line up all of my wife's and my grandmothers and grandfathers and aunts and uncles and brothers and sisters and mothers and fathers and first, second, and third cousins, and rob their wallets and purses, and maybe you'd collect about $512.

Mr. Grief was a billionaire. He could afford to check on our baby every six hours, but every six hours, my wife and I cussed him out and sent him running. My wife is beautiful and powerful and only twenty-five years old, but she is magic like a grandmother, and Indian grandmothers aren't afraid of a little man like Mr. Grief.

One night, while I guarded over our baby, my wife wrapped her braids in a purple bandana, shoved her hands into thick work clothes, sneaked up on Mr. Grief in the hallway, and beat him severely about the head and shoulders like she was Muhammad Ali.

When you're hurting, it feels good to hurt somebody else. But you have to be careful. If you get addicted to the pain-causing, then you start hurting people who don't need hurting. If you turn into a pain-delivering robot, then you start thinking everybody looks like Mr. Grief and everybody deserves a beating.

One day when my wife was crying, I swear I saw Mr. Grief hiding behind her eyes. So I yelled and screamed at her and called her all of the bad names. But I got really close to her to yell, because it's more effective to yell when you're closer to your enemy, and I smelled her true scent. I knew it was only my wife inside my wife, because she smelled like tenderness, and Mr. Grief smells like a porcupine rotting dead on the side of the road.

My wife and I didn't even name our baby. We were Indians and didn't want to carry around too much hope. Hope eats your flesh like a spider bite. But my wife and I loved our little Baby X and took turns sitting beside his bed and singing to him. The nurses and doctors let us bring in our hand drums, so we sang powwow songs to our baby. I'm a pretty good singer, and my wife is the best there is, and crowds always gathered to listen to us, and that made us feel good.

It was great to feel good about something, because my wife and I were all the way grieving. We took turns singing honor songs and falling asleep. Mr. Grief is a wizard who puts sleep spells on you. My wife spent more time sleeping than I did. I figure she was sadder because she had carried our baby inside her womb and had memorized the way he moved.

One day about a week after our baby fell into his coma, it was me who fell into a waking sleep in a hospital bathroom. Sitting on the bowl, pants wrapped around my ankles, I couldn't move. I was awake and paralyzed by the deadly venom of the grief snake. I wondered if I was going to die right there in that terrible and shameful and hilarious way. I don't want to die like Elvis, I kept saying to myself like it was a prayer.

But right then, when I was ready to roll onto the floor and crawl my way to safety like a grief soldier under grief fire, I heard two other sad men come walking into the bathroom. Those men didn't know I was trapped on the toilet, so they spoke freely and honestly about some sad woman.

"Did you see that woman?" asked man #1.

"You mean the fat one in sweatpants?" asked man #2.

"Yeah, can you believe how terrible she looked? I know our kids are sick, but that doesn't mean we have to let ourselves go like that."

"If you let yourself get ugly on the outside, you're gonna feel even worse on the inside."

"Yeah, what are your kids gonna think when they see you looking so bad?"

"They're gonna be sad."

"And things are sad enough without having to look at your fat mom wearing ugly sweatpants."

"The worst part is, that woman's kid, he isn't even that sick. He isn't terminal. He's only on the third floor."

"Yeah, put her kid on the fourth floor with our kids, and let's see how ugly she gets then."

Listening to their awfulness, I found the strength to stand and walk out of the stall. They were shocked to see me, and they went all quiet and silent and still and frozen. They were ashamed of themselves, I guess, for building a secret clubhouse out of the two-by-four boards and ten-penny nails of their pain. I could be deadly serious and deadly funny at the same time, so I washed my hands really slow, making sure each finger was cleaner than the finger before. I dried them even slower, using one towel for each hand. And then I looked at those two men. I studied the angles and shapes of them like I was taking a geometry test.

I almost yelled at them. I wanted to scream at them for being as shallow and dirty as a dog dish. But hell, their kids were dying. What else were they going to do but punish the world for it? A father with a sick child is an angry god. I know I would have earthquaked Los Angeles, Paris, and Rome, and killed a million innocent people, if it guaranteed my baby boy would rise back to his full life.

But that whole bathroom crazy-scene gave me some energy. I don't know why. I can't explain it. I felt like a good woman and I wanted to be a good mother-man. So I left the hospital and went out shopping for baby toys. The hospital was on Fifteenth and John, and over the past few days, on my journey between home and hospital, I'd been driving past a toy store over on Pike and Seventh. It was called Toys in Babeland, and that was a cute name, so I figured I'd buy some stuffed teddy bears and a rattle and maybe some of those black-and-white toys the experts say are good for babies' eyes. Those seemed like good toy ideas, but I wasn't sure. What kind of toys do you buy, exactly, for a coma baby? I walked over to the store and strolled in, feeling religious about my mission, and shocked myself to discover Toys in Babeland was a sex-toy store.

"Honey," I said to my wife later, "those women were selling vibrators and dildos and edible underwear and butt plugs and lubricants and some stuff I had no idea what the hell you were supposed to do with it. Sweetheart," I said to her, "some of those sex toys looked like a genius and a crazy scientist made them." Now, I was surely embarrassed, but I'm not a prude, so I browsed around, not expecting to buy anything but not wanting to run out of the store like a frightened Christian. Then I turned the corner and saw it, the vibrator they call Chocolate Thunder.

"Darling," I said to my wife later, "I heard that big old music from that *2001: A Space Odyssey* movie when I saw that miracle vibrator."

Chocolate Thunder was dark brown and fifteen inches long and needed a nine-volt battery. I like to think my indigenous penis is powerful. But it would take a whole war party of Indian men to equal up to one Chocolate Thunder. I was shy but quick to buy the thing and ran back to the hospital with it. I ran into the fourth-floor ICU, pulled Chocolate Thunder out of its box, held it up in the air like a magic wand, and switched it on.

Of course, all the doctors and nurses and mothers and fathers were half stunned by that vibrator. And it was a strange and difficult thing. It was sex that made our dying babies, and here was a huge old piece of buzzing sex I was trying to cast spells with. I waved it over our baby and ran around the room waving it over the other sick babies. I was laughing and hooting, and other folks were laughing and hooting, and a few others didn't know what the hell to do. But pretty soon everybody was taking their turn casting spells with Chocolate Thunder. Maybe it was blasphemous, and maybe it was stupid and useless, but we all were sick and tired of waiting for our babies to die. We wanted our babies to live, and we were ready to try anything to help them live. Maybe some people can get by with quiet prayers, but I wanted to shout and scream and vibrate. So did plenty of other fathers and mothers in that sickroom.

It was my wife who grabbed Chocolate Thunder and used it like a drumstick to pound her hand drum. She sang a brand-new song that echoed up and down the hallways of Children's Hospital. Every sick and dying and alive and dead kid heard it, and they were happy and good in their hearts. My wife sang the most beautiful song anybody ever heard in that place. She sang like ten thousand Indian grandmothers rolled into one mother. All the while, Chocolate Thunder sang with her and turned the whole thing into a healing duet.

We humans are too simpleminded. We all like to think each person, place, or thing is only itself. A vibrator is a vibrator is a vibrator, right? But that's not true at all. Everything is stuffed to the brim with ideas and love and hope and magic and dreams. I brought Chocolate Thunder back to the hospital, but it was my magical and faithful wife who truly believed it was going to bring our baby back to us. She wanted it to bring every baby back to life. Over the next week, my wife sat beside our baby's bed and held that vibrator in her two hands and sang and prayed along with its buzzing. She used up the energy of two batteries, and maybe our baby would have woken up anyway, and a few other babies never did wake up at all, but my wife still believes our son heard the magic call of Chocolate Thunder and couldn't resist it. Our beautiful, beautiful boy opened his eyes and smiled, even if he was too young to smile, but I think sick kids get old and wise and funny very fast.

And so my wife and I named him Abraham and carried him home and lay him in his crib and hung Chocolate Thunder from the ceiling above him like a crazy mobile and laughed and laughed with the joy of it. We deported Mr. Grief back to his awful country. Our baby boy was going to live a long and good life. We wondered aloud what we would tell our Abraham about the wondrous world when he was old enough to wonder about it.

This story appeared in *Ten Little Indians* (Grove Press, 2003). Sherman Alexie's other books include *The Lone Ranger and Tonto Fistfight in Heaven* (Perennial, 1998), *Reservation Blues* (Warner Books, 1996), *The Absolutely True Diary of a Part-Time Indian* (Little, Brown, 2009), *War Dances* (Grove Press, 2010), and *Blasphemy* (Grove Press, 2012).

CHAPTER TWENTY-FOUR

Despair Is a Lie We Tell Ourselves

Tony Kushner

A Chicago cab driver recently told me, "If there's a supernova sixty light-years away from here, the world will be totally wiped out. We don't stand a chance." He gave me something to think about, namely the fact that life, each individual life and our collective life on the planet, is a teleological game. It is not infinite. It has an ending, and so the future you put your faith in is not, in fact, limitless.

Given the catastrophic failure to seriously address global warming, given the sagging of the world's economy and the refusal to see any solutions beyond making poor people suffer even more than they always do in the hopes of reviving a market that only ever revives long enough to make the rich even richer, given a Supreme Court that gives corporations more rights than people, well, it's sort of optimistic to believe it's a supernova that's going to get us. It's clear that what's much more likely to get us, if we are got, is our present condition of living in a world run by miscreants while the people of the world either have no access to power or have access but have forgotten how to get it and why it is important to have it.

Since I was a little kid I've been told I have choices, the right to make a choice. Though I've never been dumb enough to believe that was literally true, I've also never been dumb enough to be literal. I have always believed I could choose to believe, or not believe, that the arc of the moral universe is long but it bends toward justice.

I do not believe the wicked always win. I believe our despair is a lie we are telling ourselves. In many other periods of history, people, ordinary citizens, routinely set aside hours, days, time in their lives for doing the work of politics, some of which is glam and revolutionary and some of which is dull and electoral and tedious and not especially pure—and the world changed because of the work they did. That's what we're starting now. It requires setting aside the time to do it, and then doing it. Not any single one of us has to or possibly can save the world, but together in some sort of concert, in even not-especially-coordinated concert, with all of us working where we see work to be done, the world will change. And we have to do it by showing up places, our bodies in places—turn off the fucking computers, leave the Web and the Net—and show up, our bodies at meetings and demos and rallies and leafleting corners.

Because this is a moment in history that needs us to begin, each of us every day at her or his own pace, slowly and surely rediscovering how to be politically active, how to organize our disparate energies into effective group action—and I choose to believe we will do what is required. Act. Organize. Assemble. Oppose. Resist. Find a place a cause a group a friend and start, today, now now now, continue continue continue. Being politically active is for the citizens of a democracy maybe the best way of speaking to God and hearing Her answer: You exist. If we are active, if we are activist, She replies to us: You specifically exist. Mazel tov. Now get busy, She replies. Maintain the world by changing the world.

So when the supernova comes to get us we don't want to be disappointed in ourselves. We should hope to be able to say proudly to the supernova, that angel of death, "Hello supernova, we have been expecting you, we know all about you, because in our schools we teach science and not creationism, and so we have been expecting you, everywhere everyone has been expecting you, except Texas. And we would like to say, supernova, in the moment before we are returned by your protean fire to our previous inchoate state, clouds of incandescent atomic vapor, we'd like to declare that we have tried our best and worked hard to make a good and just and free and peaceful world, a world that is better for our having been here, at least we believe it is."

Tony Kushner's plays include *Angels in America* (Theater Communications Group, 2003), *Homebody/Kabul* (Theater Communications Group, 2002), *Lincoln: The Screenplay* (Theater Communications Group, 2013), and *Five One-Act Plays* (Theater Communications Group, 2014). This essay is adapted from his talks at Chicago's Columbia College and New York's Cooper Union.

PART FIVE

Courage Is Contagious

TO BE OF USE

Marge Piercy

The people I love the best
jump into work head first
without dallying in the shallows
and swim off with sure strokes almost out of sight.
They seem to become natives of that element,
the black sleek heads of seals
bouncing like half-submerged balls.

I love people who harness themselves, an ox to a
heavy cart,
who pull like water buffalo, with massive patience,
who strain in the mud and the muck to move
things forward,
who do what has to be done, again and again.

I want to be with people who submerge
in the task, who go into the fields to harvest
and work in a row and pass the bags along,
who are not parlor generals and field deserters
but move in a common rhythm
when the food must come in or the fire be put out.

The work of the world is common as mud.
Botched, it smears the hands, crumbles to dust.
But the thing worth doing well done
has a shape that satisfies, clean and evident.
Greek amphoras for wine or oil,
Hopi vases that held corn, are put in museums
but you know they were made to be used.
The pitcher cries for water to carry
and a person for work that is real.

From *Circles on the Water* (Knopf, 1982). Marge Piercy's other books include *Gone to Soldiers* (Fawcett, 1988), *Woman on the Edge of Time* (Fawcett, 1985), *Colors Passing Through Us* (Knopf, 2004), and *Sex Wars* (William Morrow, 2006).

We've talked about Nelson Mandela's "multiplication of courage," whereby one individual inspires another and their example in turn inspires countless others. Suffrage pioneer Susan B. Anthony similarly challenged the debilitating effect of timidity when she wrote that "cautious, careful people, always casting about to preserve their reputation and social standing, never can bring about a reform. Those who are really in earnest must be willing to be anything or nothing in the world's estimation." Anthony challenges us to pursue our convictions without hesitation and, equally important, without fear of judgment.

I once asked former Irish president Mary Robinson how citizens could resist the kind of bullying politics by which the Bush administration forced her out of her position as United Nations High Commissioner of Human Rights after she had questioned their insistence on excluding Afghan prisoners of war from Geneva Convention protections. "People need the courage to stand up for what they believe," Robinson replied. "If I'd backed down just because the US is the most powerful nation in the world, it would have sacrificed all the moral credibility of my office. By standing up, I preserved it. You have to keep standing up even if it's hard. You have to be willing to pay the costs."

Here's a woman who turned what might be seen as a platitude—do what you think is right—into a living, breathing reality, one that challenges the rest of us to reflect upon when we would be willing to take a stand. Robinson's principled stance poses a challenge: What would it mean to apply her message, or that of any of the voices in this book, to our own lives? It would likely require that we speak out when some people would disagree with us, possibly vehemently, because that's the only way social change takes place. We might also have to accept the possibility of unpleasant consequences from those who'd prefer to silence our voices. Sometimes dissent draws heat; sometimes it draws fire. But democracy isn't a spectator sport. It's government *of the people*, *by the people*, and potentially *for the people*—but only if enough of us participate. In the words of Tom Paine, we need to be more than "summer soldiers" and "sunshine patriots."

And just as winter precedes spring, we can learn to persist even when the political climate turns harsh—drawing sustenance from the inspiring stories of others. That's the other implication of Robinson's hard decision to challenge US policy. As United Farm Workers founder Cesar Chavez once said, "Every time a man or woman stands up for justice, the heavens sing and the world rejoices." More specifically, we who hear about such actions rejoice and gain strength to match them with our own. To be sure, Robinson's example raises a tough question: "Will you, too, do the right thing, even if there are potential costs?" It also offers much-needed inspiration: "You, like me, can do the right thing, whatever the circumstances." Courage can be contagious.

Few people calling for courage are fiercer than pioneering African American lesbian poet Audre Lorde. In "The Transformation of Silence," she looks at her life "in a merciless light" after being told she likely has terminal cancer. "What I most regretted were my silences," she writes, the times she wanted to speak out about injustice but held back due to fear. We each have our own fears that silence us, she says, "of contempt, of censure, or some judgment, or recognition, of challenge, of annihilation." Lorde challenges us to get past them, overcome our own silences, and voice our own convictions, instead of burying them.

The energy released when we overcome silence is the subject of "The Small Work in the Great Work," by Victoria Safford. Her stories of ordinary people responding to "little invitations for resistance" begin with a teenage girl from a South Dakota Indian reservation who, through one spontaneous, seemingly insignificant act, transformed an athletic event marred by racism into a celebration of Native American culture and pride. Safford urges us to embrace "the possibility of living with the dignity, the bravery, and the gladness that befits a human being." In trying to realize that possibility we will be doing nothing less than what poet Marge Piercy calls "the work of the world."

In early 2011, a similar fight for dignity erupted in response to entrenched dictatorial regimes in the Middle East—a movement now known as the "Arab Spring." Most observers had long dismissed the possibility of change in this part of the world, assuming that the various governments had permanently bullied their populations into submission. But the predominantly young men and women who gathered to speak out across the Arab world didn't accept the conventional wisdom about their historical predicament. Against all expectation, they inspired each other to end the rule of Egypt's Hosni Mubarak, Tunisia's Zine El Abidine Ben Ali, Yemen's Ali Abdullah Saleh, and Libya's Muammar Gaddafi (the latter after eventual armed conflict and NATO air support). Protests also forced national leaders to step down or pledge to limit their terms in Sudan, Iraq, Jordan, and Kuwait.

As Middle East expert Stephen Zunes describes in "Arab Revolutions," the uprisings didn't come out of nowhere. They drew both on a global legacy of nonviolent change and on the courage of those who initially spoke out. During the Egyptian protests, which had been intensifying for a decade, a key Egyptian participant was Wael Ghonim, a thirty-one-year-old computer engineer. Ghonim, who rose through the ranks at Google's Middle East and North African operations to become head of marketing, had helped create the website of prominent opposition figure and Nobel Peace Prize winner Mohamed ElBaradei. But he'd done little else to challenge the regime until a friend posted a photo on Ghonim's Facebook wall of a young man named Khaled Said, whom Egyptian police had pulled from an Internet café and beaten to death. Outraged, Ghonim launched a new Facebook group page, "We Are All Khaled Said." Within a week, more than 100,000 people had joined.

Online activism can be a seductive substitute for real-world engagement. Think of those who knocked on doors or made phone calls for Barack Obama in 2008, but then retreated to sending online e-mails and signing online petitions as soon as he was elected. Meanwhile, the Tea Party held face-to-face house meetings, spoke out at public gatherings, and worked systematically to get those sympathetic with their views to the polls, a far more effective approach.

But because the Egyptian government was so repressive, sites like Ghonim's provided crucial ways for young Egyptians to voice their grievances, brainstorm ways to act, and gradually come out of the shadows to publicly voice their demands. Ghonim and his partners at "We Are All Khaled Said" began with a series of silent protests that were less likely to be physically attacked by the authorities than more confrontational protests. After getting a sense of their numbers and power, they initiated the January 25, 2011 Tahrir Square occupation that captured the attention of the rest of the region and, indeed, the world. Two days after people occupied Tahrir Square and comparable public spaces throughout Egypt, Egyptian police snatched Ghonim off the street and held him for eleven days. A global outcry led to his release, as well as to an emotional interview on Egyptian TV during which Ghonim, sobbing at times, talked about those killed in the uprising. That in turn helped inspire people to fight even more resolutely for Mubarak's resignation. When they prevailed, this brought hope to people hungering for change worldwide, including those who would eventually launch America's Occupy movement. An ordinary Egyptian pulled into politics by anger at injustice, Ghonim created a vehicle through which countless others found their voice.

Historical progress rarely proceeds in a linear fashion. During the first presidential election after Mubarak's ouster, the secular parties split their votes, leading to the election of the Muslim Brotherhood's Mohammed Morsi, who became increasingly authoritarian. Once again, massive street protests took place. Twenty-two million people signed a petition demanding that Morsi resign. The Egyptian army then overthrew Morsi and, resorting to Mubarak-like tactics, massacred nearly a thousand of his supporters when they refused to end extended sit-ins. As I write, the country seems stuck in an ugly, dangerous limbo.

Yet stories like Ghonim's can still inspire us. A month after Morsi's overthrow, I met a nineteen-year-old woman named Nada, who'd participated in the uprising in Mansoura, a city of a half million people seventy-eight miles north of Cairo. An active member of Ghonim's site since shortly after its inception, she'd been emboldened by protestors marching by her house and decided the moment had come for Egyptians finally to take a stand. "I didn't want to get hurt," she said. "But at that point, we were willing to get beaten, shot, or killed if we had to. People like us didn't matter to the people who were ruling this country. They didn't care about the poor, some of whom didn't even have bread. They were heartless and only cared about their power. But we were the ones who gave them that power and we were the ones who were going to take it back. My parents' generation kept silent. Seeing people killed on TV made me want even more to be active, to be part of the people saying that Mubarak had to leave. I didn't want to just be sitting and watching, not doing anything about this when I could."

So Nada snuck out of her house (her father later said he knew) and repeatedly joined the protests. Two years later, she participated again, this time to help overthrow Morsi. The cellphone videos she showed me depicted jubilant crowds waving flags and dancing in the street. Despite recent setbacks, Nada is convinced the uprisings taught millions of young Egyptians that they do indeed possess power and can make a difference. She believed the lessons they learned would continue to inspire them to act. Another headstrong courageous young woman is featured in Paxus Calta's David-and-Goliath tale "Not Deterred," which describes a lesser-known but equally inspirational grassroots movement that brought down Bulgaria's Communist dictatorship.

Standing up to brutal dictatorships, committing civil disobedience in the face of violent retaliation, resisting abuses of power while confined to a prison cell and utterly vulnerable: Such instances of courage are a long way from more common political activities like attending meetings, making phone calls, stuffing envelopes, canvassing neighborhoods, promoting boycotts, or registering voters. But I'm not suggesting that the latter are any less necessary. Years ago, shortly after I published my first book on the psychology of nuclear weapons workers, I was privileged to meet Phil Berrigan, the Catholic priest turned Vietnam and nuclear weapons resister, and spend an evening drinking wine with him. "When is the author going to follow his book?" he asked, fixing me with his wry gaze. The implication was uncomfortably clear. If I really believed that the nation's love affair with such massively deadly weapons risked the annihilation of humankind, I just might want to join him and his compatriots in helping dismantle them and calling attention to the threat by such nonviolent acts as pouring blood on missile nose cones.

"I don't know, Phil," I responded sheepishly. "I have a new book on the nuclear peace movement to write. And I don't think I could do that very well from jail." Berrigan laughed. A gracious, forgiving man, a man whose willingness to risk and sacrifice for his convictions brought repeated imprisonment, he had made his point and would push no further. But his words, not to mention his life, taught me a lesson I'll never forget: If we aren't going to follow a path similar to those who take the greatest risks and pay the highest costs for their beliefs—and most of us won't—then maybe we should use their deeds as a call to do what we can, in our own way, according to our own abilities and circumstances. Democracy needs us all, the heroic few and the humble many, whether our acts are performed center stage and to thunderous applause or in the wings, heralded by none but friends and family. And the heroic draw strength from the humble just as often as the humble draw strength from the heroic. That's one of the cardinal themes of this book.

Echoing Berrigan's engaged faith, Sister Rosalie Bertell, a mathematician who became a leading global campaigner to alert people to the risks of low-level radiation, provides further examples of how the bravery of a few can inspire others, including a story of Japanese grandmothers who faced down US military personnel trying to conduct exercises on sacred Mount Fuji. She concludes "In What Do I Place My Trust" by reminding us how Moses was driven by a vision of the Promised Land, even if he'd never be able to set foot on it. It's a lesson in the value of perseverance even when victory is elusive.

In the view of Jim Wallis, editor of the Christian social justice magazine *Sojourners*, the faith needed to keep on isn't something you possess but is instead "something you practice." And hope is "believing in spite of the evidence, then watching the evidence change." I admire Wallis's ability to speak truth to power consistently, but also his ability to draw on his own religious tradition—Protestant evangelical—in the service of social justice. In "Faith Works," Wallis underscores how religion fueled America's great social movements—the abolition of slavery, child labor reform, women's suffrage, civil rights. He also describes how faith strengthened participants in South Africa's anti-apartheid movement during the days when success seemed highly uncertain. Wallis calls for a movement that would link people's "desire to change their lives with a commitment to change their communities."

But what if American democracy itself is now being threatened, including the fundamental right to vote that we've long taken for granted, and that people in countries like South Africa and Egypt have fought so long and hard for? I'd be silencing my own convictions, to say nothing of the courage of people like Berrigan, Ghonim, Nada, and the Indian girl in South Dakota, were I not to address one of my own growing concerns about developments that erode both democracy and our sense that our actions can matter. I hope you will not consider what follows as unduly partisan. But I believe, and you may disagree with me, that we are facing significant attacks on the ability of ordinary citizens to shape our common future.

The United States, as many have noted, is an experiment in democracy, whose outcome can be in doubt on any given day. But during the past few decades, I've witnessed the development of a scorched-earth politics that threatens to undermine the very terms of this experiment. As I see it, a well-funded effort is concentrating power in a way that changes the fundamental rules of the game—largely to the benefit of the country's wealthiest interests. As is often the case, recent abuses of power build on long-standing injustices. A century ago, in the process of establishing racial segregation, most Confederate states barred ex-felons from voting. These laws remain in force throughout most of the South. We currently disenfranchise 4 million former felons, including 1.3 million in Florida alone (and nearly one quarter of the state's African Americans), plus another 400,000 in Virginia. No other advanced country disenfranchises former felons in this way, and thirty-five countries, including Germany and Canada, actually encourage current prison inmates to vote, as a way of giving them a stake in the system.

Both Democrats and Republicans bear responsibility for this legacy, and for worsening it by promoting a drug war that has produced the highest incarceration rate in the world. Seven hundred thousand Americans are arrested each year just for possession of marijuana, with African Americans arrested nearly four times as often as whites, despite similar rates of consumption, and Latinos arrested at similarly disproportionate rates. Thus I'm heartened by referendums in Colorado and Washington that have legalized marijuana under strict controlled conditions—limiting advertising, prohibiting sales to minors and driving under the influence, and routing funding from its taxation into areas like health care, education, combating substance abuse, and keeping troubled adolescents in school. In Washington State, key law enforcement officials such as Seattle's former police chief and Washington's former Republican US Attorney played a major role in passing the measure, which carried not only the state's more liberal areas but also many conservative rural counties. The passage of these initiatives has seemed to accelerate a public opinion shift, with 58 percent of Americans now supporting some kind of controlled legalization. In addition, it has impelled top Obama administration officials to reverse seventy-five years of federal policy and decide to wait and see how these state efforts play out, instead of intervening to shut them down. This response, which significantly furthered the legalization movement's cause, constituted a victory for all who'd worked for years to transform America's drug laws. And it reminds us once again that whomever we elect, we need to keep organizing on the issues we care about if we want them to fulfill our hopes.

But despite these shifts, and despite efforts to reverse felon disenfranchisement policies by elected officials such as Florida governor Charlie Crist and Virginia governor Bob McDonnell, this disenfranchisement continues in most of the Southern states that originally instituted it. Worse yet, these laws have become incorporated into broader attacks on the right to vote. The 2000 election may seem like ancient history. But in that year Florida governor Jeb Bush's administration not only did nothing to reverse the trend but also removed 94,000 largely poor and minority voters from the rolls for convictions that never applied even under Florida law, or never existed to begin with—if someone's name resembled an ex-con's, for instance, or if they were convicted in another state but had their voting rights restored. Staffers of ChoicePoint, the Republican-linked data-collection firm contracted to handle this effort, warned that this would disenfranchise legitimate voters. But, as reported by the BBC and the US Civil Rights Commission, Jeb's administration made no effort to verify the validity of the purges. A follow-up by BBC investigative reporter Greg Palast found that 90 percent of those scrubbed were legitimate voters, enough by far to have made Al Gore the winner in a 537-vote election eventually decided in favor of Jeb's brother George W. Bush by the US Supreme Court.

The politically driven use of disenfranchisement has continued, creating a dangerous trend. Not long ago, Supreme Court justices whom President Bush then appointed opened the floodgates to even greater dominance of money in politics through the Citizens United decision, which overturned campaign finance laws like McCain-Feingold. The Court then invalidated major sections of the Voting Rights Act, leading states previously under federal scrutiny for their history of discrimination to pass a slew of new and highly restrictive laws. North Carolina, for instance, passed a new voter ID law invalidating student IDs, public employee IDs, and photo IDs issued by public assistance agencies (while allowing gun permits as proof of identity); shortened the early voting window; banned same-day registration during early voting; and prohibited paid voter registration drives. It also prohibited extending voting hours in the event of long lines, eliminated the right to cast a provisional ballot if someone ends up at the wrong precinct, and ended a highly successful program that registered high school seniors to vote. Local election officials also began removing on-campus voting stations, relocating them sometimes miles away in areas with limited parking.

The officials who enacted these and numerous other laws restricting the franchise claimed they did so to prevent voter fraud. But a five-year Bush administration crackdown effort found no evidence of organized efforts to have ineligible voters participate, convicting just eighty-six people nationwide, most who'd simply made mistakes regarding their own eligibility status, such as ex-convicts who thought their rights had been automatically restored. Nonpartisan studies, as reported in outlets from the *New York Times* to that well-known radical magazine, *Forbes*, have repeatedly confirmed that voters rarely misrepresent themselves at the polls, and that such in-person deception, if it occurs at all, leads to no more than a handful of illegitimate votes in any given election. Meanwhile, the new laws, along with others that preceded the Voting Rights Act decision, have disenfranchised hundreds of thousands of legitimate voters—primarily African Americans, Latinos, and the young—and made voting much more difficult for far more.

That doesn't even count Ohio's Republican secretary of state allowing each county, whatever its size, just a single early-voting station, leaving Democratic cities like Cleveland and Columbus with five-hour lines—and attempting also to mandate longer early-voting hours for Republican counties than for Democratic ones. The party also conducted an unprecedented level of gerrymandering of state legislative and congressional districts to skew the vote in its favor, keeping a 17-seat majority in the House of Representatives in the 2012 election despite getting 1.4 million fewer total congressional votes.

Of course there are honorable exceptions. During the 2004 gubernatorial election in my home state of Washington, only 133 votes separated the top two candidates, but that didn't prevent the longtime Republican secretary of state, Sam Reed, from finding the courage to certify the victory of the Democrat despite strong pressure from his own party to declare it invalid. In 2012, while too many of his counterparts were doing their best to restrict the vote, Reed pioneered an agreement with Facebook and Microsoft, offering citizens secure ways to register to vote through Facebook. Reed also toured college campuses encouraging students to vote, whether or not they would support the candidates he personally preferred. I wish more elected officials were like him.

Regardless of our party identifications or stands on particular issues, we should be deeply troubled by these developments. Doing your best to get your own political supporters to the polls, so they can cast every eligible vote, is completely legitimate. Preventing potential political opponents from voting is not. Since the founding of the United States more than two hundred years ago, neither major political party has exercised a monopoly on deceit, venality, or abuse of power. That leading Republicans today wish to silence, demonize, or disenfranchise those who disagree with them doesn't mean that Democrats haven't done similarly underhanded things in the past or won't do so in the future. But we might remember that cowardice and timidity can be just as contagious as courage. Through what we permit others to do in our common name, we can allow the spread of darkness and despair just as easily as that of light and hope. So we need to challenge anyone who'd restrict the ability of American citizens to participate in our democracy.

But how do we do this when wealthy individuals and corporations seem to hold all the cards, while, with the help of their political allies, doing everything possible to further stack the deck? How do we find the courage to speak out when we wonder whether the whole game may now be irrevocably rigged? The Occupy movement briefly challenged these interests, spreading worldwide after its initial occupation of New York's Zuccotti Park and re-igniting a broader public discussion on inequality, unemployment, and the concentration of wealth. It helped shift policies, as when New York governor Andrew Cuomo reversed his initial opposition to renewing the state's "millionaire's tax" and the Los Angeles City Council passed a "responsible banking" ordinance. By encouraging discussion of these issues, it contributed to Bill de Blasio's unlikely populist victory as mayor of New York City, where he won by proposing to tax the rich to pay for services like universal pre-kindergarten. And to the rejection of Larry Summers as head of the Federal Reserve Bank after ordinary citizens became angered at how Summers had set the stage for the 2008 financial crash by helping deregulate the banks, and then had coddled them further as the head of Obama's National Economic Council. But Occupy ultimately flamed out due to the exhausting and unsustainable nature of its decision-making process, an excess of political purism, and a shift from challenging Wall Street greed to fighting with local authorities over the right to continue camping in prime city areas.

In "The Progressive Story of America," renowned journalist Bill Moyers recalls a model that might be considerably more sustainable: how grassroots citizen groups beat back attempts by America's economic royalists of a hundred years ago to create a comparable political system that would serve only their narrowest interests of wealth and greed. As Moyers notes, some of those early groups called themselves Populists, others Progressives. Both Democrats and Republicans lent a hand. They made common cause, as Moyers argues, to keep "blood pumping through the veins of democracy when others were ready to call in the mortician." And they spoke out passionately in the struggle to determine, in Moyers's words, "whether 'we, the people' is a spiritual idea embedded in a political reality—one nation, indivisible—or merely a charade masquerading as piety and manipulated by the powerful and privileged to sustain their own way of life at the expense of others."

Economic inequality is now as severe as at any point since the movements that Moyers describes. With even our basic franchise increasingly threatened, taking to heart this chapter of US history is more important than ever. As with the other examples I've gathered, I hope it will stiffen our backbones and give us the strength to resist those who'd reduce our democracy to a mere instrument for private gain. As Moyers says, it's a story that should be told again and again, inspiring each new generation of Americans.

CHAPTER TWENTY-FIVE

The Transformation of Silence

Audre Lorde

I have come to believe over and over again that what is most important to me must be spoken, made verbal and shared, even at the risk of having it bruised or misunderstood. That the speaking profits me, beyond any other effect. I am standing here as a black lesbian poet, and the meaning of all that waits upon the fact that I am still alive, and might not have been. Less than two months ago, I was told by my two doctors, one female and one male, that I would have to have breast surgery, and that there was a 60 to 80 percent chance that the tumor was malignant. Between the telling and the actual surgery, there was a three-week period of the agony of and involuntary reorganization of my entire life. The surgery was completed, and the growth was benign.

But within those three weeks, I was forced to look upon myself and my living with a harsh and urgent clarity that has left me still shaken but much stronger. This is a situation faced by many women. Some of what I experienced during that time has helped elucidate for me much of what I feel concerning the transformation of silence into language and action. In becoming forcibly and essentially aware of my own mortality, and of what I wished and wanted for in my life, however short it might be, priorities and omissions became strongly etched in a merciless light and what I most regretted were my silences.

Of what had I *ever* been afraid? To question or to speak as I believed would have meant pain, or death. But we all hurt in so many different ways, all the time, and pain will either change or end. Death, on the other hand, is the final silence. And that might be coming quickly, now, without regard for whether I had ever spoken what needed to be said, or only betrayed myself into small silences, while I planned someday to speak, or waited for someone else's words. And I began to recognize a source of power within myself that comes from the knowledge that while it is most desirable not to be afraid, learning to put fear into a perspective gave me great strength.

I was going to die, if not sooner then later, whether or not I had ever spoken myself. My silences had not protected me. Your silence will not protect you. But for every real word spoken, for every attempt I had ever made to speak those truths for which I am still seeking, I had made contact with other women while we examined the words to fit a world in which we all believed, bridging our differences. And it was the concern and caring of all those women which gave me strength and enabled me to scrutinize the essentials of my living.

The women who sustained me through that period were black and white, old and young, lesbian, bisexual, and heterosexual, and we all shared a war against the tyrannies of silence. They all gave me a strength and concern without which I could not have survived intact. Within those weeks of acute fear came the knowledge—within the war we are all waging with the forces of death, subtle and otherwise, conscious or not—I am not only a casualty, I am also a warrior.

What are the words you do not have yet? What do you need to say? What are the tyrannies you swallow day by day and attempt to make your own, until you will sicken and die of them, still in silence? Perhaps for some of you here today, I am the face of one of your fears. Because I am a woman, because I am black, because I am myself, a black woman warrior poet doing my work, come to ask you, are you doing yours?

And, of course, I am afraid—you can hear it in my voice—because the transformation of silence into language and action is an act of self-revelation and that always seems fraught with danger. But my daughter, when I told her of our topic and my difficulty with it, said, "tell them about how you're never really a whole person if you remain silent, because there's always that one little piece inside of you that wants to be spoken out, and if you keep ignoring it, it gets madder and madder and hotter and hotter, and if you don't speak it out one day it will just up and punch you in the mouth."

We can learn to work and speak when we are afraid in the same way we have learned to work and speak when we are tired. For we have been socialized to respect fear more than our own needs for language and definition, and while we wait in silence for that final luxury of fearlessness, the weight of that silence will choke us. The fact that we are here and that I speak these words is an attempt to break that silence and bridge some of those differences between us, for it is not difference which immobilizes us, but silence. And there are so many silences to be broken.

Excerpted from "The Transformation of Silence into Language and Action," originally presented at the Lesbian and Literature panel of the 1977 Modern Language Association meeting and printed in *Cancer Journals* (Aunt Lute Press, 2006, *www.auntlute.com*). Lorde's other works include *Sister Outsider: Essays and Speeches* (Crossing Press, 2007).

CHAPTER TWENTY-SIX

The Small Work in the Great Work

Victoria Safford

In his book *On the Rez,* Ian Frazier tells a story about South Dakota's Pine Ridge Reservation. In the fall of 1988, the Pine Ridge girls' basketball team played an away game in Lead, South Dakota. It was one of those times when the host gym was dense with anti-Indian hostility. Lead fans waved food stamps, yelling fake Indian war cries and epithets like "squaw" and "gut-eater." Usually, the Pine Ridge girls made their entrances according to height, led by the tallest seniors. When they hesitated to face the hostile crowd, a fourteen-year-old freshman named SuAnne offered to go first. She surprised her teammates and silenced the crowd by performing the Lakota shawl dance and then singing in Lakota—"graceful and modest and show-offy all at the same time," in Frazier's words. She managed to reverse the crowd's hostility—until they even cheered and applauded. "Of course, Pine Ridge went on to win the game."

Here's another story of daring, of the meeting of our passion and the world's great hunger for justice: Forty years ago, to march in the streets of this city, or any city, as a gay man or a lesbian, openly, must have taken wild courage, incredible courage, outrageous imagination. Those who were there will tell us, "Well, courage yes. And certainly imagination. But there was more. . . . " They will tell us that once you have glimpsed the world as it might be, as it ought to be, as it's going to be (however that vision appears to you), it is impossible to live compliant and complacent anymore in the world as it is.

To march was a dangerous risk—but not to was a risk of another kind—of living half-dead, with no name, unremembered, in the dark, surviving on scraps and crumbs and the outright threats and pious ultimatums of the hate-filled present moment. Why not risk all that, and walk out into the sun in the summer and walk around in the world as it ought to be, thereby bringing it to bear? Why not march and carry on, act out, act up, as if your life depended on it? (Bishop John Shelby Spong calls it "solar ethics"—to commit to living as the very sun itself lives, that is, to do what you were created to do, to shine and shine without regard for recognition or permanence or reward, to love and simply be for the sake of loving and living and being.)

And so you come out and walk out and march, the way a flower comes out and blooms, because it has no other calling. It has no other work. I have seen and you have seen and maybe you have been among those who have had to march in terror, on pain of dire consequences. People have marched with paper bags on their heads to guard their lives and livelihoods—teachers, police officers, neighbors, tenants, daycare providers, clergy. People took such risks, but still they were there and they still are, and we are so grateful. To march was dangerous. It still is. Not to march was dangerous—it still is now, and more so; let there be no question. This is no time for quietism.

For now, I'm going to leave these incredible stories about speaking truth to power, about making of your very self (physically, spiritually) a sacrifice, an offering to a world that doesn't even know it's hungry till it's fed on love, passion, and courage.

I don't know what kind of child, or woman-child, SuAnne really was, but clearly she had lived and breathed a mission, a way of being and seeing in the world, for a long time.

I am interested in what Seamus Heaney calls the meeting point of hope and history, where what has happened is met by what we make of it. What has happened is met midstream by people who are—among the multitude of things we are—spiritual beings and all that that implies of creativity, imagination, crazy wisdom, ancient wisdom, passionate compassion, selfless courage, and radical reverence for life. And love—for one another absolutely, and that love that rises out of us, for something larger than ourselves, call it what you will. I am interested in the place, the places, where history is met by the hope of the human soul, life's longing for itself. I am interested in hope on this side of the grave—for me there is no other kind—and in that tidal wave of justice that could rise up if only we would let it.

Six months after 9/11, our Unitarian church had a little evening forum. People were invited simply to share with one another how they were feeling. That was the only agenda and assignment, that small yet huge question; and at least for the first of the two hours, we hoped to live within its discipline. We hoped not to barrel right away into all those noisy Unitarian Universalist opinions, all those articles they're reading in *The Nation* and *The Progressive*, the *New York Times* and the *Wall Street Journal*, those Web sites that they've found, the commentaries that they've heard on NPR (some of which they've no doubt written), the positions they're defending so ably on the op-ed page, and of course the persistently wobbly but heartfelt agenda of the underfunded Social Action Committee. We knew we'd get to all that eventually, but we didn't want to go there right away. Instead we hoped to cast a different kind of circle, within and out of which people could rise to the holy occasion of hearing one another, of beholding one another. It was a gathering for prayer.

It was a lucky night. The circle held. When anybody wandered off or lost their way in the dry sands of rhetoric or opinion, the circle gently called them back, so thirsty were these people to connect with one another and with something antecedent in themselves, something original, essential, deep. There were maybe twenty people—high school students, an eighty-two-year-old member, and everybody in between. It was not long before they left off speaking about September 11, that particular, precise disaster, and began to talk instead and cogently about September 10, the mutilated world we'd known before but maybe had not seen so clearly, which is in fact the world we live in now, the world of Frederick Buechner's "great hunger," this insatiable, desperate hunger for transformation, which begs not just for our flickering attention, but for our sustained, directed passion.

Sorrow flowed into the room, like a river. Rage, decades old—or new and young and raw, straight out of the awesome youth group—stormed into the circle. Silence made its holy way. And now these were dangerous waters—and as we spoke and heard each other, inevitably we paddled close that night to the deadly shores of cynicism and despondency (which in some communions is a sin). Then someone in the circle, with more presence of mind than I could muster in the moment, saved us all from drowning, saying: "You know we cannot do this all at once. But every day offers every one of us little invitations for resistance, and you make your own responses." I wrote it down, right then, because this person is prone to neither social activism nor religious language, of any kind, but it was he who said, "It is a sacred offering, the invitation to resistance, and every day you make your own responses."

He mentioned that story from Pine Ridge, which he'd heard not long before in a Sunday-morning service, and he said, "You know, that little girl changed the world out there in South Dakota, and I know it because hearing her story has changed *me*, and ever since I heard it (and I wish I hadn't heard it), I'm moved to do things which I never would have done. I couldn't see the way. Or wouldn't." He talked about how at his job, in a large corporate setting where he's some kind of manager, he had placed a four-inch American flag upside down on the outside of his cubicle, because he feels his country is in desperate trouble, that its soul is in trouble, that its soul is sick. "I guess it's like my shawl dance," he said—so humbly, so quietly, but with trembling conviction. And we were grateful and amazed.

I have a friend who traffics in words. She is not a minister, but a psychiatrist in the health clinic at a prestigious women's college. We were sitting once not long after a student she had known, and counseled, committed suicide in the dormitory there. My friend, the doctor, the healer, held the loss very closely in those first few days, not unprofessionally, but deeply, fully—as you or I would have, had this been someone in our care.

At one point (with tears streaming down her face), she looked up in defiance (this is the only word for it) and spoke explicitly of her vocation, as if out of the ashes of that day she were renewing a vow or making a new covenant (and I think she was). She spoke explicitly of her vocation, and of yours and mine. She said, "You know I cannot save them. I am not here to save anybody or to save the world. All I can do—what I am called to do—is to plant myself at the gates of Hope. Sometimes they come in; sometimes they walk by. But I stand there every day and I call out till my lungs are sore with calling, and beckon and urge them in toward beautiful life and love."

By grace, by her will, she is planted "at the gates of Hope," regardless. There's something for all of us there, I think. Whatever our vocation, we stand, beckoning and calling, singing and shouting, planted at the gates of Hope. This world and our people are beautiful and broken, and we are called to raise that up—to bear witness to the possibility of living with the dignity, bravery, and gladness that befits a human being. That may be what it is to "live our mission."

Matthew Fox writes of "the small work in the Great Work," the place of your little life and love, daily days and earnest effort as a solitary person within the larger Life and larger Love that some call Holy, some call God, some call History, and others call simply larger than themselves. Like everybody else, we are doing small work within the Great Work of creation, and thus do we aid it and abet it in unfolding.

We stand where we will stand, on little plots of ground, where we are maybe "called" to stand (though who knows what that means?)—in our congregations, classrooms, offices, factories, in fields of lettuces and apricots, in hospitals, in prisons (on both sides, at various times, of the gates), in streets, in community groups. And it is sacred ground if we would honor it, if we would bring to it a blessing of sacrifice and risk, just as the floor of any gym in South Dakota might suddenly be sanctified by one child, one young woman's dancing and her song (ancient, holy), the interior clarity of her spirit, that spoke there to the hate-filled world, and transformed that place with faith and deep remembering.

Our mission is to plant ourselves at the gates of Hope—not the prudent gates of Optimism, which are somewhat narrower; nor the stalwart, boring gates of Common Sense; nor the strident gates of Self-Righteousness, which creak on shrill and angry hinges (people cannot hear us there; they cannot pass through); nor the cheerful, flimsy garden gate of "Everything is gonna be all right." But a different, sometimes lonely place, the place of truth-telling, about your own soul first of all and its condition, the place of resistance and defiance, the piece of ground from which you see the world both as it is and as it could be, as it will be; the place from which you glimpse not only struggle, but joy in the struggle. And we stand there, beckoning and calling, telling people what we are seeing, asking people what they see.

Not long ago I came across a photograph, a picture in a magazine that inspires me and troubles me, and calls me to account in ways that I would rather not be called. It's of a woman with two children lying on a bed, their arms flung across her body carelessly, as if it were the most natural thing in the world, the most ordinary, peaceful afternoon, one child blissfully asleep, the other just a little bit awake. The woman is lying on her side with open eyes, with an expression of alert concern, maybe fear, but also, underneath, a certain calm, and deep intensity. It is a beautiful face, for these reasons. This is the caption:

> Irene Siegel, a Jewish American, sleeps in the home of a Palestinian family in Beit Jala as part of a human shield campaign to deter Israeli shelling of Palestinian homes. She says: "Magdalene, my Palestinian hostess, looked at me sideways and said softly, 'Are you Jewish?' And I nodded. She threw her arms

> around me and said, 'You know, I love you, Irene. I love you like a sister.' And I cried. And so did she. And then she talked to me until two in the morning about everything—her fears, her pain, her experiences—everything she had held inside for so long, surrounded as she is by a community who are all suffering the same pain."

As if it were the most natural thing in the world for this American Jew to be lying on that bed, in that village, in this moment, guarding those children with her body, with her heart, with her passion, as if they were her own. This picture, this woman, is asking me a question that I don't want to answer, and yet I know that with our lives we make our answers all the time to this ravenous, beautiful, mutilated, gorgeous world. However prophetic our words, it is not enough simply to speak. And there is Irene Siegel, troubling me, shattering my illusions and delusions, redefining radically anything I might have thought about the gates of Hope, for she raises the bar alarmingly, and honestly. And there are so many other living and breathing reminders of what the small work in the Great Work might reasonably, unreasonably, look like. I am grateful for the deep, awakening trouble that her face and their stories cause me.

The Reverend Victoria Safford is the minister of White Bear Unitarian Church, in Mahtomedi, Minnesota, and the author of *Walking Toward Morning* (Skinner House, 2003) and *With or Without Candlelight* (Skinner House, 2009). For more information, see *www.whitebearunitarian.org/blog*. Ian Frazier's wonderful Pine Ridge story can be found in his *On the Rez* (Farrar, Straus and Giroux, 2000; Picador USA, 2003).

CHAPTER TWENTY-SEVEN

We Are All Khaled Said

Wael Ghonim

On June 8, 2010, while browsing on Facebook, I saw a shocking image that a friend of mine had posted on my wall. The picture linked to the official Facebook account of Dr. Ayman Nour, the former presidential candidate who was a political activist. It was a horrifying photo showing the distorted face of a man in his twenties. There was a big pool of blood behind his head, which rested on a chunk of marble. His face was extremely disfigured and bloodied; his lower lip had been ripped in half, and his jaw was seemingly dislocated. His front teeth appeared to be missing, and it looked as if they had been beaten right out of his mouth. The image was so gruesome that I wondered if he had been wounded in war. But by accessing Dr. Nour's page I learned that Khaled Mohamed Said had apparently been beaten to death on June 6 by two secret police officers in Alexandria.

My first reaction was denial. I could not believe that anyone could actually inflict such brutality on someone else. The victim was a twenty-eight-year-old from Alexandria. According to eyewitnesses, some dispute had erupted between him and the two officers, leading to their physical assault on him, which claimed the young man's life.

I could not stand by passively in the face of such grave injustice. I decided to employ all my skills and experience to demand justice for Khaled Said and to help expose his story. The logical first idea was to publish news of Khaled Said's murder on [Nobel Peace Prize winner and potential opposition candidate] Dr. Mohamed ElBaradei's Facebook page, whose members exceeded 150,000 at that time, but I reasoned that doing so would exploit an event of national concern for political gain. I discovered that a page had been launched under the title "My Name Is Khaled Mohamed Said." Their discourse was confrontational, beginning with the page's headline: "Khaled's murder will not go unpunished, you dogs of the regime." I knew that such language would not help in making the cause a mainstream one.

I decided to create another page. Out of the many options I considered for the name, "Kullena Khaled Said"—"We Are All Khaled Said"—was the best. Khaled Said was a young man just like me, and what happened to him could have happened to me. The page name was short and catchy, and it expressed the compassion that people immediately felt when they saw Khaled Said's picture. I deliberately concealed my identity, and took on the role of anonymous administrator for the page.

The first thing I posted was direct and blunt. It voiced the outrage and sadness that I felt.

> Today they killed Khaled. If I don't act for his sake, tomorrow they will kill me.
>
> 49 LIKES | 33 COMMENTS

I spoke on the page in the first person, posing as Khaled Said. What drove me, more than anything else, was the thought that I could speak for him, and if even a single victim of the regime could have the chance to defend himself, it would be a turning point.

On its first day, 36,000 people joined the page, and left more than 1,800 comments. Some wanted to learn more details about the case, some sought to offer sympathy and support, and others joined out of curiosity because they had received an invitation from a Facebook friend. Images of Khaled before and after the assault spread like wildfire. Similar crimes had taken place in the past, all too frequently, yet their stories had not spread widely. It was the visual documentation of Khaled's terrible death, along with the fact that he was from the middle class, that catalyzed this huge reaction. The image was impossible to forget, and thanks to social media, it was proliferating like crazy.

I advertised "My Name Is Khaled Mohamed Said" on the more activist site and requested that we all coordinate our efforts. To my delight, the admins of the other page reciprocated.

Several prominent opposition politicians publicly condemned Khaled Said's brutal killing. Also, a public funeral for Khaled had been announced. I publicized the funeral on the page and asked that as many people as possible attend. I also posted an edited video of various acts of torture by members of the police force, in the hope that Egyptians would finally confront the dark side of the regime and realize that any one of us could be the next victim.

About a thousand people took part in the Alexandria funeral. A protest to denounce Khaled Said's murder was also organized in Cairo by the April 6 Youth Movement, among other groups and activists. I asked the page members to join the protest, which was planned to take place outside the Ministry of Interior. But the security forces were prepared and decisive: they arrested many protesters and surrounded the rest with double their number of police officers. Worse yet, the media, under the usual pressure from State Security, ignored the protest.

The media's suppression of the physical world made the virtual world a critical alternative for promoting the cause. On the Facebook page, I began to focus on the notion that what had happened to Khaled was happening on a daily basis, in different ways, to people we never heard about.

The circumstances of Khaled Said's death were mysterious. According to eyewitnesses, he was sitting at an Internet cafe when two informers attacked and beat him severely. They then dragged him to the entrance of a nearby building, where they continued to pound him until he died. The official police account alleged that he had tried to hide a pack of marijuana by swallowing it, and that he choked and died while the informers were trying to force him to spit out the pack.

Khaled Said's family went public with a copy of the military service certificate that proved that he had completed his compulsory service, directly countering another allegation made by the Ministry of Interior. I published the certificate on the Facebook page, as well as videos of three eyewitness accounts. One was the Internet cafe owner, who said that the two secret police officers stormed the place and viciously attacked Khaled. He said he tried to interfere but that only increased their brutality. He also asserted that he did not see Khaled insert anything in his mouth. The second video featured a young boy who saw the beating and testified that others saw it as well but were too afraid to interfere.

The third witness was the porter of the building where Khaled was brutally beaten. He described the viciousness of the violence and said that the officers beat Khaled's head against the stairs while he yelled, "I will die!" But his cries did not deter them in any way. The ambulance arrived minutes later to carry his body away.

Together, we wanted justice for Khaled Said and we wanted to put an end to torture. Social networking offered us an easy means to meet. It also enabled us to defy the fears associated with voicing opposition. The virtual world seemed further from the oppressive reach of the regime, and therefore many were encouraged to speak up. The more difficult task remained, though, which was to transfer the struggle from the virtual world to the real one.

The page needed to speak directly to its members and convince them to be active participants, to break free from the barriers of fear that controlled so many of us. The first campaign suggested that members change their profile pictures to an anonymously designed banner of Khaled Said, featuring him against the backdrop of the Egyptian flag, with the caption "Egypt's Martyr." Thousands responded positively, including personal friends who had no idea that I was the page's founder.

Next I asked members to photograph themselves holding up a paper sign that said "Kullena Khaled Said." Hundreds of members did so, and we began to publish their pictures on the page. The images worked like magic. Members thanked each other for their courage and solidarity. Such admiration and instant positive interaction encouraged even more members to post their pictures. The fact that the regime had not retaliated in any way also made it easier for many people to participate. The barriers of fear were slowly being torn down.

A few days following Khaled Said's murder, opposition newspapers and some private television channels began supporting the cause. I asked page members to apply pressure to TV talk shows. Together, we compiled telephone numbers and posted them. I encouraged everyone to call in and demand that show hosts discuss the case. Earlier, some shows had attacked Khaled, while others had tried to remain neutral. A few had supported his cause, and we were hoping they would now increase in number.

The controversy grew. On June 15, Egypt's public prosecutor transferred the case to special prosecution and ordered a second autopsy to confirm the cause of death. This amounted to a small victory for our cause.

The idea for what became a turning point came from Mohamed Eisa, whose full name I didn't publish to avoid endangering his life.

> Mohamed, 26, Alexandria: How about if we all gather along the Alexandria coast on Friday? We would face the sea with our backs to the street holding hands in silent expression of our disapproval of the injustice inflicted upon Khaled Said. We should try to cover the stretch between the Alexandria Library and Muntazah. It's not a demonstration, but a silent expression of disapproval.
>
> 431 LIKES | 152 COMMENTS

A silent demonstration was proactive but not provocative. Most of the members' comments expressed agreement. I announced the date and time for the following Friday and asked for suggestions that would help bring the idea to fruition.

Scores of e-mails flowed in. The most important comment was that the effort should not turn into a typical political demonstration, so I called it the Silent Stand, to make the name a clear reminder to all participants that they were not supposed to chant or wave placards or banners. Following a suggestion from one of the members, participants were asked to bring along a copy of the Qur'an or Bible to read in peace. We wanted to send out a clear message that although we were both sad and angry, we were nevertheless nonviolent. Moreover, the way we had planned our stand along Alexandria's coastal road, the corniche—in single file—would have made us inconspicuous among the street's regular crowd, so I passed along another member's suggestion that we all wear black in order to stand out. The stand was scheduled for two days later, Friday, at 5 P.M.

> For this idea to work . . . let's all wear black T-shirts. . . . head to the corniche and stand alone. . . . turn your back to the street. . . . do not debate or argue with anyone. . . . this way no one can claim we did anything wrong. . . . we want the media to document Egyptian youth standing along 3 or 4 kilometers of the corniche. . . . What do you think?
>
> 313 LIKES | 105 COMMENTS

A lot of e-mails requested a parallel stand in Cairo along the Nile corniche. I created another event page for a similar stand at the same time. We focused on the safety of the participants, and stressed the unusualness of the idea, which would make it a strong message to the Ministry of Interior.

I called on Khaled Said's mother to participate in our Silent Stand, to provide a boost of confidence to everyone else. I had no means of reaching her or either of her two remaining children apart from the Facebook page.

> A message to Khaled Said's mother: O mother, come on Friday to see your children hand in hand for the sake of your son.
>
> 211 LIKES | 72 COMMENTS

We wrote a press release to distribute to the media. The purpose, in addition to general publicity, was to mobilize press coverage before the event in order to enable common Egyptians to participate. More than 100,000 members were reached through the page in a few short days. A call was put out to all professional graphic designers to help design logos and banners.

State-owned newspapers began to attack Facebook by claiming that it was owned by the CIA and that spies and enemies anonymously used it to brainwash Egyptian youth. The regime despised it, since people were too easily able to express their opposition and discontent. Anti-Mubarak Facebook pages had proliferated after Dr. ElBaradei's return to Egypt. Our generation was different from its predecessors, who could read only what the regime wanted them to read.

One of the page members visited Khaled Said's mother and invited her to take part. She accepted without hesitation, and I immediately posted the good news. As a result, even more people were motivated to participate. Invitations were also sent to local and international media. On Thursday night I had a chat with AbdelRahman Mansour, my co-administrator of the Facebook page. We were both very excited and optimistic, yet afraid of failure. It was hard to predict the number of people who would actually participate, yet time to take a risk. We needed another victory, this time on the street and not simply online.

On Friday afternoon, shortly before five o'clock, there was no sign of the Silent Stand at the corniche in Cairo. It became clear that the Ministry of Interior had closely followed the activity on our Facebook page and had prepared itself. Security forces were spread along the corniche. They had closed off some areas and also secured Tahrir Square, in the middle of the city. I found out from Twitter and Facebook that some people did show up in Alexandria, yet the number was very limited. I posted a message on the page, trying to create enthusiasm.

> The numbers are still very limited in both Cairo and Alexandria. . . . Where are the people who said they were coming? Where are 10,000 men and women? Hopefully they are only late. I hope that none of you are thinking they don't matter

> because many others are going. . . . Please . . . everyone must participate . . . everyone matters.
>
> 121 LIKES | 113 COMMENTS

I started imagining the level of disappointment that was going to be felt throughout the page. I hate to give up and equally despise the notion that there is no hope, but was there hope, really? This question forced itself into my mind, but I did not dare post it.

Then one activist on Twitter said that more than a hundred people were lined up along the corniche in the Cleopatra district in Alexandria. Everyone was wearing black and standing humbly reading the Qur'an or Bible or listening to something on headphones. I quickly updated:

> Guys, one of us in Cleopatra says the scene is different there and more than 100 people have showed up.
>
> 145 LIKES | 44 COMMENTS

Good news continued to flow in from Alexandria.

> Message from Ahmed Fadel: The turnout is huge. . . . people were just praying the afternoon prayer. . . . there are sooo many people. . . . there is a great increase of participants along the corniche. . . . you can barely see the sea from the blackness.
>
> 199 LIKES | 182 COMMENTS

We continued to hear news that the efforts of the Cairo participants were being frustrated in the downtown area, where the security presence had intensified. They prevented everyone wearing black from standing along the corniche.

> Security forces placed barricades and prevented movement around Tahrir. . . . Central Security cars and high-ranking officers are keeping everyone from walking. . . . are you so scared for your fragile regime that you fear young Egyptians in black?
>
> 128 LIKES | 51 COMMENTS

Shortly after 7 P.M., pictures of the stand were being uploaded by members. Even if the numbers had been small, the impact of a chain of black-clad, silent men and women was impossible to ignore. And in Alexandria the numbers had been large. AbdelRahman and I exchanged chat messages of joy as we continued to receive snapshots of young men and women standing meditatively in black attire, expressing their anger and their refusal to accept what was happening in Egypt. We were both posting the images on the page. The impact they had on everyone's morale was phenomenal. I also posted a video taken by a page member from Alexandria as she drove by slowly in her car. It lasted a full five minutes, showing one person in black after another.

Each participant stood silently next to someone he or she probably did not know. They only knew they were both members of a page on the Internet and that they believed in the same cause. They stood a meter apart, wearing black clothes. We were all concerned for Egypt. We all wanted to abolish torture. We were careful to post every photo we received. Those images helped the participants realize the worth of their achievement, and drew the envy of nonparticipants. They helped break the fear barrier inside many of us.

We even published an image of four young Egyptians along the Doha corniche in Qatar who participated. This image was very influential, because it showed that the idea succeeded beyond our borders, not just within them. A Reuters news report said that eight thousand people took part in the Silent Stand. I suspect the number was lower, but the manner in which everyone lined up created the greatest impact possible for the number of participants present. Reuters correspondent Marwa Awad said that the stand gave credence to the possible connection between the virtual world and physical reality.

It is true that movements and organizations like Kefaya, the April 6 Youth Movement, the Muslim Brotherhood, and others were the first to mobilize people on the street. But most of the Silent Stand's participants were young men and women who were not politically active. They had never participated in anything like this before. Members felt strong. They had broken the fear barrier. They had finally transferred virtual activism into real-world action.

From *Revolution 2.0: The Power of the People Is Greater Than the People in Power* (Mariner Books, 2013). Wael Ghonim's website played a key role in the overthrow of Hosni Mubarak, and Ghonim now runs a technology-focused NGO focused on fighting poverty and fostering education in Egypt.

CHAPTER TWENTY-EIGHT

Arab Revolutions

Stephen Zunes

Under Egypt's Mubarak dictatorship, a simple gathering of five or more people without a permit was considered illegal. Peaceful pro-democracy protesters were routinely beaten and jailed. Martial law had been in effect for nearly thirty years. Independent observers were banned from monitoring the country's routinely rigged elections, from which the largest opposition party was banned from participating, and other opposition parties were severely restricted. Amnesty International and other reputable human rights groups documented gross and systematic human rights abuses against perceived regime opponents, including torture, massive detention without due process, and extra-judicial killings. Targets of government repression included not just radical Islamists but leftists, liberal democrats, feminists, gay men, Coptic Christians, independent-minded scholars, and human rights activists.

Despite this, the final decade of Mubarak's rule saw an increasing number of labor strikes and small, but ever-larger, demonstrations led by such youthful, secular pro-democracy groups as Kefaya (meaning "Enough!") and the April 6 Movement (named after a nationwide strike in 2008, when low wages and rising food costs prompted workers, primarily from the state-run textile industry, to engage in a one-day general strike, and millions of Egyptians refused to go to work, open their businesses, or go shopping). The period saw increasing government repression, the murder by police of a popular blogger for exposing government corruption, worsening economic conditions, blatantly rigged elections, and the implication of security forces in a church bombing seemingly designed to stoke sectarian tensions. As a result, activists began to believe that popular sentiments against the regime were sufficiently deep and widespread to make change possible.

People were afraid, however. Most protests involved relatively few people and were faced with brutal repression. Demonstrations were violently broken up. Activists were arrested. Many were tortured. Yet a core of mostly young activists determined not to give up. In the face of repression, they created small autonomous groups to organize a broader movement.

Pro-democracy activists found that when they invited people to join them in their illegal demonstrations, even those sympathetic resisted their invitations—citing fears of losing their jobs and not being able to feed their family and of being beaten or arrested, tortured or killed. They saw no point in taking such risks to join yet another countless small protest that would inevitably be violently broken up after only a few minutes. Yet many of these same people expressed a willingness to take such risks if they felt the demonstrations would reach a large enough critical mass to provide at least some safety in numbers and potentially make a difference. A typical response, noted pro-democracy activist Ahmad Salah, would be "I'll go when everyone else goes. When I see others on, I will fight and will be on the front line."

Faced with the dilemma that in order to get people out on the streets you had to get people out on the streets, activists decided to organize neighborhood by neighborhood. They focused on the lower middle class, who tended to be politically aware but with less to lose than those more educated and affluent. A couple years earlier, thousands of Egyptians had signed on to a pro-democracy petition and boldly provided names, addresses, and official ID numbers. The activists began by drawing on this database. As more and more people were contacted, the organizers began training on such topics as how to distribute flyers without being caught and how to maintain nonviolent discipline so as not provoke even greater police repression.

As is often the case, these efforts built on years of struggle outside the media spotlight. Between 1998 and 2010, more than 2 million Egyptians participated in more than 3,300 strikes, demonstrations, and factory occupations. A 2007 sit-in by 3,000 municipal workers at the finance ministry ultimately won higher salaries and the right to form an independent union. In the spring of 2010, thousands of workers protesting privatization of their jobs staged rotating sit-ins in front of the parliament building despite efforts by police to disperse them by force. Prominent pro-Mubarak parliamentarian Nashaat al-Qasas called on the government to go beyond the use of water cannons and "shoot them." In response, hundreds of defiant protesters marched, carrying placards with targets shouting "shoot us!" As these protests grew, they won a freeze on further privatization and won other economic demands. Organizers also met with veterans of South Africa's anti-apartheid struggle, the pro-democracy uprising that overthrew Serbian dictator Slobodan Milosevic, and the nonviolent wing of the Palestinian resistance.

In December 2010, just before the nonviolent uprisings that would overthrow Tunisian dictator Abidine Ben Ali, Wael Ghonim's co-administrator at the "We Are All Khaled Said" Facebook page, AbdelRahman Mansour, came up with the idea of a national protest around the January 25 National Police Day. Ghonim got the support of the founder of the April 6 Movement, and activist networks began planning and announcing it. As the day grew closer, they needed to decide where and how to rally. Traditionally, pro-democracy demonstrators would try to gather at a large public space and hope to expand. But that made their rallies seem small and made police repression easier, making it less likely that sympathetic onlookers would join. By contrast, if they marched through narrow streets of urban neighborhoods, they would not only seem relatively large and noisy and encourage others to join in, but police would be afraid of being ambushed in the crowded alleys and some of their vehicles would be too large to enter. Since January 25 was a national holiday, they knew people would be off from work. That morning, hundreds of feeder marches surged through the back alleys of Cairo, growing block by block. By the time they fed into Tahrir Square, the marchers numbered in the hundreds of thousands. Similar scenes unfolded in cities throughout the country.

Over the next eighteen days, despite frequent attacks by police and hired thugs, the many thousands who occupied Tahrir Square and other key points around the country formed participatory councils that organized food and sanitation, first aid for the injured, and strategies for responding to repression. Young people put aside religious and ideological differences and began working together in a common cause against the Mubarak dictatorship. Mohammed Abbas, a leader in the youth wing of the Muslim Brotherhood, noted how "what happened in Tahrir was a miracle by all measures" because of "the solidarity and singularity" between Islamists and Christians, liberals and leftists. It made him and countless others realize that it was the regime that "planted in us hatred for each other . . . so that it could control us." He and countless others changed during those days, he said, enabling them to recognize the need to listen to diverse opinions and appreciate their commonalities rather than their differences. Abbas later joined other disaffected young Brotherhood activists to form a new progressive party.

The largely nonviolent insurrections that successfully toppled US-backed dictators in Egypt, Tunisia, and Yemen in what became called the "Arab Spring" have had mixed legacies so far. In each of these countries, there are ongoing struggles to ensure real democracy. Each have faced varying setbacks. However, their successes in bringing down heavily armed autocrats still mark a major triumph for Arab peoples and further confirm the power of strategic nonviolent action.

Their leaders and the vast majority of participants were not pacifists. But they recognized that using nonviolent rather than violent means would result in greater support from the population and greater divisions within the state security forces. Although some did fight back when attacked by police and thugs, this was largely limited self-defense. Those protesting maintained a remarkable degree of nonviolent discipline in their occupations of central squares and thoroughfares, including the heart of their respective capitals.

Yemen, for instance, is one of the most heavily armed countries in the world, with some estimating as many as three weapons per person. Civil war, tribal conflicts, blood feuds, terrorism, local rebellions, and secessionist movements have been factors of life for generations. Yet millions of Yemenis consciously left their guns at home when they took to the streets. At a demonstration during the height of the 2011 pro-democracy struggle in the tribal al-Bayda region, men rode into town on horseback carrying automatic weapons, only to dismount, throw them on the ground, and lift their bare hands to the sky shouting "silmiyya!" ("peacefully!") before joining the march.

During my first visit to Cairo, six months after the revolution, I was watching the news at a café near Tahrir Square. A typical Egyptian TV news show, as in many autocratic states, used to consist of the president giving a speech, greeting a foreign dignitary, visiting a widget factory, etc. That evening, however, there was a story of a labor strike in Cairo, relatives of martyrs of the revolution holding a vigil outside the Interior Ministry, continued protests in Yemen, and the initially largely nonviolent uprising in Syria. It served as a reminder of just who had become the newsmakers in the Arab world.

Years of dictatorship rarely get instantly erased. Tunisia is slowly, if unevenly, edging towards a stable democracy. In Yemen, close associates of the former dictator retain positions of influence, complicated by the presence of armed militias, including Al-Qaeda affiliates, in parts of the country. But some real progress has been made. Egypt's democratic transition has obviously faced major setbacks from a powerful military establishment and conservative Islamists, both of whom have violently suppressed pro-democratic forces and blocked badly needed economic reforms, even as they've battled each other. Despite all this, in less than two and a half years Egyptian activists have forced the removal of both the longstanding Mubarak dictatorship and the semi-autocratic Morsi regime.

Indeed, throughout the region, there has been a generational shift in the understanding of political power. People recognize that power is no longer simply in the hands of despots, military establishments, secret police, or Western governments. If enough withhold their support, even the most entrenched autocrats can still be brought down by ordinary unarmed citizens—despite their massive security apparatuses and the backing of the world's sole remaining superpower. Though the young leaders of the pro-democracy uprisings are often pessimistic about change in the short term, they are almost uniformly optimistic in the long term. They know they are the future of their countries.

Dr. Stephen Zunes is a professor of politics and international studies at the University of San Francisco, senior policy analyst for *Foreign Policy in Focus*, and chair of the academic advisory committee for the International Center on Nonviolent Conflict. He is also the principal editor of *Nonviolent Social Movements* (Blackwell Publishers, 1999), the author of *Tinderbox: U.S. Middle East Policy and the Roots of Terrorism* (Common Courage Press, 2003), and the co-author of *Western Sahara: War, Nationalism and Conflict Irresolution* (Syracuse University Press, 2010). For more information, see *www.stephenzunes.org*.

CHAPTER TWENTY-NINE

Not Deterred

Paxus Calta

The time is the winter of 1996; the place is the Bulgarian capital city of Sofia. Polina is a student who has recently gotten involved in activism. She is eighteen years old.

Unlike most of the rest of Eastern Europe, Bulgaria did not throw out its Communist rulers in the revolutions of 1989 or 1991. Instead, some minor reforms were enacted, including some freeing of the media. In the late 1990s, the Bulgarian government is widely distrusted, disliked, and recognized as deeply corrupt. Bulgaria's class structure resembles that of the United States in the 1950s, where old gray-haired men with many initials after their names dominate discussion and policy making. These figures are well represented in our story.

The Belene nuclear power plant is an unfinished reactor complex in the eastern part of the country, near the Ukrainian border. It was designed and partially built by the Russians during the Cold War and was stopped by popular protest in 1990. In December 1996 the government put together a deal with the Russians, the United States, and the European Union to complete these reactors. After a number of serious accidents, the other Bulgarian reactor complex had been identified by the US Department of Energy as one of the ten most dangerous in the world. Mostly the same people will be building and running Belene.

Polina is part of an ecological organization called For the Earth, which is fighting against the completion of Belene. They convene a national conference to discuss how to stop this reactor complex from being finished. At this conference, Professor Uzinov from the Technical University of Sofia says, "We need to promote renewable energy sources so that nuclear power will not be necessary. We can do this effectively by pursuing energy credits from the European Union."

Dr. Svetlana from the National Academy of Sciences counters with a conservation-based strategy. "We have one of the least energy-efficient countries in the world. We should rather turn our attention to the US alternative model for funding and technology to generate negawatts."

Finally Polina is recognized. "If you want to stop the construction of the Belene reactors, you need to overthrow the government," says the eighteen-year-old student. Participants smile politely as if thinking, "What a nice thing for this child to say." They continue talking about return on investment and various energy aid schemes being offered worldwide.

But Polina is not deterred. She goes with twenty friends to the steps of the Parliament and starts a daily protest against the government. The media thinks it is charming and puts them on TV. This is December 1996.

Three months later, in March 1997, there are 20,000 people on the steps every day. Bowing to popular pressure, the government resigns. Shortly thereafter, the first democratic reform government is elected. A couple of months after that, they release their energy policy—canceling the Belene project.

Paxus Calta was the lead antinuclear campaigner for Friends of the Earth International and organized nonviolent direct actions to stop reactor construction in Eastern Europe. He has also smuggled Tibetan monks across the Himalayas, danced on Soviet tanks (before Boris Yeltsin made it popular), and hitchhiked across the Pacific on sailboats. Currently, he is the board chair of the Nuclear Information and Resource Service and lives at Twin Oaks Intentional Community, in Louisa, Virginia, where he manages recruiting and marketing and teaches a class on designing revolution at a local alternative high school.

CHAPTER THIRTY

In What Do I Place My Trust?

Sister Rosalie Bertell

As I think about what keeps us going when times get tough, and how we keep on working for a more just and humane world, what first flashes through my mind is the value of stories. How could we keep going without stories like David and Goliath? Robin Hood? Florence Nightingale?

Stories alone cannot keep us motivated and active in the face of corrupt government, massive greed, lies, disregard of human rights, the monopoly of violence, and destruction of life itself. But stories like this do provide worthwhile goals and dreams of what could be. They nurture our perhaps irrational desires for a utopian life. However, it is the little things, wonderful synergies, amazing coincidences, and sudden discoveries of beauty that offer us daily nourishment. A morning sunrise can calm my soul and give me new energy for the day. The wonder of this amazing planet Earth and the knowledge that we are literally composed of stardust can erase petty complaints and grumbling. The eyes of a child can reduce me to tears and energize me for months.

In Japan, during the occupation after World War II, two grandmothers strongly objected to US military presence and military exercises on the sacred mountain Fuji. The two women had a small camp at the foot of the mountain, and during military exercises they would pop up in front of the guns and cry: "Shame on you. You should go home to your mother." This so unnerved the young men that they could not fight. The police finally came, twelve men with shields and battle armor, to arrest the two old women. Even after the women left, the troops were spooked and could no longer desecrate the sacred mountain with their war games. Life is stronger than death.

Our society places its trust in the use of violence to protect possessions and political power. We could call these our society's idols. Faith in weapons of mass destruction has produced such a pervasive toxic environment in the United States, United Kingdom, France, Russia, and China that even the wealthy cannot always secure clean air, pure water, and uncontaminated foods, and the poor often breathe, eat, and drink polluted contaminants daily. This realization has motivated me to work, for much of the past thirty-five years, challenging the decisions that cause environmental contamination of our planet. Of particular concern to me are the nuclear weapon and reactor technologies that claim to be "clean, safe, and economical" while they release their invisible poison into air and water.

Sometimes nourishing stories come from one's own family. My mother, a World War I newlywed, lived in an apartment in northeast Washington, D.C. She'd tell me how she soon noticed that black women, after working all day in white homes, would stand for an hour or more waiting for a bus to take them home. If there were only blacks at a corner, the buses did not stop. My mother went down every evening to stand with the black women so that the buses would stop—until the drivers got the point.

I remember my mother fixing supper when the word came that World War II was over. My brother and another boy ran to our church and rang the bells for fifteen minutes. Everyone was in the street singing and rejoicing: "The boys will be coming home." My mother was stirring something in a big pot on the stove, and muttering to herself over and over: "They shouldn't have done it. They shouldn't have done it." I didn't really understand at the time, but she was referring to the atomic bomb, and it made a deep impression on my teenage mind. Some people are just in tune with the pain of the world.

Later, when I took on the nuclear establishment, that dramatic pot stirring gave me a sense of being right. Rational investigations and careful research into issues are important. But the strength to stand up to forces that claim superior wisdom and a national security mandate comes from deeper down, from the fertile field of our memories.

As we grow older, our own experiences become the fuel to fire our passion. We discover for ourselves that the Creator of our magnificent Earth is concerned about each individual. No parts of the Earth are "sacrifice areas." No people are expendable. God even experiences joy at our small victories. The continuity of life, the call for making things better for the next and the next generations, blots out all hesitation. To act becomes natural, and not to be able to act, a torment.

Yet when it comes to taking direct action against the atheistic idols of violence, I tend to be timid. The story of Moses at the Red Sea always helps. Moses had done extraordinary things to convince the Pharaoh to let his people go from the oppressive conditions of slavery in Egypt. He had called down plagues and pests, and even predicted the death of the first-born sons of the Egyptians. Imagine his feelings when he had led his people out, and the angry army of the Pharaoh, men who had suffered the horrible loss of beloved children, was racing after them. Moses had women and children, undernourished former slaves and old people, not horses and chariots. They were stopped by the Red Sea. Would they all be slaughtered?

Moses had an extraordinary ability to negotiate freedom, but that did not save the Israelites. Rather, according to Jewish tradition, a man named Nachshon, of the Tribe of Yehudah, was the first to plunge into the Red Sea. When the waters did not part, Nachshon continued walking forward, driven by faith in God, until the sea finally opened a path for his tribe and for the entire Jewish people. Imagine them standing on dry land on the other side of the sea and watching the sea close over the Pharaoh's men and horses. That's a happening to hold in your memory. It can carry you forward for forty years in the desert and nourish your children's children for many generations.

Like Moses, Nachshon did not wait passively, bemoaning his fate and fearing for his people. He did not rely on his own resources or past accomplishments. He knew that the true source of those events was not himself, but God. His plan was life-oriented: to escape. He put his foot in the water with no assurance that this small act would have such a magnificent effect. I believe in significant actions, those that have totally out-of-proportion effects. Like breaking an icy silence between feuding parties, or embracing a young man who can't cry. Like Gandhi insisting that salt was a local economic right, or the hundreds of thousands of workers fighting for the justice of an eight-hour day, small acts can have disproportionate effects.

After his heroic forty-year leadership of a grumbling migrating people, Moses was not able to enter the Promised Land with them. So too, we do not need to enjoy the fruits of our longing, as we "see" them taking fruit in others who will come after us. We are part of a great chain of big-hearted people who care about the Earth, about the life that gives it fruitfulness, and about a world where rights would be respected, children would be cherished, and peace would prevail. We have to be part of something larger than ourselves, because our dreams are often bigger than our lifetimes.

Religion has a profound effect on our staying power. In spite of natural timidity, I have always felt invincible before hostile forces precisely because I have been "redeemed." This means that I have all of the power I need to face down evil. I have the power, therefore, to choose life under any circumstances. Life is stronger than death, and we surely need to understand that redemption means that we are freed from the attraction and power of evil, free to choose life-giving options and life-enhancing goals. Evil will not triumph unless we waste this power that we have of choosing life.

Sister Rosalie Bertell, PhD, was a long-time environmental activist, past president of the Association of Contemplative Sisters, and the founder of the International Institute of Concern for Public Health. She was also the author of *Planet Earth* (The Women's Press, 2002).

CHAPTER THIRTY-ONE

Faith Works

Jim Wallis

Hope is believing in spite of the evidence, then watching the evidence change. That's what I've learned after almost three decades of working for change as a person of faith. What do I mean by faith? I like the definition used by the biblical writer of the Letter to the Hebrews: "Faith is the substance of things hoped for, the evidence of things not seen." Simply put, faith makes hope possible. And hope is the single most important ingredient for changing the world. It has continued to provide the energy and sustenance I've needed, not just to keep going but to be continually renewed.

Now you know and I know that religion has not always played a positive role in the world. I think sometimes God must get very embarrassed by some of the things we human beings say we do "in God's name." In places like Northern Ireland and Bosnia, the battles are often disguised as religious, when underneath the conflicts are economic, cultural, ethnic, nationalistic, and always political. Religion is often used as a sword to divide, rather than as a balm to heal. And religious leaders and institutions can be guilty of the kind of power politics tactics that tear people apart instead of bringing them together. Toward one another, the different religious communities sometimes behave no better than rival street gangs.

Yet I have also experienced the promise and power of faith. When slavemasters put the Bible in the hands of their slaves, it was meant to control them; to turn their eyes toward heaven and away from doing anything about their plight on Earth. But in that book the slaves found Moses and Jesus. Their faith became the foundation for their liberation, and its spiritual power enabled them to "keep their eyes on the prize." I can say that, too. I know the oppressive and divisive side of religion, but I've also found the transforming power of faith that can change lives, neighborhoods, and nations. I have a long history in the streets and in the places in this world where suffering is most intense. I've seen that suffering, but I've also seen the faith that can prevail in and through it.

Perhaps the greatest heresy of twentieth-century American religion was to make faith into a purely personal matter and a private affair, which went neatly with the rise of the consumer society. With the advent of the television preachers, faith was turned into an occasion for conspicuous consumption and effective fundraising. Faith became merely another commodity: "I have it, and you don't." Or worse, "Here's how you can get it too. Our operators are standing by!"

But in the Bible, faith is not something you possess but rather something you practice. You have to put it into action or it really doesn't mean anything. Faith changes things. It's the energy of transformation, both for individuals and for a society.

As recently as the eighteenth and nineteenth centuries, both England and the United States experienced revivalist faith as a catalyst for great social movements, such as the abolition of slavery, child labor reform, and women's suffrage. In this century, American black churches led the way in the civil rights movement by putting faith into action for freedom.

It took a lot of faith for those early civil rights activists to endure the hatred and violence of the system of racial discrimination. It also required a change in the moral climate and values of the nation to end that system. People had to really believe such things could be done before they *were* possible. Change always begins with some people making decisions based in hope, and then staking their lives on those decisions. South African

Archbishop Desmond Tutu always said that people of faith are "prisoners of hope."

Perhaps my favorite story of the power of hope comes from a moment I shared with Tutu in South Africa—an extraordinary drama I witnessed at St. George's Cathedral, in Cape Town, where the Nobel Peace Prize winner and Anglican cleric preached. A political rally had just been canceled by the white government, so Tutu called for a worship service instead, inside the beautiful cathedral. The power of apartheid was frighteningly evident in the numbers of riot police and armed soldiers massing outside the church. Inside, all along the cathedral walls, stood more police openly taping and writing down every comment made from the pulpit. When Tutu rose to speak, the atmosphere was tense indeed. He confidently proclaimed that the "evil" and "oppression" of the system of apartheid "cannot prevail." At that moment, the South African archbishop was probably one of the few people on the planet who actually believed that.

I had been clandestinely sneaked into the country to support the South African churches during a time of great crisis, and to report their story back in the United States. This was the first day of my six-week stay and I had just arrived from the airport. Now I sat in the cathedral congregation and watched Tutu point his finger right at the police who were recording his words. "You may be powerful, indeed very powerful, but you are not God!" And the God whom we serve, he said, "cannot be mocked!" "You have already lost!" the diminutive preacher thundered. Then he came out from behind the pulpit and seemed to soften, flashing that signature Desmond Tutu smile. So—since they had already lost, as had just been made clear—South Africa's spiritual leader shouted with glee, "We are inviting you to come and join the winning side!" The whole place erupted, the police seemed to scurry out, and the congregation rose up in triumphal dancing. I had the blessing to be at Nelson Mandela's inauguration and to have some moments with Archbishop Tutu. He smiled when I reminded him of that day at St. George's. I said, "Today they've all joined the winning side!" They had indeed.

Many people today would like to find some way to practice their faith or spirituality, despite the excesses, corruption, or narrow regulations of religion that have turned them away. I believe the making of the modern Christian, Jew, or Muslim will be through action. When put into action, faith has the capacity to bring people together, to motivate, and to inspire, even across former dividing lines. We demonstrate our faith by putting it into practice. Conversely, if we don't keep the power of faith in the actions we undertake, our efforts can easily lead to burnout, bitterness, and despair. The call to action can preserve the authenticity of faith, while the power of faith can save the integrity of our actions. As the biblical apostle James put it, "Faith without works is dead."

Today, I see a new kind of activist emerging. Not one who is angry or burned out, but one whose belief that things can be different goes deeper than a passing optimism. We've had plenty of very sophisticated analysis of what's wrong with the world, much of it quite helpful. But what's often been missing is the vision to help people connect the desire to change their lives with a commitment to change their communities. That vision will likely be rooted in moral and spiritual values.

Adapted from *Faith Works: Lessons from the Life of an Activist Preacher* (Random House, 2000). The Reverend Jim Wallis is the executive director of Sojourners, a Christian ministry for social justice and peace. His other books include *God's Politics* (Harper San Francisco, 2006) and *On God's Side* (Brazos Press, 2013).

CHAPTER THIRTY-TWO

The Progressive Story of America

Bill Moyers

On my 16th birthday, I went to work for the daily newspaper in the small East Texas town where I grew up. It was a good place to be a cub reporter and I soon had a stroke of luck. Some of the old timers were on vacation or out sick and I got assigned to cover what came to be known as the Housewives' Rebellion. Fifteen women in my home town decided not to pay the Social Security withholding tax for their domestic workers. They argued that Social Security was unconstitutional, that imposing it was taxation without representation, and that—here's my favorite part—"requiring us to collect [the tax] is no different from requiring us to collect the garbage." They hired themselves a lawyer but eventually the women wound up holding their noses and paying the tax.

That hooked me, and in one way or another—after a detour through seminary and then into politics and government for a spell—I've been covering the class war ever since. Those women in Marshall, Texas, were its advance guard. They were not bad people. They were regulars at church, their children were my friends, many of them were active in community affairs, their husbands were pillars of the business and professional class in town. They were respectable and upstanding citizens all. So it took me awhile to figure out what had brought on that spasm of reactionary rebellion. It came to me one day, much later. They simply couldn't see beyond their own prerogatives. Fiercely loyal to their families, to their clubs, charities and congregations—fiercely loyal, in other words, to their own kind—they narrowly defined membership in democracy to include only people like them. The women who washed and ironed their laundry, wiped their children's bottoms, made their husband's beds, and cooked their family meals—these women, too, would grow old and frail, sick and decrepit, lose their husbands and face the ravages of time alone, with nothing to show from their years of labor but the crease in their brow and the knots on their knuckles; so be it; even on the distaff side of laissez-faire, security was personal, not social, and what injustice existed this side of heaven would no doubt be redeemed beyond the Pearly Gates. God would surely be just to the poor once they got past Judgment Day.

In one way or another, this is the oldest story in America: the struggle to determine whether "we, the people" is a spiritual idea embedded in a political reality—one nation, indivisible—or merely a charade masquerading as piety and manipulated by the powerful and privileged to sustain their own way of life at the expense of others.

Look at our history. All of us know that the American Revolution ushered in what one historian called "The Age of Democratic Revolutions." Not surprisingly, the previous winners often resisted. In the early years of constitution-making in the states and emerging nation, aristocrats wanted a government of propertied "gentlemen" to keep the scales tilted in their favor. Battling on the other side were moderates and even those radicals harboring the extraordinary idea of letting all white males have the vote. Luckily, the weapons were words and ideas, not bullets. Through compromise and conciliation the draftsmen achieved a Constitution of checks and balances that is now the oldest in the world, even as the revolution of democracy that inspired it remains a tempestuous adolescent whose destiny is still up for grabs. For all the rhetoric about "life, liberty, and the pursuit of happiness," it took a civil war to free the slaves and another hundred years to invest their freedom with meaning. Women only gained the right to vote in my mother's time.

Much of our country's movement toward a society whose arrangements roughly serve all its citizens came through the progressive movement that started late in the 19th century and remade the American experience piece by piece until it peaked in the last third of the 20th century. Its aim was to keep blood pumping through the veins of democracy when others were ready to call in the mortician. Progressives exalted and extended the original American revolution. They spelled out new terms of partnership between the people and their rulers. And they kindled a flame that lit some of the most prosperous decades in modern history, not only here but in aspiring democracies everywhere, especially those of western Europe.

Step back with me to the curtain-raiser, the founding convention of the People's Party—better known as the Populists—in 1892. The members were mainly cotton and wheat farmers from the recently reconstructed South and the newly settled Great Plains, and they had come on hard, hard times, driven to the wall by falling prices for their crops on the one hand and racking interest rates, freight charges and supply costs on the other. This in the midst of a booming and growing industrial America. They were angry, and their platform—issued deliberately on the 4th of July—pulled no punches. "We meet," it said, "in the midst of a nation brought to the verge of moral, political and material ruin. . . . Corruption dominates the ballot box, the [state] legislatures and the Congress and touches even the bench. . . . The newspapers are largely subsidized or muzzled, public opinion silenced. . . . The fruits of the toil of millions are boldly stolen to build up colossal fortunes for a few."

Furious words from rural men and women who were traditionally conservative and whose memories of taming the frontier were fresh and personal. But in their fury they invoked an American tradition as powerful as frontier individualism—the war on inequality and especially on the role that government played in promoting and preserving inequality by favoring the rich.

The Populists knew it was the government that granted millions of acres of public land to the railroad builders. It was the government that gave the manufacturers of farm machinery a monopoly of the domestic market by a protective tariff that was no longer necessary to shelter "infant industries." It was the government that contracted the national currency and sparked a deflationary cycle that crushed debtors and fattened the wallets of creditors. And those who made the great fortunes used them to buy the legislative and judicial favors that kept them on top. So the Populists recognized one great principle: the job of preserving equality of opportunity and democracy demanded the end of any unholy alliance between government and wealth.

But how? How was the democratic revolution to be revived? The promise of the Declaration reclaimed? How were Americans to restore government to its job of promoting the general welfare? And here, the Populists made a breakthrough to another principle. In a modern, large-scale, industrial and nationalized economy it wasn't enough simply to curb the government's outreach. That would simply leave power in the hands of the great corporations whose existence was inseparable from growth and progress. The answer was to turn government into an active player in the economy at the very least enforcing fair play, and when necessary being the friend, the helper and the agent of the people at large in the contest against entrenched power. So the Populist platform called for government loans to farmers about to lose their mortgaged homesteads—for government granaries to grade and store their crops fairly—for governmental inflation of the currency, which was a classical plea of debtors—and for some decidedly non-classical actions like government ownership of the railroad, telephone and telegraph systems and a graduated—i.e., progressive—tax on incomes and a flat ban on subsidies to "any private corporation." And to make sure the government stayed on the side of the people, the "Pops" called for the initiative and referendum and the direct election of Senators.

Predictably, the Populists were denounced, feared and mocked as fanatical hayseeds ignorantly playing with socialist fire. They got twenty-two electoral votes for their candidate in '92, plus some Congressional seats and state houses, but it was downhill from there for many reasons. America wasn't—and probably still isn't—ready for a new major party. The People's Party was a spent rocket by 1904. But if political organizations perish, their key ideas don't—keep that in mind, because it gives perspective to your cause today. Much of the Populist agenda would become law within a few years of the party's extinction. And that was because it was generally shared by a rising generation of young Republicans and Democrats who, justly or not, were seen as less outrageously outdated than the embattled farmers. These were the progressives.

Here is what the celebrated William Allen White, a Kansas country editor, and a Republican, wrote about them:

> What the people felt about the vast injustice that had come with the settlement of a continent, we, their servants—teachers, city councilors, legislators, governors, publishers, editors, writers, representatives in Congress and Senators—all made a part of our creed. Some way, into the hearts of the dominant middle class of this country, had come a sense that their civilization needed recasting, that their government had fallen into the hands of self-seekers, that a new relationship should be established between the haves and the have-nots.

They were a diverse lot, held together by a common admiration of progress—hence the name—and a shared dismay at the paradox of poverty stubbornly persisting in the midst of progress like an unwanted guest at a wedding. Of course they welcomed, just as we do, the new marvels in the gift-bag of technology: the telephones, the autos, the electrically powered urban transport and lighting systems, the indoor heating and plumbing, the processed foods and home appliances and machine-made clothing that reduced the sweat and drudgery of home-making and were affordable to an ever-swelling number of people. But they saw the underside, too—the slums lurking in the shadows of the glittering cities, the exploited and unprotected workers whose low-paid labor filled the horn of plenty for others, the misery of those whom age, sickness, accident or hard times condemned to servitude and poverty with no hope of comfort or security.

What troubled our progressive forebears and should trouble us now was not only the miasma of poverty in their nostrils, but the sour stink of a political system for sale. Because all of them, whatever party they subscribed to, were inspired by the gospel of democracy. Inevitably, this swept them into the currents of politics, whether as active officeholders or persistent advocates.

Here's a small, but representative, sampling of their ranks. Jane Addams forsook the comforts of a middle-class college graduate's life to live in Hull House in the midst of a disease-ridden and crowded Chicago immigrant neighborhood, determined to make it an educational and social center that would bring pride, health and beauty into the lives of her poor neighbors. She was inspired by "an almost passionate devotion to the ideals of democracy," to combating the prevailing notion "that the well-being of a privileged few might justly be built upon the ignorance and sacrifice of the many." Community and fellowship were the lessons she drew from her teachers, Jesus and Abraham Lincoln. But people simply helping one another couldn't move mountains of disadvantage. She came to see that "private beneficence" wasn't enough. To bring justice to the poor would take more than soup kitchens and fundraising prayer meetings. Not individual regeneration or the magic of the market, but conscious, cooperative effort.

The social reformer Jacob Riis lugged his heavy camera up and down the staircases of New York's disease-ridden, firetrap tenements to photograph the unspeakable crowding, the inadequate toilets, the starved and hollow-eyed children and the filth on the walls so thick that his crude flash equipment sometimes set it afire. Bound between hard covers, with Riis's commentary, they showed comfortable New Yorkers "How the Other Half Lives." They were powerful ammunition for reformers who eventually brought an end to tenement housing by state legislation.

There are many more to call to the witness stand. Sociologist Edward A. Ross believed that the function of "social science" wasn't simply to dissect society for non-judgmental analysis and academic promotion, but to help in finding solutions to social problems. "The man who picks pockets with a railway rebate," he wrote in 1907, "murders with an adulterant instead of a bludgeon, burglarizes with a 'rake-off' instead of a jimmy, cheats with a company instead of a deck of cards, or scuttles his town instead of his ship, does not feel on his brow the brand of a malefactor." In other words, upstanding individuals could plot corporate crimes and sleep the sleep of the just without the sting of social stigma or the pangs of conscience.

And there is Tom Johnson, the progressive mayor of Cleveland in the early nineteen hundreds—a businessman converted to social activism. His major battles were to impose regulation, or even municipal takeover, on the private companies that were meant to provide affordable public transportation and utilities but in fact crushed competitors, overcharged customers, secured franchises and licenses for a song, and paid virtually nothing in taxes—all through their pocketbook control of lawmakers and judges. Johnson's argument for public ownership was simple: "If you don't own them, they will own you. It's why advocates of Clean Elections today argue that if anybody's going to buy Congress, it should be the people." When advised that businessmen got their way in Washington because they had lobbies and consumers had none, Tom Johnson responded: "If Congress were true to the principles of democracy it would be the people's lobby." What a radical contrast to the House of Representatives today!

Our political, moral, and intellectual forbearers occupy a long and honorable roster. They include wonderful characters like Dr. Alice Hamilton, a pioneer in industrially caused diseases, who spent long years clambering up and down ladders in factories and mineshafts—in long skirts!—tracking down the unsafe toxic substances that sickened the workers whom she would track right into their sickbeds to get leads and tip-offs on where to hunt. Or Harvey Wiley, the chemist from Indiana who, from a bureaucrat's desk in the Department of Agriculture, relentlessly warred on foods laden with risky preservatives and adulterants with the help of his "poison squad" of young assistants who volunteered as guinea pigs. Or lawyers like the brilliant Harvard graduate Louis Brandeis, who took on corporate attorneys defending child labor or long and harsh conditions for female workers.

To be sure, these progressives were not saints. Their glory years coincided with the heyday of lynching and segregation, of empire and the Big Stick and the bold theft of the Panama Canal, of immigration restriction and ethnic stereotypes. But their common enemy was unchecked privilege, their common hope was a better democracy, and their common weapon was an informed public opinion.

In a few short years the progressive spirit made possible the election not only of reform mayors and governors but of national figures like Senator George Norris of Nebraska, Senator Robert M. La Follette of Wisconsin, and even that hard-to-classify political genius, Theodore Roosevelt. All three of them Republicans. Here is the simplest laundry-list of what was accomplished at state and federal levels: publicly regulated or owned transportation; sanitation and utilities systems; the partial restoration of competition in the marketplace through improved antitrust laws; increased fairness in taxation; expansion of the public education and juvenile justice systems; safer workplaces and guarantees of compensation to workers injured on the job; oversight of the purity of water, medicines and foods; conservation of the national wilderness heritage against overdevelopment; and honest bidding on any public mining, lumbering and ranching. We take these for granted today—or we did until recently. All were provided not by the automatic workings of free enterprise but by implementing the idea in the Declaration of Independence that the people had a right to governments that best promoted their "safety and happiness."

The progressive wave peaked in 1912. But the ideas unleashed by it forged the politics of the 20th century. Like his cousin Theodore, Franklin Roosevelt argued that the real enemy of enlightened capitalism was "the malefactors of great wealth"—the "economic royalists"—from whom capitalism would have to be saved by reform and regulation. Progressive government became an embedded tradition of Democrats—the heart of FDR's New Deal and Harry Truman's Fair Deal, both honored by Dwight D. Eisenhower, who didn't want to tear down the house that progressive ideas had built—just to put it under different managers. The progressive impulse had its final fling in the landslide of 1968 when LBJ, who was a son of the West Texas hill country, where the Populist rebellion had been nurtured in the 1890s, won the public endorsement for what he meant to be the capstone in the arch of the New Deal.

I had a modest role in that era. I shared in its exhilaration and its failures. We went too far too fast, overreached at home and in Vietnam, failed to examine some assumptions, and misjudged the rising discontents and fierce backlash engendered by war, race, civil disturbance, violence and crime. Democrats grew so proprietary in this town that a fat, complacent political establishment couldn't recognize its own intellectual bankruptcy or the beltway that was growing around it and beginning to separate it from the rest of the country.

The failure of democratic politicians and public thinkers to respond to popular discontents—to the daily lives of workers, consumers, parents, and ordinary taxpayers—allowed a resurgent conservatism to convert public concern and hostility into a crusade to resurrect social Darwinism as a moral philosophy, multinational corporations as a governing class, and the theology of markets as a transcendental belief system.

What will it take to get back in the fight? Understanding the real interests and deep opinions of the American people is the first thing. And what are those? That a Social Security card is not a private portfolio statement but a membership ticket in a society where we all contribute to a common treasury so that none need face the indignities of poverty in old age without that help. That tax evasion is not a form of conserving investment capital but a brazen abandonment of responsibility to the country. That self-interest is a great motivator for production and progress, but is amoral unless contained within the framework of community. That the rich have the right to buy more cars than anyone else, more homes, vacations, gadgets and gizmos, but they do not have the right to buy more democracy than anyone else. That public services, when privatized, serve only those who can afford them and weaken the sense that we all rise and fall together as "one nation, indivisible." That concentration in the production of goods may sometimes be useful and efficient, but monopoly over the dissemination of ideas is evil. That prosperity requires good wages and benefits for workers. And that our nation can no more survive as half democracy and half oligarchy than it could survive "half slave and half free"—and that keeping it from becoming all oligarchy is steady work—our work.

Ideas need legs. The eight-hour day, the minimum wage, the conservation of natural resources and the protection of our air, water, and land, women's rights and civil rights, free trade unions, Social Security and a civil service based on merit—all these were launched as citizen's movements and won the endorsement of the political class only after long struggles and in the face of bitter opposition and sneering attacks. It's just a fact: democracy doesn't work without citizen activism and participation, starting at the community. What's right and good doesn't come naturally. You have to stand up and fight for it—as if the cause depends on you, because it does. Allow yourself that conceit—to believe that the flame of democracy will never go out as long as there's one candle in your hand.

So go for it. Never mind the odds. Remember what the progressives faced. Their story is your story—the progressive story of America.

Adapted from a speech to the annual conference of the Campaign for America's Future. Bill Moyers was the press secretary for Lyndon Johnson, helped run the Peace Corps, and is the host of Moyers & Company on PBS. See *www.Billmoyers.com* for his wonderful interviews and commentaries. His books include *Moyers on America: A Journalist and His Times* (Anchor, 2005) and *Bill Moyers Journal: The Conversation Continues* (New Press, 2011).

PART SIX

The Global Stage

IMAGINE THE ANGELS OF BREAD

Martín Espada

This is the year that squatters evict landlords,
gazing like admirals from the rail
of the roofdeck
or levitating hands in praise
of steam in the shower;
this is the year
that shawled refugees deport judges
who stare at the floor
and their swollen feet
as files are stamped
with their destination;
this is the year that police revolvers,
stove-hot, blister the fingers
of raging cops,
and nightsticks splinter
in their palms;
this is the year
that darkskinned men
lynched a century ago
return to sip coffee quietly
with the apologizing descendants
of their executioners.

This is the year that those
who swim the border's undertow
and shiver in boxcars
are greeted with trumpets and drums
at the first railroad crossing
on the other side;
this is the year that the hands
pulling tomatoes from the vine
uproot the deed to the earth that sprouts the vine,
the hands canning tomatoes
are named in the will
that owns the bedlam of the cannery;
this is the year that the eyes
stinging from the poison that purifies toilets
awaken at last to the sight
of a rooster-loud hillside,
pilgrimage of immigrant birth;
this is the year that cockroaches
become extinct, that no doctor
finds a roach embedded
in the ear of an infant;
this is the year that the food stamps
of adolescent mothers
are auctioned like gold doubloons,
and no coin is given to buy machetes
for the next bouquet of severed heads
in coffee plantation country.

If the abolition of slave-manacles
began as a vision of hands without manacles,
then this is the year;
if the shutdown of extermination camps
began as imagination of a land
without barbed wire or the crematorium,
then this is the year;
if every rebellion begins with the idea
that conquerors on horseback
are not many-legged gods, that they too drown
if plunged in the river,
then this is the year.

So may every humiliated mouth,
teeth like desecrated headstones,
fill with the angels of bread.

From Martín Espada, *Imagine the Angels of Bread* (W. W. Norton, 1996). Martín Espada's other books include *A Mayan Astronomer in Hell's Kitchen* (W. W. Norton, 2002), *Alabanza: New and Selected Poems* (W. W. Norton, 2004), *The Republic of Poetry* (W. W. Norton, 2008), and *The Trouble Ball* (W. W. Norton, 2012).

Most of us are familiar with the Serenity Prayer, the Alcoholics Anonymous maxim (adapted from theologian Reinhold Niebuhr): "God, grant me the serenity to accept the things I cannot change, the courage to change the things I can, and the wisdom to know the difference."

It will come as no surprise that I value most the courage to change the things we can—whether in our communities or halfway around the world. The rest of the prayer has its wisdom, too. Some kinds of sorrow we have no choice but to accept, as when a loved one falls severely ill or suddenly dies, or when a cherished relationship ends. In the public sphere, when even our most admirable efforts at social change fail to bear fruit, sometimes we have to accept setbacks and move on. In such circumstances, resistance and rage do more harm than good, even to ourselves. Better to accept the loss, the disappointment, than to tie ourselves in knots by endlessly fuming about it. But this widely promoted prescription for serenity, courage, and wisdom becomes more complex when applied to the largest and most overwhelming global issues of our time: climate change, poverty, economic injustice, violence and war.

Consider the following example. Shortly after the September 11 attacks, I visited the website of the respected Christian hunger advocacy organization, Bread for the World. There I learned that each day in developing countries more than sixteen thousand children—five times the World Trade Center toll—die of hunger-related causes. That's every day of every week of every year. Satisfying the basic health and nutrition needs of the world's poorest people, thereby putting an end to this invisible carnage, might seem impossible, one of the inevitable aspects of modern life that wisdom dictates we shouldn't even try to rectify. But in fact, hunger isn't inevitable. Nor would alleviating it require extraordinary measures. According to Bread for the World, all it would take is $13 billion a year. That's roughly a tenth of the $130 billion that the only partially rescinded 2001 and 2002 Bush tax cuts gave to the wealthiest 1 percent of Americans, or less than one-fiftieth of the $729 billion the United States currently spends each year on military-related expenditures.

My point? The Serenity Prayer is too easily misread as a gospel of resignation. That's because it's impossible to predict precisely what people can and cannot change. Wisdom comes not from anticipation but from action. The only way to find out what's possible is through our deeds. And that's true whether we're tackling issues that affect the whole world or just our neighborhoods. Niebuhr himself would have acknowledged this; he spoke out for social justice all of his life. To read the future as already determined, be it implacable darkness or rosy dawn, is to give up on precisely what can make the greatest difference—giving our all to the present.

One person who understands the power of action to enlarge possibility is Mel Yost, a retired Safeway truck driver from Denver who is active in a national hunger action network called Results. When a $10 million congressional outlay to fight the global resurgence of tuberculosis was threatened, volunteers nationwide mounted a campaign to petition their legislators. Yost hesitated, since only a few days earlier he'd contacted the office of his then-congressman, Mark Udall, regarding another request, and was afraid of appearing pushy. He picked up the phone, put it down; then, thinking about lives that might depend on his actions, he picked it up again and dialed the number. After Yost convinced Udall's aide to support the appropriation, she persuaded her boss. And Udall and others successfully fought to retain the TB funding. When he heard the news, Yost realized that he'd "just saved 10 million dollars for something really important." Only after he'd acted was Yost in any position to discover what was possible and what was not.

History is replete with examples of ordinary people unexpectedly transforming situations that appeared impossible to change. Rebecca Solnit describes how she joined thousands of others protesting US nuclear tests in Nevada in the late 1980s. "We didn't shut down our test site," she writes. But soon afterward, the efforts of Solnit and her peers inspired the Kazakh poet Olzhas Suleimenov to take an action of his own. Scheduled to recite poetry on live Kazakh TV, Suleimenov instead read a manifesto demanding the shutdown of a Soviet nuclear test site in Semipalatinsk, Kazakhstan. He also called a meeting. The next day, five thousand Kazakhs gathered at the Writers' Union headquarters to form what they called the Nevada-Semipalatinsk Antinuclear Movement, to honor the American demonstrations that had inspired them. They ended up shutting down the Soviet test site. Hope isn't an abstract theory about where human aspirations end and the impossible begins; rather, it's a never-ending experiment, continually expanding the boundaries of the possible.

This approach applies to even the gravest issues, like global climate change. Mark Hertsgaard dreams large when envisioning solutions to global environmental crises. For the past twenty years, he's been traveling to the remotest places on the planet, finding both ecological destruction and growing environmental concern. In "Kids, Trees, and Climate Change," he grounds his hope in some of the amazing grassroots initiatives that have been emerging worldwide. African farmers, for instance, have begun reclaiming their arid lands by spreading manure on fields to let embedded seeds naturally germinate into trees. In Niger alone, this has resulted in 200 million new trees. Efforts like the Sierra Club's Beyond Coal campaign have blocked 166 proposed coal plants in the past dozen years, largely in conservative states like Kentucky, South Dakota, and Oklahoma. The deployment of wind and solar technologies has been skyrocketing worldwide. Denmark now gets more than a quarter of its electricity from wind, aiming for 50 percent by the end of the decade. Portugal has passed 50 percent. Here in the United States, Iowa has passed 25 percent, California's aiming for 30 percent or more from renewables by 2020, and wind now constitutes the largest source of recent new US electricity production. Solar projects, though initially slower to take hold, are even more rapidly increasing their deployment. Hertsgaard draws hope from these concrete manifestations of new possibilities. (I get a similar sense of tangible alternatives by generating power from our rooftop solar panels, even in cloudy Seattle, and driving an electric car, charged largely by these same panels, which removes all reliance on gas.) Hertsgaard is also inspired by his young daughter, Chiara, because what we do—or do not do—to address climate change today will shape her future. Having founded a group called Climate Parents, he's begun to engage others based on their love for their own children.

"Most people want to do right by the environment," Hertsgaard says, "and, if given the chance, they will—as long as they are not penalized too much economically for it." He argues for setting a price on carbon while rolling the proceeds back to US taxpayers, so they can drive the necessary shifts with their choices. He also explores how the United States and other affluent countries could create the equivalent of the Marshall Plan, which rebuilt Europe after World War II, so the developing world isn't forced to choose between poverty and environmental devastation. The solutions are there, Hertsgaard makes clear. We just need to find the courage to fight for them.

As Mary Pipher points out in "Reluctant Activists," Bill McKibben's *Eaarth* was the inspiration for her to act on climate change. In 1989 McKibben wrote the first popular book on the subject, *The End of Nature*, and he's been a tireless voice for environmental sustainability ever since. He has also become a major activist, founding the Step-It-Up campaign in 2007 with seven students from his Middlebury classes when he felt national environmental groups weren't doing enough to engage local communities. Step-It-Up set a date for a decentralized day of protest, sent out materials, and used then-new Google Maps technology to help people connect with each other at 1,400 local events. The next year, McKibben took this model to a global stage with 350.org, named for the level of sustained atmospheric CO_2 presence above which climate disruption risks spiraling out of control. When I started the nonpartisan Campus Election Engagement Project in 2008, I was inspired not only by my own election volunteering but also by McKibben's shift from writing about critical issues to organizing people to act on them, and by his jumping in to fill the gaps when existing institutions weren't adequately responding. I solicited McKibben's advice before initiating this project, and by 2012, we reached 750 campuses, and have continued to expand our efforts. You could say our successes represent further ripples of McKibben's powerful work.

In "Curitiba," he offers further evidence that Hertsgaard's notion of what's possible isn't as outlandish as proponents of complacency might think. McKibben describes visiting a Brazilian city of 1.5 million people that's become a global model for development that both safeguards the natural environment and delights its inhabitants. Using special right-of-ways on the streets and transparent advance-boarding tubes, its metropolitan buses carry more passengers than those of New York City. Architects help low-income residents build their own houses on city-deeded land. Pedestrian malls abound, initiated when the mayor ripped up a key street in one weekend and enlisted dozens of children to block off cars by sitting down and painting pictures.

Instead of enclosing rivers in costly flood-control channels, the citizens of Curitiba built a system of lakes and parks. "If the rains were heavy," McKibben writes, "the lake might rise a foot or two—perhaps the jogging track would get a little soggy or the duck in the big new zoo would find itself swimming a few feet higher than usual." The result is an abundance of green space. As former Curitiba mayor Jaime Lerner explains, many cities have "a lot of people who are specialists in proving change is not possible. What I try to explain to them when I go visit is that it takes the same energy to say why something can't be done as to figure out how to do it."

Inspired by McKibben, I made my own journey to Curitiba in 2010, which I write about immediately following McKibben's piece. The city has continued to experiment with creative ways of reconciling development and sustainability, even as the population became more affluent and mushroomed into a metro area of 3 million. And the Bus Rapid Transit that it pioneered has been adopted in 150 cities worldwide, just as cities like New York and Chicago have recently copied Copenhagen's protected bike lanes.

Climate change threatens the very ground we stand on with floods, droughts, out-of-control wildfires, and hurricanes. Yet we've devoted far more of our attention and national resources to the violence unleashed by our fellow human beings, focusing particularly, since the September 11 attacks, on how to combat global terrorism. One lesson I hope America has learned in recent years is that a single nation, even a global superpower, cannot and should not control everything that happens worldwide, especially since we've so often intervened in ways that increase rather than diminish bitterness, anger, and a desire for revenge. US support of the anti-Soviet Mujahideen in Afghanistan, for instance, sowed the seeds for the Taliban and helped create the horror of September 11 by bringing Osama bin Laden into politics. Iran was once a democracy, but in 1953 the United States not only overthrew an elected prime minister who had dared to nationalize the country's oil but also installed the Shah in his place, then armed and trained his notoriously brutal secret police, the Savak. After twenty-six years, the only forces capable of overthrowing the Shah were fundamentalists loyal to Ayatollah Khomeini. A decade later, the United States helped bring Saddam Hussein's Baath Party to power in Iraq by sponsoring a 1963 coup against OPEC co-founder General Abdul Karim Qasim.

Keep this history in mind while reading "Come September," in which Arundhati Roy examines global justice issues in the wake of September 11. Roy's essay is radical, provocative. You may not agree with everything she says. I find myself unsettled by the starkness of her indictment, the power of her anger, and the disturbing history she cites. But Roy's passion for justice—her insistence that "every humiliated mouth" be fed, as poet Martín Espada phrases it—inspires social activists worldwide. She has made me think, in challenging ways, about the root causes of the crises we face. Roy also matches her words with brave acts. She's been intensely active in India, where she has defied environmentally destructive dams and a corrupt legal system, among other things. "Whether there's hope or despair is a way of seeing," Roy told *Democracy Now* radio host Amy Goodman. "But even if there wasn't hope, I would still be doing what I do. Because that's what I do; that's who I am."

Roy is anything but serene. She offers a scathing critique of unchecked global capitalism at its most destructive. She reminds us that the attacks on the Twin Towers and the Pentagon weren't the only assaults on human dignity on that sorrowful date, citing the shameful Chilean coup of September 11, 1973. The story bears repeating. Salvador Allende's democratically elected administration, trying to create a humane alternative to authoritarian socialism and predatory capitalism, peacefully initiated fundamental reforms, in the belief that people have a right to determine their common economic as well as political destiny. While protecting civil liberties, including those of its opponents, the government took control of critical national resources, among them the copper mines, which had long been owned by foreign companies and exploited for their benefit. But Allende's agenda conflicted with US foreign policy. When CIA financial support for Allende's opponents failed to subvert his election, the agency orchestrated the kidnapping and assassination of General René Schneider, the strongly constitutionalist head of the armed forces. Then the CIA, together with disgruntled members of the Chilean military and corporations such as International Telephone & Telegraph and Kennecott Copper, worked covertly to overthrow Allende. The coup ushered in the dictator Augusto Pinochet and nearly twenty years of political oppression.

As much as this episode was a setback for human freedom, it also demonstrates that predictions regarding the limits of the possible are notoriously unreliable. Pinochet's regime was extraordinarily brutal. Those living in Chile and hungering for freedom could be forgiven for choosing a quiet retreat over courage. But many individuals refused to allow others to narrate their lives, as Chilean novelist and playwright Ariel Dorfman puts it, and gradually began to defy the regime. Eventually, Pinochet was driven from power. Dorfman still draws strength from the Allende government's initial promise—a time of real joy, when he felt as if it were "the first day in history and the world was about to begin in all its beauty and that all it would take to give birth to that beauty which was just within our reach was to dare to invent it, dare to name it." But in "The Black Hole," Dorfman also acknowledges the Allende movement's blind spots, such as arrogance toward those who disagreed. He exposes the dilemmas that underlie any attempt at fundamental change: If we actually gain power, how should we treat dissenters? How can we respond to ruthless opponents without becoming ruthless ourselves? How do we keep alive the hunger for freedom and justice even when the obstacles seem insurmountable?

Another global phenomenon that affects our sense of the possible is the proliferation of social and cultural distractions, especially in urban industrial countries. Carla Seaquist explores this problem in "Behemoth in a Bathrobe," an imagined dialogue between the still small voice of conscience and an American psyche walled off from reality by an endless barrage of distractions and meaningless preoccupations. If we're willing to turn away, Seaquist suggests, from the siren songs of advertising, material acquisition, and superficial entertainment, we actually stand a better chance of finding genuine fulfillment—and successfully engaging the common challenges of our country. To settle for being passive spectators is to accept things as they are. Acting on our convictions, by contrast, helps broaden the human horizon.

CHAPTER THIRTY-THREE

Kids, Trees, and Climate Change

Mark Hertsgaard

Talk about a problem that tests one's capacity for hope! I've spent much of the past twenty years traveling around the world, investigating maybe the greatest question of our time: Will humanity act quickly and decisively enough to avoid environmental self-destruction? I returned home from my first round of travels in 1997 and wrote a book (*Earth Odyssey*) that tried to provide answers. Since then, I've written two more books and countless articles, and I confess there have been moments when I've doubted our species' long-term prospects.

But in 2005 I became a father, and that fundamentally changed my outlook. The birth of my daughter Chiara awakened a profound instinct to protect her. I remember, not long after she came home from the hospital, cradling her napping body in the crook of my arm and suddenly realizing that I would not hesitate to give my life to save hers if I had to. This instinct arises in most new parents, I think, and gives me fresh hope that the climate crisis can be overcome. In fact, writing my book *HOT* led me to join with others to create the organization Climate Parents. Our goal is to awaken parents to what climate change implies for our beloved children and to mobilize both parents and kids to demand prompt and forceful action to defuse the threat.

Let's be honest: many of us find the climate crisis scary—so scary, we'd rather not think about it. I understand that reaction. No one who has reported and written about climate change for as long as I have, from so many places around the world, could deny that the problem is super-wicked. Nevertheless, I insist upon what I call the imperative of hope. It's what sustains me when things look dark, along with my love for Chiara and my determination that she and her generation will inherit a livable planet.

Chiara was born in San Francisco, but our family spent the first few years of her life in a small coastal town an hour's drive north. It took five minutes to walk from our front door to the beach, fifteen minutes if Chiara toddled along with me. The beach was mainly rocky at our end, covered by shale that trickled down from cliffs that towered fifty to a hundred feet into the air. Low tide exposed a black, slippery reef where Chiara loved to explore tide pools that teemed with mussels, baby crabs, and other aquatic life. At least twice a week she played at this beach or a sandy one in town, where she quickly wiggled out of her shoes and ran off, blond curls blowing in the wind, to splash in the chilly surf and build sandcastles.

Once I asked her what part of the ocean she liked best: The water? The beach? The tide pools? Cocking her head, Chiara looked up at me as if those were pretty silly questions. "All of it, Daddy," she replied. "I like all of it."

Sadly, climate change has now put "all of it" under grave threat. Rising global temperatures are already causing sea levels to rise—so much so that, at present rates, the road connecting our town to the main highway could frequently be underwater by the time Chiara is my age. What's more, carbon dioxide normally remains in the atmosphere for many decades, so unless humans employ methods to extract that CO_2, oceans will continue to warm and expand, causing sea levels to climb for the rest of Chiara's lifetime and beyond. In California, sea levels are projected to rise between 3 and 4.5 feet by 2100, according to a landmark study commissioned by the state government. This outcome would endanger $100 billion worth of property in California alone—for example, putting the airports of San Francisco and Oakland underwater unless protective measures are taken. It would also threaten the dwellings of 480,000 people, many of whom will lack the economic resources to move or protect themselves.

Climate change also profoundly threatens the water supply in Chiara's home state. Rising temperatures will shrink the snow pack atop the Sierra Nevada Mountains that are the source of roughly 40 percent of California's fresh water. That poses difficulties not only for state residents but also for the rest of the United States. California's Central Valley is the source of most of the fruits and vegetables Americans consume, and its agriculture is overwhelmingly dependent on irrigation water from the Sierras.

These and other projected impacts of climate change are more than worrisome—they are so potentially overwhelming that people can feel that it's futile to resist. What difference can one person make against a problem so big and relentless?

Easy as it is to succumb to despair, we can't afford it. Take comfort instead in the imperative of hope, which I define as an active, determined conviction to work for what is right, even in the face of long odds. Sound sentimental? Not really. Hope has triumphed numerous times in recent history: think of the falls of South African apartheid and Soviet totalitarianism in the early 1990s, or the overthrow of tyrants in 2011's Arab Spring. This kind of militant hope is now also indispensable to humanity's chances of creating an environmentally sustainable future.

Let me be clear: hope is not mere trust that everything will be okay despite the dark clouds billowing on the horizon. There must be factual reasons for hope and, above all, concerted efforts made on its behalf. Which is one of the reasons why resisting despair is essential: despair paralyzes us, when what we need to do is take action.

A second reason to resist despair: it is factually incorrect that nothing can be done about climate change. We know perfectly well what needs to be done; the solutions are there for the taking and increasingly they are being grasped. As I describe in my book *HOT*, there are many people, governments, citizen groups, and even businesses that are doing the right things today: quitting coal; making solar and wind the fastest-growing energy sources on Earth; blocking the Keystone XL pipeline; fortifying communities against future storms, droughts, and other impacts of climate change; and much more. If they can do it, so can the rest of us.

Want specifics?

The biggest recent victory against climate change is one that most Americans haven't heard of because the corporate media didn't bother to report it. I'm referring to the de facto moratorium on new coal plants that was put in place during the 2000s. What makes this moratorium important is that coal-fired power plants have long been the source of roughly one-quarter of America's greenhouse gas emissions. The federal government, under the George W. Bush administration, wanted to extend that trajectory by building 150 more coal plants. Instead, by April 2012, a national network of grassroots activists had helped to block 166 proposed plants.

Equally heartening is *how* this victory was won, and where. The vast majority of these proposed coal plants were defeated in the supposedly "red" states of the Midwest and the South—places like Kentucky, South Dakota, and Oklahoma, "not the usual liberal bastions where you'd expect environmental victories," said Mary Ann Hitt, who helped direct this "Beyond Coal" campaign for the Sierra Club. And what turned the tide was the mobilization of ordinary citizens, not the insider lobbying and Big Money pressures that are the coin of the realm in Washington, DC.

The Beyond Coal movement's strength was grounded in the tried-and-true tactics of retail politics: people talking with friends and neighbors, pestering local media, packing regulatory hearings, protesting before state legislatures, filing legal challenges, and more. The movement had no formal membership rolls; it was populated by clean-energy advocates, public health professionals, community organizers, faith leaders, farmers, attorneys, students, and other people like you and me. Besides opposing coal, this movement also championed a positive vision: shifting our energy supply to clean alternatives—solar, wind, and energy efficiency, each of which can employ more workers in better, safer jobs than fossil fuels can, and all of which have been growing dramatically in recent years. Working far from the limelight of the national media, these unheralded activists brought about what's been called "the most significant achievement of American environmentalists since the passage of the Clean Air Act and the Clean Water Act" in the 1970s.

The single most hopeful story I told in *HOT* took place not in the US but overseas. It was in Africa, the continent that scientists say will be the hardest hit by climate change, both because the impacts will be especially severe there and because Africa's people and economies are relatively poor. In the West African nations of Burkina Faso and Mali, I observed a quiet green miracle that convinced me that all is not lost in the climate battle.

The miracle workers were some of the poorest farmers in the world, deploying a weapon often overlooked in wealthier places: trees. Most of these farmers were illiterate and did not know the term "climate change," but they knew what they were experiencing and resolved to take action. I should emphasize that these farmers were not planting trees; they were *growing* them. Planting was impossible: these farmers could not afford to buy seedlings, much less to install the irrigation systems that would have been needed to keep them alive in the face of the region's dry, scorching heat. But an elderly farmer named Yacouba Sawadogo discovered that when he added manure to his fields, small trees began to sprout amid his rows of millet and sorghum. The manure, after all, contained seeds of vegetation that the livestock had eaten. Instead of cutting down the small trees, as farmers had long done, Sawadogo let them grow.

As one season followed another, it became apparent that the growing trees were increasing the yields of millet and sorghum while also restoring the degraded soil's vitality. Mixing trees and crops—a technique specialists call "agro-forestry"—brings a range of benefits. The trees' shade and bulk offer crops relief from the overwhelming heat, not to mention gusting winds that can cover crops with sand. After the trees' leaves fall to the ground, they act as mulch, boosting soil fertility; they also provide fodder for livestock if no other food is available. Perhaps most valuable, the roots of the trees extend downwards into the earth, opening passageways that enable the soil to receive and store what rainfall there is, rather than the rain flashing off of a hardened surface. As a result, underground water tables were rising. Most heartening of all, crop yields had doubled and in some cases even tripled, which led to sizable declines in child malnutrition rates. In Niger alone, farmers have grown an estimated 200 million trees and rehabilitated 12.5 million acres of land—enough that the transformation is visible from outer space on US government satellites.

If some of the poorest people on Earth can achieve so much in the face of climate change, surely those of us who enjoy more comfortable circumstances should be able to do our part, no?

Many of us are. By 2012, solar and wind power were growing so fast worldwide that giant investment banks agreed with environmental activists that clean, renewable energy would displace fossil fuels much sooner than usually thought.

In the US, wind power was the largest source of new electrical generation in 2012. Solar was expanding even faster, thanks to plummeting production costs and innovative financing programs that enabled consumers to put solar on their roofs with no money down, yet lower monthly bills. "Solar is growing so fast it is going to overtake everything," Jon Wellinghoff, the chairman of the US Federal Electricity Regulatory Commission, which oversees the US electricity market, said in August 2013. "It's going to be the dominant player. Everybody's roof is out there."

Meanwhile, Deutsche Bank was projecting much the same for the global market—and saying government subsidies will soon be unnecessary. Within 18 months, said this investment giant, solar would not need subsidies to compete in three-quarters of the world's electricity markets. The industry was climbing the learning curve, driving down costs of solar panels in much the same way computer manufacturers did. "Like Moore's law predicts, every doubling in [production] volume has led to an 18 percent reduction in price," said Danny Kennedy, a former activist who left Greenpeace in 2007 to help found the global solar company Sungevity.

In Germany, which has pledged to leave both fossil fuels and nuclear power behind, "there are now 30 gigawatts of solar on rooftops—that's the equivalent of 30 nuclear power plants," Kennedy added. "There will be another 4 gigawatts by end of this year and another 4 the year after that." In China, renewables will make up more than half of the power capacity added through 2030, when their capacity will equal coal's, projects Bloomberg New Energy Finance. "There is nothing else like these rates of adopting a new technology," Kennedy said. "They're faster than the adoption rates for cell phones."

I could provide many additional examples (you can find some in *HOT*), but the point is that we humans know, or are learning, what it will take to survive and prosper in the face of climate change. If we're smart, we could make restoring the environment the biggest economic enterprise of our time—a huge source of jobs, profits, and the alleviation of poverty.

I have dubbed my proposal to achieve this vision the Global Green Deal. Similar ideas under different names have been proposed by others—including former US Vice President Al Gore and the former chief climate advisor to the German government, Hans Schellenhuber. But the name matters less than the concept: putting people and businesses to work in environmentally healing rather than destructive ways. The idea is to renovate civilization from top to bottom, in rich and poor countries alike. People would remake everything from farms to factories, schools, houses, offices, and everything inside them. The economic activity such environmental renovations would generate is enormous. Better yet, it would be labor-intensive, providing jobs and addressing problems of poverty that are the irreducible other half of our environmental challenge. And it would reinforce the key positive trends that are already happening.

Governments would not have to spend more money, so much as spend it differently. Every year the United States government buys some 56,000 new vehicles for official use. Washington could help bring green cars to market by requiring these cars to be hybrid-electrics or hydrogen-fueled, and produced domestically. We know such government pump-priming works; it's how the computer industry and the Internet went from being government projects in the 1960s to the key engines of the 1990s productivity boom.

In Germany, Chancellor Angela Merkel's conservative government has subsidized energy efficiency investments that were initially devised by the left-of-center Green Party. Not only are they promoting solar adoption, but every year the government has funded the renovation of 5 percent of the nation's pre-1978 housing stock, covering the up-front costs of installing more efficient insulation, heating, and electrical systems. The program is a win-win-win. Residents' energy costs go down, enough to recoup the annual 1.5 billion euros of government subsidies. Greenhouse gas emissions decline. And perhaps most important for a nation struggling with high unemployment rates, the program has generated thousands of jobs for construction workers, jobs that by their nature cannot be sent abroad.

Of course, much more needs to be done. Both the pace and the scope of progress need to accelerate if we are to bring climate change under control and manage now-unavoidable future impacts. So, if you care about climate change, join the movement that's mobilizing against it. You can start by changing your individual consumer choices—taking a bus or biking rather than driving a car; it gives you something concrete to do in your daily life and provides openings to suggest that others do the same. But while individual lifestyle changes can be a good place to begin fighting climate change, they are a poor place to stop. As long as the basic rules of our economy encourage—indeed, subsidize—the overheating of the atmosphere, individual lifestyle changes can never by themselves make a decisive difference.

What's needed is to put a price on carbon emissions. At the moment, there is no cost to emitting greenhouse gases, even though these gases are causing enormous amounts of human suffering and economic deterioration and promise to do much worse in the years to come. We do not allow other polluters to emit deadly chemicals for free; government prohibits the practice outright (as in the case of lead) or imposes monetary penalties. The same should hold true for the greenhouse gases destabilizing our climate.

The trick is to increase the price of carbon but give the money that is raised in the process *back to the public*, rather than letting government keep it. This idea is usually called "cap-and-dividend," because government would raise the price of carbon emissions to a certain cap and then pass the revenues of the increased price on to the general population in the form of a monthly dividend check, similar to the check that every Alaskan has received for the last 30-plus years from the state's oil revenues.

Like a Global Green Deal, cap-and-dividend is in the majority of people's self-interest and thus should attract strong political support. But both of these programs would take billions of dollars away from some of the most powerful interests in the world—above all, the fossil fuel industries. Such fundamental change will happen only if government officials are pushed by intense and sustained public pressure—the same kind of grassroots pressure that has stopped new US coal plants and that citizens have levied to try and stop the Keystone XL pipeline.

In short, politics must be committed. Now, if you're like many Americans, you find politics distasteful, especially electoral politics. Politicians are all the same, goes the argument: you can't trust them; they just do what Big Money tells them; there's no point trying to change this. But not so fast: you may not be interested in politics, but politics is very interested in you. Politics decides whether you or someone you know gets sent overseas to fight a war, often a war related to oil. Politics helps decide what kind of college loans and health coverage are available to you. Politics decides whether climate change will be contained in time to preserve a livable climate on Earth—for Chiara's future and that of all of our children and children yet to come.

As those who've worked for change have taught us, politics can be transformed if enough people make up their minds and commit their lives to doing it. "Change can come fast once the times are right," said former Greenpeace USA executive director John Passacantando. "In 1957, Lyndon Johnson was voting against the Civil Rights Act as the Senate Majority Leader, but by 1965 he was signing that Act as President—not because he had changed, but because the world around him had changed. Now our world is changing. So I do have hope."

Mark Hertsgaard is an independent journalist and author who has published six books in sixteen languages. His most recent titles are *Earth Odyssey: Around the World in Search of Our Environmental Future* (Broadway Books, 1999), *The Eagle's Shadow: Why America Fascinates and Infuriates the World* (Picador USA, 2003), and *HOT: Living Through the Next Fifty Years on Earth* (Houghton Mifflin Harcourt, 2011). Hertsgaard's article on how grassroots citizens have stopped new coal plants can be found at *www.motherjones.com/environment/2012/04/beyond-coal-plant-activism*. See also *www.climateparents.org* for information on Climate Parents and *www.markhertsgaard.com* for information on Mark's other work.

CHAPTER THIRTY-FOUR

Curitiba

Bill McKibben,
with a Postscript by Paul Rogat Loeb

The first time I went there, I had never heard of Curitiba. I had no idea that its bus system was the best on Earth or that a municipal shepherd and his flock of 30 sheep trimmed the grass in its vast parks. It was just a midsize Brazilian city where an airline schedule forced me to spend the night midway through a long South American reporting trip. I reached my hotel, took a nap, and then went out in the early evening for a walk—warily, because I had just come from crime-soaked Rio.

But the street in front of the hotel was cobbled, closed to cars, and strung with lights. It opened onto another such street, which in turn opened into a broad and leafy plaza, with more shop-lined streets stretching off in all directions. Though the night was frosty—Brazil stretches well south of the tropics, and Curitiba is in the mountains—people strolled and shopped, butcher to baker to bookstore. There were almost no cars, but at one of the squares, a steady line of buses rolled off, full, every few seconds. I walked for an hour, and then another. I felt my shoulders, hunched from the tension of Rio (and probably New York as well), straightening. Though I flew out the next day as scheduled, I never forgot the city.

From time to time over the next few years, I would see Curitiba mentioned in planning magazines or come across a short newspaper account of it winning various awards from the United Nations. Its success seemed demographically unlikely. For one thing, it's relatively poor—average per capita (cash) income is about $2,500. Worse, a flood of displaced peasants has tripled its population to a million and a half in the last 25 years. It should resemble a small-scale version of urban nightmares like São Paulo or Mexico City. But I knew from my evening's stroll it wasn't like that, and I wondered why.

Maybe an effort to convince myself that a decay in public life was not inevitable was why I went back to Curitiba to spend some real time, to see if its charms extended beyond the lovely downtown. For a month, my wife and baby and I lived in a small apartment near the city center. Morning after morning I interviewed cops, merchants, urban foresters, civil engineers, novelists, planners; in the afternoons, we pushed the stroller across the town, learning the city's rhythms and habits. And we decided, with great delight, that Curitiba is among the world's great cities.

Not for its physical location; there are no beaches, no broad bridge-spanned rivers. Not in terms of culture or glamour; it's a fairly provincial place. But measured for "livability," I have never been anyplace like it. In a recent survey, 60 percent of New Yorkers wanted to leave their rich and cosmopolitan city; 99 percent of Curitibans told pollsters that they were happy with their town; and 70 percent of the residents of São Paulo said they thought life would be better in Curitiba.

This city has slums: Some of the same shantytown *favelas* that dominate most Third World cities have sprouted on the edge of town as the population has rocketed. But even they are different, hopeful in palpable ways. They are clean, for instance—under a city program, a slum dweller who collects a sack of garbage gets a sack of food from the city in return. And Curitiba is the classic example of decent lives helping produce a decent environment. Because of its fine transit system, and because its inhabitants are attracted toward the city center instead of repelled out to a sprawl of suburbs, Curitibans use 25 percent less fuel per capita than other Brazilians, even though they are actually more likely to own cars.

Curitiba started out as a backwater town, a good stopover on the way to São Paulo. By 1940, there were 125,000 residents. By 1950, the number had jumped to 180,000, and by 1960, doubled to 361,000—the explosive, confident growth that marked the entire country was under way in Curitiba as well. And with many of the same effects: Traffic downtown started to snarl, and the air was growing thick with exhaust. It was clear that the time had come to plan, and, as in almost every other city, planning meant planning for automobiles.

The official scheme called for widening the main streets of the city to add more lanes—which would have meant knocking down the turn-of-the-century buildings that lined the downtown—and for building an overpass that would link two of the city's main squares by going over the top of Rua Quinze de Novembro, the main shopping street. But resistance to the plan was unexpectedly fierce. Opposition was centered in the architecture and planning departments of the local branch of the federal university, and the loudest voice belonged to Jaime Lerner.

Jaime Lerner is a chubby man with a large, friendly, and open face. He looks like Norm, the guy at the end of the bar in *Cheers*. He also looks silly stuffed into a suit; so even though he's been mayor of Curitiba on and off for the last two decades, he normally wears a polo shirt. In the late 1960s, however, he was just a young planner and architect who had grown up in the city, working in his Polish father's dry goods store. And he organized the drive against the overpass, out of what might almost be called nostalgia. "They were trying to throw away the story of the city," he recalls.

It was a good thing that Jaime Lerner had grown up loving the mix of people in Curitiba. Because through a chain of political flukes, Lerner found himself the mayor of Curitiba at the age of 33. All of a sudden, his friends and colleagues were pulling their plans out of the cupboards. All of a sudden, they were going to get their chance to remake Curitiba—not for cars, but for people.

And so the story of Curitiba begins with its central street, Rua Quinze—the one that the old plan wanted to obliterate with an overpass. Lerner insisted instead that it should become a pedestrian mall, an emblem of his drive for a human-scale city. "I knew we'd have a big fight," he says. "I had no way to convince the store owners a pedestrian mall would be good for them, because there was no other pedestrian mall in Brazil. But I knew if they had a chance to actually see it, everyone would love it."

To prevent opposition, he planned carefully. "I told my staff, 'This is like war.' My secretary of public works said the job would take two months. I got him down to one month. Maybe one week, he said, but that's final. I said, 'Let's start Friday night, and we have to finish by Monday morning.'" And they did—jackhammering the pavement, putting down cobblestones, erecting streetlights and kiosks, and putting in tens of thousands of flowers.

"It was a horrible risk—he could easily have been fired," said Oswaldo Alves, who helped with the work. But by midday Monday, the same storeowners who had been threatening legal action were petitioning the mayor to extend the mall. The next weekend, when offended members of the local automobile club threatened to "reclaim" the street by driving their cars down it, Lerner didn't call out the police. Instead, he had city workers lay down strips of paper the length of the mall. When the auto club arrived, its members found dozens of children sitting in the former street painting pictures. The transformation of Curitiba had begun.

Cheapness is one of the three cardinal dictates of Curitiban planning. Many of the city's buildings are "recycled." The planning headquarters is in an old furniture factory; the gunpowder depot became a furniture factory; a glue plant was turned into the children's center. An old trolley stationed on the Rua Quinze has become a free babysitting center where shoppers can park their kids for a few hours. The city's parks provide the best example of brilliance on the cheap. When Lerner took office for the first time in 1971, the only park in Curitiba was smack downtown—the Passeio Publico, a cozy zoo and playground with a moat for paddleboats and a canopy of old and beautiful ipé trees, which blossom blue in the spring. "In that first term, we wanted to develop a lot of squares and plazas," recalls Alves. "We picked one plot, we built a lot of walls, and we planted a lot of trees. And then we realized this was very expensive."

At the same time, as luck would have it, most Brazilian cities were installing elaborate flood-control projects. Curitiba had federal money to "channelize" the five rivers flowing through town, putting them in concrete viaducts so that they wouldn't flood the city with every heavy summer rain and endanger the buildings starting to spring up in the floodplain.

"The bankers wanted all the rivers enclosed," says Alves; instead, city hall took the same loan and spent it—on land. At a number of sites throughout the city, engineers built small dams and backed up the rivers into lakes. Each of these became the center of a park; and if the rains were heavy, the lake might rise a foot or two—perhaps the jogging track would get a little soggy or the duck in the big new zoo would find itself swimming a few feet higher than usual. "Every river has a right to overflow," insists parks chief Nicolau Klupel.

Mostly because of its flood-control scheme, in 20 years—even as it tripled in population—the city went from 2 square feet of green area per inhabitant to more than 150 square feet per inhabitant. From every single window in Curitiba, I could see as much green as I could concrete. And green begets green; land values around the new parks have risen sharply, and with them tax revenues.

Though the population continues to grow steadily, it's indeed possible that Curitiba may have broken the back of its social problems. Since many of the people in the *favelas* have been evicted from their homes in the countryside, a house is an urgent need. Not just a shelter—a house they own, on a lot they own.

Until the mid-1980s, COHAB, Curitiba's public housing program, was fairly standard. It built more units per capita than any other Brazilian city and did a good job of scattering them around in small pockets so they blended in with neighborhoods. But the main source of funding, the national housing bank, collapsed in 1985. At the same time, the demand for housing skyrocketed as the countryside poured into the *favelas*. Abandoning the policy of small scattered sites, the city bought one of the few large plots of land left within its limits, a swath of farmland bounded by several rivers called Novo Bairro, or New Neighborhood.

We stood on a rise in Novo Bairro and watched as bulldozers scraped and contoured the hills. This cleared field would soon be home to 50,000 families, perhaps 200,000 people. Small houses crept like a tidemark across the land. The city was not building the homes—the new landowners were, sometimes with the aid of a city mortgage on a small pile of bricks and windows. Every third house seemed to be doubling as a building supply store; and everywhere, people plastered, framed, roofed.

"Sixty percent of the lower-income people are involved in the construction industry anyhow," says one COHAB executive. "They know how to build." And here is the moving part: With your plot of land comes not only a deed and a pair of trees (one fruit bearing and one ornamental), but also an hour downtown with an architect. "The person explains what's important to him—a big window out front, or room in the kitchen. They tell how many kids they have, and so on. And then we help draw up a plan," says one architect, who has more than 3,000 of "his" homes scattered around the city.

"Most people can only afford to build one room at a time, so we also show them the logical order to go in," another designer explains.

At the moment, in the center of Novo Bairro, COHAB is building "Technology Street," an avenue of twenty-four homes, each built using some different construction technique—bamboo covered with plaster, say—so that people can get ideas for the kind of house they might want. The houses are all smaller than most Americans would want to live in, but they all say something about the people who built them. “It’s a house built out of love,” says the housing chief. “And because of that, people won’t leave it behind. They’re going to consolidate their lives there, become part of the city.”

One of the first structures to go up at Novo Bairro was a glass tube bus station, linking this enclave to the rest of the city. “Integration” is a word one hears constantly from official Curitiba, another of its mantras. It means knitting together the entire city—rich, poor, and in-between—culturally and economically and physically. Hitoshi Nakamura is the city parks commissioner and one of Lerner’s longtime collaborators. “We have to have communication with the people of the slums,” he said one day as we were talking about the problems posed by settlers invading fragile bottomlands along the rivers. “If we don’t, if they start to feel like *favelados* [slumdwellers], then they will go against the city. . . . If we give them attention, they don’t feel abandoned. They feel like citizens.”

To learn from Curitiba, the rest of the world would have to break some longstanding habits. And the hardest habit to break, in fact, may be what Lerner calls the “syndrome of tragedy, of feeling like we’re terminal patients.” Many cities have “a lot of people who are specialists in proving change is not possible. What I try to explain to them when I go visit is that it takes the same energy to say why something can’t be done as to figure out how to do it.”

Bill McKibben is the founder of the climate-change action network *www.350.org*. His books include *Hope, Human and Wild* (Milkweed Editions, 2007), from which this essay was adapted; *Deep Economy* (St. Martin’s Griffin, 2008); *Eaarth: Making a Life on a Tough New Planet* (St. Martin’s Griffin, 2011); *The Global Warming Reader: A Century of Writing About Climate Change* (Penguin, 2012); and *Oil and Honey: The Education of an Unlikely Activist* (Times Books, 2013). This essay was also excerpted in *Yes* magazine (*www.yesmagazine.org*).

Postscript: Curitiba Revisited

Paul Rogat Loeb

Inspired by Bill McKibben's description, I visited Curitiba in 2010. Sixteen years after McKibben's extended visit, the metro area had almost doubled again, to 3.2 million people. It had also become more affluent, with a thirty-year economic growth rate nearly twice as high as that of the rest of Brazil. One hundred and fifty cities worldwide had adapted its model of Bus Rapid Transit, including Bogota, Jakarta, Guangzhou, Istanbul, Johannesburg, Los Angeles, and Cleveland.

Curitiba's express buses still move nearly as fast as subways, and at a fraction of the cost. As the city has expanded, the biggest transportation challenge has been incorporating more distant, sparsely populated, and generally poorer suburbs. But Curitiba has managed the problem while keeping the transit system affordable, and without any public subsidies until a 2008 rise in fuel prices. Local buses feed into the express routes, with their trademark transparent boarding tubes. Encouraged by zoning laws, high-rise apartment buildings line the new transit corridors, while the municipality offers health, education, and recreational services at transit hubs, supporting local businesses and walking neighborhoods. Because of its increasing affluence, Curitiba now has more cars per capita than any other major Brazilian city (1 per 1.6 inhabitants, running primarily on sugar cane–based ethanol blends). But most are reserved for recreation or errands, and the bus system carries 2.3 million people each day.

The city's recycling program is also a global model. Costumed characters from the environmental ministry visit schools so that children can teach their families how to separate compostable organic materials from everything else, and "garbage that is not garbage" from trash. Builders re-use wooden beams and ironwork and embed old bricks in concrete. Collectors with pull carts pick up recyclables, complementing the main city trucks. In the poorest communities, where trucks can't traverse the narrowest streets, the city continues to underwrite the exchange of bags of garbage and recyclables for transit tokens or fresh vegetables and fruit. At hangar-size sorting facilities, previously unemployed workers wear protective gloves and breathing masks while filling hundreds of bins and dumpsters with glass bottles, plastic containers, computer keyboards, disassembled metal office desks, and the frames and legs of baby strollers. High piles of cardboard and newspapers sit next to bundled plastic bags that will become plastic fence posts. The city supplies technical consulting and social services. Purchases by nearby companies, including a major paper plant that no longer uses virgin wood pulp, pay for the collection and sorting process. The prime municipal landfill was projected to become full by the mid-1990s, but it lasted more than twenty additional years.

The most striking shift has been the continued growth of green spaces, transforming Curitiba from a city of concrete to one where these spaces constitute nearly a fifth of the land. Curitibans still pack the Passeio Publico, watching toucans preen themselves and monkeys swing from trees. But the park is now complemented by thirty-five others, most located either on flood plains or on various former eyesores. At one, ponds and bridges connect two former quarries, while people look down from a high covered overlook. At another, hundred-pound capybaras graze on an island in the middle of a pond. Other parks include heavy-duty outdoor exercise equipment and buildings honoring local ethnic groups like the Poles, Germans, and Ukrainians. Especially on weekends and after work, city residents fill the parks and the equally crowded pedestrian streets and squares. On a weekend Sunday during my stay, the Botanical Garden, a former refuse dump, was packed with people walking, picnicking, kissing (including gay couples), and taking cell-phone pictures of their friends.

Together, these amenities have transformed a once more reticent and private culture in which people socialized mostly at home. At the end of our visit, my wife and I stayed with a couple who'd grown up in the city, Cesar and Marcia. Cesar ran an import/export business, targeting areas where the country had shortages like specialized printing cartridges. Marcia worked as a teacher. They'd lived in Curitiba all their lives, though Cesar had traveled widely abroad. He talked about how the city had changed. "When I grew up here," Cesar said, "this was not that agreeable a city. People lived here. People worked. But it was all concrete and stone, no parks, nothing green. It was not that agreeable. Now it is."

CHAPTER THIRTY-FIVE

Come September

Arundhati Roy

The theme of much of what I write, fiction as well as nonfiction, is the relationship between power and powerlessness and the endless, circular conflict they're engaged in. John Berger, that most wonderful writer, once wrote: "Never again will a single story be told as though it's the only one." There can never be a single story. There are only ways of seeing. So when I tell a story, I tell it not as an ideologue who wants to pit one absolutist ideology against another, but as a storyteller who wants to share her way of seeing. Though it might appear otherwise, my writing is not really about nations and histories; it's about power. About the paranoia and ruthlessness of power. About the physics of power. I believe that the accumulation of vast unfettered power by a State or a country, a corporation or an institution—or even an individual, a spouse, a friend, a sibling—regardless of ideology, results in excesses such as the ones I will recount here.

Living as I do, as millions of us do, in the shadow of the nuclear holocaust that the governments of India and Pakistan keep promising their brainwashed citizenry, and in the global neighborhood of the War Against Terror (what President Bush rather biblically called "The Task That Never Ends"), I find myself thinking a great deal about the relationship between Citizens and the State.

In India, those of us who have expressed views on Nuclear Bombs, Big Dams, Corporate Globalization, and the rising threat of communal Hindu fascism—views that are at variance with the Indian government's—are branded "anti-national." While this accusation doesn't fill me with indignation, it's not an accurate description of what I do or how I think. Because an "anti-national" is a person who is against his or her own nation and, by inference, is pro some other one. But it isn't necessary to be "anti-national" to be deeply suspicious of all nationalism, to be anti-nationalism. Nationalism of one kind or another was the cause of most of the genocide of the twentieth century. Flags are bits of colored cloth that governments use first to shrink-wrap people's brains and then as ceremonial shrouds to bury the dead.

The term "anti-American" is usually used by the American establishment to discredit and, not falsely—but shall we say inaccurately—define its critics. Once someone is branded anti-American, the chances are that he or she will be judged before they are heard, and the argument will be lost in the welter of bruised national pride.

But what does the term "anti-American" mean? Does it mean you are anti-jazz? Or that you're opposed to freedom of speech? That you don't delight in Toni Morrison or John Updike? That you have a quarrel with giant sequoias? Does it mean that you don't admire the hundreds of thousands of American citizens who marched against nuclear weapons, or the thousands of war resisters who forced their government to withdraw from Vietnam? Does it mean that you hate all Americans?

This sly conflation of America's culture, music, literature, the breathtaking physical beauty of the land, the ordinary pleasures of ordinary people with criticism of the US government's foreign policy (about which, thanks to America's "free press," sadly most Americans know very little) is a deliberate and extremely effective strategy. It's like a retreating army taking cover in a heavily populated city, hoping that the prospect of hitting civilian targets will deter enemy fire. But there are many Americans who would be mortified to be associated with their government's policies. The most scholarly, scathing, incisive, hilarious critiques of the hypocrisy and the contradictions in US government policy come from American citizens.

Similarly, in India, not hundreds, but millions of us would be ashamed and offended if we were in any way implicated with the present Indian government's policies which, apart from the perpetration of State terrorism in the valley of Kashmir (in the name of fighting terrorism), have also turned a blind eye to the recent state-supervised pogrom against Muslims in Gujarat. It would be absurd to think that those who criticize the Indian government are "anti-Indian"—although the government itself never hesitates to take that line.

It is dangerous to cede to the Indian government or the American government, or *anyone* for that matter, the right to define what "India" or "America" is or ought to be.

To call someone "anti-American," indeed to *be* anti-American (or for that matter, anti-Indian or anti-Timbuktuan), is not just racist, it's a failure of the imagination. An inability to see the world in terms other than those the establishment has set out for you. If you're not a Bushie, you're a Taliban. If you don't love us, you hate us. If you're not Good, you're Evil. If you're not with us, you're with the terrorists.

None of us need anniversaries to remind us of what we cannot forget. So it's no more than coincidence that I happen to be here, on American soil, in September—this month of dreadful anniversaries. Uppermost on everybody's mind of course, particularly here in America, is the horror of what has come to be known as 9/11. Nearly 3,000 civilians lost their lives in that lethal terrorist strike. The grief is still deep. The rage still sharp. The tears have not dried. And a strange, deadly war is raging around the world. Yet, each person who has lost a loved one surely knows secretly, deeply, that no war, no act of revenge, no daisy-cutters dropped on someone else's loved ones or someone else's children, will blunt the edges of their pain or bring their own loved ones back. War cannot avenge those who have died.

War is only a brutal desecration of their memory.

To fuel yet another war—most recently against Iraq—by cynically manipulating people's grief, by packaging it for TV specials sponsored by corporations selling detergent and running shoes, is to cheapen and devalue grief, to drain it of meaning. What we are seeing now is a vulgar display of the *business* of grief, the commerce of grief, the pillaging of even the most private human feelings for political purpose. It is a terrible, violent thing for a State to do to its people.

It's not a clever enough subject to speak of from a public platform, but what I would really love to talk to you about is Loss. Loss and losing. Grief, failure, brokenness, numbness, uncertainty, fear, the death of feeling, the death of dreaming. The absolute relentless, endless, habitual unfairness of the world. What does loss mean to individuals? What does it mean to whole cultures, whole people who have learned to live with it as a constant companion?

Since it is September 11 we're talking about, perhaps it's in the fitness of things that we remember what that date means, not only to those who lost their loved ones in America last year, but to those in other parts of the world to whom that date has long held significance. This historical dredging is not offered as an accusation or a provocation. But just to share the grief of history. To thin the mists a little. To say to the citizens of America, in the gentlest, most human way: "Welcome to the World."

In Chile, on September 11, 1973, General Pinochet overthrew the democratically elected government of Salvador Allende in a CIA-backed coup. "Chile should not be allowed to go Marxist just because its people are irresponsible," said Henry Kissinger, Nobel Peace Laureate, then the US secretary of state.

After the coup, President Allende was found dead inside the presidential palace. Whether he was killed or whether he killed himself, we'll never know. In the regime of terror that ensued, thousands of people were killed. Many more simply "disappeared." Firing squads conducted public executions. Concentration camps and torture chambers were opened across the country. The dead were buried in mine shafts and unmarked graves.

In 1999, following the arrest of General Pinochet in Britain, thousands of secret documents were declassified by the US government. They contain unequivocal evidence of the CIA's involvement in the coup as well as the fact that the US government had detailed information about the situation in Chile during General Pinochet's reign. Yet Kissinger had assured the general of his support: "In the United States as you know, we are sympathetic to what you're trying to do," he said. "We wish your government well."

Sadly, Chile was not the only country in South America to be singled out for the US government's attentions. Guatemala, Costa Rica, Ecuador, Brazil, Peru, the Dominican Republic, Bolivia, Nicaragua, Honduras, Panama, El Salvador, Mexico, and Colombia—they've all been the playground for covert (and overt) operations by the CIA. Hundreds of thousands of Latin Americans have been killed or tortured or have simply disappeared under the despotic regimes that were propped up in their countries. If this were not humiliation enough, the people of South America have had to bear the cross of being branded as people who are incapable of democracy—as if coups and massacres are somehow encrypted in their genes.

This list does not, of course, include countries in Africa or Asia that suffered US military interventions—the Congo, Vietnam, Korea, Indonesia, Laos, and Cambodia.

September 11 has a tragic resonance in the Middle East, too. On September 11, 1922, ignoring Arab outrage, the British government proclaimed a mandate in Palestine, a follow-up to the 1917 Balfour Declaration which imperial Britain issued, with its army massed outside the gates of Gaza. The Balfour Declaration promised European Zionists a national home for the Jewish people.

In 1937, Winston Churchill said of the Palestinians, I quote, "I do not agree that the dog in a manger has the final right to the manger even though he may have lain there for a very long time. I do not admit that right. I do not admit, for instance, that a great wrong has been done to the red Indians of America or the black people of Australia. I do not admit that a wrong has been done to these people by the fact that a stronger race, a higher-grade race, a more worldly wise race, to put it that way, has come in and taken their place." That set the trend for the Israeli State's attitude toward the Palestinians. In 1969, Israeli Prime Minister Golda Meir said, "Palestinians do not exist." Her successor, Prime Minister Levi Eschol, said, "What are Palestinians? When I came here (to Palestine), there were 250,000 non-Jews, mainly Arabs and Bedouins. It was a desert, more than underdeveloped. Nothing." Prime Minister Menachem Begin called Palestinians "two-legged beasts." Prime Minister Yitzhak Shamir called them "grasshoppers" who could be crushed. This is the language of Heads of State, not the words of ordinary people.

Over the decades there have been uprisings, wars, intifadas. Tens of thousands have lost their lives. Accords and treaties have been signed. Ceasefires declared and violated. But the bloodshed doesn't end. Palestine still remains illegally occupied. Its people live in inhuman conditions, in virtual Bantustans, where they are subjected to collective punishments, twenty-four-hour curfews, where they are humiliated and brutalized on a daily basis.

Young Palestinians who cannot control their anger turn themselves into human bombs and haunt Israel's streets and public places, blowing themselves up, killing ordinary people, injecting terror into daily life, and eventually hardening both societies' suspicion and mutual hatred of each other. Each bombing invites merciless reprisal and even more hardship on Palestinian people. But then suicide bombing is an act of individual despair, not a revolutionary tactic. Although Palestinian attacks strike terror into Israeli citizens, they provide the perfect cover for the Israeli government's daily incursions into Palestinian territory.

What lessons should we draw from this tragic conflict? Is it really impossible for Jewish people who suffered so cruelly themselves—more cruelly perhaps than any other people in history—to understand the vulnerability and the yearning of those whom they have displaced? Does extreme suffering always kindle cruelty? What hope does this leave the human race with? What will happen to the Palestinian people in the event of a victory? When a nation without a state eventually proclaims a state, what kind of state will it be? What horrors will be perpetrated under its flag? Is it a separate state that we should be fighting for, or the rights to a life of liberty and dignity for everyone regardless of their ethnicity or religion?

In another part of the Middle East, September 11 strikes a more recent chord. It was on September 11, 1990, that George Bush, Sr., then president of the United States, made a speech to a joint session of Congress announcing his government's decision to go to war against Iraq.

The US government said that Saddam Hussein was a war criminal, a cruel military despot who has committed genocide against his own people. That was a fairly accurate description of the man. In 1988, Saddam Hussein razed hundreds of villages in northern Iraq, used chemical weapons and machine guns to kill thousands of Kurdish people. Today we know that that same year the US government provided him with $500 million in subsidies to buy American farm products. The next year, after he had successfully completed his genocidal campaign, the US government doubled its subsidy to $1 billion. It also provided him with high-quality germ seed for anthrax, and helicopters and dual-use material that could be used to manufacture chemical and biological weapons. So it turns out that while Saddam Hussein was carrying out his worst atrocities, the US and the UK governments were his close allies.

So what changed? In 1990, Saddam Hussein invaded Kuwait. His sin was not so much that he had committed an act of war, but that he had acted independently, without orders from his master.

Recently the United States played an important part in forcing India and Pakistan back from the brink of war. Is it so hard for it to take its own advice? Who is guilty of feckless moralizing? Of preaching peace while it wages war? The United States, which George W. Bush has called "the most peaceful nation on Earth," has been at war with one country or another every year for the last fifty.

Wars are never fought for altruistic reasons. They're usually fought for hegemony, for business. And then of course there's the business of war.

Nobody puts it more elegantly than the *New York Times* columnist, Thomas Friedman. In an article called "Craziness Pays," he said, "The US has to make it clear to Iraq and US allies that . . . America will use force without negotiation, hesitation or UN approval." His advice was well taken—in the wars against Iraq and Afghanistan as well as in the almost daily humiliation the US government heaps on the UN. In his book on globalization, *The Lexus and the Olive Tree*, Friedman says, and I quote, "The hidden hand of the market will never work without the hidden fist. McDonald's cannot flourish without McDonnell Douglas . . . and the hidden fist that keeps the world safe for Silicon Valley's technologies to flourish is called the US Army, Air Force, Navy, and Marine Corps." Perhaps this was written in a moment of vulnerability, but it's certainly the most succinct, accurate description of the project of corporate globalization that I have read.

In the last ten years of unbridled Corporate Globalization, the world's total income has increased by an average of 2.5 percent a year. And yet the numbers of poor in the world have increased by 100 million. Of the top hundred biggest economies, fifty-one are corporations, not countries. The top 1 percent of the world has the same combined income as the bottom 57 percent and that disparity is growing. And now, under the spreading canopy of the War Against Terror, this process is being hustled along.

The men in suits are in an unseemly hurry. While bombs rain down on us, and cruise missiles skid across the skies, while nuclear weapons are stockpiled to make the world a safer place, contracts are being signed, patents are being registered, oil pipelines are being laid, natural resources are being plundered, water is being privatized, and democracies are being undermined.

There is a notion gaining credence that the Free Market breaks down national barriers, and that Corporate Globalization's ultimate destination is a hippie paradise where the heart is the only passport and we all live happily together inside a John Lennon song. ("Imagine there's no country. . . . ") But this is a canard.

What the Free Market undermines is not national sovereignty, but democracy. As the disparity between the rich and poor grows, the hidden fist has its work cut out for it. Multinational corporations on the prowl for "sweetheart deals" that yield enormous profits cannot push through those deals and administer those projects in developing countries without the active connivance of State machinery—the police, the courts, sometimes even the army. Today Corporate Globalization needs an international confederation of loyal, corrupt, preferably authoritarian governments in poorer countries to push through unpopular reforms and quell the mutinies. It needs a press that pretends to be free. It needs courts that pretend to dispense justice. It needs nuclear bombs, standing armies, sterner immigration laws, and watchful coastal patrols to make sure that it's only money, goods, patents, and services that are being globalized—not the free movement of people, not a respect for human rights, not international treaties on racial discrimination or chemical and nuclear weapons, or greenhouse gas emissions, climate change, or, God forbid, justice. It's as though even a gesture toward international accountability would wreck the whole enterprise.

Meanwhile, down at the mall there's a mid-season sale. Everything's discounted—oceans, rivers, oil, gene pools, fig wasps, flowers, childhoods, aluminum factories, phone companies, wisdom, wilderness, civil rights, ecosystems, air—all 4,600 million years of evolution. It's packed, sealed, tagged, valued, and available off the rack. (No returns.) As for justice—I'm told it's on offer, too. You can get the best that money can buy.

But fortunately, power has a shelf life. When the time comes, maybe this mighty empire will, like others before it, overreach itself and implode from within. It looks as though structural cracks have already appeared. As the War Against Terror casts its net wider and wider, America's corporate heart is hemorrhaging.

Soviet-style communism failed, not because it was intrinsically evil but because it was flawed. It allowed too few people to usurp too much power. Twenty-first-century market-capitalism, American style, will fail for the same reasons. Both are edifices constructed by the human intelligence, undone by human nature.

The time has come, the Walrus said. Perhaps things will become worse and then better. Perhaps there's a small god up in heaven readying herself for us. Another world is not only possible, she's on her way. Maybe many of us won't be here to greet her, but on a quiet day, if I listen very carefully, I can hear her breathing.

Excerpted from a longer version of this essay in *War Talk* (South End Press, 2003), based on a Lannan Foundation reading. Arundhati Roy's other books include *Power Politics* (South End Press, 2001); *The God of Small Things* (Random House, 2008), which won the Booker Prize; *Field Notes on Democracy* (Haymarket Books, 2009); *Walking with the Comrades* (Penguin, 2011); and *The Folded Earth* (Free Press, 2012).

CHAPTER THIRTY-SIX

The Black Hole

Ariel Dorfman

This is the bedrock of who I am: a man who cannot live in this world unless he believes there is hope.

In front of me as I write is a photograph of the balcony of the palace of La Moneda in Santiago, snapped on November 4, 1970, the day Salvador Allende was inaugurated President of the Republic. In that photo, he waves a handkerchief from the balcony, greeting an unseen crowd that is gathered in the plaza below him.

Next to that photo I have hung another one, of the same balcony, almost three years later, a few days after the Hawker Hunter planes under the control of General Pinochet attacked the palace on September 11, 1973. Their bombs left a black yawning gap where the balcony stood. Where the president once waved his handkerchief, there is nothing. Allende is dead. And we can sense that outside the frame, below where the balcony jutted out, there is only emptiness, that only the cold, implacable solitary lens of the camera witnesses the scene. Nothing else. All too soon, I will be forced to face the black hole of that photo.

For now, I want to return to the day when that balcony was as intact as our dreams, when these eyes of mine and all the thousands of other eyes in the crowd did not have an inkling of the destruction that awaited us. There was no room for absurd premonitions: This was a turning point in history, the first peaceful, democratic revolution the world had ever known. Who could stop us? Who would dare to even try?

It was then, in the midst of that multitude of men and women I had never met and did not know, it was then, as I breathed in the air that they were breathing out, that I had an experience which I hesitate to call mystical but which was as near to a religious epiphany as I have had in my life.

Allende was making a brief speech, something about how we were now going to be the masters of our own destiny, the owners of our own land and the metals under the ground and the streets we walked through, how we would have to fight for the possession of everything in Chile, from the state to the city to the fields, how this country belonged to the people who had suffered in it, something like that. At some point during that speech I stopped listening and let my eyes wander over the crowd, thousands and thousands of hopeful faces as far as I could see.

Since their birth, those men and women had been told the limits they could not cross, the questions they could not ask. They had been told that their failure in life was deserved, that the very fact that they had not found a way out of their destitution proved that they deserved it, that they were by nature subhuman, incompetent, inferior, worthless, lazy, all their lives treated like something disposable and defective, all their lives taught to bow their heads and lower their eyes so as to survive, warned to obey or else, the doctrine of submission drilled into every nerve of their bodies, taught that the only road out of their misery was individual and solitary, each person scratching his way to the top, where, if he was lucky or ruthless enough, he could then become the exploiter of his brothers.

Above all, they had been warned that any collective attempt to change their lot was doomed to failure and pain. And they had defied that warning, they were about to break out of the script dreamt for them, they were about to start telling their own stories in their own way after having lived endlessly under the shadow of somebody else's story. And if they could do it, so could I, and then it was as if I had stepped out of that space and inhabited some other zone where I could watch myself and the multitude as well, suddenly all the voices went silent and in the silence I felt reality begin to crack open under my feet, as if a real, physical crack had opened in the very architecture of the universe, and that was when, peering into the crack that my own life had become, immensely vulnerable and open, I felt life quicken and accelerate, I felt the giddiness of those few great moments in your existence when you know that everything is possible, that anything is possible.

I felt as if I were the first man on Earth and this was the first day in history and the world was about to begin in all its beauty and that all it would take to give birth to that beauty which was just within our reach was to dare to invent it, dare to name it.

It was a magnificent vision and I kept it inside me all during the Chilean revolution; it was so intense that even now, more than forty years later, I am able to commune with it. Everything was new and crying out to be written. I shared a glorious language with the people who were writing the text of reality itself and I wanted to put every last word of it down on paper. I wrote essays and screenplays and poems and magazine articles and television programs and pamphlets and newspaper ads and radio jingles and political slogans and propaganda tracts and an experimental novel and cultural policy reports and political diatribes and songs and plays, all of them juxtaposed, all of them given equal attention in my life.

A typical day might see me rise at dawn and frenetically type a surrealistic short story, take my son Rodrigo to school, teach a class at the university, burst into my office to scribble part of an essay at noon, then lunch with the producer of a quiz show for adolescents I was hosting on TV, rush off to a powdered-milk factory whose workers had called for volunteers to help load and unload trucks, run back all sweaty to the center of town to collaborate with some writers who were issuing a cultural manifesto, talk over the phone with a colleague at the university about the possibility of our Spanish Department joining forces with a trade union to launch a poetry festival, and then, as the afternoon began to wane, meet with a Socialist Party committee that was deciding what political slogan we would issue, to be painted by the brigades, and then that night, after a quick dinner with my wife Angélica, who had been through an equally hectic schedule, and after a goodnight story to my son, my wife and I would join our group of comrades to splash the walls of the city with the very message I myself had conjured up a few hours before. And then, if there was time and energy—and there was, there always was—off we'd go to somebody's house to dance and drink and celebrate the fact that we were alive.

When General Pinochet stopped the revolution in its tracks, I was lucky enough to be expelled and not executed or held endlessly in jail. Next to me in the police van taking me to the airport was a worker. I will call him Juan.

He was one of the scant handful of workers who, like me, had sought refuge in the Argentine Embassy to save his life. We had struck up a conversation several times. He had worked, he told me, in a factory that produced canned food and when Allende's Unidad Popular coalition had come, he and his fellows had found themselves facing a major crisis. During Allende's first year in office, the president's policies had created an economic boom: Increased salaries and benefits led to skyrocketing consumption and that led, in turn, to a major increment in production. So, more goods sold and a better life for Juan and his co-workers, right?

Not at all. The owner of the factory, opposed to Allende's government, even if it did not threaten his property, had decided to sabotage production: He had stopped reordering machine parts, he had blocked distribution deals that were already in place, he refused to hire new workers and threatened to fire those who complained. He should have been making money in buckets and instead was secretly preparing bankruptcy proceedings, pulling his capital out of the industry, getting ready to flee the country. The workers had watched this class warfare patiently for months and, finally, when the owner had announced he was shutting down the whole operation, they had taken over the premises. It was the only way to save their jobs and keep producing the food that Chile needed.

Allende's government intervened in the conflict, negotiated compensation for the owner, and put the workers in control.

Juan had been elected to head the council that, for a couple of years, ran that factory, and in spite of inevitable mistakes, it had been an economically successful venture.

But it was another kind of success that stirred in Juan when he spoke to me about that time: The Chilean revolution had given him a chance to prove his dignity as a full human being, had dared to conceive through him and millions of others the pale possibility of a world where things did not have to be the way they had always been. That is why the rulers of the world had reacted with such ferocity. And Juan understood this and explained it to me with chilling simplicity that day as we crossed the city of Santiago on our way to exile.

"We are paying," he told me, gesturing toward the streets filled with subdued citizens and rampant military patrols, in the general direction of the factory that was at that very moment being returned to the owner, who had come back to exercise his dominion. "We are being punished. We are paying for our joy."

He understood that General Pinochet's military coup was meant to return to their previous owners the levers of economic and political power. But it was just as clear to him that the counterrevolution was conceived as an admonitory lesson for those who had surfaced from the depths of anonymity and set themselves squarely in the middle of a history which was not supposed to belong to them.

His body and the body of all our compañeros were, ultimately, being disciplined for an act of the imagination. Pinochet was trying to make him and millions like him admit that they had been mistaken—not so much in their tactics as in their human strategy, the very rebellion itself, the fact that they had dared to dream of an alternative to the life charted out for them since before their birth.

Pinochet was preparing the world as we know it now, where the word *revolution* has been relegated to ads for jogging shoes and greed has been proclaimed as good and profits have become the only basis to judge value and cynicism is the prevailing attitude and amnesia is vaunted and justified as the solution to all the pain of the past.

The emptiness of the La Moneda balcony drilled itself into me as we passed through the plaza and turned the corner, and then it was gone from view, it was behind us, out of sight, but I could feel it growing inside me, its darkness threatening to engulf me in its void, to erase us all forever from the memory of Chile just as it had extirpated the presence of Allende, left nothing of that day when he had stood there defiantly, inaugurating the future. I fought back against the black hole that was sucking me into despair, I told myself that I would keep alive that other balcony, that if we could keep it fiercely alive and warm inside during the years to come, we would be able to return Chile to all its glory, we could ourselves return to the country we would resurrect.

But first I had to face the most painful political question of my life. If the past under Allende was so luminous and promising and participatory, how is it that it became the black hole of the present? How could we have been so wrong that day we started our revolution, how could we have been so blind not only to the impending disaster but also to the mistakes we made which, all that time, were paving the way for that disaster?

It was not a question that would go away; it demanded a collective answer from all Chileans who had supported Allende as well as an individual answer from each of us. That black hole devouring us would not disappear by stubbornly and nostalgically reiterating and validating the past, because that past was responsible for this future we were living, and until we recognized that responsibility, our responsibility in the catastrophe, there would be no change. We could blame the CIA, the United States, the oligarchy, and the military all we wanted, but they would never have prevailed if we had been able to get the majority of Chileans behind our reforms. That had not been the case, however, and unless we now built the vast coalition that we had failed to build during the Allende years we would never rid ourselves of Pinochet; he would stay in power as long as the past continued to divide us.

Let me make this as concrete as possible, this need that inevitably awaited me to scrutinize the past for mistakes.

For the very people who should have been our allies then and were indispensable as allies against Pinochet in the years to come, for the people we had to convince to join us against Pinochet, the past that I remembered as glorious and enthralling was perceived as painful and traumatic.

No better way to illustrate this dichotomy than to focus on someone who had been unjustly hurt by the Unidad Popular, someone I recalled with regret many times in exile: Don Patricio, a friend and neighbor of ours in Santiago and the father of Rodrigo's favorite playmate. A calm, decent, quiet man, a progressive Christian Democrat who had worked as an accountant in the government center for the distribution of flour, he had been more than willing, he told me several times over afternoon tea, to contribute to the change in Chile that Allende had inaugurated, even if he did feel himself to be in the opposition.

But Don Patricio had been shunted aside, humiliated, left at his desk with no work to do for months, discriminated against merely because he was not an Allendista. I remember the day he told me, fighting back tears, that he had resigned, that he couldn't stand so much hatred. I didn't know what to say. I commiserated with him, pointed out that these were probably temporary misunderstandings, suggested that perhaps these small sacrifices were necessary for the country to be liberated.

Later, back home, a stone's throw from where he was staring into space, right there next door to him, I lamely told myself, recalling his anger and frustration, that I had never done anything directly to hurt him. But neither did I denounce the way he was being treated, nor recognize that it was the very way in which I was treating (and I was one of the most tolerant and empathetic of the militants!) many of my own colleagues who legitimately disagreed with me and whom I publicly excoriated and privately dismissed as traitors. I did not take the opportunity to comprehend that we were being insufficiently democratic, that we were accelerating the revolution beyond what was reasonable, that we had swept people like Don Patricio under the carpet of history, as if they didn't count, as if their dissidence was to be despised instead of valued, as if consensus were a crime.

And yet, no matter how many mistakes we had made, I had made, we did not deserve that balcony at La Moneda, the black hole in that balcony which threatened to engulf us all. I was not willing then, in that van, and I am not willing now, so many years later, to say that our joy was unreal.

It is the recognition of these mistakes and many more that the balcony at La Moneda is demanding of us, demanding of me. As the years go by, I will reluctantly, painstakingly, corner that young man and those three years he lived, I will slowly turn him into the man who writes these words, I will tell him what I have learned from this defeat, how I was one of those who inadvertently helped to bring the black hole of that balcony into being.

I will tell him that he should not have trusted the state to solve all the problems of Chile or the revolution to solve all his problems. I will tell him that it was unfair to burden a whole people with his salvation. I will tell him that the desire for purity may lead to fanaticism and ethnic strife and fundamentalism. I will tell him that the poor do not need to be represented by a paternal voice, no matter how benevolent. I will tell him that if you reduce everything to politics and ideology, you end up totalizing, squeezing the mystery out of life and explaining away too easily what at times has no explanation; you end up not leaving space for your own imperfections. I will tell him he should not have turned a blind eye to human rights violations in socialist countries out of insensitivity and political expediency. I will tell him how women's rights were postponed in the revolution and how we did not even conceive that our attitude toward nature was one that pillaged and polluted it.

I will tell him this and much more from the retrospect of the future, everything that I think he did wrong. But there is one thing I will not tell him, that young man I used to be. I will not tell him, I have never told that alter ego of mine in the past, that he was wrong to rebel.

One more story.

In the voyages that were to come, that still awaited me, I met a woman who had been tortured in Chile.

What saved her at the worst moments, she told me, was her unending repetition of some lines by Neruda or Machado—strange, she couldn't remember the author or the lines themselves anymore—verses that contained water in them, trees, she thought, something about the wind. What matters is that she concentrated on them ferociously so she could make clear to herself over and over how different she was from the men who were making her suffer. She discovered that, inside her, beyond those hands and what they were doing to her, there was a space all her own which could remain intact. One small zone in the world that she could keep from them. Some dead poet was providing her with this shield, with this guardian angel of language. As she silently repeated those words to herself, she expected to be extinguished forever.

Who can doubt that at this very moment, in this abominable world where General Pinochet is alive and Allende is dead, there are many others just like her, anonymous, unknown people, enduring other attempts to obliterate them, suck them into the black hole of history? Perhaps they will not survive, as she did, to tell the tale. But perhaps they are also sending us messages. We cannot be sure. We can only answer those words as if they are being transmitted.

We do know that the woman, even if there was nobody there, was hoping to be heard. Not only by herself. And what she was saying was simple. She was not willing, even if nobody was listening, even if her fate was to disappear from the face of the Earth, to be treated like an object. She was not willing to let others narrate her life and her death.

As for me, while there is one person like her in this world, I will find myself defending both her right to struggle and our obligation to remember.

Adapted from *Heading South, Looking North* (Penguin, 1999). Ariel Dorfman's other books include *Death and the Maiden* (Penguin, 1994), *Blake's Therapy* (Seven Stories Press, 2001), *Widows* (Seven Stories Press, 2002), and *Feeding on Dreams: Confessions of an Unrepentant Exile* (Houghton Mifflin Harcourt, 2011). Augusto Pinochet died in 2006.

CHAPTER THIRTY-SEVEN

Behemoth in a Bathrobe

The Small Voice of Conscience Converses with the American Psyche

Carla Seaquist

BEHEMOTH: Huh? Who's there?

VOICE: I'm that still, small voice—inside, at the back—that says, "I can." And I've pushed my way to the front, because, even a dozen years after 9/11, "the day everything changed," I'm hearing, "I can't." *What has happened to us?* We need to talk.

BEHEMOTH: About what?

VOICE: Our spark. Our élan vital, our can-do spirit. America's unique quality—once upon a time—the quality that, just two hundred years after the nation's founding, put a man on the moon. We need to recover that spark.

BEHEMOTH: Who says it's gone?

VOICE: Well, look at us. We're consuming trash TV and "reality" shows that exalt humiliation, violence, sex—a tawdry reality to convey to our kids. After a stint of admiring real heroes, like the rescue workers of 9/11, we've reverted to the unreal kind—celebrities—who behave ever more moronically—

BEHEMOTH: I need a sandwich.

VOICE:—and we're feeding our faces, far too much. Sure, with everything we're facing, we need distraction, but we've gotten silly. Meanwhile, vital issues get past us. Too many of us stayed passive when the Bush administration took us to war in Iraq and, shame of shame, into torture. We raised few peeps about Enron and other corporate scandals. We did raise our voices about the 2008 financial crash—with Occupy Wall Street—but then slunk back to our sofas. We sit out Congressional elections, then complain about a do-nothing Congress. We're in bad psychic shape. The behemoth is still in his bathrobe. We need to get a grip—

BEHEMOTH: Oh, look, a rerun of the Victoria's Secret documentary!

VOICE: All this mindless activity—we must become *more mindful.*

BEHEMOTH: What? Think *more* about more 9/11s, think *more* about the planet being destroyed, the god-awful mess of the economy, America's decline?

VOICE: Deep down, we know what's going on, don't we. Avoidance. *A-void-ance*.

BEHEMOTH: Where's my remote control?

VOICE: Ralph Waldo Emerson, early American *thinker,* in his essay "Self-Reliance"—

BEHEMOTH: Where *is* my remote control?

VOICE: *I'm* your remote control! Who must ask: Would you, if the walls came tumbling down, want to be caught watching women tumbling out of their underwear?

(*Pause*)

BEHEMOTH: No. But I don't like to think about walls tumbling down.

VOICE: Understandable, but we must—or be blindsided. Any terrorist, any declinist would be thrilled we've retreated to our bathrobe. Now: What are we avoiding?

BEHEMOTH: The still, small voice raises the *very* big thing. Fear.

VOICE: Yes, fear. Of the worst kind: of annihilation. Physical annihilation, financial annihilation, planetary annihilation. Capital-F Fear, feeling like "zero at the Bone."

BEHEMOTH: Emily Dickinson.

VOICE: Yes, another early American.

BEHEMOTH: Keep talking.

VOICE: In our historical crises—the Revolution, the Civil War, the Great Depression, two world wars—there was fear, but we faced it together. But no matter: Feeling fear that's "zero at the Bone," the question becomes. . . .

BEHEMOTH: How to live.

VOICE: Yes, and live fully, not just exist. Realizing that most of humankind shares this fear may help.

BEHEMOTH: Sharing the fear is good, I suppose. Still, I feel like I'm on the *Titanic* heading for the iceberg!

VOICE: So, what to do, what to do?

BEHEMOTH: Reduce the fear, for starters. But what concrete steps *can* we take?

VOICE: What's been our theme here?

BEHEMOTH: Mindfulness. But that's not a concrete step.

VOICE: On the contrary! In this carnival of fear, to question, to protest, to think—and think clearly—is capital-A Action. Question the use of labels—"good," "evil." Question premises, motives—Main Street must get *much* better at questioning Wall Street, *and* the politicians in its pocket. And question any administration's resorting to "national security" as justification for use of force, for snooping and spying on us—

BEHEMOTH:—and don't let our fear be manipulated. History is replete with people manipulated by fear, which is why so much history is tragic.

VOICE: Brilliant!

BEHEMOTH: But, is it too late to act?

VOICE: Who knows, but we Americans must learn to live in our new world, not retreat. Harness the fear and use it. Live with questions as well as answers—in a word, accept complication. Learn self-critique—vital for a behemoth. Get over our narcissism—and come together again. And understand that, while our security is gone, it was an illusion, and isn't life better without illusion? This is our opportunity to mature.

In fact, metaphysically, this could lead to an American existentialism—yes!—taking action in a hostile universe—

BEHEMOTH: Let's not get ahead of ourselves. Tell me: Will we ever laugh again?

VOICE: Our easy smile has gone, but an earned one will come. Our work is not about grimness, but passion.

BEHEMOTH: Let's keep talking. I find this dialogue bracing, in fact—this is antique vocabulary—tonic, inspiriting.

VOICE: Favorite words of Ralph Waldo Emerson, who said, to close our loop: "Nothing is at last sacred but the integrity of our own mind." Now, about the bathrobe: Shall we suit up? . . .

An earlier version of this piece originally appeared in the *Christian Science Monitor*. Carla Seaquist now writes for *The Huffington Post*. Her play *Who Cares? The Washington-Sarajevo Talks* was produced in the Festival of Emerging American Theatre 2003.

PART SEVEN

Radical Dignity

HOW HAVE YOU SPENT YOUR LIFE?

Jalaluddin Rumi

On Resurrection Day God will ask,
"During this reprieve I gave you,
what have you produced for Me?
Through what work have you reached your
life's end?
For what end have your food
and your strength been consumed?
Where have you dimmed the luster of your eye?
Where have you dissipated your five senses?
You have spent your seeing, hearing,
intelligence
and the pure celestial substances;
what have you purchased from the earth?
I gave you hands and feet as spade and mattock
for tilling the soil of good works;
when did they by themselves become existent?"

From *The Pocket Rumi Reader*, translated and edited by Kabir Helminski (Shambhala Press, 2001). Jalaluddin Rumi was a thirteenth-century Sufi poet. "How Have You Spent Your Life?" originally appeared in Rumi's great work, the six-volume *Mathnawi*. Rumi's other books include *The Rumi Collection*, translated and edited by Kabir Helminski (Shambhala Press, 2000).

There's a paradox in living with a sense of responsibility to our communities: The first and most enduring measure of success is what we see in the mirror at the end of each day. Have we displayed integrity? Have we done our best to serve the truth? All efforts to change the world—or, more realistically, small parts of it—spring from a fundamental respect for the dignity of human beings, starting with the person in the mirror, then expanding to encompass everyone else. But without the first, the second is impossible. Hope, Tony Kushner has said, is "a moral obligation, a human obligation, an obligation to the cells in your body. . . . Hope is not naïve, hope grapples endlessly with despair. Real, vivid, powerful, thunderclap hope, like the soul, is at home in darkness, is divided; but lose your hope and you lose your soul." We all have our flaws, doubts, and uncertainties, but when we do our best to create a more just world, we also honor the best in ourselves.

In "Letter from Birmingham Jail," Martin Luther King Jr., offers a classic example of this moral equation as he reflects on the deep personal cost of ignoring, obscuring, or excusing the suffering of our fellow human beings. What makes King's words so powerful, and worth reading and rereading, is his challenge to the white moderates, ministers of ostensible goodwill who'd explained, in public statements, that although they personally favored an end to segregation, the black community was simply being too impatient. King said he'd almost come to believe that the greatest stumbling block toward freedom was "not the White Citizen's Counciler or the Ku Klux Klanner, but the white moderate who is more devoted to 'order' than to justice." Underscoring one of the common ways that democracy is undermined, he warned: "We will have to repent in this generation not merely for the vitriolic words and actions of the bad people, but for the appalling silence of the good people."

A comparable silence pervades American society today, as immensely destructive actions proceed with the tacit acceptance of most of the media and of far too many elected officials and economic and civic leaders. They encourage the view that circumstances are simply out of our control, or that it's best to defer action until conditions are perfect, as King's critics had urged. They say that we shouldn't take action because we don't know enough or aren't powerful enough, or that the process of raising controversial issues isn't likely to be effective anyway. But as King writes, "Human progress never rolls in on wheels of inevitability." It comes instead through tenacious, step-by-step effort without which "time itself becomes an ally of the forces of social stagnation." By virtue of such work, we redeem ourselves as well as "reconstitute the world," to borrow Adrienne Rich's words.

The historical moment that first called King to his mission was the Montgomery bus boycott. According to the prevailing myth, it all started when Rosa Parks appeared out of nowhere, too tired to move, as people of color were expected to do, to the back of the bus. In "The Real Rosa Parks," I explore how this cartoon version of history obscures key elements of Parks's journey, including her own history of engagement and the support and guidance she received from an existing activist community. Like other movement participants, Rosa Parks took a decisive moral stand to affirm her own humanity. But she didn't make that choice within a social vacuum, or in isolation. No one ever does. Like her, we can reclaim our dignity most powerfully by acting in concert with others.

Although the civil rights movement ended legal segregation, African American communities still suffer from poverty and neglect, a neglect that has significantly worsened since the

2008 economic crash, and despite the election of America's first African American president. Meanwhile, the sense of shared destiny that once motivated resistance to injustice has eroded, although events like the shooting of unarmed African American teenager Trayvon Martin have revived some of it. In "Prisoners of Hope," Cornel West meditates on this spiritual corrosion. If we don't offer an alternative to despair, West warns, the resulting rage and bitterness will tear society apart. But change won't be easy or swift. In a time when those who seek more justice must, by necessity, be "stepping out on nothing, hoping to land on something," West challenges us to look squarely at the ills of the world while not letting them overwhelm us. "To live is to wrestle with despair," he writes, "yet never to allow despair to have the last word."

Too often, this despair indeed undermines our ability to act, whatever our experience, and whatever issues we care about most. It is resignation disguised as realism, betraying not only our integrity but also that of generations to come. Hope, Wendell Berry says, is "one of our duties . . . part of our obligation to our own being and to our descendants." By the same token, the absence of hope creates what psychologist Robert Jay Lifton calls "the broken connection," which severs the connections between past, present, and future and prevents us from engaging with a broader public world.

King, Parks, West, and Berry were raised in engaged religious traditions that provide transcendent frameworks for social commitment. Whatever setbacks or frustrations we face, they and others who share this sense of faith can rely for moral support on an infinitely patient and benevolent God. No matter how difficult the task before them, no matter how unlikely success might seem, their faith in the divine gives them the strength to persevere and a reminder that they are never alone: that, as in the phrase from the 23rd psalm, "Yea, though I walk through the valley of the shadow of death, I will fear no evil. For Thou art with me." Many also believe in the inevitable triumph of good over evil, however long it may take: that the arc of the moral universe really does bend toward justice.

Those whose basic outlook is secular, by contrast, can't appeal to eternity or inevitability. They live with no equivalent promise that justice will inevitably prevail. Instead, they turn to history, culture, and nature for that same sense of larger connection. Like those steeped in explicit faith traditions, they take heart from movements for justice that began long before them and will continue long after they're gone. They draw strength from the flow of a river or the flight of an eagle, from communion with the majesty of the natural world and the richness, resilience, and sweep of ordinary life. They keep in mind those who will inherit the world, like Mark Hertsgaard grounding his actions in his daughter Chiara's future, and gain inspiration from those who have spoken out for human dignity even in the darkest situations and bleakest times.

We've talked about some of the voices that can inspire us, from Nelson Mandela and Václav Havel to pioneering gay activists. One of the most impressive examples of someone reclaiming dignity and acting for justice under all-but-impossible conditions is Billy Wayne Sinclair, who spent over forty years in Louisiana's Angola Prison for killing a convenience store clerk. While serving a life sentence, Sinclair was offered the chance to buy his freedom for $15,000 in a pardon-selling scheme. He seriously considered the opportunity, having seen others pay and be released. But he'd spent half his life struggling to become, as he puts it, a "moral man," and finally had been able to "see more than a 'convicted murderer' in the mirror." So Sinclair contacted the FBI. The corrupt Pardon Board chair went to jail, as did the crooked governor who appointed him. But Sinclair remained in prison, isolated in protective custody, punished additionally for blowing the whistle.

Sinclair redeemed not only himself but, in part, the brutal world he inhabited. In addition to exposing the bribery scandal, he helped integrate the prison and edited *The Angolite*, a pioneering, nationally recognized inmate newspaper. Those with far more freedom and resources would be proud to have attempted a fraction of his accomplishments. He found a way, under the most discouraging of circumstances, to "replace fear with truth," in the terms of Peter Ackerman and Jack DuVall.

In "Resisting Terror," Ackerman and DuVall describe astounding, yet largely unknown instances of radical dignity in terrifying and daunting situations. They tell how the nonviolent resistance of the "Mothers of the Disappeared" helped overthrow a murderous Argentinean dictatorship. They also recount the courageous acts of non-Jewish women in Berlin, under Hitler, whose Jewish husbands had been arrested. The wives gathered outside the police station and stayed until their loved ones—including some men already sent to Auschwitz—were freed. Their love was stronger than real threats of torture and death. Ackerman and DuVall's essay highlights the transformative power of ordinary people who assert their dignity, even in contexts where action seems unthinkable, like the participants in the Arab Spring. Their stories, all too frequently ignored or forgotten, cannot help but give us heart. For if these "ordinary" individuals can take a stand, persist, and prevail, so can we.

Whatever our sources of strength, we all live in a society in which troubling social ills are ignored, idealism is denigrated, and citizens are too often discouraged from reflecting upon, debating, and taking action to check the excesses of the powerful and to remedy the plight of the powerless. We need to counter this culture of willful blindness if we're to be true to the core of who we are, and to the values we believe in. Yet balancing the personal and the public can be challenging, even overwhelming, and most of us seek a roadmap to navigate the constantly changing territory we'll have to traverse. These changes will be anything but linear or predictable, says anthropologist Mary Catherine Bateson. Her essay is more about personal than public life but nonetheless offers essential lessons for anyone working to transform society, particularly about the value of living with ambiguity. Indeed, some of the very writers in this book have cited Bateson as helping them keep that balance in their own lives. Echoing Cornel West, Bateson reminds us that change of any kind is improvisatory, proceeding with interruptions, disappointments, and unexpected detours. The contours of what we've accomplished may not be apparent until long after we take action for a particular cause. But whether we're striving toward personal or political change, if we risk sufficient leaps of faith, enlist enough allies, and persist long enough, we can simultaneously be true to ourselves and help create a society that fosters greater dignity for all.

CHAPTER THIRTY-EIGHT

Letter from Birmingham Jail

Martin Luther King, Jr.

While confined here in the Birmingham City Jail, I came across your recent statement calling our present activities "unwise and untimely." You deplore the demonstrations that are presently taking place in Birmingham. But I am sorry that your statement did not express a similar concern for the conditions that brought the demonstrations into being.

Frankly, I have never yet engaged in a direct action movement that was "well timed," according to the timetable of those who have not suffered unduly. For years now I have heard the word "Wait!" It rings in the ear of every Negro with a piercing familiarity. This "Wait" has almost always meant "Never." We must come to see with the distinguished jurist of yesterday that "justice too long delayed is justice denied."

I guess it is easy for those who have never felt the stinging darts of segregation to say, "Wait." But when you have seen vicious mobs lynch your mothers and fathers at will and drown your sisters and brothers at whim; when you have seen hate-filled policemen curse, kick, brutalize, and even kill your black brothers and sisters with impunity; when you see the vast majority of your 20 million Negro brothers smothering in an air-tight cage of poverty in the midst of an affluent society; when you suddenly find your tongue twisted and your speech stammering as you seek to explain to your six-year-old daughter why she can't go to the public amusement park that has just been advertised on television, and see tears welling up in her eyes when she is told that Funtown is closed to colored children, and see the depressing clouds of inferiority begin to form in her little mental sky, and see her begin to distort her little personality by unconsciously developing a bitterness toward white people; when you have to concoct an answer for a five-year-old son asking in agonizing pathos: "Daddy, why do white people treat colored people so mean?"; when you take a cross-country drive and find it necessary to sleep night after night in the uncomfortable corners of your automobile because no motel will accept you; when you are humiliated day in and day out by nagging signs reading "white" and "colored"; when your first name becomes "nigger," your middle name becomes "boy" (however old you are), and your last name becomes "John," and your wife and mother are never given the respected title "Mrs."; when you are harried by day and haunted by night by the fact that you are a Negro, living constantly at tip-toe stance never quite knowing what to expect next, and plagued with inner fears and outer resentments; when you are forever fighting a degenerating sense of "nobodiness"; then you will understand why we find it difficult to wait. There comes a time when the cup of endurance runs over, and men are no longer willing to be plunged into an abyss of despair.

I must confess that over the last few years I have almost reached the regrettable conclusion that the Negro's great stumbling block in the stride toward freedom is not the White Citizen's Counciler or the Ku Klux Klanner, but the white moderate who is more devoted to "order" than to justice; who prefers a negative peace which is the absence of tension to a positive peace which is the presence of justice; who constantly says "I agree with you in the goal you seek, but I can't agree with your methods of direct action"; who paternalistically feels he can set the timetable for another man's freedom; who lives by the myth of time and who constantly advises the Negro to wait until a "more convenient season." Shallow understanding from people of goodwill is more frustrating than absolute misunderstanding from people of ill will. Lukewarm acceptance is much more bewildering than outright rejection.

I had hoped that the white moderate would understand that law and order exist for the purpose of establishing justice, and that when they fail to do this they become dangerously structured dams that block the flow of social progress. I had hoped that the white moderate would understand that the present tension in the South is merely a necessary phase of the transition from an obnoxious negative peace, where the Negro passively accepted his unjust plight, to a substance-filled positive peace, where all men will respect the dignity and worth of human personality. Actually, we who engage in nonviolent direct action are not the creators of tension. We merely bring to the surface the hidden tension that is already alive. We bring it out in the open where it can be seen and dealt with.

I had also hoped that the white moderate would reject the myth of time. I received a letter this morning from a white brother in Texas which said: "All Christians know that the colored people will receive equal rights eventually, but it is possible that you are in too great of a religious hurry. It has taken Christianity almost 2,000 years to accomplish what it has. The teachings of Christ take time to come to Earth." All that is said here grows out of a tragic misconception of time. It is the strangely irrational notion that there is something in the very flow of time that will inevitably cure all ills. Actually time is neutral. It can be used either destructively or constructively. I am coming to feel that the people of ill will have used time much more effectively than the people of goodwill. We will have to repent in this generation not merely for the vitriolic words and actions of the bad people, but for the appalling silence of the good people. We must come to see that human progress never rolls in on wheels of inevitability. It comes through the tireless efforts and persistent work of men willing to be co-workers with God, and without this hard work time itself becomes an ally of the forces of social stagnation. We must use time creatively, and forever realize that the time is always ripe to do right. Now is the time to make real the promise of democracy, and transform our pending national elegy into a creative psalm of brotherhood. Now is the time to lift our national policy from the quicksand of racial injustice to the solid rock of human dignity.

Now [our] approach is being dismissed as extremist. I must admit that I was initially disappointed in being so categorized. But as I continued to think about the matter I gradually gained a bit of satisfaction from being considered an extremist. Was not Jesus an extremist for love—"Love your enemies, bless them that curse you, pray for them that despitefully use you." Was not Amos an extremist for justice—"Let justice roll down like waters and righteousness like a mighty stream." Was not Paul an extremist for the gospel of Jesus Christ—"I bear in my body the marks of the Lord Jesus." Was not Martin Luther an extremist—"Here I stand; I can do none other so help me God." Was not John Bunyan an extremist—"I will stay in jail to the end of my days before I make a butchery of my conscience." Was not Abraham Lincoln an extremist—"This nation cannot survive half slave and half free." Was not Thomas Jefferson an extremist—"We hold these truths to be self-evident, that all men are created equal." So the question is not whether we will be extremist but what kind of extremist will we be. Will we be extremists for hate or will we be extremists for love? Will we be extremists for the preservation of injustice—or will we be extremists for the cause of justice? In that dramatic scene on Calvary's hill, three men were crucified. We must not forget that all three were crucified for the same crime—the crime of extremism. Two were extremists for immorality, and thusly fell below their environment. The other, Jesus Christ, was an extremist for love, truth, and goodness, and thereby rose above his environment. So, after all, maybe the South, the nation, and the world are in dire need of creative extremists.

I had hoped that the white moderate would see this. Maybe I was too optimistic. Maybe I expected too much. I guess I should have realized that few members of a race that has oppressed another race can understand or appreciate the deep groans and passionate yearnings of those that have been oppressed, and still fewer have the vision to see that injustice must be rooted out by strong, persistent, and determined action. I am thankful, however, that some of our white brothers have grasped the meaning of this social revolution and committed themselves to it. They are still all too small in quantity, but they are big in quality. Some like Ralph McGill, Lillian Smith, Harry Golden, and James Dabbs have written about our struggle in eloquent, prophetic, and understanding terms. Others have marched with us down nameless streets of the South. They have languished in filthy roach-infested jails, suffering the abuse and brutality of angry policemen who see them as "dirty nigger lovers." They, unlike so many of their moderate brothers and sisters, have recognized the urgency of the moment and sensed the need for powerful "action" antidotes to combat the disease of segregation.

In spite of my shattered dreams of the past, I came to Birmingham with the hope that the white religious leadership of this community would see the justice of our cause and, with deep moral concern, serve as the channel through which our just grievances would get to the power structure. I had hoped that each of you would understand. But again I have been disappointed. I have heard numerous religious leaders of the South call upon their worshippers to comply with a desegregation decision because it is the *law*, but I have longed to hear white ministers say, "Follow this decree because integration is morally *right* and the Negro is your brother." In the midst of blatant injustices inflicted upon the Negro, I have watched white churches stand on the sideline and merely mouth pious irrelevancies and sanctimonious trivialities. In the midst of a mighty struggle to rid our nation of racial and economic injustice, I have heard so many ministers say, "Those are social issues with which the gospel has no real concern." And I have watched so many churches commit themselves to a completely other-worldly religion which made a strange distinction between body and soul, the sacred and the secular.

There was a time when the church was very powerful. It was during that period when the early Christians rejoiced when they were deemed worthy to suffer for what they believed. In those days the church was not merely a thermometer that recorded the ideas and principles of popular opinion; it was a thermostat that transformed the mores of society. Whenever the early Christians entered a town the power structure got disturbed and immediately sought to convict them for being "disturbers of the peace" and "outside agitators." But they went on with the conviction that they were "a colony of heaven," and had to obey God rather than man. They were small in number but big in commitment. They were too God-intoxicated to be "astronomically intimidated." They brought an end to such ancient evils as infanticide and gladiatorial contest.

Things are different now. The contemporary church is often a weak, ineffectual voice with an uncertain sound. It is so often the arch supporter of the status quo. Far from being disturbed by the presence of the church, the power structure of the average community is consoled by the church's silent and often vocal sanction of things as they are.

But even if the church does not come to the aid of justice, I have no despair about the future. I have no fear about the outcome of our struggle in Birmingham, even if our motives are presently misunderstood. We will reach the goal of freedom in Birmingham and all over the nation, because the goal of America is freedom. Abused and scorned though we may be, our destiny is tied up with the destiny of America. Before the pilgrims landed at Plymouth, we were here. Before the pen of Jefferson etched across the pages of history the majestic words of the Declaration of Independence, we were here. For more than two centuries our fore-parents labored in this country without wages; they made cotton king; and they built the homes of their masters in the midst of brutal injustice and shameful humiliation—and yet out of a bottomless vitality they continued to thrive and develop. If the inexpressible cruelties of slavery could not stop us, the opposition we now face will surely fail.

One day the South will recognize its real heroes. They will be the James Merediths, courageously and with a majestic sense of purpose, facing jeering and hostile mobs and with the agonizing loneliness that characterizes the life of the pioneer. They will be old, oppressed, battered Negro women, symbolized in a seventy-two-year-old woman of Montgomery, Alabama, who rose up with a sense of dignity and with her people decided not to ride the segregated buses, and responded to one who inquired about her tiredness with ungrammatical profundity, "My feet is tired, but my soul is rested." They will be the young high school and college students, young ministers of the gospel and a host of their elders courageously and nonviolently sitting-in at lunch counters and willingly going to jail for conscience's sake. One day the South will know that when these disinherited children of God sat down at lunch counters they were in reality standing up for the best in the American dream and the most sacred values in our Judeo-Christian heritage, and thusly, carrying our whole nation back to those great wells of democracy.

Excerpted from "Letter from Birmingham Jail." The full text can be found in James Washington, ed., *A Testament of Hope: The Essential Writings and Speeches of Martin Luther King, Jr.* (Harper San Francisco, 2003).

CHAPTER THIRTY-NINE

The Real Rosa Parks

Paul Rogat Loeb

We learn much from how we present our heroes. A few years ago, on Martin Luther King Day, I was interviewed on CNN. So was Rosa Parks, by phone from Los Angeles. "We're very honored to have her," said the host. "Rosa Parks was the woman who wouldn't go to the back of the bus. She wouldn't get up and give her seat in the white section to a white person. That set in motion the year-long bus boycott in Montgomery. It earned Rosa Parks the title of 'mother of the civil rights movement.'"

I was excited to hear Parks's voice and to be part of the same show. But it occurred to me that the host's description—the story's standard rendition—stripped the Montgomery boycott of all of its context. Before refusing to give up her bus seat, Parks had been active for twelve years in the local NAACP chapter, serving as its secretary. The summer before her arrest, she had attended a ten-day training session at Tennessee's labor and civil rights organizing school, the Highlander Center, where she'd met an older generation of civil rights activists, including South Carolina teacher Septima Clark, and discussed the recent Supreme Court decision banning "separate-but-equal" schools. During this period of involvement and education, Parks had become familiar with previous challenges to segregation: Another Montgomery bus boycott, fifty years earlier, successfully eased some restrictions; a bus boycott in Baton Rouge won limited gains two years before Parks was arrested; and the previous spring, a young Montgomery woman had also refused to move to the back of the bus, causing the NAACP to consider a legal challenge until they realized that she was unmarried and pregnant, and therefore a poor symbol for a campaign.

In short, Rosa Parks didn't make a spur-of-the-moment decision. She didn't single-handedly give birth to the civil rights efforts, but she was part of an existing movement for change, at a time when success was far from certain. We all know Parks's name, but few of us know about Montgomery NAACP head E. D. Nixon, who served as one of her mentors and first got Martin Luther King, Jr., involved. Nixon carried people's suitcases on the trains and was active in the Brotherhood of Sleeping Car Porters, the union founded by legendary civil rights activist A. Philip Randolph. Nixon played a key role in the campaign. But no one talks of him, any more than they talk of JoAnn Robinson, who taught nearby at an underfunded and segregated black college and whose Women's Political Council distributed the initial leaflets following Parks's arrest. Without the often lonely work of people like Nixon, Randolph, and Robinson, Parks would likely have never taken her stand, and if she had, it would never have had the same impact.

This in no way diminishes the power and historical importance of Parks's refusal to give up her seat. But it reminds us that this tremendously consequential act, along with everything that followed, depended on all the humble and frustrating work that Parks and others undertook earlier on. It also reminds us that Parks's initial step of getting involved was just as courageous and critical as the stand on the bus that all of us have heard about.

People like Parks shape our models of social commitment. Yet the conventional retelling of her story creates a standard so impossible to meet, it may actually make it harder for us to get involved, inadvertently stripping away Parks's most powerful lessons of hope.

The conventional portrayal suggests that social activists come out of nowhere, to suddenly take dramatic stands. It implies that we act with the greatest impact when we act alone, at least initially. And that change occurs instantly, as opposed to building on a series of often-invisible actions. The myth of Parks as lone activist reinforces a notion that anyone who takes a committed public stand, or at least an effective one, has to be a larger-than-life figure—someone with more time, energy, courage, vision, or knowledge than any normal person could ever possess. This belief pervades our society, in part because the media tend not to represent historical change as the work of ordinary human beings, which it almost always is.

Once we enshrine our heroes on pedestals, it becomes hard for mere mortals to measure up in our eyes. However individuals speak out, we're tempted to dismiss their motives, knowledge, and tactics as insufficiently grand or heroic. We fault them for not being in command of every fact and figure, or being unable to answer every question put to them. We fault ourselves as well, for not knowing every detail, or for harboring uncertainties and doubts. We find it hard to imagine that ordinary human beings with ordinary flaws might make a critical difference in worthy social causes.

Yet those who act have their own imperfections, and ample reasons to hold back. "I think it does us all a disservice," says a young African American activist in Atlanta named Sonya Tinsley, "when people who work for social change are presented as saints—so much more noble than the rest of us. We get a false sense that from the moment they were born they were called to act, never had doubts, were bathed in a circle of light. But I'm much more inspired learning how people succeeded despite their failings and uncertainties. It's a much less intimidating image. It makes me feel like I have a shot at changing things too."

Sonya had recently attended a talk given by one of Martin Luther King's Morehouse professors, in which he mentioned how much King had struggled when he first came to college, getting only a C, for example, in his first philosophy course. "I found that very inspiring, when I heard it," Sonya said, "given all that King achieved. It made me feel that just about anything was possible."

Our culture's misreading of the Rosa Parks story speaks to a more general collective amnesia, where we forget the examples that might most inspire our courage, hope, and conscience. Apart from obvious times of military conflict, most of us know next to nothing of the many battles ordinary men and women fought to preserve freedom, expand the sphere of democracy, and create a more just society. Of the abolitionist and civil rights movements, we at best recall a few key leaders—and often misread their actual stories. We know even less about the turn-of-the-century populists who challenged entrenched economic interests and fought for a "cooperative commonwealth." Who these days can describe the union movements that ended eighty-hour work weeks at near-starvation wages? Who knows the origin of the Social Security system, now threatened by systematic attempts to privatize it? How did the women's suffrage movement spread to hundreds of communities and gather enough strength to prevail?

As memories of these events disappear, we lose the knowledge of mechanisms that grassroots social movements have used successfully in the past to shift public sentiment and challenge entrenched institutional power. Equally lost are the means by which their participants managed to keep on and eventually prevail in circumstances at least as harsh as those we face today.

Think again about the different ways one can frame Rosa Parks's historic action. In the prevailing myth, Parks decides to act almost on a whim, in isolation. She's a virgin to politics, a holy innocent. The lesson seems to be that if any of us suddenly got the urge to do something equally heroic, that would be great. Of course most of us don't, so we wait our entire lives to find the ideal moment.

Parks's real story conveys a far more empowering moral. She begins with seemingly modest steps. She goes to a meeting, and then another, helping build the community that in turn supported her path. Hesitant at first, she gains confidence as she speaks out. She keeps on despite a profoundly uncertain context, as she and others act as best they can to challenge deeply entrenched injustices, with little certainty of results. Had she and others given up after her tenth or eleventh year of commitment, we might never have heard of Montgomery.

Parks's journey suggests that change is the product of deliberate, incremental action, whereby we join together to try to shape a better world. Sometimes our struggles will fail, as did many earlier efforts of Parks, her peers, and her predecessors. Other times they may bear modest fruits. And at times they will trigger a miraculous outpouring of courage and heart—as happened with her arrest and all that followed. For only when we act despite all our uncertainties and doubts do we have the chance to shape history.

Adapted from Paul Rogat Loeb, *Soul of a Citizen: Living with Conviction in Challenging Times* (St. Martin's Press, 2010), *www.soulofacitizen.org.*

CHAPTER FORTY

Prisoners of Hope

Cornel West

> He who has never despaired has no need to have lived.
>
> —GOETHE

A specter of despair haunts America. The quality of our lives and the integrity of our souls are in jeopardy. Wealth inequality and class polarization are escalating—with ugly consequences for the most vulnerable among us. The lethal power of global corporate elites and national managerial bosses is at an all-time high. Spiritual malnutrition and existential emptiness are rampant. The precious systems of caring and nurturing are eroding. Market moralities and mentalities—fueled by economic imperatives to make a profit at nearly any cost—yield unprecedented levels of loneliness, isolation, and sadness. And our public life lies in shambles, shot through with icy cynicism and paralyzing pessimism.

This bleak portrait is accentuated in black America. The fragile black middle class fights a white backlash. The devastated black working class fears further underemployment or unemployment. And the besieged black poor struggle to survive. Over forty years after the cowardly murder of Martin Luther King, Jr., and despite the election of an African American President, black America sits on the brink of collective disaster.

Yet most of our fellow citizens deny this black despair, downplay this black rage, and blind themselves to the omens in our midst. So now, as in the past, we prisoners of hope in desperate times must try to speak our fallible truths, expose the lies, and bear our imperfect witness.

In 1946, when the great Eugene O'Neill's play *The Iceman Cometh* was produced, he said America was the greatest example of a country that exemplifies the biblical question, "For what shall it profit a man, if he shall gain the whole world but lose his own soul?" Artists like Harry Belafonte and John Coltrane and Toni Morrison and others have been asking the same question, as the young people say, "How do we keep it real?"

When we look closely at jazz, or the blues, for example, we see a profound sense of the tragic linked to human agency. This music does not wallow in a cynicism or a paralyzing pessimism, but it also is realistic enough not to project excessive utopia. It responds in an improvisational, undogmatic, creative way to circumstances, helping people still survive and thrive.

How can we be realistic about what this nation is about and still sustain hope, acknowledging that we're up against so much? When I talk to young people these days, there's a sense in which they're in an anti-idealist mode and mood. They want to keep it real. And keeping it real means, in fact, understanding that the white supremacy you thought you could push back permeates this nation so deeply that you ought to wake up and recognize how deep it is. Think of the 30% of Republicans who believe Obama is a Muslim or the 49% of white Americans who believed George Zimmerman's acquittal for shooting the unarmed Trayvon Martin was justified. They'll say the level of hope is based on the reality.

Now, what do we say back to them? Part of my response has to do with a certain kind of appeal to their moral sense. Part of it has to do with their connection to a tradition, from grandmother to grandfather to father to mother, that has told them it is often better to be right and moral as opposed to being simply successful in the cheapest sense. And yet we all know that there must be some victories, some successes, if we're going to keep alive this tradition and the legacy of King, Harry Belafonte, Paul Robeson, and others. To convince them that what we're talking about is real, what do we say? This is what I struggle with every day.

I think that rage is an understandable and appropriate response to an absurd situation, namely, black people facing white supremacist power. The question becomes, "How do you channel the rage?" Because it's going to come out. It's going to be manifest in some way. Too often it's manifested in cowardly ways not guided by political consciousness, in self-destructive ways, like physical violence. Malcolm X's great insight, among many, was that we need to have some moral channels through which this rage can flow. Malcolm wasn't the only one who pointed this out; he learned it from Elijah Muhammad and Marcus Garvey and others. We also get it from other traditions, from King and A. Philip Randolph. This rage needs some targeting and direction. It has to reflect a broad moral vision, a sharp political analysis of wealth and power. Most important, it's got to be backed up with courage and follow-through.

When there's a paucity of courage and follow-through, you can have the broadest vision and the most sophisticated analysis in the world, and it's still sounding like brass and tinkling cymbals. It's empty, if you don't have follow-through. Again this is where young people have so much to teach us. Because when they say, "Make it real," in part they're saying they want to see a sermon, not hear one. They want an example. They want to be able to perceive in palpable concrete form how these channels will allow them to vent their rage constructively and make sure that it will have an impact. What Malcolm, I think, was able to perceive is: Look, we're going to have to deal with black rage one way or another. Let's at least try to channel it.

The country is in deep trouble. We've forgotten that a rich life consists fundamentally of serving others, trying to leave the world a little better than you found it. This is true at the personal level. But there's also a political version, which has to do with what you see when you get up in the morning and look in the mirror and ask yourself whether you are simply wasting your time on the planet or spending it in an enriching manner.

We need a moral prophetic minority of all colors who muster the courage to question the powers that be, the courage to be impatient with evil and patient with people, and the courage to fight for social justice. In many instances we will be stepping out on nothing, hoping to land on something. That's the history of black folks in the past and present, and of those of us who value history and struggle. Our courage rests on a deep democratic vision of a better world that lures us and a blood-drenched hope that sustains us.

This hope is not the same as optimism. Optimism adopts the role of the spectator who surveys the evidence in order to infer that things are going to get better. Yet we know that the evidence does not look good. The dominant tendencies of our day are unregulated global capitalism, racial balkanization, social breakdown, and individual depression. Hope enacts the stance of the participant who actively struggles against the evidence in order to change the deadly tides of wealth inequality, group xenophobia, and personal despair. Only a new wave of vision, courage, and hope can keep us sane—and preserve the decency and dignity requisite to revitalize our organizational energy for the work to be done. To live is to wrestle with despair yet never to allow despair to have the last word.

Adapted from Cornel West, *Restoring Hope: Conversations on the Future of Black America*, edited by Kelvin Shawn Sealey (Beacon Press, 1997). This essay also includes material adapted from West's comments in bell hooks and Cornel West, *Breaking Bread* (South End Press, 1991). Cornel West's other books include *The Cornel West Reader* (BasicCivitas, 2000); *Race Matters* (Vintage Books, 2004); *African American Religious Thought: An Anthology*, co-edited with Eddie Glaude (Westminster John Knox Press, 2004); *Democracy Matters* (Penguin, 2005); and *Brother West: Living and Loving Out Loud, A Memoir* (Smiley Books, 2010).

CHAPTER FORTY-ONE

Road to Redemption

Billy Wayne Sinclair

Seven of my thirty-eight years in Louisiana's prison system were spent on Angola's death row, doing time for murder. In 1965, as a twenty-year-old punk looking for fast money, I ordered a convenience store clerk to open the cash register. He refused and chased me out of the store. Running toward my car, I fired over my shoulder to frighten him. The last time I saw the clerk, he was sitting on the sidewalk yelling for the police. He bled to death.

In 1972 the US Supreme Court overturned the death penalty nationwide in the case of *Furman v. Georgia*. I was resentenced to life without parole.

Apart from the time on death row, I spent two years in one of Angola's maximum-security tiers in lockdown, an unspeakably violent environment. One year was spent working in Angola's fields under slave labor conditions, another in the office as a clerk. Nine were spent as a prison journalist, working on *The Angolite*, the prison magazine, written by inmates for inmates. As a result of my testimony in a bribery case, the rest of my years in the prison system have been spent in protective custody away from Angola.

Battles against Louisiana's prison system are hard-won. But they show that the system is vulnerable. And small victories can fuel larger ones. Change is a potent force behind bars that inspires desperate acts.

In February 1951, thirty-one inmates slashed their heel tendons to protest their brutal treatment at Angola. Newspapers across the state headlined the story. The public reeled in shock. The heel stringers succeeded in improving conditions for a few years. But old ways died hard. It would take repeated assaults to tame Angola.

While I was on the "row," I won the first prisoner rights lawsuit in the history of Louisiana in 1971 with the help of a young VISTA attorney from New York. *Sinclair v. Henderson* dramatically improved conditions on death row. It was the first in a long string of jailhouse lawsuits I have successfully filed against Louisiana's callous prison system.

Other prisoners followed my legal assault. In 1973, four black inmates filed suit against Angola alleging discrimination. The suit charged that conditions at the prison were "cruel and unusual punishment." The court found that Angola "would shock the conscience of any right-thinking person."

"Life," a militant black inmate from New Orleans, was my best friend. He was a crusader against homosexual rape who was not afraid to take on the criminal subculture. No brother, Life said, should take another brother for a woman. A few years after the US Supreme Court decision that released me from death row, the US Justice Department demanded that the prison be integrated. Together Life and I went into the most dangerous dormitories and cellblocks at Angola to argue for integration. It came without violence. But Life was knifed to death for his stand against sexual predators.

In 1976, in an effort to quell violence at the prison, the administration unshackled *The Angolite*, which was little more than a newsletter when it was set free. A hard-nosed reformer, Warden Ross Maggio, appointed me to the staff. My expertise as a jailhouse lawyer won me the spot. Administrators felt that uncensored inmate voices would help decrease the level of violence. The warden's gamble worked. But it had an unintended consequence. *The Angolite* rose to national prominence. Stories that my co-editor Wilbert Rideau wrote, and others that I wrote, won national awards—the Robert F. Kennedy Award for Special Interest Journalism, the Sidney Hillman Award, and the George Polk Award, among others.

With the breeze of success in its sails, *The Angolite* journeyed into uncharted waters for prison journalism. Rideau and I covered stories on sexual violence, prison suicides, inmate killings, and a host of other issues. We were a black/white writing team in a Southern prison rife with repressed racism and potential violence. Along with our awards, we became the subjects of stories on television networks, in national magazines, and in the foreign press.

The Angolite's success lifted me out of a pit of despair in Angola's fields and cellblocks. Rideau and I traveled the state on overnight speaking trips to schools and civic groups. We could pick up the telephone in *The Angolite* office and arrange for calls to journalists all over the country. We had influence with the administration and the free world. We were the envy of other prisoners.

I lost it all in 1986 when I turned down a ranking prison official's offer to sell me a pardon. It was a ticket to freedom I felt that I had earned after twenty years at Angola. I yearned to be free with every breath I took. I was a lifer without benefit of parole. I would never leave Angola unless a governor commuted my sentence. In 1986, the governor's mercy was in short supply as the nation escalated its war on crime. Most lifers in Angola's clutches knew they would die there.

In 1982, I had married Jodie Bell, a television reporter I met when she came to the prison to do a series on the death penalty for the CBS affiliate in Baton Rouge. The need to be with her shredded my days. Angola did not allow conjugal visits. I lived and breathed sexual desire. Craving to be at home with my wife haunted me. I knew, as she knew, that turning down the opportunity to buy a pardon in 1986 might leave me at Angola forever.

When I left death row in 1972, I carried its stigma with me. I came to understand that the free world would always see me as a "convicted murderer." But I could not accept that label. Seeds of decency waited to sprout inside my soul, sowed by Sundays in fire-and-brimstone Southern Baptist churches. But I had never matured. Parental abuse, neglect, and cruelty crippled me as I grew up. Prison was the only place left in which I could save my soul.

Change did not come with a glorious, religious awakening. It came in painful increments, from education and the self-awareness that education fosters. As I looked in the mirror every day, I began to see a killer. The familiar contours of my flesh covered an animal's bones. I had to accept responsibility for an undeserved death. But I could not accept a label that placed me beyond the pale of human salvation.

I am not the only prisoner who has ever chosen that road. But each and every one who takes it knows that it tempts a shank in the gut. The rehabilitated inmate steps away from social acceptance and stands in opposition to the natural order in his prison environment. He becomes a target of inmate scorn—"riding the religious pony" or "sucking up to the man" to get out of prison. Scorn easily escalates into violence. I walked a fine line for two years before I was moved from a Big Yard dormitory, where I lived with some of the most dangerous prisoners in Angola, to a safer dormitory.

The offer to sell a pardon confirmed rumors that I had been hearing for months in 1986 about corruption in Governor Edwin Edwards's third administration. [The four-time governor of Louisiana served eight years in a federal penitentiary for selling state licenses to build casinos.] In the late 1980s, his Pardon Board chairman sold pardons for a golf cart, cash, gold jewelry, and sex with inmates' wives. He and the prison official who offered to help me buy a pardon were convicted of public bribery.

The offer of an illegal pardon ignited a firestorm in my brain. I had spent years changing myself. Now, I could reap the full reward only if I dismantled the moral framework I had struggled to erect. I could only be released if I committed the crime of bribery.

Whispers from my criminal past urged me to do it. The hard, practical side of my nature agreed. But I could not. I was a prisoner of the moral man I had become. The striving to see more than a "convicted murderer" in the mirror drove me to reject the offer.

Neither could I betray my wife. My rehabilitation was the foundation of our marriage. She is a Catholic who believes in forgiveness and redemption. Her moral heritage—instilled by the nuns who taught her in parochial schools—put her on a plane I revered. "My child," the nuns would say, "virtue is its own reward."

I could not involve my wife in an illegal act that would destroy her faith in me and make her liable for a criminal charge. Jodie had the price of a pardon—$15,000 in a bank account in Texas. She wrestled with her own demons in rejecting the offer. She was a woman in her forties married to a lifer. She ached to have me at home and knew how unlikely it was. Buying a pardon might be the only way we would ever be together.

Had she decided to pay the bribe without telling me, I might not have known until I was set free or we were charged with public bribery. But she would not betray me. Instead, she contacted the FBI for me. Jodie understood my struggle for self-respect.

Cooperation with the federal government doomed me to a life in protective custody—one of the most restrictive environments in prison. Otherwise, I would be killed as the "snitch" who slammed the door on freedom. Inmates who bought pardons were released. Governor Edwards claimed he knew nothing of the scheme.

In 1992, Louisiana governor Buddy Roemer commuted my life sentence to ninety years, making me eligible for parole.

On Sunday, June 8, 2003, my wife and I celebrated our twenty-first wedding anniversary in the cellblock lobby with a cup of coffee that I was allowed to bring to the table where we visit. I have nearly a decade left to serve in prison. I have been denied parole eight times since 1992. I will not be discharged until 2011, after I have served half of a ninety-year sentence.

My wife will be seventy-two years old when I finally go home, and I will be sixty-six.

God knows how much life will be left to us. But I will leave prison knowing that I am more than a "convicted murderer." I did not fail my wife or myself. Striving for change saved my soul and left its marks on a prison system without one.

Billy Wayne Sinclair is the author of *Capital Punishment: An Indictment by a Death Row Survivor* (Arcade Publishing, 2011) and *A Life in the Balance: The Billy Wayne Sinclair Story* (Arcade Publishing, 2012), a book he wrote with his wife, Jodie Sinclair. He was finally paroled and released from prison on April 21, 2006, and now lives with Jodie and works in the law firm of the lawyer who secured his release.

CHAPTER FORTY-TWO

Resisting Terror

Peter Ackerman and Jack DuVall

Berlin, 1943: "Let Our Husbands Go!"

On February 27, 1943, SS soldiers and Gestapo agents began seizing the remaining Jews of Berlin. They loaded them onto trucks and took them to an administration building at Rosenstrasse 2–4, in the heart of the city. The goal was finally to make the city *judenfrei* (free of Jews), through forcible collection of Jews with German spouses and mixed ancestry children. These Jews had previously escaped the Holocaust because they or their spouses were essential for the war effort. But the military defeat at Stalingrad had led Hitler to call for "Total War" against all Jews as well as Allied armies.

Before long a group of non-Jewish wives gathered on the Rosenstrasse with food and other items for their Jewish husbands who were inside. Soon they began demanding their spouses' release. One woman's brother, a soldier on leave, approached an SS guard and said, "If my brother-in-law is not released, I will not return to the front." The crowds grew, with women waiting outside day and night, holding hands and chanting "Let our husbands go!" By the second day, over six hundred women were keeping a vigil.

Hitler had always sidestepped domestic opposition, and until this point the regime had largely managed to keep the genocide against the Jews a secret. But now that secrecy was jeopardized. Berlin—never a city enthusiastic about the Nazis—was the German base for foreign news organizations that still operated during the war. If political malcontents or the wire services were to get wind of the protest, the myth of omnipotent Nazi control could be fractured.

By the third day SS troops were ordered to train their guns on the crowd but fire only warning shots. That scattered the women to nearby alleyways, but they returned. Jailing the women would have been the rankest hypocrisy: According to Nazi theories, women were intellectually incapable of political action. So women dissenters were the last thing the Nazis wanted Germans to hear about.

The crowd soon expanded to include people not in mixed marriages, bulging to a thousand, with people taunting SS soldiers. To stop more from arriving, Joseph Goebbels closed down the nearest streetcar station, but women walked a mile from another station. By the end of the week Goebbels saw no alternative but to let the prisoners go. Some thirty-five Jewish men, already sent to Auschwitz, were ordered to board a passenger train back to Berlin.

Without fully realizing what they had done, the Rosenstrasse women had forced the Nazis to make a choice: They could pay a finite cost—1,700 prisoners set free, if all the intermarried Jewish men were released. Or they could open a Pandora's box of opposition in the center of the capital and brutalize German women in the bargain. For the Nazis, maintaining social control was more important. The regime that terrorized Europe found itself unable to use violence against a challenge on its very doorstep.

As it happened, many more than thirty-five Jewish men were eventually set free. Adolf Eichmann's deputy in Paris wanted to know what he should do about intermarried Jews. On May 21 they were all released, everywhere in Europe, from the camps. Five years earlier Mohandas Gandhi had been asked about the Nazis. "Unarmed men, women, and children offering nonviolent resistance," he predicted, "will be a novel experience for them."

In February 1943 Ruth Gross was a ten-year-old girl who went down to the Rosenstrasse so she could glimpse her father, one of the men interned there. One day she saw him, and he waved back. "This thing with Rosenstrasse," she said years later, "that was always a bond between us, my father and me." When she visited him in the hospital at the end of his life, each time she left he would stand up and wave at her. "I have always been convinced that he too was always thinking about this scene there on Rosenstrasse. About how he stood there and waved." When love comes to rescue life, no one forgets.

Buenos Aires, 1977: "We Will Walk Until We Drop"

On the first day, there were only fourteen—an improbable troop of women in their middle years, anonymous and ordinary, not knowing whether the gray hand of authority would crush them or merely brush them away. Through the low light of that autumn afternoon, they filed across the stone paths of the city's most historic square, collecting near the obelisk erected to celebrate the nation's nineteenth-century break with Spanish rule.

They had gone to the Plaza de Mayo, in the civic heart of Buenos Aires, on this last day of April 1977, in search of another kind of independence—freedom from an uncertainty more haunting than grief. "We arrived separately," recalled one of the women, Maria del Rosario de Cerruti. "We wore flat shoes so we could make a run for it if they came after us. To demonstrate in front of Government House was very dangerous." But they were linked as securely as climbers on a rock cliff by the rope line of what they had in common: All were mothers; all had children who had disappeared.

Not until two months later, after weekly demonstrations, were three mothers allowed to see the minister of the interior, a general who said he had a file with the names of the disappeared.

But he did not know who had taken them; he said "that there were paramilitary groups out there who couldn't be controlled," Rosario recalled. "Then he said that perhaps our sons had run away with a woman, that perhaps our daughters were working as prostitutes somewhere."

At that moment, the women's fear gave way to anger. "We told him that they were cowards, because even a cruel dictator like Franco had signed the death sentences with his own hand . . . and we told him that we would come back every week until they gave us an answer and that we would walk in the square every Thursday until we dropped." Although they did not know it, these grieving women had declared war.

The mothers' enemy was a military government whose roots reached back half a century, marked by several coups and only two free elections. When political repression spiked in the late 1960s, secret militias on the right were joined in the field by leftist counterparts, and kidnappings and car bombs proliferated. In just one year, one rightist group murdered seventy intellectuals and lawyers.

In 1974, the army's hands were untied. With webs of spies and paramilitaries, the army fashioned a kind of clandestine armed service and managed to quench the violence. But a year later, when the nation tipped toward mayhem again, a new junta dissolved the congress, provincial governments, and the Supreme Court, forbade political or trade union activity, and made civilians subject to trial by military courts.

The goal was to obliterate subversion, and this meant all-out war—a dirty war, using any means. In every region covert detention centers were set up and special task forces were trained to capture and interrogate suspects. "First we will kill all the subversives," explained the military governor of Buenos Aires, "then we will kill their collaborators; then . . . those who remain indifferent; and finally we will kill the timid."

To do this, they simply made people disappear—into the forests and into the rivers and oceans, dropped from helicopters. In time, as many as 30,000 Argentines would disappear, and each disappearance was concealed and denied; survivors were left with only an empty place, as if the loved one had never existed.

Typically, a victim was taken by a squad of armed men in mufti, arriving in a fleet of blue Ford Falcons, which became their signature car. At first they worked only late at night, but as they smelled the fear rising around them, they began snatching people in broad daylight. People were disappeared because they were only a few degrees of separation from another disappeared person. The terror might favor the taking of journalists, academics, and politicians, but it also did not hesitate to seize ordinary men, women, and even children.

At first the mothers of the disappeared felt only numb loss. But as they realized that no one else would act, they began a melancholy migration from the world of their families and homes out onto Argentina's cold plains of political lawlessness. Yet the mothers sensed that they were not alone: If they had no one else, they had each other.

Ironically, this realization dawned as they came to sit in the Interior Ministry. There a policewoman would take down their names, addresses, the names of missing children, the names of their associates—names, the mothers realized too late, that would become grist for the mill of terror. Soon they had begun to share their unspeakable stories—grief bound them into an association, a force.

Short on political experience, they nonetheless understood instinctively that the terror was sustained less by the junta's physical might than by the frightened stillness of victims' families. So, searching for a weapon they might raise against this enemy, they resolved to deny the junta what it most needed: silence.

"Our first problem was how we were going to organize meetings if we didn't know each other," recalled Dora de Bazze. "There were so many police and security men everywhere that you never knew who was standing next to you. . . . So we carried different things so we could identify each other. For example one would hold a twig in her hand . . . one would pin a leaf to her lapel, anything to let us know this was a Mother."

The women also made signs that asked "Where are our disappeared children?" or declared "The military have taken our children." Dora de Bazze remembered that they "went out at night to stick them on the buses and underground trains. . . . And we wrote messages on peso notes so that as many people as possible would see them. . . . If a journalist reported us, he disappeared; the television and radio were completely under military control."

Azucena de Villaflor de De Vincente quickly emerged as the first leader. Her parents had been trade union leaders, but, once married, she had become a homemaker, never looking outward—until 1976, when her son, Néstor, and his wife, Raquel, were disappeared. From that moment on she was a whirlwind, rallying the mothers, offering her home as a meeting place, organizing letter-writing campaigns to Amnesty International. It was she who suggested that they take their grievance into the bright light of the Plaza de Mayo.

"At first we didn't march together in the square," remembered Maria del Rosario. "We sat on the benches with our knitting or stood in small groups. . . . Then, when the police . . . began pointing their rifles at us and telling us to move on . . . we began to walk in twos around the edge of the square. . . . There were so few of us we were hardly noticed and we had to make sure the public knew we existed . . . so we began to walk in the center of the square, around the monument."

Eddying about on the plaza, they piled up belongings of disappeared children, and often they carried carpenter's nails to show their solidarity with the Holy Mother, whose son had also been detained and tortured to death. In September 1977 they decided to join an annual pilgrimage to Luján, thirty miles outside Buenos Aires, so they could tell their stories to strangers during the long walk. But how to identify themselves?

"Azucena's idea," said Aida de Suárez, "was to wear as a head scarf one of our children's nappies, because every mother keeps something like this, which belonged to your child as a baby. It was very easy to spot the head scarves . . . so we decided to use the scarves at other meetings and then every time we went to Plaza de Mayo . . . and we embroidered on the names of our children. Afterwards we put on them '*Aparicion con Vida*'"—literally, reappearance with life—"because we were no longer searching for just one child but for all the disappeared."

By the last months of 1977, *las Madres de la Plaza de Mayo* had grown from fourteen reluctant housewives to about 150 protesting mothers, who were in touch with hundreds more. On October 5 of that first year, they managed to place a half-page Mother's Day advertisement in the newspaper *La Prensa*, addressed to the president of the Supreme Court, armed forces commanders, junta leaders, and the Church. A few weeks later they followed with a petition with 24,000 signatures, and the names of 537 *desparecidos*.

Around the world, news media and governments began to take notice. But as the mothers revealed what was wrong in Argentina, they became a target. "They started calling us '*las locas*'"—the madwomen—recalled Aida de Suárez. "When . . . the foreign journalists began to ask about us, they used to say, 'Don't take any notice of those old women, they're all mad.' Of course they called us mad. How could the armed forces admit they were worried by a group of middle-aged women? And anyway we were mad. When everyone was terrorized we didn't stay at home crying—we went to the streets to confront them directly. We were mad but it was the only way to stay sane."

According to Marina de Curia, the government had waited too long to take them seriously. "They didn't destroy us immediately because they thought we couldn't do anything and when they wanted to, it was too late. We were already organized."

One day when the mothers were putting the final touches on their second advertisement, men appeared as if from nowhere and began hitting mothers and hauling them away. Two days later Azucena was taken. The authorities thought that "by kidnapping the fourteen Mothers, they would destroy our movement," Aida de Suárez said. "They didn't realize this would only strengthen our determination. We said, no, they're not going to destroy us, we will continue, stronger than ever. They thought we would be too afraid to go back to the square. It was difficult to go back . . . but we went back."

Returning to the Plaza de Mayo, the mothers now understood that their once-spontaneous protest had become a strategic thrust. Where the generals had thrown a cape of legitimacy over their crimes, the mothers lifted it. Despite threats and kidnappings, they refused to submit. They were now, in their way, as unassailable as the regime had been, having shown an audacity in the face of what was thought to be unopposable.

Argentina hosted the World Cup of soccer in 1978, and at first, the mothers were forgotten in the excitement. But journalists who came to cover soccer were drawn to their weekly promenade. When Argentina won the World Cup, domestic television showed the generals in a throng of fans; on Dutch TV, there were *las Madres*.

Having rebuked the regime at home, they proceeded to lacerate it abroad. Three of the mothers embarked on an international tour heralded by the simple statement "We are the Mothers of the disappeared from Buenos Aires, Argentina, and we are coming to discuss human rights." They acquired a kind of celebrity, which tended to protect them: The famous, both they and the junta understood, are not easily disappeared.

Other human rights organizations in Argentina now sprang up in the mothers' wake. In August 1979 the Association of the Mothers of the Plaza de Mayo was formally registered. That same year the Inter-American Commission on Human Rights was able to visit Argentina and document illegal detention, torture, and disappearances, later condemning the regime.

Finally seams became visible within the junta, as the air force split from the army and navy. Tensions borne of fighting the Dirty War and maintaining a fictitious normality were now worsened by a collapsing economy. Yet another coup occurred, led by a hard-line general who decided to produce a splendid diversion. In March 1982 Argentine marines landed on the Falkland Islands (or *Malvinas*), a British possession claimed by Argentines. It was a ruinous miscalculation. Argentine forces were unceremoniously routed by a British naval armada dispatched by Prime Minister Margaret Thatcher. Before another year elapsed, the control of Argentina passed to a constitutional, elected government.

For the mothers of the Plaza de Mayo, this might have meant the end of a long, often lonely struggle. In fact, it was only a point of new departure. They now resisted the military's attempt to declare an amnesty for the malefactors of the Dirty War, declaring that their children's assassins had to face justice.

Today, the oldest survivors among the original mothers are in their seventies and eighties. Many still feel the effects of the days of marching, of beatings and detentions. But the force they fashioned became a permanent feature of the political landscape, as Argentine women, and aggrieved women elsewhere in Latin America, put on white scarves. In the twentieth century there was no better emblem of the fact that replacing fear with truth is the first step toward freedom.

Václav Havel said that those who acquiesce to a dictator's rule are "living a lie" and that when they begin to "live in the truth," it opens up "explosive, incalculable political power" in the society. To do that requires courage, especially when the ruler's authority is poised on the point of a bayonet.

Thirty years before *las Madres de la Plaza de Mayo*, the non-Jewish wives of Jewish men being rounded up for the Holocaust stood for a week on the streets of Berlin and demanded their husbands' release. The Nazis' will to terrorize did not make them invulnerable: They were alarmed at protest at the seat of their power, and the cost of suppressing that—though trifling in blood and time—was too high politically. So the evil they embodied was, in that place and at that moment, impotent.

Strutting narcissistically, the uniformed regimes of Germany and Argentina were confounded by unyielding groups of unpretentious women. There are perhaps no two stories in the long development of nonviolent conflict involving a starker contrast of opponents: storm troopers using terror and women without weapons.

History continues to show little correlation between the degree of a regime's brutality and its ability to maintain control. Throughout the 1990s, Serbian president Slobodan Milosevic had brought genocide to Bosnia, ethnic cleansing to Kosovo, and political oppression to his own people. But in the year 2000, a broad-based, nonviolent civilian movement, sparked initially by young students and unifying around a single new leader, prevented Milosevic from stealing an election and then forced him from power by subverting his control of his own police and military. The man who had been called "the butcher of the Balkans" was brought down without a single violent death.

Today one-quarter of the world is still held in subjection by rulers who refuse to listen to their own people. Their days are numbered, because, as Archbishop Desmond Tutu has said, "when people decide they want to be free, there is nothing that can stop them"—not the evil of any regime nor the terror it can inflict on a few. Resistance begins with a few. But it can end with liberation.

Peter Ackerman and Jack DuVall are authors of *A Force More Powerful: A Century of Nonviolent Conflict* (St. Martin's Press, 2000), from which parts of this chapter were drawn. They also produced the PBS documentary series by the same name. Ackerman is chairman of the Board of Overseers of the Fletcher School of Law and Diplomacy and executive producer of the Peabody Award–winning film *Bringing Down a Dictator,* on the fall of Serbia's Slobodan Milosevic. DuVall is president and Ackerman founding chair of the International Center on Nonviolent Conflict (*www.nonviolent-conflict.org*), which supports the study and use of civilian-based, nonmilitary strategies aimed at establishing and defending human rights, democratic self-rule, and justice worldwide.

CHAPTER FORTY-THREE

Composing a Life Story

Mary Catherine Bateson

There are advantages in having access to multiple versions of your life story. I am not referring to a true version versus a false version, or to one that works in a particular therapeutic context as opposed to others, or to one that will sell to *People* magazine as opposed to ones that won't. I am referring to the freedom that comes not only from owning your memory and your life story but also from knowing that you make creative choices in how you look at your life. It can be very difficult to recognize the ways in which one situation or event in your life is linked to others. When you are able to see multiple levels of changes and consistency, you are empowered to make your own decisions.

When I was working on my memoir of my parents, *With a Daughter's Eye*, I found an example of this in my father's life. Some of you may know my father, Gregory Bateson, as a great anthropologist, a great thinker. But in the middle of his life, he went through a difficult period that went on for some time. From year to year he didn't know whether he would have a salary, whether there would be anything to live on.

His career at that time must have seemed totally discontinuous. First he was a biologist. Then he got interested in anthropology and went to New Guinea, where he made a couple of field trips that he never wrote up. Then to Bali.

During the war he wrote an analysis of propaganda films and worked in psychological warfare. Then he did a study of communication in psychotherapy. Then he worked on alcoholism and schizophrenia, and then on dolphins and octopuses. Somehow he turned into a philosopher.

One of the things that I realized while I was putting together the memoir is that only when he drew together a group of his articles—all written in very different contexts for very different audiences, with apparently different subject matters—and put them into the book called *Steps to an Ecology of Mind,* did it become clear to him that he had been working on the same kind of question all his life: The continuous thread through all of his work was an interest in the relationships between ideas.

The interruptions that forced him to change his research focus were absolutely critical to pushing him up the ladder of logical types, so that ultimately he could see continuity at a very abstract level. His insight, his understanding of what he had been working on all his life, was a result of a sometimes desperate search for a continuity beyond the discontinuities.

When I started writing *Composing a Life*, the issue that I wanted to write about was the issue of discontinuity. Part of my interest in this was based on two events in my own life. One was that I had just gone through the experience of losing, in a rather painful way, a job that I cared about. I had been forced to change jobs before, because of my husband changing jobs, and I had had to adapt to that situation. So what I set out to do was to look at a group of women who had been through a lot of transitions and who were able to cope with the changes. I was asking the question, "How on Earth does one survive this kind of interruption?"

The other circumstance that made me focus on the issue of discontinuity had to do with my experiences in Iran. At the time of the Iranian revolution, my husband and I had been living and working there for seven years. We, and a great many of our friends, had to make fresh starts; many Iranians became refugees. The way they interpreted their situation was absolutely critical to their adjustment. I could see very clearly, among them, that there were those who came into the refugee situation with a sense that they had skills and adaptive patterns that they could transfer to the new situation. They were emphasizing continuity. Other people came into the refugee situation feeling that their lives had ended and they had to start from zero. You could see that the choices people made about how to interpret the continuities and discontinuities in their lives had great implications for the way they approached the future.

There are three meanings that "composing a life," as a phrase, has to me. Two of those meanings refer to different arts, in that I see the way people live their lives as, in itself, an artistic process. An artist takes ingredients that may seem incompatible, and organizes them into a whole that is not only workable, but finally pleasing and true, even beautiful. As you get up in the morning, as you make decisions, as you spend money, make friends, make commitments, you are creating a piece of art called your life. The word "compose" helps me look at two aspects of that process.

Very often in the visual arts, you put together components to find a way that they fit together and balance each other in space. You make a visual composition of form and color. One thing that you do in composing a life is to put together disparate elements that need to be in some kind of balance, like a still life with tools, fruit, and musical instruments. This sense of balance is something that women have been especially aware of in recent years because they cannot solve the problem of composing the different elements of their lives simply by making them separate, as men have.

Of course, less and less are men able to do so. But for a long time it was possible for men to think in terms of a line between the public and the private. A man would go to the workplace and then, at a certain point, he would switch that off and go home to a different world where the atmosphere was different. He could switch gears from one aspect of his life to the other.

But it hasn't been possible for women to separate their commitments in quite the same way. It is one thing in the traditional nuclear family for the husband to go to the office and stop thinking about his family during the day because he has left his wife in charge. It is quite a different thing for both parents to go off and feel that they can completely forget what is happening with the family. Many women have the sense that the combining of different areas in their lives is a problem that is with them all the time.

What this has meant is that women have lived their lives experiencing multiple simultaneous demands from multiple directions. Increasingly men are also living that way. So thinking about how people manage this is becoming more and more important. One way to approach the situation is to think of how a painter composes a painting: by synchronously putting together things that occur in the same period, and finding a pattern in the way they fit together.

But of course "compose" has another meaning in music. Music is an art in which you create something that happens over time, that goes through various transitions over time. Looking at your life in this way, you have to look at the change that occurs within a lifetime—discontinuities, transitions, and growth of various sorts—and the artistic unity, like that of a symphony with very different movements, that can characterize a life.

Those two meanings of composing a life—one that relates to visual art and the other that relates to music—will crop up again in this essay. But what I want to emphasize is a third meaning, one that has to do with the ways in which you compose your own versions of your life. I'm referring to the stories you make about your life, the stories you tell first to yourself and then to other people, the stories you use as a lens for interpreting experience as it comes along. What I want to say is that you can play with, compose, multiple versions of a life.

For instance, most people can tell a version that emphasizes the continuities in their lives, to make a single story that goes in a clear direction. But the same people can also tell their life stories as if they were following on this statement: "After lots of surprises and choices, or interruptions and disappointments, I have arrived some place I could never have anticipated."

For example, one version of my life story goes like this: I already thought of myself as a writer when I was in high school, and there hasn't been a year since college that I haven't published something. Now I spend half the year writing full-time and half the year writing and teaching. Many of my students are future writers.

That's one version of me. The other version goes like this: I planned in high school to be a poet. But I gave up writing poetry in college. The only writing I did for years was academic publish-or-perish writing. When I became unemployed because of the Iranian revolution, shortly after my mother died, I dealt with unemployment by starting to write a memoir. I suddenly found that I could write nonfiction. Now I'm considering switching again and writing a novel.

Both of these are true stories. But they are very different stories.

One person told me that there had been so much discontinuity in her life that it wasn't hard to think of a discontinuous version, but it was painful to tell it. I think that is a problem many people have. Because our society has preferred continuous versions of stories, discontinuities seem to indicate that something is wrong with you. A discontinuous story becomes a very difficult story to claim.

I would say that the most important effect of my book, *Composing a Life*, has been to give people who feel that they've been bumped from one thing to another, with no thread of continuity, a way of positively interpreting their experience. You might be uncomfortable with your life if it has been like the *Perils of Pauline*, yet many of us have lives like that. One strategy for working with that is to make a story that interprets change as continuity. One of my favorites was someone who said, "My life is like surfing, with one wave coming after another." He unified his whole life with that single simile.

Of course, in composing any life story, there is a considerable weight of cultural pressure. Narratives have canonical forms.

One of the stories that we, as a culture, respond to is the story in which the hero or heroine's end is contained in the beginning. For example, there is a film about Henry Ford that I happened to see recently on television. In one scene, he sees his first horseless carriage as a little boy and falls in love with it. In other words, you have an episode in childhood that prefigures all that is to come. Think about how many biographies you have read in which the baby who grew up to be a great violinist loved lullabies, or loved listening to the radio: stories about talent that was visible from the very beginning.

Another popular plot is one that we can think of as the conversion narrative. It's a simple plot. Lives that in reality have a lot of zigzags in them get reconstrued into before-and-after narratives with one major discontinuity. One very interesting example of this is the *Confessions of St. Augustine*, which tells the story of his life before and after his conversion to Christianity. The narrative structure requires that he depict himself before conversion as a terrible sinner, that he devalue all that he did before he was converted, and that he dredge up sins to talk about so that he can describe a total turnaround.

Reading this book today, what strikes me is that St. Augustine after his conversion to Christianity was not that different from St. Augustine before his conversion to Christianity. He pursued a reasonable intellectual life. He was a seeker. He experimented with different things. After his conversion, it is true, he disowned his mistress, who had borne him a son, which is construed, in this story, as a sign of virtue. But he continued to be, as he is throughout the narrative, profoundly self-centered. The universe was apparently organized around bringing him to God, and other people were very peripheral. In that sense, you can follow the same story throughout the book.

The conversion narrative can be a very empowering way of telling your story, because it allows you to make a fresh start. The more continuous story, in which the end is prefigured in the beginning, is powerful in different ways. But what I want to emphasize are the advantages of choosing a particular interpretation at a particular time, and the even greater advantage of using multiple interpretations.

The availability of multiple interpretations of a life story is particularly important in terms of how different generations communicate with each other. When we, as parents, talk to our children about our lives, there is a great temptation to edit out the discontinuities, to reshape our histories so that they look more coherent than they are. But when we tell stories to our children with the zigzags edited out, it causes problems for many of those children.

A lot of young people have great difficulty committing themselves to a relationship or to a career because of the feeling that once they do, they're trapped for a long, long time. On the other hand, they feel they've got to get on the right "track" because, after all, this is a long and terrifying commitment. I think it is very liberating for college students when an older person says to them, "Your first job after college need not be the beginning of an ascending curve that's going to take you through your life. It can be a zigzag. You might be doing something different in five years." That's something that young people need to hear: that the continuous story, where the whole of a person's life is prefigured very early on, is a cultural creation, not a reflection of life as it is really lived.

The ways in which we interpret our life stories have a great effect on how our children come to define their own identities. An example of this occurred in my own life when my daughter was about to become a teenager. She said to me, "Gee Mom, it must be awfully hard on you and Daddy that I'm not interested in any of the things you're interested in." I said, "What do you mean?" She said, "Well, you're professors. You write books about social science. I'm an actress. I care about theater." I said a secret prayer because it was clearly a very tricky moment. Maybe she needed to believe in that discontinuity. Maybe it was worrying her and she needed to get away from that discontinuity.

But what I said to her was, "Well, to be a social scientist, to be an anthropologist, you have to be a good observer of human behavior. You have to try and understand how people think and why they behave as they do. It strikes me that that's pretty important for a good actor." She has been telling that story ever since because it gave her permission, first, to pursue what she deeply wanted to pursue without feeling she was betraying me and her father. But it also gave her permission to use anything she might pick up from us by giving her a way of construing the cross-generational relationship as a continuity.

The choice you make affects what you can do next. Often people use the choice of emphasizing either continuity or discontinuity as a way of preparing for the next step. They interpret the present in a way that helps them construct a particular future.

Much of coping with discontinuity has to do with discovering threads of continuity. You cannot adjust to change unless you can recognize some analogy between your old situation and your new situation. Without that analogy you cannot transfer learning. You cannot apply skills. If you can recognize a problem that you've solved before, in however different a guise, you have a much greater chance of solving that problem in a new situation. That recognition is critical to the transfer of learning.

If you create continuity by freezing some superficial variable, the result, very often, is to create deep change. This is something my father used to talk about in relation to evolutionary theory. He used the example of a tightrope walker. The tightrope walker is walking along a high wire, carrying a very light bamboo rod. To keep his balance, he continually moves the rod. He keeps changing the angle of the rod to maintain a constancy, his balance in space. If you froze the rod, what would happen to him? He would fall off. In other words, the superficial variation has the function of maintaining the deeper continuity. In evolution, the deeper continuity is survival. For the tightrope walker, it's staying on the high wire.

Among the people I've talked to, it's clear that those who stay the course with their commitments are those who are able to ride the changes and to adapt. At some fundamental level, they are able to bridge all the superficial changes, and to say,

"My commitment is the same commitment that brought me here in the first place." They are people with an extraordinary capacity to translate.

Adapted from a talk on the value for individuals of alternative interpretations of their past in creating the future. Mary Catherine Bateson is the author of *Composing a Life* (Grove Press, 2001), *Willing to Learn: Passages of Personal Discovery* (Steerforth Press, 2004), and *Composing a Further Life: The Age of Active Wisdom* (Vintage, 2011). Used with permission of Mary Catherine Bateson.

PART EIGHT

Beyond Hope

ORIGAMI EMOTION

Elizabeth Barrette

Hope is
folding paper cranes
even when your hands get cramped
and your eyes tired,
working past blisters and
paper cuts,
simply because something in you
insists on
opening its wings.

Elizabeth Barrette's books include *Prismatica: Science Fiction Poetry Spanning the Spectrum* (Diminuendo Press, 2010) and *From Nature's Patient Hands* (Diminuendo Press, 2010).

From THE NEW YORK POEM

Sam Hamill

. . . a mute sadness settles in,
like dust, for the long, long haul. But if
I do not get up and sing,
if I do not get up and dance again,
the savages will win . . .

Excerpted from "The New York Poem." Sam Hamill is the founding editor of Copper Canyon Press. His books include *Dumb Luck* (BOA editions, 2002) and *Border Songs* (Word Temple Press, 2012), and he edited *Poets Against the War* (Thunders Mouth Press/Nation Books, 2003), in which this poem appears. See *www.poetsagainstthewar.org*).

Sometimes we achieve the impossible sooner than we expect. Knowing that can stiffen our resolve. But relying on quick victories can also tempt us to place too much emphasis on outcomes; it can cause us to become unduly impatient, brittle, with our will easily broken by setbacks. A deeper, more farseeing hope, by contrast, combines realism with resilience, acknowledging suffering and despair without giving in to them.

There is even a kind of hope beyond hope, which happens only when we're willing to act whether or not we ever see results. By letting go of impatient hope we can persist no matter how hard it gets. Certainly tangible victories matter; if we're facing an important election we need to do everything possible to ensure that more humane values prevail, even if the candidates are less than ideal. We need to be as intentional as possible as we think through our approaches, figure out how to tell our story, devise plans to gather crucial allies, and reach out to key constituents—all in the process of building momentum for change. But since we won't always win, we need ways to continue regardless of the outcome. The more we accept that we can't always dictate the results of our actions, the more we free ourselves to keep doing the work that seems most necessary.

Mary-Wynne Ashford outlines this paradox in "Staying the Course": If we let go of immediate expectations, yet refuse to quit when our plight seems bleakest, she says, we can rediscover not only our own sense of meaning and purpose but also a deeper and more grounded hope. Ashford, former president of the Nobel Peace Prize–winning International Physicians for the Prevention of Nuclear War, begins by exploring her own temptation to despair. She compares the experience to that of Sisyphus as he endlessly rolls his rock up the hill, but with one crucial difference: Sisyphus acted alone. "We sustain each other in dark times," Ashford writes, "sometimes simply by being present together. . . . Whether or not we succeed in pushing the rock up the hill, there is meaning in the journey, not in the hope that one time we'll be able to shed the rock forever and live in a perfect world." We can't predict the future, Ashford says, but for all our doubt and hesitation, we can choose how to live and what to fight for. She therefore urges us to join with others in the pursuit of what may seem impossible, drawing strength from community, as Sisyphus, acting alone, could not.

Acting together is essential if we're going to keep on. We've explored this theme before: Nelson Mandela and his fellow prisoners passing news from cell to cell on toilet paper, John Lewis's image of children holding hands in a storm, the mothers of the Plaza de Mayo communing in silent witness, Mary Pipher holding a potluck with her friends to challenge a seemingly inevitable Keystone XL pipeline. There's no more important lesson if we're going to learn to persist: Isolation, whether physical or psychological, starves the human spirit; connection feeds and heals it. In her book *Small Wonder*, Barbara Kingsolver draws on this sense of connection to resist those "who say it's ridiculous to imagine that the world could be made better than it is. When I come down to this feeling that I am an army of one standing out on the broad plain waving my little flag of hope, I call up a friend or two and offer to make dinner for us. We remind ourselves that we aren't standing apart from the crowd, we are a crowd. We're a prairie fire, a church choir, a major note in the American chord. . . . We're the theater of the street, the accurate joy of children's hearts, the literature of tomorrow's wisdom arrived today, just in time. I'm with Emma Goldman: Our revolution will have dancing—and excellent food. In the long run, the choice of life over death is too good to resist."

Embracing life also means opening ourselves up to suffering. Though community heals our souls, we're taught to keep our pain to ourselves, especially when it's the result of powerful political or economic interests. Yet sharing outrage and grief is a critical part of keeping going. In "The Elm Dance," Buddhist activist Joanna Macy describes the Soviet city of Novozybkov. A decade after the nuclear meltdown at Chernobyl and fifteen years before the disastrous nuclear meltdown in Fukushima, Japan, residents were riddled with cancers and birth defects. The superintendent of schools carried a Geiger counter in his car so that he could tell children where not to play on a given day. Surrounding forests remain so radioactive that generations to come will never be able to walk among the trees. Yet those affected began to recover from their losses by grieving together publicly, talking about the spring day when white ash fell from a clear sky. "It feels like my heart is breaking open," said a mother who had asked what good her tears were if they couldn't protect her daughters. "Maybe it will keep breaking again and again every day, I don't know." The simple act of telling what happened made her feel more connected to others. Through public mourning she found another kind of community.

But what if we're torn away from our communities? Under Stalin, prisoners were deliberately isolated in Siberia. Nadezhda Mandelstam recalls struggling to avoid drowning in despair when she and her husband, the poet Osip Mandelstam, were deported to a Stalinist labor camp. They didn't know whether they'd ever be released. Osip eventually died in another camp. But Nadezhda refused to resign herself to the fate the dictatorship had designed for her. Silence, she concluded, "is the real crime against humanity."

Most of us will never experience conditions remotely as ghastly as those suffered by the Mandelstams. But that doesn't mean that we won't sometimes feel powerless, as if the future were out of our hands—particularly regarding the largest and most overwhelming issues. When political powerlessness overwhelms us, it's tempting simply to give up, or to rage at the world, convinced that no matter what we do, no one will listen and nothing will change. Like the caller on Diane Ackerman's suicide line, we see no options, no way to proceed, just an endless dark tunnel of bleakness with no windows or doors, albeit in a more limited sphere. Most of us have had times when we've felt so politically helpless that we can think of nothing to do except curse those whose greed or arrogance knows no bounds. One way out of this dilemma is to identify modest tasks that have at least a decent chance to move us in the right direction.

While listening to the news, for example, I'll often feel boxed in, helpless before vast institutional forces. Then I'll stop, take a breath, and think of some small way to act—a letter I can write, a phone call I can make, a campaign I can help promote, some person or community I can approach who might just get others engaged. Instead of obsessing about how awful the situation is, I'll focus on ways to chip away at the problem. For all the inevitable frustrations, and whether or not my efforts achieve their immediate goals, concentrating on useful, readily doable tasks helps me shift gears and put my strengths in service of what I believe. At least, as Howard Zinn would say, I'm back in the game.

It helps in this regard to cultivate what we might call radical stubbornness, the willingness to continue acting even when we feel temporarily defeated. I remember a week where nothing was going right for the Campus Election Engagement Project that's been the prime focus of my time and energy over the past few years. As with any challenging project, we've faced more than a few of those weeks. Anticipated donations fell through. Sympathetic contacts at major foundations unexpectedly left. Health issues sandbagged key staffers. At one point I was close to tears. But then I thought about the importance of what we were doing. I took a break, went for a run, and got back on the phone the next day. Over the following week, our community of existing supporters began to come through. The week afterward, we got the largest contribution in the history of the project. It was a reminder of the importance of keeping on.

Focusing on taking action also allows us to be moved by human suffering without feeling paralyzed and overwhelmed by this recognition. Coming to grips with what we're doing to our fellow human beings and to the earth isn't always easy. But it lets us take the next step. And to stare the horrors of the world in the face and still take action, no matter now minor it may seem, can be surprisingly empowering. As Macy's Novozybkov residents made clear, sharing sorrow and anger can also, paradoxically, lift our spirits. It can help us break out of the gated community of the heart that separates us both from each other and from any common future.

There will always be times when the deck seems stacked against us. Money already dominates our country's political and cultural life in a profoundly destructive way, yet institutions like the Supreme Court grant ever more power to those who already treat democracy as their private Monopoly game. To make matters worse, far too many poor, working-class, and even middle-class people—those who are being shortchanged—either withdraw from the political process altogether or elect representatives who make their lives still harder by gutting critical common services, ramming through tax packages that benefit only the rich, and undermining the ability to vote. Although engaged citizens like the Progressives and the Populists overcame a similar erosion of democracy in the past, it's an open question whether we'll get past our culture's omnipresent distractions and omnipresent reasons for cynicism to meet the even more consequential challenges of our time.

But in struggles for justice, neither victory nor failure is certain. As K. C. Golden writes in "The Inevitability Trap," defeat—even regarding seemingly intractable issues like climate change—is certain only if we accept it as such. What we often call preordained only becomes so through our resignation. So the only way to discover what's achievable is by taking action, trying new approaches, expanding the bounds of the possible. Golden's group, Climate Solutions, mixes environmental advocacy on issues like coal exports with climate-change consulting for Pacific Northwest corporations, small businesses, and local governments. The sponsors of the group's annual breakfast recently included Boeing and Alaska Airlines, with which Climate Solutions is working to develop algae-based and other sustainable bio-fuels—a partnership that would have been nearly unimaginable a short while ago.

Will efforts like these be enough? In "Is There Hope on Climate Change?" David Roberts of the wonderful online environmental magazine *Grist* ponders this question, knowing full well that failure spells catastrophe. Echoing Howard Zinn, Roberts takes heart from community, from the intrinsic value of acting, and from the very uncertainty of prediction. Hope isn't "about the future," Roberts argues, "as much as it is about the present." In other words, it's the choices we make here and now that have the potential to rescue us from despair—and by so doing, alter a common future. Or as Roberts concludes, "We don't know when history might unlock the door, so we have no choice but to keep pushing on it."

History, in short, is contingent. Nothing is guaranteed, anything can happen. And this is precisely why hoping beyond hope, rather than accepting the transient impositions placed on us by particular social and political circumstances, holds such promise. As Atlanta activist Sonya Vetra Tinsley reminds us, we'll never know who will ultimately prevail, so we have to pick the "team" we want to be on. And who wouldn't choose to join the team that keeps working for change over the team of cynical despair?

In a *Salon* article, novelist Anne Lamott gives this attitude toward the world a name that you might not have expected in this book: hopelessness. "The reason I never give up hope," she writes, "is because everything is so basically hopeless. Hopelessness underscores everything—the deep sadness and fear at the center of life, the holes in the heart of our families, the animal confusion within us. . . . But when you do give up hope, a lot can happen. When it's not pinned wriggling onto a shiny image or expectation, it sometimes floats forth and opens like one of those fluted Japanese blossoms, flimsy and spastic, bright and warm. This almost always seems to happen in community."

It would be easy to misunderstand Lamott. She's not celebrating bleakness. She's saying that if we can detach ourselves from the consequences of our actions and concentrate instead on, to employ Thomas Merton's terms, "the value, the rightness, the truth" of the actions themselves, we gain the strength to do what needs to be done.

Again, none of this removes the need for conscious, intentional action. But sometimes we really don't know the impact of what we do until long afterward. Change can be transmitted by communities unknown to each other, or existing in different places or historical times. Our impact on those whose actions we seek to change or whose power we seek to curtail can also be hidden. In 1969, Richard Nixon's envoy, Henry Kissinger, told the North Vietnamese that the president would escalate the Vietnam War, and even use nuclear strikes, unless they capitulated and forced the National Liberation Front in the South to surrender as well. Nixon had military advisers prepare detailed plans, including mission folders with photographs of potential nuclear targets. But two weeks before the president's November 1 deadline, there was a nationwide day of protest, the Moratorium; millions of Americans joined local demonstrations, vigils, church services, petition drives, and other forms of opposition. The next month, more than half a million people marched in Washington. An administration spokesperson announced that Nixon had watched the Washington Redskins football game and that the demonstrators wouldn't affect his policies in the slightest—thereby feeding the frustration of far too many in the peace movement and accelerating the descent of a few into violence. Yet privately, as we now know from Nixon's memoirs, he decided that the movement had, in his words, so "polarized" American opinion that he couldn't carry out his threat. Moratorium participants had no idea that their efforts may have helped stop a nuclear attack.

Since we can't predict the future or even always read the present's impact, perhaps, as Margaret Wheatley suggests in "From Hope to Hopelessness," we should let go of expectations altogether. "Anytime we hope for a certain outcome," she writes, "and work hard to make it happen, then we also introduce fear—fear of failing, fear of loss." Instead, Wheatley suggests concentrating less on the measurable impact of what we do, and more on the value and appropriateness of our work and on the communities we build in the process. It's no accident that many of those who've devoted their lives to creating a more humane world while also having experienced the worst forms of oppression share this outlook. "When I was younger," says Abe Osheroff, a friend of mine who fought in the Spanish Civil War, and died, still politically engaged, at ninety-two, "I acted because I hoped to achieve a certain something. Now I'm path-oriented. I act to get in contact with the best part of who I am. I do the work whether we win or lose."

There's a paradox here as well. If we let go of consequences altogether, we can delude ourselves into thinking that critical life-and-death outcomes don't matter. Yet if we base our commitment solely on whether we'll prevail, we run the risk of giving up before the full promise of history is fulfilled. "The only kinds of fights worth fighting are those you are going to lose," wrote the radical journalist I. F. Stone, "because somebody has to fight them and lose and lose and lose until someday, somebody who believes as you do wins. In order for somebody to win an important, major fight a hundred years hence, a lot of other people have got to be willing—for the sheer fun and joy of it—to go right ahead and fight, knowing you're going to lose. You mustn't feel like a martyr. You've got to enjoy it."

CHAPTER FORTY-FOUR

Staying the Course

Mary-Wynne Ashford

I once borrowed five hours of tapes from a popular radio series about current environmental crises, and listened to them one after another over a weekend. By Monday, I was paralyzed with despair. I felt like the mythical Sisyphus in his task of endlessly pushing a rock uphill. Onto the weight of the nuclear arms race, I had now cemented overpopulation, ozone depletion, drift-net fishing, destruction of the rain forests, the Great Lakes dying. And this was before I started thinking about global warming. For a time, I couldn't put my shoulder to the rock at all.

How do you find hope when there is no rational reason for optimism? How do you deal with evidence that the situation is worsening despite your best efforts? Does your life make any difference? How do you continue in the face of despair?

Albert Camus, in his 1947 novel *The Plague*, explores the same questions, using an epidemic of bubonic plague to represent evil and suffering, specifically the Nazi occupation of France and the collusion of the Vichy regime. The protagonist, Dr. Rieux, fights against suffering and death, not as a hero, but as a weary, somewhat detached man, who through his struggle gives his life meaning. His friend, Tarrou, speaks of having had the plague when he discovered as a child that his father's role as a judge was to sentence and preside over death.

In choosing how to respond to the plague, Camus's characters are motivated not by hope, but by an inner imperative similar to that often described by those who chose to risk their lives saving Jews from the Holocaust. The rescuers say that they were faced with someone at the door, and simply did what had to be done. Viktor Frankl also writes that finding meaning in life is independent of hope or freedom, as he describes life in a Nazi concentration camp, where daily tasks of living often represent a refusal to acquiesce.

Joanna Macy writes of visiting a group of monks in Tibet. The monks were reconstructing their ancient monastery, which had been reduced to rubble by the Chinese. Her heart fell at the magnitude of the task and its almost foolhardy nature. When the monks were asked about Chinese policies and the likelihood of another period of repression, Macy saw that such calculations were conjecture to the monks. Since you cannot see into the future, you simply proceed to put one stone on top of another, and another on top of that. If the stones get knocked down, you begin again, because if you don't nothing will get built.

The planetary crises raise existential and spiritual questions we are usually able to avoid in our affluent society. I find that the question of how to face hopelessness is one I cannot answer with consistency and intellectual rigor. On the one hand, optimism probably represents denial of the facts: The scientific research offers little evidence that nature can recover from the man-made destruction wrought in this century. I know, therefore, that I cannot rationally base my decisions on the hope that we will turn things around. On the other hand, I find that I cherish the small signs that people are taking action to promote change, and when I see them, I feel a tiny surge of optimism that I am unwilling to repress. My compromise is to work without depending on hope that it will make a difference, while at the same time treasuring the signs that I am one of many.

In spite of my despair after hearing the radio series, I found myself continuing my efforts in disarmament, not because it seemed to be the most urgent problem, or the most terrifying, but because there were things to be done in disarmament that were clear to me. Whether or not I could really make a difference, leaving them undone was a resignation to despair. At the very least, the individual can challenge the silence of assumed consensus. By breaking the silence, by refusing to collude with evil and insanity, one resists the darkness.

Breaking the silence is, I think, the most significant thing we do as individuals. Sometimes even without speaking, one can challenge the silence, as did the women in Argentina during the military regime. These women, *las Madres de la Plaza*, refused to be intimidated by death squads. They kept their regular vigil, their presence alone a blatant accusation of murder and brutality. They also showed that the power of one is acted out in community, not in solitude. We sustain each other in dark times, sometimes simply by being present together.

The result of "speaking truth to power," as the Quakers put it, is often subtle and unpredictable. Men who left their jobs in US military industries as a result of a crisis of conscience describe individuals who forced them to confront the meaning of their work on nuclear weapons. One senior official told of the impact of passing a solitary man who stood every day outside the entrance to the Lawrence Livermore Laboratory, holding a placard opposing nuclear weapons. The anonymous protester played a significant role in the official's eventual decision to resign his job.

Sometimes, we look to great individuals like Mother Teresa or Nelson Mandela to see that one person can effect change. I find it more inspiring to see the impact of ordinary people who did what they saw had to be done without becoming great symbols of resistance. I think, for example, of hearing the executive director of the Manila YWCA speaking at a peace meeting in Honolulu. She was asked whether the YWCA had had any part in the overthrow of dictator Ferdinand Marcos and the election of Corazón Aquino.

Well, yes," she admitted, "we did."

"What did you do?" the audience demanded.

"Well, I lay on the road to keep the tanks from coming into the downtown, and the other women brought food and water."

Whether or not we succeed in pushing the rock up the hill, there is meaning in the journey, not in the hope that one time we'll be able to shed the rock forever and live in a perfect world. In the end, we stay the course in our everyday actions—shouldering the burden, working in community, speaking truth to power, and refusing to join forces with the pestilence.

Mary-Wynne Ashford, MD, is the former president of the Nobel Peace Prize–winning organization International Physicians for the Prevention of Nuclear War and teaches at the University of Victoria. An earlier version of this article appeared in Canada's *Peace* magazine.

CHAPTER FORTY-FIVE

The Elm Dance

Joanna Macy

It was Harasch who insisted that we come to Novozybkov. A Russian psychologist practicing in Moscow, he had flown to Chernobyl within hours of the 1986 nuclear disaster, to give support to the operators of the doomed reactor. In the years that followed, he traveled to towns throughout the region to help the survivors, and none had touched his heart more deeply than this city and its fate.

Now, six years after Chernobyl's nuclear meltdown, our team of four—Harasch, Yuri, my husband Fran, and I—had been traveling from one town to another in Byelorussia and Ukraine, offering workshops to people living in contaminated areas. Our last stop was Novozybkov, an agricultural and light industrial city of 50,000 a hundred miles east of Chernobyl, in the Bryansk region of Russia.

Drawing on what we learned from years of leading workshops on despair and empowerment, we came to offer, as we put it to the authorities, "psychological tools for coping with the effects of massive, collective trauma." We had entitled the workshops "Building a Strong Post-Chernobyl Culture." The name had a nice Soviet ring to it, but I soon realized that the word "post" was in error. "It suggests that the disaster is over," I said to Fran, "but it has become obvious to us that it isn't over. It compounds itself through time in vicious circles, in positive feedback loops." The radioactivity was still spreading silently through wind, water, and food, creating new toxins as it mixed with industrial pollution and sickening bodies already weakened from previous exposures. Our workshops, we soon realized, were meant not to help people recover from a previous catastrophe, but to live with an ongoing one.

On the train, as we headed east from Minsk toward the Russian border, Harasch pulled out the map and told us the story once more. The burning reactor was a volcano of radioactivity when the winds shifted to the northeast, carrying the clouds of poisoned smoke in the direction of Moscow. To save the millions of people in the metropolitan area, a fast decision was taken to seed the clouds and cause them to precipitate. An unusually heavy late April rain, bearing intense concentrations of radioactive iodine, strontium, cesium, and particles of plutonium, drenched the towns and fields and forests of the Bryansk region, just across the Russian border from Chernobyl.

The highest Geiger-counter readings were measured, as they still are, in and around Novozybkov. As with some of the US nuclear releases of the 1940s and 1950s, the people there were not informed of their government's choice—who wants to tell people they're disposable? By now it's common knowledge that the clouds were seeded, but it is rarely mentioned. That silence is part of the tragedy for the people of Novozybkov.

In a big open room of a school for special education, fifty people of Novozybkov, mostly teachers and parents, women predominating, were seated in a large circle. Carefully, almost formally dressed, they sat upright, eyes riveted on the speaker, and stood up when they spoke, the way their children stand in school when called to recite.

As I explained the nature and purpose of the work we'd come to do, I was glad for Yuri's swift and cogent translations. A young physician and social activist, he had used my books extensively in Moscow, and had his own things to say about how people can overcome feelings of isolation and powerlessness, and reconnect to take charge of their lives. To interpret from Russian to English for me, without delaying things, Fran murmured in my ear. By mid-morning there had been so many words. I was glad for a respite from them. I put on the tape of the Elm Dance and showed the simple steps. It's a circle dance we do in every workshop and class I teach, whether on systems theory, Buddhism, or deep ecology. It came from a German friend, created from a Latvian song. We all joined hands and moved together to the music.

We were too many to dance in one circle, so formed concentric rings. The movements are easy to learn, and soon the rings were slowly orbiting to the music. Each time we stepped toward the middle, raising our linked hands high, we looked like a giant sunflower, or a many-petaled lotus.

As we danced, I wondered what the mayor of Novozybkov would think to see us. Our team had called on him upon our arrival the previous day to explain what we'd come to do. The handsome, heavyset man of about forty listened guardedly. "It is good of you to come to undertake psychological rehabilitation," he said.

That was the term now in vogue: psychological rehabilitation. I was glad that the emotional toll of the disaster was at last acknowledged by the authorities, especially since, in the three years following the accident, doctors were ordered by the Ministry of Health to dismiss its effects. When people insisted that their sickness and exhaustion, their cancers, miscarriages, and deformed babies, had something to do with Chernobyl, they were diagnosed as afflicted with "radiophobia," an irrational fear of radiation. Still the phrase "psychological rehabilitation" irked me; I considered it an affront to the people of Chernobyl. It reduced their suffering to a pathology, as if it were something to be corrected.

How could we convey to the mayor the basic difference in our assumptions? "Mr. Mayor, we do not imagine that we can take away the suffering of your people," I said. "That would be presumptuous on our part. But what we can do is look together at two main ways we respond to collective suffering. The suffering of a people can bring forth from them new strengths and solidarity. Or it can breed isolation and conflict, turning them against each other. There is always a choice."

At that the mayor's demeanor totally changed. Leaning back in his chair, he spread his hands on the table and said, "There is not a single day, nor a single encounter in this office, that does not reveal the anger that stirs just under the surface. Whatever the matter at hand, there is this anger that is barely contained, ready to explode." Then, after a pause, "Tell me if there is anything I can do to support your work here."

It became clear, however, on that first day of the workshop, that these people had little desire to talk about Chernobyl and its ongoing presence in their lives. They referred to it in passing as "the event," and went on to speak of other things. People in less contaminated towns than this had told us in detail of the exhaustion, the chronic infections, the emerging patterns of cancers and birth defects. Now I'd come to the most toxic place of all, to be with these people in their suffering, and they didn't want to talk about it. Even when a married couple took turns leaving in the morning and afternoon, they said no word about their little girl in the hospital, to whose bedside they hurried.

The group's silence seemed to say, "This we don't need to talk about. We have to deal with this nightmare all the rest of our time. Here, at last, we can think about something else. We can look together at how we can achieve some sanity and harmony in family life." On that last, they were explicit. They wanted to know how to deal with defiant children, sullen, absent spouses, backbiting neighbors.

Okay, we'll focus on family life. It was lively, as people took partners to enact encounters between parents and children, switching roles, practicing how to listen to each other. This led them to remember their own childhoods—not only the adolescent frustrations that could help them empathize with their own offspring, but the good times, too. They shared reminiscences of harvest seasons with the grandparents, and sleigh parties, and fishing outings to the Dneiper.

Why did this feel so important? "We're strengthening our cultural immune system," I thought to myself, then said aloud.

Just as radiation attacks the integrity of the body, so does it assault our society, eroding its sense of wholeness and continuity. To bolster our cultural immune system, we need to remember who we are and the sources of our strength; memories help us do that, don't they?

Evening now, and before disbanding to go home, we are circling once more to the music—guitar music with a woman singing. She sings in Latvian in honor of the elm and in hope of its healing, for that tree ails in the Baltics as in my own country. Her words, I'm told, disguise other meanings as well—a call for freedom from Soviet occupation, and for the will to endure and resist. It doesn't matter that we don't know Latvian; it's the lilt of her voice that we dance to, and the haunting melody, stately and filled with yearning.

By now the simple steps are so familiar that some people are dancing with eyes closed. Their faces grow still, as if listening for something almost out of reach. Once they had their own folk dances. When did those old traditions die away, relegated to a useless past? Was it under Lenin, Stalin?

Our hosts, Fran's and mine, live in a fourth-floor apartment in a cement housing block. Covering one wall of their parlor is a beautiful woodland scene: sunlight flickers through birch trees into a grassy glade. In the room crowded with overstuffed furniture, that wallpaper vista provides a refreshing sense of space and natural beauty. I commented on it that evening, as I took tea with Vladimir Ilyich, our host's father and the Novozybkov school superintendent. Sitting there with his ten-year-old grandson, he was showing me the large Geiger counter he carries in his car; it shows him where the poison has newly appeared, and where to tell the children not to play.

Following my eyes, Vladimir Ilyich said, "That is where the children may not go—or any of us, for that matter. You see, the trees stay radioactive a long time. Our ancestors were of the forest. During the Nazi occupation, our partisans fought from the forest. Even in the hardest times under Stalin, we went into the woodlands every holiday, every weekend—walking, picnicking, mushrooming. Yes, we were always people of the forest." Quietly, he repeated "people of the forest."

I asked him, "When will you be able to go back into the forest?" With a tired little smile he shrugged. "Not in my lifetime," he said, and looking at his grandson, he added, "and not in his lifetime either." Then he gestured to the wallpaper. "This is our forest now."

It is the second morning of our three days together, and the people entering the school assembly room take each other's hands and, before any words are spoken, move into the Elm Dance. Every fourth measure, between moving right or left, forward or backward, we pause for four beats, gently swaying. To my eyes this morning, we could be trees, slender trunks swaying from firm roots, and our arms, as we raise them, look like branches meeting, interlacing. Do we dance for the forests we can no longer enter?

That afternoon the grief broke open.

It happened unexpectedly, at the close of a guided journey in which I invited these people of Novozybkov to connect with their ancestors and harvest their strengths. Standing and moving through the room, as on a vast wheel turning, they moved backward in time through all preceding generations.

Yuri's voice guiding them enriched my words. Then they moved forward through time, retracing their steps to gather, for their own present use, the gifts of the ancestors. But on that return trip, when we reached the year of 1986, they balked. They did not want to come any further into the present. They refused to accept the horror of what happened to them then—and that very refusal compelled them to speak of it.

Talk exploded, releasing memories of that unacceptable spring—the searing hot wind from the southwest, the white ash that fell from a clear sky, the children running and playing in it, the drenching rain that followed, the rumors, the fear. Remember how it was? Remember, remember? Our team had laid out paper and colored pencils for people to use to draw the gifts they'd harvested from the ancestors, but now there was one theme only. A number of the drawings featured trees, and a road to the trees, and across the road a barrier, or large X, blocking the way.

When we finally reassembled in the large circle, the good feelings that had grown since the workshop began shattered in anger, directed at me. "Why have you done this to us?" a woman cried out. "What good does it do? I would be willing to feel the sorrow—all the sorrow in the world—if it could save my daughters from cancer. Each time I look at them I wonder if tumors will grow in their little bodies. Can my tears protect them? What good are my tears if they can't?"

Angry, puzzled statements came from others, as well. Our time together had been so good until now, so welcome a respite from what their lives had become; why had I spoiled it?

Listening to them all, I felt deeply chastened and silently blamed myself for my insensitivity. What, now, could I possibly say? When I finally broke the silence that followed the long outburst, I was surprised that the words that came were not about them or their suffering under Chernobyl, but about the people of Germany who had given me the dance.

"I have no wisdom with which to meet your grief. But I can share this with you: After the war that almost destroyed their country, the German people determined that they would do anything to spare their children the suffering they had known. They worked hard to provide them a safe, rich life. They created an economic miracle. They gave their children everything—except for one thing. They did not give them their broken hearts. And their children have never forgiven them."

The next morning, as we took our seats after the Elm Dance, I was relieved to see that all fifty were still there. Behind us, still taped to the walls, hung the drawings of the previous afternoon, the sketches of the trees and the slashing X's that barred the way to the trees. "It was hard yesterday," I said. "How is it with you now?"

The first to rise was the woman who had expressed the greatest anger, the mother of the two daughters. "I hardly slept. It feels like my heart is breaking open. Maybe it will keep breaking again and again every day, I don't know. But somehow—I can't explain—it feels right. This breaking connects me to everything and everyone, as if we were all branches of the same tree."

Of the others who spoke after her that last morning, the one I recall most clearly was the man I recognized as the father who regularly stepped out to visit his little girl in the hospital. This was the first time he had addressed the whole group, and his bearing was as stolid, his face as expressionless, as ever. "Yes, it was hard yesterday," he said. "Hard to look at the pain, hard to feel it, hard to speak it. But the way it feels today—it is like being clean, for the first time in a long time." *Chisti*, the word he used for clean, also means uncontaminated.

At my turn, I spoke of the meeting I would attend the following week in Austria, the World Uranium Hearing, where native peoples from around the world would testify to their experiences of nuclear contamination. Navajo and Namibian miners would come, Marshall Islanders, Kazakhs, Western Shoshone downwinders from American testing sites, and many others to speak out about the disease and death that follow in the wake of nuclear power and weapons production. I wanted them to know they are not alone in their suffering, but part of a vast web of people determined to use their painful experience to help restore the health of our world. "At the hearing, I will speak of you in Novozybkov, and I will tell your story to my own people back home. I promise you."

I have kept the promise I made to my friends in Novozybkov. I spoke of them at the World Uranium Hearing, and then to every group I met. Soon I was telling their story around the world by sharing the Elm Dance they loved. Everywhere I lead workshops, I ask people to imagine they are dancing with the men and women of Novozybkov and that the hands they hold are the hands of Vladimir, Elena, Olga, Igor, Misha. I want them to feel, more strongly than they can through words alone, how their lives are interlaced with the people of Chernobyl.

Joanna Macy's books include *Widening Circles* (New Society Publishers, 2000), from which this essay is adapted; *Coming Back to Life* (New Society Publishers, 1998); *World as Lover, World as Self* (Parallax Press, 2007); and *Active Hope: How to Face the Mess We're in Without Going Crazy* (with Chris Johnson, New World Library, 2012). Based on five decades of activism, she leads workshops worldwide on psychological and spiritual issues of the nuclear age, the cultivation of ecological awareness, and the resonance between Buddhist thought and contemporary science. For more information, see *www.joannamacy.net*.

CHAPTER FORTY-SIX

Is There Hope on Climate Change?

David Roberts

Over the last 10 years, I've been asked one question more than any other: Is there any hope of avoiding civilization-threatening climate disruption? If there is, the US and other nations must act immediately and aggressively on an unprecedented scale.

On the other side, we have the many forces that retard or prevent change. Cognitively, we suffer from status quo bias and loss aversion. Psychologically and physiologically, we are designed to heed immediate threats with teeth and eyes, not long-term, incremental, invisible dangers. Socioeconomically, power is concentrated in the hands of wealthy incumbents who benefit from the carbon-intensive status quo: fossil fuel companies, the sprawl industry (roads, real estate), Big Ag, airlines, heavy manufacturers, and so on. Politically, we are gripped by polarization, dysfunction, and paralysis. Individually and collectively, we are extremely poor judges of risk, particularly the sort of risk posed by climate change. That makes social change, what sociologist Max Weber called the "slow boring of hard boards," halting and painful at best.

And so we are stuck between the impossible and the unthinkable.

It's difficult to see a way out of this dilemma that doesn't involve considerable suffering. Limiting global temperature rise to 2 degrees Celsius, the widely agreed-upon threshold beyond which climate impacts are expected to become severe and irreversible, is likely off the table. Widespread adaptive measures are slow in coming, far more expensive than prevention would have been (and still would be), and subject to enormous inequality of impact based on wealth and class.

So, in this grim situation, do I have hope? It's complicated.

What does it mean, exactly, to have hope? It's not a prediction. If we're being coldly rational, we look to the climate and economic models that show current trends in fossil fuel use and carbon emissions extending out as far as the eye can see. A Vegas bookie making odds would probably say that the good money's against us.

And hope is surely not just about possibility. Sure, it's possible we could stop rising temperatures at 2 degrees. There are scenarios floating around that demonstrate how it could happen, if we decided to make it happen. If all hope required was possibility, people wouldn't be asking the question.

So, if not a prediction and not mere possibility, what are we asking about when we ask about hope?

I don't think it's about the future as much as it is about the present. It's about whether it's worth it to learn about this stuff, carry the weight of it, talk about it with other people when they don't want to hear it, fight against overwhelmingly steep odds, suffer daily disappointments and setbacks. If tomorrow we die, would it not be better just to eat, drink, and be merry? What good is all this anxiety, pain, and yearning?

We fear heartbreak. That's why we reach out for hope.

The sad truth is that there's no guarantee against heartbreak, in this or anything else. It looks like things are going to get bad, possibly really bad, even within my children's lifetimes. The decisions we're making today will reverberate for centuries, and so far we're blowing it.

With no obvious path to victory (where victory means minimizing suffering and maximizing resilience in the face of climate change), the question is how to proceed. How do we maintain our equilibrium, our happiness and fighting spirit, with disappointments so common, victories so rare, and unthinkable loss looming?

Though it may seem odd, I find comfort in chaos theory. For all our sophistication, we remain terribly inept at the simple task of predicting what will happen more than a few years out. All our models fail. That means those who predict a steady extension of the status quo will be wrong, too.

The outcome of the climate crisis depends not just on physical forces but on human beings and on complex economic, social, and technological systems—and complex systems are nonlinear. We forget this; our instinct is to think the future will look like the recent past, only more so. We don't anticipate the lateral moves, the lurches, the phase shifts. Because of this, the Very Serious thing to do is always to predict that things will not substantially change. If you say, "There will be a series of brilliant innovations that make clean energy cheap," or, "There will be a sea change in public opinion on climate," or, "Young people will take over and revive politics," you sound like a hippie dreamer. Those aspirations are a matter of faith, a triumph of hope over experience.

And yet: things change! History unfolds along the lines of what Stephen Jay Gould called "punctuated equilibrium." Things can appear stable for years and years while tensions gather beneath the surface, hairline fractures develop, and the whole system becomes highly sensitive to small perturbations. We do not know what those perturbations will be or when they will emerge, but we know from history that what Donald Rumsfeld called "unknown unknowns" are inevitable. The North American natural gas boom, the precipitous decline in solar photovoltaic prices, the financial crisis—none were widely predicted. And there will be more like them.

Will unexpected, rapid changes in coming decades be good or bad, positive or negative? That depends on millions of individual choices made in the interim. Some of those choices, if they happen at just the right moment, could be just the perturbations that spark cascading changes in social, economic, or technological systems. Some of those choices, in other words, will be incredibly significant.

Which ones? That we cannot know. It could be any of them, any time. Precisely because we cannot know—because any one of our choices might be key—we must act. We must take advantage of every affordance, grasp every opportunity. We don't know when history might unlock the door, so we have no choice but to keep pushing on it.

And really, what else are we going to do?

Remember, there is no "too late" here, no "game over"—it will be a tragedy to shoot past 2 degrees to 3, but 4 is worse than 3, and 5 is worse than 4. Being unprepared for any of those will be much worse than being prepared. The future always forks; there are always better and worse paths ahead. There's always a difference to be made.

When we ask for hope, then, I think we're just asking for fellowship. The weight of climate change, like any weight, is easier to bear with others. And if there's anything I've learned in these last 10 years, it's that there are many, many others. They are out there, men and women of extraordinary imagination, courage, and perseverance, pouring themselves into this fight for a better future.

You are not alone. And as long as you are not alone, there is always hope.

David Roberts is a staff writer for *www.Grist.org*, where this piece originally appeared. He and his colleagues do top-level environmental reporting, mixed with a sense of humor.

CHAPTER FORTY-SEVEN

The Inevitability Trap

K. C. Golden

It's time to rally around an embattled concept: free will.

Having aligned myself against a battalion of seemingly irresistible forces over the years, I've become a student of "inevitability." How do environmentally destructive *choices* become inevitable? Near as I can tell, it starts when the people who will benefit from these choices simply begin to assert their inevitability. We're especially receptive to inevitability right now. We're comforted by the notion that amid all the uncertainty and confusion, from the economy to climate disruption—some larger forces are at work toward predetermined outcomes. We're sort of relieved to hear that something's inevitable, even if it's not necessarily something we like. It clarifies things. It's more pragmatic to be resigned to the inevitable than to chart a new course through the chaos. Plus, it spares us the disappointment of pinning false hopes on dysfunctional democratic institutions—or working to change them. So the myth of inevitability spreads and the prophecy fulfills itself. If the proponents of a particular course can get a critical mass of folks to believe that it's a foregone conclusion, pretty soon it will be.

Those who assert that conservation and renewables will never replace fossil fuels are using the only strategy available to them. They propound the myth of inevitability because they know that few of us would actually choose more waste, and eternal dependence on coal, oil, and gas extracted in ever-more risky and destructive ways. Having little chance of convincing people that these outcomes are desirable, they tell us we have no choice in the matter.

Think about the arguments that have blocked serious US action on climate change. First, it wasn't happening. Then it was happening but it wasn't human-caused. (Damn those sun spots.) Now maybe it is human-caused but there's nothing we can do because China and India's emissions will swamp us anyway—never mind the American corporations whose manufacturing facilities get counted in their carbon impact. So we might as well shovel and ship their coal because otherwise they'll just burn someone else's. Responsibility is no one's. Resistance is futile.

But *inevitably* we do have choices to make. Failing to make them consciously isn't failing to make them at all; it's just falling for the inevitability trap. It's just giving ourselves an excuse for allowing the wrong choices to be made, and a feeble excuse at that. Among all the reasons for continuing to choose the path of evading responsibility for climate disruption, I think the least satisfying, the least noble, the hardest one to forgive ourselves for is: "It wasn't up to me."

Well, it's up to somebody. Who's it gonna be?

K. C. Golden is policy director of Climate Solutions (*www.climatesolutions.org*), which promotes clean and efficient energy sources. He is also the former director of energy policy for the state of Washington.

CHAPTER FORTY-EIGHT

Hoping Against Hope

Nadezhda Mandelstam

The coach gradually filled with other passengers. The door to our compartment was guarded by a soldier who turned back passengers eager to find places—the rest of the coach was crammed. M. [Osip Mandelstam] stayed by the window, desperate for contact with the two men on the other side, but no sound could penetrate the glass. Our ears were powerless to hear, and the meaning of their gestures hard to interpret. A barrier had been raised between us and the world outside. It was still a transparent one, made of glass, but it was already impenetrable. The train started for Sverdlosk.

At the moment I entered the coach and saw our brothers through the glass, my world split into two halves. Everything that had previously existed now vanished to become a dim memory, something beyond the looking glass, and the future no longer meshed with the past. I am not trying to be literary—this is just a modest attempt to put into words the mental dislocation that is probably felt by all the many people who cross this fateful line. Its first result was utter indifference to what we had left behind.

Until a short time before, I had been full of concern for all my friends and relatives, for my work, for everything I set store by. Now this concern was gone—and fear, too. Instead there was an acute sense of being doomed—it was this that gave rise to an indifference so overwhelming as to be almost physical, like a heavy weight pressing down on the shoulders. I also felt that time, as such, had come to an end—there was only an interlude before the inescapable swallowed us with our "Europe" and our handful of last thoughts and feelings.

How would it come, the inescapable? Where, and in what form? It really didn't matter. Resistance was useless. Having entered a realm of non-being, I had lost the sense of death. In the face of doom, even fear disappears. Fear is a gleam of hope, the will to live, self-assertion. It is a deeply European feeling, nurtured on self-respect, the sense of one's own worth, rights, needs, and desires. A man clings to what is his, and fears to lose it. Fear and hope are bound up with each other. Losing hope, we lose fear as well—there is nothing to be afraid for.

When a bull is being led to the slaughter, it still hopes to break loose and trample its butchers. Other bulls have not been able to pass on the knowledge that this never happens and that from the slaughterhouse there is no way back to the herd. But in human society there is a continuous exchange of experience. I have never heard of a man who broke away and fled while being led to his execution. It is even thought to be a special form of courage if a man about to be executed refuses to be blindfolded and dies with his eyes open. But I would rather have the bull with his blind rage, the stubborn beast who doesn't weigh his chances of survival with the prudent dull-wittedness of man, and doesn't know the despicable feeling of despair.

Later I often wondered whether it is right to scream when you are being beaten and trampled underfoot. Isn't it better to face one's tormentors in a stance of satanic pride, answering them with contemptuous silence? I decided that it is better to scream. This pitiful sound, which sometimes, goodness knows how, reaches into the remotest prison cell, is a concentrated expression of the last vestige of human dignity. It is a man's way of leaving a trace, of telling people how he lived and died.

By his screams he asserts his right to live, sends a message to the outside world demanding help and calling for resistance. If nothing else is left, one must scream. Silence is the real crime against humanity.

Excerpted from *Hoping Against Hope: A Memoir*, by Nadezhda Mandelstam (Modern Library, 1999).

CHAPTER FORTY-NINE

You Have to Pick Your Team

Sonya Vetra Tinsley, as told to Paul Rogat Loeb

Every day presents infinite reasons to believe that change can't happen, infinite reasons to give up. But I always tell myself, "Sonya, you have to pick your team." It seems to me that there are two teams in this world. And that you can find evidence to support the arguments of both. The trademark of one team is cynicism. They'll tell you why what you're doing doesn't matter, why nothing is going to change, why no matter how hard you work, you're going to fail. They seem to get satisfaction out of explaining how we'll always have injustice. You can't change human nature, they say. It's foolish to try. From their experience, they might be right.

Then there's another group of people who admit that they don't know how things will turn out, but have decided to work for change. I see Martin Luther King on that team, Alice Walker, Howard Zinn. I see my chaplain from college and my activist friends. They're always telling stories of faith being rewarded, of ways things could be different, of how their own lives have changed. They'll give you reasons why you shouldn't give up, testimonials why we've yet to see our full potential as a species. They believe we're partners in God's creation, and that change is really possible.

There are times when both teams seem right. Both have evidence. We'll never know who's really going to prevail. So I just have to decide which team seems happier, which side I'd rather be on. And for me that means choosing on the side of faith. Because on the side of cynicism, even if they're right, who wants to win that argument anyway? If I'm going to stick with somebody, I'd rather stick with people who have a sense of possibility and hope. I just know that's the side I want to be on.

Excerpted from *Soul of a Citizen: Living with Conviction in Challenging Times*, by Paul Rogat Loeb (St. Martin's Press, 2010). Sonya Vetra Tinsley is a singer, songwriter, and activist in Atlanta.

CHAPTER FIFTY

From Hope to Hopelessness

Margaret Wheatley

As the world grows ever darker, I've been forcing myself to think about hope. I watch as the world and the people near me experience increased grief and suffering. As aggression and violence move into all relationships, personal and global. As decisions are made from insecurity and fear. How is it possible to feel hopeful, to look forward to a more positive future? The biblical psalmist wrote that "without vision the people perish." Am I perishing?

I don't ask this question calmly. I am struggling to understand how I might contribute to reversing this descent into fear and sorrow, to help restore hope to the future. In the past, it was easier to believe in my own effectiveness. If I worked hard, with good colleagues and good ideas, we could make a difference. Now, I sincerely doubt that. Yet without hope that my labor will produce results, how can I keep going? If I have no belief that my visions can become real, where will I find the strength to persevere?

To answer these questions, I've consulted some who have endured dark times. They have led me on a journey into new questions, one that has taken me from hope to hopelessness.

My journey began with a little booklet entitled *The Web of Hope*. It lists the signs of despair and hope for Earth's most pressing problems. Foremost among these is the ecological destruction humans have created. Yet the only thing the booklet lists as hopeful is that the Earth works to create and maintain the conditions that support life. As the species of destruction, humans will be kicked off if we don't soon change our ways.

E. O. Wilson, the well-known biologist, comments that humans are the only major species that, were we to disappear, every other species would benefit (except pets and houseplants). The Dalai Lama has been saying the same thing in many recent teachings.

This didn't make me feel hopeful.

But in the same booklet, I read a quote from East German dissident Rudolf Bahro that did help: "When the forms of an old culture are dying, the new culture is created by a few people who are not afraid to be insecure." Could insecurity, self-doubt, be a good trait? I find it hard to imagine how I can work for the future without feeling grounded in the belief that my actions will make a difference. But Bahro offers a new prospect, that feeling insecure, even groundless, might actually increase my ability to stay in the work. I've read about groundlessness—especially in Buddhism—and recently have experienced it quite a bit. I haven't liked it at all, but as the dying culture turns to mush, could I give up seeking ground to stand on?

Václav Havel helped me become further attracted to insecurity and not-knowing: "Hope," he states, "is not the conviction that something will turn out well, but the certainty that something makes sense regardless of how it turns out."

Havel seems to be describing not hope, but hopelessness. Being liberated from results, giving up outcomes, doing what feels right rather than effective. He helps me recall the Buddhist teaching that hopelessness is not the opposite of hope. Fear is. Hope and fear are inescapable partners. Anytime we hope for a certain outcome, and work hard to make it happen, then we also introduce fear—fear of failing, fear of loss. Hopelessness is free of fear and thus can feel quite liberating. I've listened to others describe this state. Unburdened of strong emotions, they describe the miraculous appearance of clarity and energy.

Thomas Merton, the late Christian mystic, clarified further the journey into hopelessness. In a letter to a friend, he advised: "Do not depend on the hope of results . . . you may have to face the fact that your work will be apparently worthless and even achieve no result at all, if not perhaps results opposite to what you expect. As you get used to this idea, you start more and more to concentrate not on the results, but on the value, the rightness, the truth of the work itself. . . . You gradually struggle less and less for an idea and more and more for specific people. . . . In the end, it is the reality of personal relationship that saves everything."

I know this to be true. I've been working with colleagues in Zimbabwe as their country descends into violence and starvation by the actions of a mad dictator. Yet as we exchange e-mails and occasional visits, we're learning that joy is still available, not from the circumstances, but from our relationships. As long as we're together, as long as we feel others supporting us, we persevere. Some of my best teachers of this have been young leaders. One in her twenties said: "How we're going is important, not where. I want to go together and with faith." At the end of a conversation that moved us all to despair, another young Danish woman quietly spoke: "I feel like we're holding hands as we walk into a deep, dark woods." A Zimbabwean, in her darkest moment, wrote: "In my grief I saw myself being held, us all holding one another in this incredible web of loving kindness. Grief and love in the same place. I felt as if my heart would burst with holding it all."

Thomas Merton was right: We are consoled and strengthened by being hopeless together. We don't need specific outcomes. We need each other.

Hopelessness has surprised me with patience. As I abandon the pursuit of effectiveness, and watch my anxiety fade, patience appears. Two visionary leaders, Moses and Abraham, both carried promises given to them by their God, but they had to abandon hope that they would see these in their lifetime. They led from faith, not hope, from a relationship with something beyond their comprehension. This is how I want to journey through this time of increasing uncertainty. Groundless, hopeless, insecure, patient, clear. And together.

Margaret (Meg) Wheatley speaks, writes, and consults around the world about new ways to organize. Her books include *Leadership and the New Science* (Berrett-Koehler, 2006), *Turning to Each Other* (Berrett-Koehler, 2009), *Walk Out Walk On: A Learning Journey into Communities Daring to Live the Future Now* (with Deborah Frieze, Berrett-Koehler, 2011), and *So Far from Home: Lost and Found in Our Brave New World* (Berrett-Koehler, 2012). For more information, see *www.margaretwheatley.com*.

PART NINE

Only Justice Can Stop a Curse

STILL I RISE

Maya Angelou

You may write me down in history
With your bitter, twisted lies,
You may trod me in the very dirt
But still, like dust, I'll rise.

Does my sassiness upset you?
Why are you beset with gloom?
'Cause I walk like I've got oil wells
Pumping in my living room.

Just like moons and like suns,
With the certainty of tides,
Just like hopes springing high,
Still I'll rise.

Did you want to see me broken?
Bowed head and lowered eyes?
Shoulders falling down like teardrops,
Weakened by my soulful cries?

Does my haughtiness offend you?
Don't you take it awful hard
'Cause I laugh like I've got gold mines
Diggin' in my own back yard.

You may shoot me with your words,
You may cut me with your eyes,

You may kill me with your hatefulness,
But still, like air, I'll rise.

Does my sexiness upset you?
Does it come as a surprise
That I dance like I've got diamonds
At the meeting of my thighs?

Out of the huts of history's shame
I rise
Up from a past that's rooted in pain
I rise
I'm a black ocean, leaping and wide,
Welling and swelling I bear in the tide.

Leaving behind nights of terror and fear
I rise
Into a daybreak that's wondrously clear
I rise
Bringing the gifts that my ancestors gave,
I am the dream and the hope of the slave.
I rise
I rise
I rise.

From Maya Angelou, *And Still I Rise* (Random House, 1978).

Focusing on the journey rather than the destination, valuing the work and those who join us in it, seeking the deeper form of hope that awaits us on the other side of hopelessness: All this is sound practice. But looking clear-eyed at the many ills of the world still carries a risk. Not only may we find ourselves promoting a needlessly bleak view that alienates others, we may also overdose on anger, leaving our own souls inflexible and raw. "We activists," Naomi Klein writes, "whether grassroots organizers, researchers, or theorists, tend to hop from one atrocity to the next—sweatshops, poisons, sickness, war—until we are pickled in horrors. Gradually, our beliefs, rather than flowing from love for what we are protecting or building, start to flow from more dangerous sources: rage and bitterness."

How can we avoid this? Inspired by an ancient curse collected by anthropologist and novelist Zora Neale Hurston, Alice Walker meditates, in "Only Justice Can Stop a Curse," on the all-too-human impulse to seek revenge: "That the South wind shall scorch their bodies and make them wither. . . . That the North wind shall freeze their blood and numb their muscles. . . . That the West wind shall blow away their life's breath." Deeply upset at those "who have never met any new creature without exploiting, abusing, or destroying it," Walker contemplates the annihilation of humanity. Perhaps it would be best, she wonders, if the ills we've created were indeed to end our tenure on this planet. But she cannot ignore the taste of fresh peaches and the courage of "people at their best, reaching toward their fullness." And that expands her spirit, making her larger than her rage. Never complacent, never willing to compromise, never blind to man-made horror, Walker nonetheless chooses life. Call it defiant generosity.

Many of the battles we need to take on seem like David vs. Goliath situations. And if we persist long enough, sometimes David will win. But as Van Jones points out, that model doesn't always fit the challenges we face. "If you're an activist," Jones writes, "that has a positive side: you want to confront unjust authority, fight against long odds, hold out the possibility of miraculous outcomes. And that's a good thing. But there's a shadow side to David and Goliath, which is that there's got to be some big mean other. You've got to be the small underdog all the time and there's got to be some confrontation between absolute good (you) and absolute evil (the other)."

Plus, Jones suggests, "it could be that you're just in the wrong book of the Bible altogether. It could be that it's not really about David and Goliath; it's really about Noah." If we're dealing with issues like climate change, it's not enough to say that there are evil Goliaths who are letting bad things happen to good people. Because even if they were "to leave the planet, we've still got major, major climate destabilization to deal with. And so it could be that we need to figure out new ways to win—to be open to the possibility that sometimes we can win [some of the Goliaths] over to helping us build the ark."

Although Terry Tempest Williams has every legitimate claim to righteous anger, she, like Walker and Jones, advocates a fierce form of love with the potential, as she's said, "to find a language that opens hearts rather than closes them." Nine women in Tempest Williams's immediate family have had mastectomies from radiation-linked cancers, most likely due to living downwind from 1950s nuclear bomb tests. Seven have died, and her brother died from lymphoma. "The Clan of One-Breasted Women" tells her "family nightmare," the American counterpart to the Chernobyl downwinders. But Tempest

Williams does more than bear witness to the cost of the US government's deceit and neglect: She demands that scarred lives and a wounded Earth be reclaimed. When this essay came out in the pre-Internet days of 1990, activists everywhere passed around faded copies as if they were talismans of hope, and it soon became a classic. "The women couldn't bear it any longer," Tempest Williams writes, describing a dream that inspired her during a later nonviolent protest. "They were mothers. They had suffered labor pains but always under the promise of birth. The red hot pains beneath the desert promised death only, as each bomb became a stillborn. A contract had been made and broken between human beings and the land. A new contract was being drawn by the women, who understood the fate of the Earth as their own."

Through her passionate writing and activism, Tempest Williams urges us to recognize that the fate of others is ours as well, that we cannot break that human contract without doing harm to everyone, including ourselves. Instead, we must continue strengthening it as we go. In an interview with the online magazine *Guernica*, Tempest Williams describes a bridge in Maine that offers a metaphor for our times.

> When we would drive from Bucksport to Belfast, we had to cross this bridge. For years, we would cross this rickety, rusted green bridge, and every time we crossed it, we would hold our breath and think, "I hope we make it across." You'd see these large cables that were holding the bridge up, splitting, sagging, and the car would start rocking. And then, whew! Thank god, you'd be on the other side. We'd all sigh with relief.
>
> And then, some time down the line, we noticed a new bridge was being built. We were still driving on the old bridge, but I was mindful, each time we crossed the old bridge, of the beauty and the design, and at times, the precariousness of this new bridge that was under construction. I kept thinking, "I hope we make it to the new bridge before the old bridge falls down." And then, one miraculous day, the new bridge was

> built and we were driving across it. The old bridge was no longer in use. I feel like we are building this new bridge. I hope we can finish it in time.

Picture a world where all of us work steadily, stubbornly, persistently, to create the bridges between a culture that destroys lives and futures from short-sightedness and greed, and one that respects our fellow humans and the planet that sustains us. Building those bridges won't be easy. We'll need to break through the walls of fear, denial, and timidity that separate us, and challenge the resistance of powers and principalities that know no other ways to act. We're going to need to cultivate Nelson Mandela's "multiplication of courage" at every turn.

That's the challenge the contributors to this book have taken on, and the world they've worked to build. If, like Moses, we never set foot in such a world, and view its full contours only from a distance, we will still have had the satisfaction of glimpsing it and devoting our days to helping others reach it. For as Alice Walker writes, echoing the poet Rumi, "All we own, at least for the short time we have it, is our life. With it we write what we come to know of the world."

For the moment, though, our world remains beautiful but broken. And among our most critical tasks is that of interrupting the cycles of vengeance and violence that emerge when justice is denied or deferred. And reaching out and engaging those who may not be part of our tribe—those with radically different and perhaps radically conflicting perspectives, experiences, and lives. Starhawk works with the International Solidarity Movement, a nonviolent resistance effort uniting Palestinians and Jews. Her essay, "Next Year in Mas'Ha," wrestles with her own temptations toward bitterness after an Israeli soldier drives a bulldozer over one of her comrades, Rachel Corrie, and Israeli soldiers shoot two others. Starhawk feels in a mood to "smash something," she writes, which doesn't mean she will, only that she understands too well the rage that boils over when desperate people see no alternative to self-destructive violence. Instead, she travels on an Israeli settlers' bus, "full of elderly women who could have been my aunts and old men who could have been my uncles," eventually reaching a Palestinian town where ancient olive groves are about to be uprooted and buried to make way for Israel's new "security" wall. Surrounded by anguish, she experiences an unlikely moment of hope during a Seder that brings together Palestinians and their young Israeli supporters. While watching "a people who, faced with utter destruction of everything they need and hold dear, [open] their hearts to the children of the enemy and [ask] for help," Starhawk feels redeemed and renewed.

The Israeli-Palestinian conflict is also the manifest subject of "The Gruntwork of Peace," by the noted Israeli novelist and peace activist Amos Oz. He describes how a promising new peace plan emerged in the midst of near-total despair because long-standing enemies—such as the former commander of the Israel Defense Forces in the Gaza Strip, the Palestinian Authority's minister for prisoner affairs, and a leader of the Tanzim, a Palestinian guerrilla group—were willing to sit down in the same room, speak honestly but respectfully, and then compromise on issues they cared about passionately. Each side resisted, then listened, then gave still more. The plan has now been distributed to almost every household in Israel and the West Bank.

As an American Jew who has cousins in Jerusalem and Tel Aviv, I was deeply moved by these two essays—especially since neither my Israeli relatives nor the Palestinians will be safe until occupation is replaced by a durable peace. Oz and Starhawk do not agree about exactly how to view their common Jewish heritage or what should be done to create a just Middle East peace—whose absence feeds cycles of violence that continue to echo globally—but they both value dialogue, negotiation, and reconciliation. I've included them in this book not as policy experts but as witnesses to the value of sitting down, again and again, to make peace with one's longtime enemies or build bridges to those of differing backgrounds or political views. Talking to one's enemies—or just those in a different political camp—may be as hard, in its own way, as willingly going to jail or facing down a bulldozer to protect a house or an olive grove.

But if we're willing to do the moral and spiritual gruntwork and take the necessary leaps of courage, we can slow down, interrupt, and sometimes even halt seemingly intractable destructive cycles. And we can take a similar approach of broadening our reach when we tackle other seemingly impossible challenges, like climate change and ever-widening economic divides.

No more convincing example of healing based on reconciliation exists than the extraordinary events that have taken place in South Africa since the end of apartheid, described by Desmond Tutu in "No Future Without Forgiveness." That country certainly is no paradise, but as Martin Luther King reminds us, just because our victories are inevitably partial, that makes them no less significant. "A final victory," King says, "is an accumulation of many short-term encounters. To lightly dismiss a success because it does not usher in a complete order of justice is to fail to comprehend the process of achieving full victory."

And South Africa's bloodless revolution and its historically unprecedented attempt at telling the buried stories of injustice in a way that invites everyone into a reconciling community have inspired the world. "Who in their right minds," Tutu asks, "could ever have imagined South Africa to be an example of anything but the most ghastly awfulness, of how not to order a nation's race relations and its governance?" The long-awaited, seemingly inevitable bloodbath did not occur, proving that the "centrifugal force of alienation, brokenness, division, hostility, and disharmony" can be reversed.

Now, Tutu continues to speak out on issues like climate change, and as a voice for those whose voices are rarely heeded. He is called, he says, by the 3 billion poorest people in the world, "who are not responsible for global warming" but "will pay the highest price if wealthy countries refuse to do their fair share." History, as Barbara Ehrenreich rightly observes, has given us "no operating manual, no step-by-step instructions. Nothing is promised, nothing is guaranteed." South Africa has proven that retribution isn't inevitable, that seemingly miraculous victories for human dignity can occur. People can persist even in the most difficult of circumstances, until at last they prevail. Displaying compassion in a situation that might easily have produced only rage, Mandela, Tutu, and their fellow countrymen have shown us the truth in W. H. Auden's admonition, "We must love one another or die." Or Dostoyevsky's recognition that "each one of us is responsible to all others for everything."

South Africa's victory will persist in memory, speaking fierce love to paralyzing rage, solidarity to isolation, and hope to despair, as long as the human experiment continues.

CHAPTER FIFTY-ONE

Only Justice Can Stop a Curse

Alice Walker

Let me start (but not end) with a curse-prayer that Zora Neale Hurston, novelist and anthropologist, collected in the 1920s. And by then it was already old. I have often marveled at it. At the precision of its anger, the absoluteness of its bitterness. Its utter hatred of the enemies it condemns. It is a curse-prayer by a person who would readily, almost happily, commit suicide, if it meant her enemies would also die. Horribly.

> To the Man God: O Great One, I have been sorely tried by my enemies and have been blasphemed and lied against. My good thoughts and my honest actions have been turned to bad actions and dishonest ideas. My home has been disrespected, my children have been cursed and ill-treated. My dear ones have been backbitten and their virtue questioned. O Man God, I beg that this that I ask for my enemies shall come to pass:
>
> That the South wind shall scorch their bodies and make them wither. . . . That the North wind shall freeze their blood and numb their muscles. . . . That the West wind shall blow away their life's breath and will not leave their hair grow, and that their fingernails shall fall off and their bones shall crumble. That the East wind shall make their minds grow dark, their sight shall fail and their seed dry up so that they shall not multiply.

> I ask that their fathers and mothers from their furthest generation will not intercede for them before the great throne, and the wombs of their women shall not bear fruit except for strangers, and that they shall become extinct. I pray that the children who may come shall be weak of mind and paralyzed of limb and that they themselves shall curse them in their turn for ever turning the breath of life into their bodies. I pray that disease and death shall be forever with them and that their worldly goods shall not prosper, and that their crops shall not multiply and that their cows, their sheep, and their hogs and all their living beasts shall die of starvation and thirst. I pray that their house shall be unroofed and that the rain, the thunder and lightning shall find the innermost recesses of their home and that the foundation shall crumble and the floods tear it asunder. I pray that the sun shall not shed its rays on them in benevolence, but instead it shall beat down on them and burn them and destroy them. I pray that the Moon shall not give them peace, but instead shall deride them and decry them and cause their minds to shrivel. I pray that their friends shall betray them and cause them loss of power, of gold and of silver, and that their enemies shall smite them until they beg for mercy which shall not be given them. I pray that their tongues shall forget how to speak in sweet words, and that it shall be paralyzed and that all about them will be desolation, pestilence and death. O Man God, I ask you for these things because they have dragged me in the dust and destroyed my good name; broken my heart and caused me to curse the day that I was born. So be it.

I am sure it was a woman who first prayed this curse. And I see her—black, yellow, brown, or red, "*aboriginal*" as the Ancient are called in South Africa and Australia and other lands invaded, expropriated, and occupied by whites. And I think, with astonishment, that the curse-prayer of this colored woman—starved, enslaved, humiliated, and carelessly trampled to death—over centuries, is coming to pass. Indeed, like ancient peoples of color the world over, who have tried to tell the white man of the destruction that would inevitably follow from the uranium mining plunder of their sacred lands, this woman—along with millions and billions of obliterated sisters, brothers, and children—seems to have put such enormous energy into her hope for revenge, that her curse seems close to bringing it about.

When I have considered the enormity of the crimes against humanity of the rich white men. Against women. Against every living person of color. Against the poor. Against my mother and my father. Against me. . . . When I consider that at this very moment they have taken away education, medicine, housing, and food, in Florida the right to vote. . . . That prominent commentators say the problems of blacks spring from genetic inferiority. When I consider that they are a real and present threat to my life and the life of my daughter, my people, I think—in perfect harmony with my sister of long ago: *Let the Earth marinate in poisons. Let the bombs cover the ground like rain. Let the heated atmosphere go mad, leaving us a world of fires and droughts, floods and hurricanes, the oceans swallowing our cities. For nothing short of total destruction will ever teach them anything.*

And it would be good, perhaps, to put an end to the species in any case, rather than let these wealthy white men continue to subjugate it, and continue their lust to dominate, exploit, and despoil not just our planet, but the rest of the universe, which is their clear and stated intention, leaving their arrogance and litter not just on the moon, but on everything else they can reach.

If we have any true love for the stars, planets, and the rest of Creation, we must do everything we can to keep men like these away from them. They who have appointed themselves our representatives to the rest of the universe. They who have never met any new creature without exploiting, abusing, or destroying it. They who say we poor and colored and female and elderly blight neighborhoods, while they blight worlds.

However, just as the sun shines on the godly and the ungodly alike, so does our destruction of our environment. And with this knowledge it becomes increasingly difficult to embrace the thought of extinction purely for the assumed satisfaction of—from the grave—achieving revenge. Or even of accepting our demise as a planet as a simple and just preventive medicine administered to the Universe. Life is better than death, I believe, if only because it is less boring, and because it has fresh peaches in it. In any case, Earth is my home—though for centuries white people have tried to convince me I have no right to exist, except in the dirtiest, darkest corners of the globe.

So let me tell you: I intend to protect my home. Praying—not a curse—only the hope that my courage will not fail my love. But if by some miracle, and all our struggle, the Earth is spared, only justice to every living thing (and everything is alive) will save humankind.

And we are not saved yet.

My activism—cultural, political, spiritual—is rooted in my love of nature and my delight in human beings. It is when people are at peace, content, *full*, that they are most likely to meet my expectation, selfish, no doubt, that they be a generous, joyous, even entertaining experience for me. I believe people exist to be enjoyed, much as a restful or engaging view might be. As the ocean or drifting clouds might be. Or as if they were the human equivalent of melons, mangoes, or any other kind of attractive, seductive fruit. When I am in the presence of other human beings I want to revel in their creative and intellectual fullness, their uninhibited social warmth. I want their precious human radiance to wrap me in light. I do not want fear of war or starvation or bodily mutilation to steal both my pleasure in them and their own birthright. Everything I would like other people to be for me, I want to be for them. I have been an activist all my adult life, though I have sometimes felt embarrassed to call myself one. In the Sixties, many of us were plagued by the notion that, given the magnitude of the task before us—the dismantling of American apartheid—our individual acts were puny. There was also the apparent reality that the most committed, most directly confrontational people suffered more. The most "revolutionary" often ended up severely beaten, in prison, or dead. Shot down in front of their children, blown up in cars or in church, run over by racist drunks, raped and thrown in the river.

In Mississippi, where I lived from 1967 to 1974, people who challenged the system anticipated menace, battery, even murder, every day. In this context, I sometimes felt ashamed that my contributions at the time were not more radical. I taught in two local black colleges, I wrote about the Movement, and I created tiny history booklets which were used to teach the teachers of children enrolled in Head Start. And, of course, I was interracially married, which was illegal. It was perhaps in Mississippi during those years that I understood how the daily news of disaster can become, for the spirit, a numbing assault, and that one's own activism, however modest, fighting against this tide of death, provides at least the possibility of generating a different kind of "news." A "news" that empowers rather than defeats.

There is always a moment in any kind of struggle when one feels in full bloom. Vivid. Alive. One might be blown to bits in such a moment and still be at peace. Martin Luther King, Jr., at the mountaintop. Gandhi dying with the name of God on his lips. Sojourner Truth baring her breasts at a women's rights convention in 1851. Harriet Tubman exposing her revolver to some of the slaves she had freed, who, fearing an unknown freedom, looked longingly backward to their captivity, thereby endangering the freedom of all. To be such a person or to witness anyone at this moment of transcendent presence is to know that what is human is linked, by a daring compassion, to what is divine. During my years of being close to people engaged in changing the world I have seen fear turn into courage. Sorrow into joy. Funerals into celebrations. Because whatever the consequences, people, standing side by side, have expressed who they really are, and that ultimately they believe in the love of the world and each other enough *to be that*—which is the foundation of activism. It has become a common feeling, I believe, as we have watched our heroes falling over the years, that our own small stone of activism, which might not seem to measure up to the rugged boulders of heroism we have so admired, is a paltry offering toward the building of an edifice of hope. Many who believe this choose to withhold their offerings out of shame.

This is the tragedy of our world.

For we can do nothing substantial toward changing our course on the planet, a destructive one, without rousing ourselves, individual by individual, and bringing our small, imperfect stones to the pile.

In this regard, I have a story to tell.

In the mid-Sixties during a voter-registration campaign in South Georgia, my canvassing partner, Beverly, a local black teenager, was arrested on a bogus moving-violation charge. This was meant to intimidate her, "show her her place," and terrify her family. Those of us who feared for her safety during the night held a vigil outside the jail. I remember the raw vulnerability I felt as the swaggering state troopers—each of them three times Beverly's size, and mine—stomped in and out of the building, scowling at us. The feeling of solidarity with Beverly and our friends was strong, but also the feeling of being alone, as it occurred to me that not even my parents knew where I was. We were black and very young: We knew no one in white America paid the slightest attention to the deaths of such as us. It was partly because of this that we sometimes resented the presence of the white people who came to stand, and take their chances, with us. I was one of those to whom such resentment came easily. I especially resented blond Paul from Minnesota, whose Aryan appearance meant, when he was not with us, freedom and almost worship in the race-obsessed South. I had treated him with coolness since the day we met. We certainly did not invite him to our vigil. And yet, at just the moment I felt most downhearted, I heard someone coming along the street in our direction, whistling. A moment later Paul appeared. Still whistling a Movement spiritual that sounded strange, even comical, on his lips, he calmly took his place beside us. Knowing his Nordic presence meant a measure of safety for us, and without being asked, he offered it. This remains a moment as bright as any I recall from that time.

All we own, at least for the short time we have it, is our life. With it we write what we come to know of the world. I believe the Earth is good. That people, untortured by circumstance or fate, are also good. I do not believe the people of the world are naturally my enemies, or that animals, including snakes, are, or that Nature is. Whenever I experience evil, and it is not, unfortunately, uncommon to experience it in these times, my deepest feeling is disappointment. I have learned to accept the fact that we risk disappointment, disillusionment, even despair, every time we act. Every time we decide to believe the world can be better. Every time we decide to trust others to be as noble as we think they are. And that there might be *years* during which our grief is equal to, or even greater than, our hope. The alternative, however, not to act, and therefore to miss experiencing other people at their best, reaching toward their fullness, has never appealed to me.

Only justice can stop a curse.

This essay includes material adapted and updated from *In Search of Our Mothers' Gardens* (Harcourt, 1983) and from *Anything We Love Can Be Saved* (Random House, 1997). Alice Walker's newest books are *The Cushion in the Road: Meditation and Wandering as the Whole World Awakens to Being in Harm's Way* (New Press, 2013) and *The World Will Follow Joy: Turning Madness into Flowers* (poems) (New Press, 2013).

CHAPTER FIFTY-TWO

The Clan of One-Breasted Women

Terry Tempest Williams

I belong to a Clan of One-Breasted Women. My mother, my grandmothers, and six aunts have all had mastectomies. Seven are dead. The two who survive have just completed rounds of chemotherapy and radiation.

I've had my own problems: two biopsies for breast cancer and a small tumor between my ribs diagnosed as a "borderline malignancy."

This is my family history.

Most statistics tell us breast cancer is genetic, hereditary, with rising percentages attached to fatty diets, childlessness, or becoming pregnant after thirty. What they don't say is living in Utah may be the greatest hazard of all.

We are a Mormon family with roots in Utah since 1847. The "word of wisdom" in my family aligned us with good foods—no coffee, no tea, tobacco, or alcohol. For the most part, our women were finished having their babies by the time they were thirty. And only one faced breast cancer prior to 1960. Traditionally, as a group of people, Mormons have a low rate of cancer.

Is our family a cultural anomaly? The truth is, we didn't think about it. Those who did, usually the men, simply said, "Bad genes." The women's attitude was stoic. Cancer was part of life. On February 16, 1971, the eve of my mother's surgery, I accidentally picked up the telephone and overheard her ask my grandmother what she could expect.

"Diane, it is one of the most spiritual experiences you will ever encounter."

I quietly put down the receiver.

Two days later, my father took my brothers and me to the hospital to visit her. She met us in the lobby in a wheelchair. No bandages were visible. I'll never forget her radiance, the way she held herself in a purple velvet robe, and how she gathered us around her.

"Children, I am fine. I want you to know I felt the arms of God around me."

We believed her. My father cried. Our mother, his wife, was thirty-eight years old.

A little over a year after Mother's death, Dad and I were having dinner together. He had just returned from St. George, where the Tempest Company was completing the gas lines that would service southern Utah. He spoke of his love for the country, the sandstoned landscape, bare-boned and beautiful. He had just finished hiking the Kolob trail in Zion National Park. We got caught up in reminiscing, recalling with fondness our walk up Angel's Landing on his fiftieth birthday and the years our family had vacationed there.

Over dessert, I shared a recurring dream of mine. I told my father that for years, as long as I could remember, I saw this flash of light in the night in the desert—that this image had so permeated my being that I could not venture south without seeing it again, on the horizon, illuminating buttes and mesas.

"You did see it," he said.

"Saw what?"

"The bomb. The cloud. We were driving home from Riverside, California. You were sitting on Diane's lap. She was pregnant. In fact, I remember the day, September 7, 1957. We had just gotten out of the Service. We were driving north, past Las Vegas. It was an hour or so before dawn, when this explosion went off. We not only heard it, but felt it. I thought the oil tanker in front of us had blown up. We pulled over and suddenly, rising from the desert floor, we saw it, clearly, this golden-stemmed cloud, the mushroom. The sky seemed to vibrate with an eerie pink glow. Within a few minutes, a light ash was raining on the car."

I stared at my father.

"I thought you knew that," he said. "It was a common occurrence in the Fifties."

It was at this moment that I realized the deceit I had been living under. Children growing up in the American Southwest, drinking contaminated milk from contaminated cows, even from the contaminated breasts of their mothers, my mother—members, years later, of the Clan of One-Breasted Women.

It is a well-known story in the Desert West, "The Day We Bombed Utah," or more accurately, the years we bombed Utah: Above-ground atomic testing in Nevada took place from January 27, 1951, through July 11, 1962. Not only were the winds blowing north covering "low-use segments of the population" with fallout and leaving sheep dead in their tracks, but the climate was right. The United States of the 1950s was red, white, and blue. The Korean War was raging. McCarthyism was rampant. Ike was it, and the Cold War was hot. If you were against nuclear testing, you were for a Communist regime.

Much has been written about this "American nuclear tragedy." Public health was secondary to national security. The Atomic Energy Commissioner, Thomas Murray, said, "Gentlemen, we must not let anything interfere with this series of tests, nothing."

Again and again, the American public was told by its government, in spite of burns, blisters, and nausea, "It has been found that the tests may be conducted with adequate assurance of safety under conditions prevailing at the bombing reservations." Assuaging public fears was simply a matter of public relations. "Your best action," an Atomic Energy Commission booklet read, "is not to be worried about fallout." A news release typical of the times stated, "We find no basis for concluding that harm to any individual has resulted from radioactive fallout."

On August 30, 1979, during Jimmy Carter's presidency, a suit was filed, *Irene Allen v. The United States of America*. Mrs. Allen's case was the first on an alphabetical list of twenty-four test cases, representative of nearly twelve hundred plaintiffs seeking compensation from the United States government for cancers caused by nuclear testing in Nevada.

Irene Allen lived in Hurricane, Utah. She was the mother of five children and had been widowed twice. Her first husband, with their two oldest boys, had watched the tests from the roof of the local high school. He died of leukemia in 1956. Her second husband died of pancreatic cancer in 1978.

In a town meeting conducted by Utah senator Orrin Hatch, shortly before the suit was filed, Mrs. Allen said, "I am not blaming the government, I want you to know that, Senator Hatch. But I thought if my testimony could help in any way so this wouldn't happen again to any of the generations coming up after us . . . I am happy to be here this day to bear testimony of this."

God-fearing people. This is just one story in an anthology of thousands.

On May 10, 1984, Judge Bruce S. Jenkins handed down his opinion. Ten of the plaintiffs were awarded damages. It was the first time a federal court had determined that nuclear tests had been the cause of cancers. For the remaining fourteen test cases, the proof of causation was not sufficient. In spite of the split decision, it was considered a landmark ruling. It was not to remain so for long.

In April 1987, the Tenth Circuit Court of Appeals overturned Judge Jenkins's ruling on the ground that the United States was protected from suit by the legal doctrine of sovereign immunity, a centuries-old idea from England in the days of absolute monarchs.

In January 1988, the Supreme Court refused to review the appeals court decision. To our court system it does not matter whether the United States government was irresponsible, whether it lied to its citizens, or even that citizens died from the fallout of nuclear testing. What matters is that our government is immune: "The King can do no wrong."

In Mormon culture, authority is respected, obedience is revered, and independent thinking is not. I was taught as a young girl not to "make waves" or "rock the boat."

"Just let it go," Mother would say. "You know how you feel, that's what counts."

For many years, I have done just that—listened, observed, and quietly formed my own opinions, in a culture that rarely asks questions because it has all the answers. But one by one, I have watched the women in my family die common, heroic deaths. We sat in waiting rooms hoping for good news, but always receiving the bad. I cared for them, bathed their scarred bodies, and kept their secrets. I watched beautiful women become bald as Cytoxan, Cisplatin, and Adriamycin were injected into their veins. I held their foreheads as they vomited green-black bile, and I shot them with morphine when the pain became inhuman. In the end, I witnessed their last peaceful breaths, becoming a midwife to the rebirth of their souls.

The price of obedience has become too high.

The fear and inability to question authority that ultimately killed rural communities in Utah during atmospheric testing of atomic weapons is the same fear I saw in my mother's body. Sheep. Dead sheep. The evidence is buried.

I cannot prove that my mother, Diane Dixon Tempest, or my grandmothers, Lettie Romney Dixon and Kathryn Blackett Tempest, along with my aunts, developed cancer from nuclear fallout in Utah. But I can't prove they didn't.

My father's memory was correct. The September blast we drove through in 1957 was part of Operation Plumbbob, one of the most intensive series of bomb tests to be initiated. The flash of light in the night in the desert, which I had always thought was a dream, developed into a family nightmare. It took fourteen years, from 1957 to 1971, for cancer to manifest in my mother—the same time, Howard L. Andrews, an authority in radioactive fallout at the National Institutes of Health, says radiation cancer requires to become evident. The more I learn about what it means to be a "downwinder," the more questions I drown in.

What I do know, however, is that as a Mormon woman of the fifth generation of Latter-day Saints, I must question everything, even if it means losing my faith, even if it means becoming a member of a border tribe among my own people. Tolerating blind obedience in the name of patriotism or religion ultimately takes our lives.

When the Atomic Energy Commission described the country north of the Nevada Test Site as "virtually uninhabited desert terrain," my family and the birds at Great Salt Lake were some of the "virtual uninhabitants."

One night, I dreamed women from all over the world circled a blazing fire in the desert. They spoke of change, how they hold the moon in their bellies and wax and wane with its phases. They mocked the presumption of even-tempered beings and made promises that they would never fear the witch inside themselves. The women danced wildly as sparks broke away from the flames and entered the night sky as stars.

And they sang a song given to them by Shoshone grandmothers:

Ah tie nah, nah	Consider the rabbits
nin nah nah—	How gently they walk on the earth—
ah ne nah, nah	Consider the rabbits
nin nah nah—	How gently they walk on the earth—
Nyaga mutzi	We remember them
oh ne nay—	We can walk gently also—
Nyaga mutzi	We remember them
oh ne nay—	We can walk gently also—

The women danced and drummed and sang for weeks, preparing themselves for what was to come. They would reclaim the desert for the sake of their children, for the sake of the land.

A few miles downwind from the fire circle, bombs were being tested. Rabbits felt the tremors. Their soft leather pads on paws and feet recognized the shaking sands, while the roots of mesquite and sage were smoldering. Rocks were hot from the inside out and dust devils hummed unnaturally. And each time there was another nuclear test, ravens watched the desert heave. Stretch marks appeared. The land was losing its muscle.

The women couldn't bear it any longer. They were mothers. They had suffered labor pains but always under the promise of birth. The red hot pains beneath the desert promised death only, as each bomb became a stillborn. A contract had been made and broken between human beings and the land. A new contract was being drawn by the women, who understood the fate of the Earth as their own.

Under the cover of darkness, ten women slipped under a barbed-wire fence and entered the contaminated country. They were trespassing. They walked toward the town of Mercury, in moonlight, taking their cues from coyote, kit fox, antelope squirrel, and quail. They moved quietly and deliberately through the maze of Joshua trees. When a hint of daylight appeared they rested, drinking tea and sharing their rations of food. The women closed their eyes. The time had come to protest with the heart, that to deny one's genealogy with the Earth was to commit treason against one's soul.

At dawn, the women draped themselves in Mylar, wrapping long streamers of silver plastic around their arms to blow in the breeze. They wore clear masks, which became the faces of humanity. And when they arrived at the edge of Mercury, they carried all the butterflies of a summer day in their wombs. They paused to allow their courage to settle.

The town that forbids children and pregnant women to enter because of radiation risks was asleep. The women moved through the streets as winged messengers, twirling around each other in slow motion, peeking inside homes and watching the easy sleep of men and women. They were astonished by such stillness and periodically would utter a shrill note or low cry just to verify life.

The residents finally awoke to these strange apparitions. Some simply stared. Others called authorities, and in time, the women were apprehended by wary soldiers dressed in desert fatigues. They were taken to a white, square building on the other edge of Mercury. When asked who they were and why they were there, the women replied, "We are mothers and we have come to reclaim the desert for our children."

The soldiers arrested them. As the ten women were blindfolded and handcuffed, they began singing:

You can't forbid us everything
You can't forbid us to think—
You can't forbid our tears to flow
And you can't stop the songs that we sing.

The women continued to sing louder and louder, until they heard the voices of their sisters moving across the mesa:

Ah tie nah, nah
nin nah nah—
ah ne nah, nah
nin nah nah—
Nyaga mutzi
oh ne nay—
Nyaga mutzi
oh ne nay—

"Call for reinforcements," one soldier said.

"We have," interrupted one woman, "we have—and you have no idea of our numbers."

I crossed the line at the Nevada Test Site and was arrested with nine other Utahns for trespassing on military lands. They are still conducting nuclear tests in the desert. Ours was an act of civil disobedience. But as I walked toward the town of Mercury, it was more than a gesture of peace. It was a gesture on behalf of the Clan of One-Breasted Women.

As one officer cinched the handcuffs around my wrists, another frisked my body. She found a pen and a pad of paper tucked inside my left boot.

"And these?" she asked sternly.

"Weapons," I replied.

Our eyes met. I smiled. She pulled the leg of my trousers back over my boot.

"Step forward, please," she said as she took my arm.

We were booked under an afternoon sun and bused to Tonopah, Nevada. It was a two-hour ride. This was familiar country. The Joshua trees standing their ground had been named by my ancestors, who believed they looked like prophets pointing west to the Promised Land. These were the same trees that bloomed each spring, flowers appearing like white flames in the Mojave. And I recalled a full moon in May, when Mother and I had walked among them, flushing out mourning doves and owls.

The bus stopped short of town. We were released.

The officials thought it was a cruel joke to leave us stranded in the desert with no way to get home. What they didn't realize was that we were home, soul-centered and strong, women who recognized the sweet smell of sage as fuel for our spirits.

Reprinted from *Refuge: An Unnatural History of Family and Place* (Vintage Books, 1992). Terry Tempest Williams's other books include *Red: Passion and Patience in the Desert* (Vintage Books, 2002), *The Open Space of Democracy* (Wipf and Stock, 2004), *Finding Beauty in a Broken World* (Vintage, 2009), and *When Women Were Birds* (Picador, 2013).

CHAPTER FIFTY-THREE

Next Year in Mas'Ha

Starhawk

During a month I spent in the occupied territories of Palestine working with the International Solidarity Movement, one of our people, Rachel Corrie, was deliberately run over by a bulldozer driven by an Israeli soldier, and two young men were deliberately shot, one in the face, one in the head. On the eve of Passover, I found myself unable to face the prospect of a Seder, even with my friends in the Israeli peace movement. I couldn't sit and bewail our ancient slavery or celebrate our journey to the Promised Land. I was afraid that I might spew bitterness and salt all over any Seder table I graced, and smash something.

So I went to the peace encampment at Mas'Ha. Mas'Ha needed people, and the moon was full, and I thought I could just lie down on the land under the moonlight and let some of the bitterness drain away.

Mas'Ha is a village on the line of the new so-called "security wall," where a peace camp has been set up at the request of the local people, mostly farmers who are faced with the confiscation of 98 percent of their land.

Mas'Ha, on one of the main roads into Israel proper, once had a thriving trade, until the Israelis closed the road. The farmers grow olives and figs and grapes and wheat, but now the land has been confiscated for the building of the wall, with no compensation offered. In places the wall is a thirty-foot-high concrete barrier, complete with guard towers. Elsewhere it is an electrified fence in a deep ditch surrounded by a swathe of bare, scraped ground, flanked by roads to be continually patrolled by soldiers. It will soon separate the village from the neighboring settlement of Elcanah, with which it has always had peaceful relations. No armed resistance, no suicide bombers, have ever come from Mas'Ha.

Faced with this prospect, given only a few short weeks notice, the village council came to an amazing conclusion. With every reason to hate Israelis, they decided to invite Israelis in, in company with internationals from the International Women's Peace Service (IWPS) and the International Solidarity Movement (ISM). We set up an encampment on the edge of the bulldozers' route, to witness and document the destruction.

To be at Mas'Ha is to be on the absolute edge of the conflict. The roadblock that separates the village from the settlement is the divide between two realities. I got to Elcanah from Tel Aviv on the settlers' bus, full of elderly women who could have been my aunts and old men who could have been my uncles and a few young people, everyone wishing each other Hag Sameach—"happy holiday," for Passover or, in Hebrew, *Pesach*. We drove through one settlement to let people off, and I got a tour of what looks like a transplanted Southern California suburb, complete with lush gardens and new houses, all with an aura of prosperity and complacent security—provided by armed guards and razor wire and the Israeli military. The landscaping featured olive trees in the street dividers: I suspected they had been transplanted from some farmer's stolen fields—the Palestinians' livelihood turned into a decorative element of the settlements. From Elcanah, I walked down the road a few hundred yards and climbed over the roadblock bulldozed to keep Palestinians out of Israel. I was in a dusty village of old stone and new cement houses and shuttered shops, backing onto open hillsides of ancient olives.

The camp at Mas'Ha is on a knoll, two pink tents set up in an olive grove on stony ground studded with wildflowers, yellow broom, and prickly pear. The olives give shade and sometimes a backrest. If you look in one direction, the groves are spread out below the hilltop for miles of a soft gray-green with blue hills in the background and small villages beyond. But encircling the hill, and cutting a gray swath across the hillsides, is the zone of destruction, a wide band of uprooted trees and bare subsoil, where a giant backhoe is wallowing like some giant, prehistoric beast, grabbing and crushing stones, gouging the earth, filling the air with dust and the mechanical bellowing of its engines.

A young man is sitting under a tree as I arrive, writing on stones with a black marker. He's a farmer, he tells me. In Arabic, he writes, "Don't cut the trees." He thinks for a moment, and adds another graceful line. I ask him to translate. He gives me a sweet smile, and points to the ground. "What is this?" "Earth?" I ask, not knowing if he means earth or land or soil. "The earth speaks Arabic," he tells me.

All the Israelis but one have gone, to celebrate *Pesach* with their families. There are only two of us from the ISM and one woman from IWPS who stay over, along with two of the Palestinians, to guard the camp.

As the full moon rises, I lie on the stones and meditate. I am hoping to find some peace or healing, but the Earth is tortured here and all I can feel is her anguish. Down and down, through layers and centuries and epochs, I hear the ancestors weeping. The land is soaked in blood, and generations have faced ruthless powers and been cut down, and why should we be any different?

I am woken up at 3:00 A.M. to take my shift on watch. I sit by the fire, exhausted, and finally drift back into sleep, waking again in the morning feeling sick at heart.

But people begin to arrive, for a midday meeting. The women from the IWPS, and the men from the village, and dozens of Israelis. We sit under the tent with its sides raised, talking about building an international campaign against the wall. One of the men, a stonemason, makes miniature buildings out of the stones at our feet as we talk. "Maybe we can't stop it here," one man from the village says, "but maybe we can stop it other places."

The Israelis who come are mostly young. They are anarchists and punks and lesbians and wild-haired students, and it strikes me that the mayor of Mas'Ha and the village leaders in a very socially conservative society might actually have more in common with the Orthodox Jews who hate them than with these wild social rebels. But the village accepts them all with good grace and a warm-hearted Palestinian welcome. One woman is from the group Black Laundry, which requires a somewhat complicated three-way translation of a Hebrew play on words. She explains that it is a lesbian direct action group, and asks our translator if that's a problem. "Not for me," he says with a slightly quizzical shrug, and the meeting goes on.

Later we meet with the village women, who want to know if we can help them in any way. They are about to lose their source of livelihood: Is there anything we can do? We have a long discussion about what we do in the ISM, and promise to research organizations that do community development work. They are excited to learn that we watch checkpoints and help people get through them. Students from the village who go to the university often get stopped at the checkpoints, or have to walk round through the mountains. Maybe we can help them.

Back at the camp, all the young *shabob*—the term for young unmarried men—have come out for the evening. We sit around the fire while two of the men prepare us dinner, laughing and talking. And suddenly I realize something wonderful is happening. The Israelis and the Palestinians can talk to each other, because most of the young men speak Hebrew. They are hanging out around the fire and talking and telling stories, laughing and relaxing together. They are hanging out just like any group of young people around a fire at night, as if they weren't bitter enemies, as if it could really be this simple to live together in peace.

So it was a strange Seder this year, pita instead of matzoh, the eggs scrambled with tomato, hummous instead of chicken soup, water instead of wine, and instead of the maror, the bitter herbs that I have already tasted, a slight sweet hint of hope.

I can't ever again say "next year in Jerusalem." I can no longer believe in the promise of a land which requires the building of concrete walls and guard towers and ongoing murder to defend it. Far better that we should abandon the old stones of Jerusalem than to practice torture in order to claim it.

But I would like to believe in the promise of Mas'Ha, in the example of a people who, faced with utter destruction of everything they need and hold dear, opened their hearts to the children of the enemy and asked for help. I would like to believe in the Israel reflected in the eyes of those who answer that call. That somehow, on this chasm between the conquerors and those who resist being finally conquered, the bridges and connections and meetings are happening that can tear down the walls of separation.

By next year, the camp at Mas'Ha will most likely be gone. Already the contractors who work for the Israeli military have begun blasting a chasm that will soon cut the olive groves off from the village. An international campaign to stop the building of the wall has begun; but the reality is that they have the capacity to build it faster than we can organize to stop it.

And yet I say it again, as an act of pure faith:

Next year in Mas'Ha.

Starhawk is an activist and organizer who trains people worldwide for involvement in peace and global justice movements. Her books include *The Spiral Dance* (Harper San Francisco, 1999), *Webs of Power: Notes from the Global Uprising* (New Catalyst Books, 2008), *The Earth Path* (Harper One, 2005), and *The Empowerment Manual: A Guide for Collaborative Groups* (New Society Publishers, 2011). Her works have been translated into eight languages. For more information, see *www.starhawk.org*.

CHAPTER FIFTY-FOUR

The Gruntwork of Peace

Amos Oz

I went to the Israeli-Palestinian conference in Jordan in a skeptical frame of mind. I estimated that, as so often in the past, we might succeed in drafting a joint declaration of principles about the need to make peace, to halt terror, to end the occupation and oppression, to mutually recognize each other's rights, and to live as neighbors in two states for two peoples.

We have done all that many times before, at all kinds of conferences and gatherings and with agreements and public statements and what have you. At many points in the past ten years we have been in striking distance of peace, only to slide again into the abyss of violence and despair.

The same old points of dispute would, I feared, trip us up again: "The right of return" or a solution to the refugee problem? "Return to the 1967 borders" or a logical map that also takes the present into account, and not just history? Open and explicit recognition of the national rights of the Jewish and Palestinian peoples to live each in its own country, or just some equivocating platitude about "peaceful coexistence"? Explicit Palestinian assent to finally and absolutely renounce any additional future claims, or "black holes" that would permit an eventual renewal of conflict and violence?

In previous agreements, including the Oslo agreement, the two sides were very careful not to get caught in the "radioactive core" of the conflict. Refugees, Jerusalem, end of the conflict, permanent borders—all these minefields were marked off by white ribbons and their resolution put off to a better future. The Camp David conference collapsed, after all, the minute it trod on those mines.

On the first evening, the members of the two groups meet for an opening talk. It is a few days after the murder of families and children at the Maxim restaurant in Haifa, a few hours after the killing of several innocent Palestinians in Rafiah, children also among them. A strange ambience pervades the room. Here and there someone tries to crack a joke, perhaps in order to mask the mixture of emotion, resentment, suspicion, and goodwill.

Colonel Shaul Arieli, former commander of the Israel Defense Forces in the Gaza Strip, sits facing Samir Rantisi, a cousin of Hamas leader Abd al-Aziz Rantisi. The son of the late Faisal Husseini, Abd al-Qader al-Husseini (named after his grandfather, who in my childhood was referred to as the commander of the Arab gangs, and who was killed in 1948 in a battle with Israeli forces), sits facing Brigadier General Shlomo Brom, a former deputy commander of the Israeli army's strategic planning division. Next to David Kimche, formerly senior Mossad official and director-general of Israel's foreign ministry, sits Fares Kadura, a leader of the Tanzim, a Palestinian militant guerrilla group.

Through the window, beyond the Dead Sea, we can see the small cluster of lights that marks Kibbutz Kalia, which the Geneva document would transfer to Palestinian control. We also see the large dome of lights marking Ma'aleh Adumim, the Jerusalem suburb along the road to Jericho that, according to the same document, would become an inalienable part of the State of Israel.

We talk and debate (in fluent Hebrew) until after midnight with Hisham Abd al-Raziq, who spent twenty-one years—half his life—in Israeli prisons. Now he serves as the Palestinian Authority's minister for prisoners' affairs. He is almost certainly the world's only cabinet minister for prisoners' affairs.

But our own minister-prisoner, Natan Scharansky, is apparently the only person in the entire world who bears the title "minister for diaspora affairs." Some day, Palestine will most likely have a minister for diaspora affairs instead of a minister for prisoners' affairs.

There is a certain intimacy at such meetings: The Israelis and Palestinians are enemies, but not strangers. The Swiss observer at the conference was certainly astonished to see the frequent switches that took place here, in the rooms and in the corridors, between anger and back-slapping and between jabs as sharp as slivers of glass and simultaneous outbursts of laughter. (Nervous but liberating laughter was brought on by unintentional double entendres, such as when an Israeli said "Could I detain you for a moment?" and when a Palestinian said "I'll blow up the meeting on this point.")

When the day comes for the Israelis to sit down with the Syrians, faces will be rigid and stern on both sides of the negotiating table. So the Palestinians are, they say, with the Saudis. But here, in the hotel on the Dead Sea shore (Israeli Knesset member Chaim Oron and former Palestinian cabinet minister Yasir Abd-Rabbo walk around in sandals and shorts), we are more like a long-married couple in their divorce attorney's waiting room. They and we can joke together, shout, mock, accuse, interrupt, place a hand on a shoulder or waist, throw invective at each other, and once or twice even shed a tear.

Because we and they have experienced thirty-six years of intimacy. Yes, a violent, bitter, warped intimacy, but intimacy, because only they and we, not the Jordanians and not the Egyptians and certainly not the Swiss, know exactly what a roadblock looks like and what a car bomb sounds like and exactly what the extremists on both sides will say about us. Because since the Six Day War, we are as close to the Palestinians as a jailer is to the prisoner handcuffed to him. A jailer cuffing his wrist to that of a prisoner for an hour or two is a matter of routine. But a jailer who cuffs himself to his prisoner for thirty-six long years is himself no longer a free man. The occupation has also robbed us of freedom.

This conference was not meant to inaugurate a honeymoon between the two nations. Quite the opposite—it was aimed at, finally, attenuating this warped intimacy. At drafting a fair divorce agreement. A painful, complicated divorce, but also one that unlocks the handcuffs. They will live in their home and we will live in ours. The Land of Israel will no longer be a prison, or a double bed. It will be a two-family house. The handcuffed link between the jailer and his prisoner will become a connection between neighbors who share a stairwell.

Nabil Qasis, a former president of Bir-Zeit University and the Palestinian Authority's minister of planning, is a polite, introverted, melancholy man. He is also a tough negotiator. He is perhaps the only member of the Palestinian group who has no inclination to jest or trade mild jabs with the Israelis. He stops me by the bathroom door to say: "Try, please, to understand: For me, giving up the right of return to the cities and villages we lost in 1948 is to change my identity from here on out."

I really do "try to understand." What the words mean is that Qasis's identity is conditional on the eradication of my identity.

Afterwards, during a discussion in the meeting room, Nabil Qasis raises his voice and demands that the word "return" appear in the document. In exchange, he and his associates will consent to the word being accompanied by reservations. Avraham Burg, a religious Labor member of the Knesset and its former speaker, also raises his voice. He, too, is angry: Let Nabil Qasis give up part of his national identity just as I, Avraham Burg, hereby relinquish no less than a part of my religious faith, inasmuch as I am prepared to agree, with a broken heart, to Palestinian sovereignty on the Temple Mount.

For my part, I say that as far as I'm concerned, "return" is a code name for the destruction of Israel and the establishment of two Palestinian states on its ruins. If there's return, there's no agreement. Furthermore, I will be a party only to a document that contains explicit recognition of the Jewish people's national right to their own country.

This was one of any number of difficult moments of crisis during the conference. In the end, neither the term "right of return" nor the word "return" appear anywhere in the document. It speaks of a comprehensive solution of the entire Palestinian refugee problem, outside the borders of the State of Israel. Moreover, the document we signed, the Geneva Initiative, recognizes, unequivocally, the right of the Jewish people to their own country, alongside the state of the Palestinian people.

As far as I am aware, we have never heard from any representative Palestinian actor the words "the Jewish people," and we have certainly not heard any word of recognition of the Jewish people's national right to establish an independent state in the Land of Israel.

At 2:30 A.M., over the fifteenth cup of coffee, in a break between argument and drafting and between discussion and bargaining, I tell Yasir Abd-Rabbo and several of his associates: Some day we will have to erect a joint memorial to horrible folly, yours and ours. After all, you could have been a free people fifty-five years ago, five or six wars ago, tens of thousands of dead ago—our dead and your dead—had you signed a document similar to this one in 1948. And we Israelis could have long ago lived in peace and security had we offered the Palestinian people in 1967 what this document offers them now. Had we not been inebriated with victory after the conquests of the Six Day War.

There is no point at all to the hysteria that the document's opponents are now encouraging. Its authors know very well that Sharon and his cabinet are the legal government of Israel. They also knew that their initiative, which is the fruit of an intense series of meetings between the parties, conducted in strict secrecy during a period of two years, is no more than an exercise.

The goal of the exercise is solely to present the Israeli and Palestinian publics with a window through which they can view a different landscape—no more car bombs and suicide bombers and occupation and oppression and expropriation, no more endless war and hatred. Instead, here is a detailed, cautious solution that does not circumvent any one of the fundamental questions.

Its fundamental principle is: We end the occupation and the Palestinians end their war against Israel. We give up the dream of Greater Israel and they give up the dream of Greater Palestine. We surrender sovereignty in parts of the Land of Israel where our hearts lie, and they do the same. The problem of the 1948 refugees, which is really the heart of our national security predicament, is resolved comprehensively, completely, and absolutely outside the borders of the State of Israel and with broad international assistance.

If this initiative is put into action, not a single Palestinian refugee camp, afflicted with despair, neglect, hatred, and fanaticism, will remain in the Middle East. In the document we have in hand, the Palestinian side accepts contractually, finally, and irrevocably that it does not have and will never have any future claims against Israel.

At the end of the conference, after the signing of the Geneva Initiative, a representative of the Tanzim told us that we now perhaps see on the horizon the end of the hundred-year war between the Jews and the Palestinians. It will be replaced, he said, by a bitter struggle between those on both sides who promote compromise and peace, and a fanatical coalition of Israeli and Palestinian extremists.

That struggle is now in full force. Sharon opened it even before the Geneva Initiative was published, and the leaders of Hamas and Islamic Jihad rushed to support him, using the very same vocabulary of vituperation.

What does the Geneva Initiative document not have? It has no teeth. It is no more than fifty pages of paper. But if the people on both sides accept it, tomorrow or the day after, they will find that the gruntwork of making peace has already been done. Almost to the last detail. If Sharon and Arafat want to use this paper as a basis for an agreement, its authors will not insist on their copyright. What if Sharon presents a different, better, more intricate, more patriotic plan that is also accepted by the other side? Let him do it. We'll congratulate him. Even though Sharon, as everyone knows, is a weighty personage, my friends and I will bear him on our shoulders.

Amos Oz is the internationally acclaimed author of numerous novels and essays that have been translated into more than thirty languages. He is also one of the founders of Peace Now and lives in Arad in Israel. His books include *The Same Sea* (Harvest Books, 2002), *A Tale of Love and Darkness* (Mariner Books, 2005), *My Michael* (Mariner Books, 2005), and *Between Friends* (Houghton Mifflin Harcourt, 2013). This essay originally appeared in *The Guardian* and is translated by Haim Watzman.

CHAPTER FIFTY-FIVE

No Future Without Forgiveness

Desmond Tutu

A year after the genocide in Rwanda, when at least half a million people were massacred, I visited that blighted land. I went as the president of the ecumenical body, the All Africa Conference of Churches. In my ten-year, two-term presidency, I had tried to take the AACC to its member churches through pastoral visits, especially to those countries that were experiencing crises of one sort or another. Other officers and I also went to celebrate successes when, for instance, democracy replaced repression and injustice in Ethiopia.

In Rwanda we visited Ntarama, a village near the capital, Kigali. In Ntarama, Tutsi tribespeople had been mown down in a church. The new government had not removed the corpses, so that the church was like a mortuary, with the bodies lying as they had fallen the year before during the massacre. The stench was overpowering. Outside the church building was a collection of skulls, some still stuck with *pangas* (machetes) and daggers. I tried to pray. Instead I broke down and wept.

The scene was a deeply disturbing and moving monument to the viciousness that, as human beings, we are capable of unleashing against fellow human beings. Those who had turned against one another in this gory fashion had often lived amicably in the same villages and spoken the same language. They had frequently intermarried and most of them had espoused the same faith—most were Christians. The colonial overlords had sought to maintain their European hegemony by favoring the main ethnic group, the Tutsi, over the other, the Hutu, thus planting the seeds of what would in the end be one of the bloodiest episodes in modern African history.

A few kilometers from this church, some women had begun to build a settlement which they named the Nelson Mandela Village. It was to be a home for some of the many widows and orphans created by the genocide. I spoke to the indomitable leaders of this women's movement. They said, "We must mourn and weep for the dead. But life must also go on, we can't go on weeping." Over at Ntarama, we might say, there was Calvary, death and crucifixion. Here in the Nelson Mandela Village was Resurrection, new life, new beginning, new hope.

I also attended a rally in the main stadium of Kigali. It was amazing that people who had so recently experienced such a devastating trauma could sing and laugh and dance as they did at that rally. Most of the leading politicians were present, from the president on down. I had been asked to preach. I began by expressing the deepest condolences of all their sisters and brothers in other parts of Africa, for people elsewhere had been profoundly shocked at the carnage and destruction.

I said that the history of Rwanda was typical of a history of "top dog" and "underdog." The top dog wanted to cling to its privileged position and the underdog strove to topple the top dog. When that happened, the new top dog engaged in an *orgy* of retribution to pay back the new underdog for all the pain and suffering it had inflicted when it was top dog. The new underdog fought to topple the new top dog, storing in its memory all the pain and suffering it was enduring, forgetting that the new top dog was in its view only retaliating for all that it remembered it had suffered when the underdog had been its master. It was a sad history of reprisal provoking counter reprisal.

I reminded the Tutsi that they had waited for thirty years to get their own back for what they perceived to be the injustices that had been heaped on them. I said that extremists among the Hutu were also quite capable of waiting thirty years or more for one day when they could topple the new government, in which the Tutsi played a prominent role, and in their turn unleash the devastation of revenge and resentment.

I said there was talk about tribunals because people did not want to tolerate allowing the criminals to escape punishment. But what I feared was that, if retributive justice was the last word in their situation, then most Hutu would feel that they had been found guilty not because they *were* guilty but because they were Hutu and they would wait for the day when they would be able to take revenge. Then they would pay back the Tutsi for the horrendous prison conditions in which they had been held.

I told them that the cycle of reprisal and counter reprisal that had characterized their national history had to be broken and that the only way to do this was to go beyond retributive justice to restorative justice, to move on to forgiveness, because without it there was no future.

The president of Rwanda responded to my sermon with considerable magnanimity. They were ready to forgive, he said, but even Jesus had declared that the devil could not be forgiven. I do not know where he found the basis for what he said, but he was expressing a view that found some resonance, that there were atrocities that were unforgivable. My own view was different, but I had been given a fair and indeed friendly hearing. Later I addressed the parliamentary and political leadership of that country and I was not shouted down as I repeated my appeal for them to consider choosing forgiveness and reconciliation rather than their opposites.

Why was I not rebuffed? Why did these traumatized people, who had undergone such a terrible experience, listen to an unpopular point of view? They listened to me particularly because something had happened in South Africa that gave them reason to pause and wonder. The world had expected that the most ghastly bloodbath would overwhelm South Africa. It had not happened. Then the world thought that, after a democratically elected government was in place, those who for so long had been denied their rights, whose dignity had been trodden underfoot, callously and without compunction, would go on the rampage, unleashing an orgy of revenge and retribution that would devastate their common motherland.

Instead there was this remarkable Truth and Reconciliation Commission to which people told their heart-rending stories, victims expressing their willingness to forgive and perpetrators telling their stories of sordid atrocities while also asking for forgiveness from those they had wronged so grievously. Was this not a viable way of dealing with conflict? Might those who had been at one another's throats try to live amicably together?

It was courageous leaders who gave the sides hope that negotiations could lead to a good outcome. At that time we were fortunate to have as President F. W. De Klerk, leader of the Nationalist Party. Whatever the reasons may have been that impelled him to do what he did, he deserves his niche in history for having announced those very courageous decisions in February of 1990: amongst them the unbanning of the African National Congress, the Pan African Congress, and the Communist Party and the release of political prisoners. That wasn't done lightly. Had De Klerk been maybe more apprehensive, he might not have done it. Had he been his granite-like predecessor, we might still be struggling against a vicious system. It was even more fortunate for us that Mr. De Klerk had, as his opposite number, not someone consumed by bitterness, eager for revenge and retribution, saying we are going to give them the same dose of medicine that they gave us once we come to power.

It was our good fortune that on the other side De Klerk found Nelson Mandela, who despite twenty-seven years of incarceration, instead of being consumed by a lust for revenge, demonstrated an extraordinary magnanimity, a nobility of spirit wishing to be able to forgive. Very many in his constituency were saying "We're going to fight to the last drop of blood." There were many, especially young ones, who felt that they could no longer take what had happened to their people for so long and for their own integrity's sake they really had to clobber the other side. By agreeing to negotiations with the Nationalists, Nelson Mandela was putting his reputation and his life, in a sense, on the line. He knew how to inspire hope.

The world could not quite believe what it was seeing. South Africans managed an extraordinary, reasonably peaceful transition from the awfulness of repression to the relative stability of democracy. They confounded everyone by their novel manner of dealing with a horrendous past. They had perhaps surprised even themselves at first by how much equanimity they had shown as some of the gory details of that past were rehearsed. It was a phenomenon that the world could not dismiss as insignificant. It was what enabled me to address my sisters and brothers in Rwanda in a manner that under other circumstances could have been seen as insensitive and presumptuous.

Believers say that we might describe most of human history as a quest for that harmony, friendship, and peace for which we appear to have been created. The Bible depicts it all as a God-directed campaign to recover that primordial harmony when the lion will again lie with the lamb and they will learn war no more because swords will have been beaten into plowshares and spears into pruning hooks. Somewhere deep inside us we seem to know that we are destined for something better than strife. Now and again we catch a glimpse of the better thing for which we are meant—for example, when we work together to counter the effects of natural disasters and the world is galvanized by a spirit of compassion and an amazing outpouring of generosity; when for a little while we are bound together by bonds of a caring humanity, a universal sense of *ubuntu;* when victorious powers set up a Marshall Plan to help in the reconstruction of their devastated former adversaries; when we establish a United Nations organization where the peoples of the Earth can parley as they endeavor to avoid war; when we sign charters on the rights of children and of women; when we seek to ban the use of antipersonnel land mines; when we agree as one to outlaw torture and racism. Then we experience fleetingly that we are made for community, for family, that we are in a network of interdependence.

There is a movement to reverse the awful centrifugal force of alienation, brokenness, division, hostility, and disharmony. God has set in motion a centripetal process, a moving toward harmony, goodness, peace, and justice, a process that removes barriers. Jesus says, "And when I am lifted up from the Earth I shall draw everyone to myself" as He hangs from His cross with outflung arms, thrown out to clasp all, everyone and everything, in a cosmic embrace, so that all, everyone, everything, belongs. None is an outsider—all are insiders, all belong. There are no aliens—all belong in the one family, God's family, the human family.

With all its imperfections, what we have tried to do in South Africa has attracted the attention of the world. This tired, disillusioned, cynical world, hurting so frequently and so grievously, has marveled at a process that holds out considerable hope in the midst of much that negates hope. People in the different places that I have visited and where I have spoken about the Truth and Reconciliation process see in this flawed attempt a beacon of hope, a possible paradigm for dealing with situations where violence, conflict, turmoil, and sectional strife have seemed endemic, conflicts that mostly take place not between warring nations but within the same nation. At the end of their conflicts, the warring groups in the Middle East, the Balkans, Afghanistan, Angola, the Sudan, the two Congos, and elsewhere are going to have to sit down together to determine just how they will be able to live together amicably, how they might have a shared future devoid of strife, given the bloody past that they have recently lived through. Many already have, like those in Northern Ireland, Sri Lanka, Burma, and El Salvador, and this should give us hope.

God does have a sense of humor. Who in their right minds could ever have imagined South Africa to be an example of anything but the most ghastly awfulness, of how not to order a nation's race relations and its governance? We South Africans were the unlikeliest lot and that is precisely why God has chosen us. We cannot really claim much credit ourselves for what we have achieved. We were destined for perdition and were plucked out of total annihilation. We were a hopeless case if ever there was one. God intends that others might look at us and take courage. God wants to point to us as a possible beacon of hope, a possible paradigm, and to say, "Look at South Africa. They had a nightmare called apartheid. It has ended. Your nightmare will end too. They had a problem regarded as intractable. They are resolving it. No problem anywhere can ever again be considered to be intractable. There is hope for you too."

Archbishop Desmond Tutu won the Nobel Peace Prize in 1984. This essay is adapted from *No Future Without Forgiveness* (Doubleday, 2000) and from his recent speeches. With his daughter, Mpho Tutu, he is also the author of *Made for Goodness: And Why This Makes All the Difference* (Harper, 2011).

Acknowledgments

First, thanks to Craig Comstock. I've appreciated Craig's skill, sensibility, and intellect since I met him thirty-five years ago. As a Harvard student, he came up with the idea that became the Peace Corps and convinced then-Senator John F. Kennedy's staff to make it part of Kennedy's platform. During the Reagan era, Craig pioneered the US-Soviet citizen exchanges that eventually helped end the Cold War. I brought Craig in on this project to help me edit down some of the pieces I'd assembled. Not only did he help ensure that every excerpt spoke as powerfully as possible to this book's purpose, he also brainstormed on its mix, balance, and sequence, making valuable suggestions in every possible area, and has played an integral role in updating this new edition. Craig, who has also co-edited three excellent books, can be reached at *www.bookcreationcoach.com*. I'd recommend him to anyone as an exemplary editor and coach. Liz Gjelten helped as always on framing and structure. And Edwin Dobb added his masterful touch in both the initial and revised editions to ensure that I said what I meant with more grace than I could ever have achieved on my own. Both Ed and Liz have been there for me since the beginning of my writing career.

I began this book by compiling all the authors who most sustained my hope, so appreciation to all I've included and to all the others who've fed my vision. I'd also like to thank the community of readers who regularly receive my articles (you can join at *www.paulloeb.org/subscribe.html*) and particularly those who responded when I asked for pieces that most inspired them. Some of my favorite pieces are the result of this outreach, and *The Impossible* would be far weaker without them. Glen Gersmehl gets the prize for suggesting the most authors that I included.

I would never have built this community without the success of my previous book, *Soul of a Citizen*. Thanks to Nichole Argyres and especially Peter Janssen for helping it find its audience, and to Becky Koh for commissioning it originally. Thanks to Harvey McKinnon for his innovative promotional ideas, which have played a key role in helping both *Soul* and *The Impossible* reach major audiences. Other friends who've helped keep me doing this work in the face of inevitable obstacles and setbacks include Alan Bernstein, Jerry Chroman, Lenny Dee, Gary Drieblatt & Nancy Sinkoff, Carolyn Fancher, Jaki & Henry Florsheim, Jorge Garcia & Barbara Schinzinger, Wayne Grytting & Kevin Castle, Tim Harris, Barbara Kidder, Pete Knutson & Hing Lau Ng, Sue & Dan May, Jean Moshofsky, Katherine Oldfield, Geov Parrish, Magdeleno Rose-Avila, Norman Solomon, John Weeks & Jeana Kimball, Betsy & Bill Vandercook, Magda Waingrow, and Laura Zanieski. Thanks as well to my Campus Election Engagement Project team of Jonathan Romm, Marcie Smith-West, Sam Menefee-Libey, and Dick Kinsley, to previous core staffer Erica Kay, and to the state Campus Compact directors and all who've supported the project financially.

At Basic, JoAnn Miller commissioned *The Impossible*'s original edition and John Sherer helped make it a success. I'm now delighted to work with a great team of Lara Heimert, Clay Farr, Katy O'Donnell, Leah Strecher, Katie O'Neill, Rachel King, and Michele Jacob. Chris Arden did a superb job in meticulously editing the final revised manuscript. My agent Geri Thoma continues to be my wise navigator through the perilous shoals of publishing, including saving me from endless permissions nightmares. No one could ask for a better or more supportive literary partner. My wonderful wife, Rebecca Feather Hughes, helped in immeasurable ways from the beginning of this book and of *Soul*, and we continue savoring our now-nineteen-year journey. My stepson, William Hughes Martin, is already as fine a writer as I'll ever be, while staking out his own path studying law. Rebecca and William not only share my passion for the written word but also keep reminding me how much more life has to offer.

Credits

"A Slender Thread" by Diane Ackerman. Adapted from *A Slender Thread: Rediscovering Hope at the Heart of Crisis* by Diane Ackerman, copyright © 1996 by Diane Ackerman. Used by permission of Diane Ackerman and Random House, Inc.

"Resisting Terror" by Peter Ackerman and Jack DuVall. Adapted from *A Force More Powerful: A Century of Nonviolent Conflict* by Peter Ackerman and Jack DuVall, copyright © 2000 by Peter Ackerman and Jack DuVall. Reprinted by permission of Peter Ackerman, Jack DuVall, and Palgrave Macmillan.

"Do Not Go Gentle" by Sherman Alexie. Excerpted from *Ten Little Indians* by Sherman Alexie, copyright © 2003 by Sherman Alexie. Used by permission of Sherman Alexie and Grove/Atlantic, Inc.

"Still I Rise" by Maya Angelou. Copyright © 1978 by Maya Angelou. From *And Still I Rise* by Maya Angelou. Used by permission of Random House, Inc.

"Staying the Course" by Mary-Wynne Ashford. Copyright © by Mary-Wynne Ashford. Used by permission of Mary-Wynne Ashford. First appeared in *Peace* magazine.

From "September 1, 1939" by W. H. Auden. Copyright © 1940 and renewed 1968 by W. H. Auden. Excerpted from *Collected Poems* by W. H. Auden. Used by permission of Random House, Inc.

"Origami Emotion" by Elizabeth Barrette. Copyright © 2003 by Elizabeth Barrette. Used by permission of Elizabeth Barrette.

"Composing a Life Story" by Mary Catherine Bateson. Copyright © 1993, 2003 by Mary Catherine Bateson. Reprinted by permission of Mary Catherine Bateson.

"Getting Our Gaze Back" by Rose Marie Berger. Copyright © 2003 by Rose Marie Berger. Used by permission of Rose Marie Berger. First appeared in *Sojourners* magazine.

"The Peace of Wild Things" by Wendell Berry. Excerpted from *Collected Poems: 1957–1982* by Wendell Berry, copyright © 1985 by Wendell Berry. Reprinted by permission of Wendell Berry and Counterpoint Press.

"In What Do I Place My Trust?" by Rosalie Bertell. Copyright © 2003 by Rosalie Bertell. Used by permission of Rosalie Bertell.

"Not Deterred" by Paxus Calta. Copyright © 2003 by Paxus Calta. Used by permission of Paxus Calta.

"The Black Hole" by Ariel Dorfman. Adapted from *Heading South, Looking North* by Ariel Dorfman. Copyright © 1998 by Ariel Dorfman. Reprinted by permission of Ariel Dorfman and Farrar, Straus and Giroux, LLC.

"Imagine the Angels of Bread" by Martín Espada. Excerpted from *Imagine the Angels of Bread: Poems* by Martín Espada. Copyright © 1996 by Martín Espada. Used by permission of Martín Espada and W. W. Norton & Company, Inc.

"Celebration of the Human Voice" by Eduardo Galeano. "Celebration of Human Voices/2," from *The Book of Embraces* by Eduardo Galeano, translated by Cedric Belfrage with Mark Schaefer. Copyright © 1989 by Eduardo Galeano. English translation copyright © 1991 by Cedric Belfrage. Used by permission of Eduardo Galeano and W. W. Norton & Company, Inc.

"We Are All Khaled Said" by Wael Ghonim. From *Revolution 2.0: The Power of the People Is Greater Than the People in Power, A Memoir*. Copyright © 2012 by Wael Ghonim. Used by permission of Houghton Mifflin Harcourt publishing company, all rights reserved.

"The Inevitability Trap" by K. C. Golden. Copyright © 2013 by K. C. Golden. Used by permission of K. C. Golden.

"Political Paralysis" by Danusha Veronica Goska. Copyright © 2003 by Danusha Veronica Goska. Used by permission of Danusha Veronica Goska.

"To Love the Marigold" by Susan Griffin. Copyright © 2003 by Susan Griffin. Used by permission of Susan Griffin. First appeared in *Whole Earth Review* and the *Utne Reader*.

From "The New York Poem" by Sam Hamill. Copyright © 2003 by Sam Hamill. Used by permission of Sam Hamill.

"An Orientation of the Heart" by Václav Havel. Excerpted from *Disturbing the Peace: A Conversation with Karel Hvizdala* by Václav Havel, translated by Paul Wilson, copyright © 1990 by Václav Havel. Used by permission of Alfred A. Knopf, a division of Random House, Inc.

"You are Brilliant and the Earth Is Hiring" by Paul Hawken. Copyright © 2008 by Paul Hawken. Used with permission of Paul Hawken.

From "The Cure at Troy" by Seamus Heaney. Excerpted from *The Cure at Troy: A Version of Sophocles' Philoctetes* by Seamus Heaney. Copyright © 1990 by Seamus Heaney. Reprinted by permission of Farrar, Straus and Giroux, LLC, and Faber and Faber.

"Kids, Trees, and Climate Change" by Mark Hertsgaard. Copyright © 2013 by Mark Hertsgaard. Used by permission of Mark Hertsgaard.

"Stories from the Cha Cha Cha" by Vern Huffman. Copyright © 2003 by Vern Huffman. Used by permission of Vern Huffman.

"Letter from Birmingham Jail" by Martin Luther King. Copyright © 1963 by Martin Luther King, Jr., copyright renewed © 1991 by Coretta Scott King. Reprinted by arrangement with the Estate of Martin Luther King, Jr., c/o Writers House as agent for the proprietor, New York, NY.

"Ordinary Resurrections" by Jonathan Kozol. Adapted from *Ordinary Resurrections* by Jonathan Kozol, copyright © 2000 by Jonathan Kozol. Used by permission of Jonathan Kozol and Crown Publishers, a division of Random House, Inc.

"Despair Is a Lie We Tell Ourselves" by Tony Kushner. Copyright © 2003 by Tony Kushner. Used by permission of Tony Kushner.

"Walking with the Wind" by John Lewis. Excerpted with slight changes from the Prologue to *Walking with the Wind: A Memoir of the Movement* by John Lewis. Copyright © 1998 by John Lewis.

Used by permission of John Lewis and Simon & Schuster Adult Publishing Group.

"The Real Rosa Parks" by Paul Rogat Loeb. Adapted from *Soul of a Citizen: Living by Conviction in a Cynical Time* (St. Martin's Press, 1999), copyright © 1999 by Paul Rogat Loeb. Reprinted by permission of Paul Rogat Loeb and St. Martin's Press.

"The Transformation of Silence" by Audre Lorde. Copyright © 1977 by Audre Lorde. From *Cancer Journals* (Aunt Lute Press, 2006, www.auntlute.com). Reprinted with permission of Aunt Lute Press.

From "Last Night as I Was Sleeping" by Antonio Machado. Excerpted from *Times Alone: Selected Poems of Antonio Machado* by Antonio Machado, translated by Robert Bly, copyright © 1983 by Robert Bly. Reprinted by permission of Wesleyan University Press.

"The Elm Dance" by Joanna Macy. Adapted from *Widening Circles: A Memoir* by Joanna Macy, copyright © 2000 by Joanna Macy. Reprinted by permission of Joanna Macy and New Society Publishers, Ltd.

"The Dark Years" by Nelson Mandela. Excerpted from *Long Walk to Freedom* by Nelson Mandela. Copyright © 1994, 1995 by Nelson Rolihlahla Mandela. By permission of Little, Brown, and Company, Inc.

"Hoping Against Hope" by Nadezhda Mandelstam. Reprinted with the permission of Scribner, an imprint of Simon & Schuster Adult Publishing Group, from *Hoping Against Hope: A Memoir* by Nadezhda Mandelstam. Copyright © 1970 by Atheneum Publishers.

"Curitiba" by Bill McKibben. Excerpted from *Hope, Human and Wild* by Bill McKibben. Copyright © 1995 by Bill McKibben. By permission of Bill McKibben and Little, Brown, and Company, Inc.

"Rough Translation" by Toni Mirosevich. Excerpted from *The Rooms We Make Our Own* by Toni Mirosevich, copyright © 1996 by Toni Mirosevich. Reprinted by permission of Toni Mirosevich and Firebrand Books, Ann Arbor, Michigan.

"The Progressive Story of America" by Bill Moyers. Copyright © 2003 by Bill Moyers. Used with permission of Bill Moyers.

"Childhood and Poetry" by Pablo Neruda, translation by Robert Bly. From *Neruda and Vallejo: Selected Poems* translated by Robert Bly.

Copyright © 1971, 1993 by Robert Bly. Reprinted by permission of Georges Borchardt, Inc., for Robert Bly.

"Fragile and Hidden" by Henri Nouwen. Excerpted from *The Road to Peace: Writings on Peace and Justice* by Henri Nouwen, copyright © 1998 by Henri Nouwen, edited by John Dear. Reprinted by permission of Orbis Books. First appeared as "The Journey from Despair to Hope" in *Praying* magazine.

"Gate A-4" by Naomi Shihab Nye. Copyright © 2008 by Naomi Shihab Nye. Used with permission of Naomi Shihab Nye.

"The Gruntwork of Peace" by Amos Oz. Copyright © 2003 by Amos Oz. Reprinted by permission of Amos Oz. First appeared as "We Have Done the Gruntwork of Peace" in *The Guardian* on October 17, 2003.

"There Is a Season" by Parker Palmer. Adapted from *Let Your Life Speak: Listening for the Voice of Vocation* by Parker Palmer. Copyright © 1999 by Parker Palmer. This material is used by permission of Parker Palmer and John Wiley & Sons, Inc. New material provided by Parker Palmer, by permission.

"To Be of Use" by Marge Piercy. From *Circles on the Water* by Marge Piercy, copyright © 1982 by Marge Piercy. Used by permission of Alfred A. Knopf, a division of Random House, Inc.

"Reluctant Activists" by Mary Pipher. From *The Green Boat: Reviving Ourselves in Our Capsized Culture*, copyright © 2013 by Mary Pipher. Used by permission of Riverhead Books, a division of Penguin Group (USA) LLC.

From "Natural Resources" by Adrienne Rich. Excerpted from *The Fact of a Doorframe: Selected Poems 1950–2001* by Adrienne Rich, copyright © 2002 by Adrienne Rich, copyright © 1978 by W. W. Norton & Company, Inc. Used by permission of Adrienne Rich and W. W. Norton & Company, Inc.

"Is There Hope on Climate Change?" by David Roberts. Copyright © 2013 by David Roberts. Used by permission of David Roberts and *Grist* magazine.

"Come September" by Arundhati Roy. Excerpted from *War Talk* by Arundhati Roy, copyright © 2003 by Arundhati Roy. Based on a talk originally given in Santa Fe, New Mexico, September 18,

2002, sponsored by the Lannan Foundation. Reprinted by permission of Arundhati Roy and South End Press.

"How Have You Spent Your Life?" by Jalaluddin Rumi. From *The Pocket Rumi Reader*, edited by Kabir Helminski, copyright © 2001 by Kabir Helminski. Reprinted by arrangement with Shambhala Publications, Inc., Boston, www.shambhala.com.

"The Small Work in the Great Work" by Victoria Safford. Copyright © 2003 by Victoria Safford. Used by permission from Victoria Safford.

"Mountain Music" by Scott Russell Sanders. Adapted from *Hunting for Hope: A Father's Journeys* by Scott Russell Sanders. Copyright © 1998 by Scott Russell Sanders. Reprinted by permission of Scott Russell Sanders and Beacon Press, Boston.

"On Being Different" by Dan Savage. From *American Savage: Insights, Slights, and Fights on Faith, Sex, Love, and Politics*, copyright © 2013 by Dan Savage. Used by permission of Dutton, a division of Penguins Group (USA) LLC.

"Behemoth in a Bathrobe" by Carla Seaquist. Copyright © 2013 by Carla Seaquist. Used by permission of Carla Seaquist. First appeared in *Christian Science Monitor*.

"Road to Redemption" by Billy Wayne Sinclair. Copyright © 2003 by Billy Wayne Sinclair. Used by permission of Billy Wayne Sinclair.

"Next Year in Mas'Ha" by Starhawk. Copyright © 2003 by Starhawk. Used by permission of Starhawk.

"The Clan of One-Breasted Women" by Terry Tempest Williams. Excerpted from *Refuge: An Unnatural History of Family and Place* by Terry Tempest Williams, copyright © 1991 by Terry Tempest Williams. Reprinted by permission of Terry Tempest Williams and Pantheon Books, a division of Random House, Inc.

"You Have to Pick Your Team" by Sonya Vetra Tinsley, as told to Paul Rogat Loeb. Excerpted from *Soul of a Citizen: Living by Conviction in a Cynical Time* (St. Martin's Press, 1999), copyright © 1999 by Paul Rogat Loeb. Reprinted by permission of Sonya Vetra Tinsley, Paul Rogat Loeb, and St. Martin's Press.

"No Future Without Forgiveness" by Desmond Tutu. Adapted from the author's speeches and from *No Future Without Forgiveness* by Desmond Tutu, copyright © 1999 by Desmond Tutu. Used by permission of Desmond Tutu and Doubleday, a division of Random House, Inc.

"Only Justice Can Stop a Curse" by Alice Walker. Adapted from *Anything We Love Can Be Saved* by Alice Walker (Random House, 1997), copyright © 1997 by Alice Walker, and *In Search of Our Mothers' Gardens: Womanist Prose* by Alice Walker (Harcourt, 1983), copyright © 1983 by Alice Walker. Used by permission of Alice Walker, Random House, Inc., and Harcourt, Inc.

"Faith Works" by Jim Wallis. Adapted from *Faith Works: Lessons from the Life of an Activist Preacher* by Jim Wallis, copyright © 2000 by Jim Wallis. Used by permission of Jim Wallis and Random House, Inc.

"The Sukkah of Shalom" by Arthur Waskow. Excerpted, in part, from " We All Live in a Sukkah," from *From the Ashes: A Spiritual Response to the Attack on America*, collected by the editors of Beliefnet, copyright © 2001 by Rodale, Inc. and Beliefnet, Inc. Permission granted by Arthur Waskow and Rodale, Inc., Emmaus, PA 18098. New material added by Arthur Waskow.

"Prisoners of Hope" by Cornel West. Adapted from *Breaking Bread: Insurgent Black Intellectual Life* by bell hooks and Cornel West (South End Press, 1991), copyright © 1991 by bell hooks and Cornel West; and *Restoring Hope: Conversations on the Future of Black America* by Cornel West, Kelvin Shawn Sealey, and the Obsidian Society (Beacon Press, 1997), copyright © 1997 by Cornel West and Kelvin Shawn Sealey. Reprinted by permission of Cornel West, South End Press, and Beacon Press, Boston.

"From Hope to Hopelessness" by Margaret Wheatley. Copyright © 2003 by Margaret Wheatley. Used by permission of Margaret Wheatley.

"Jesus and Alinsky" by Walter Wink. Copyright © 2003 by Walter Wink. Used by permission of Walter Wink.

"Standing Up for Children" by Marian Wright Edelman. Copyright © 2013 by Marian Wright Edelman. Used by permission of Marian Wright Edelman.

"The Optimism of Uncertainty" by Howard Zinn. Adapted from *Howard Zinn on History: Collected Lectures of Howard Zinn* by Howard Zinn

(Seven Stories Press, 2000), copyright © 2000 by Howard Zinn; and *You Can't Be Neutral on a Moving Train: A Personal History of Our Times* by Howard Zinn (Beacon Press, 1994), copyright © 1994 by Howard Zinn. Reprinted by permission of Howard Zinn, Seven Stories Press, and Beacon Press, Boston. Includes an excerpt from "Once" by Alice Walker, from *Once: Poems* by Alice Walker, copyright © 1968 and renewed 1996 by Alice Walker, reprinted by permission of Alice Walker and Harcourt, Inc.

"Arab Revolutions" by Stephen Zunes. Copyright © 2013 by Stephen Zunes. Used with permission of Stephen Zunes.

Index

About the Editor

Paul Rogat Loeb has spent over forty years researching and writing about citizen responsibility and empowerment—asking what makes some people choose lives of social commitment, while others abstain. Born in California in 1952, Loeb attended Stanford University and New York's New School for Social Research, and worked in both places to end the Vietnam War. Loeb has written for a range of publications including the *New York Times*, *Washington Post*, *USA Today*, *Los Angeles Times*, *Huffington Post*, *AARP Bulletin*, *Redbook*, *Psychology Today*, *Chronicle of Higher Education*, *Boston Globe*, *Christian Science Monitor*, *The Nation*, *Utne Reader*, *Salon*, *Parents Magazine*, *Mother Jones*, *Technology Review*, *Atlanta Journal-Constitution*, *Baltimore Sun*, *San Francisco Chronicle*, *Cleveland Plain Dealer*, *Detroit News*, *San Jose Mercury*, *St. Louis Post Dispatch*, *Academe*, *Sojourners*, *National Catholic Reporter*, *Teaching Tolerance*, *Inside Higher Ed*, and the *International Herald-Tribune*.

Loeb's first book, *Nuclear Culture* (Coward, McCann, and Geoghegan, 1982; New Society Publishers, 1986), explores the daily world of atomic weapons workers in Hanford, Washington. *Hope in Hard Times* (Lexington Books, 1987) examines the lives and visions of ordinary Americans involved in grassroots peace activism. *Generation at the Crossroads: Apathy and Action on the American Campus* (Rutgers University Press, 1994) explores the values and choices of American college students. *Soul of a Citizen* (St. Martin's Press 1999, 2nd edition 2010) looks at what it takes to lead lives of social commitment despite all the obstacles. Including this wholly updated edition, *Soul* has more than 150,000 copies in print. Loeb's anthology on political hope, *The Impossible Will Take a Little While* (Basic Books, 2004, second edition 2014), was named the No. 3 political book of 2004 by the

History Channel and the American Book Association; it also won the Nautilus Award for best social change book.

Because it offers uniquely intimate perspectives on the fundamental questions of our time, Loeb's work has sparked widespread attention. His writing has also been praised, quoted, and discussed in most of the publications above, as well as in *Time*, *Newsweek*, *The Economist*, *AARP Magazine*, *Harper's*, *New York Review of Books*, the *London Sunday Times*, *The Guardian*, *USA Weekend*, *Teacher Magazine*, *NEA Today*, *Family Circle*, *Toronto Globe and Mail*, *Daily Age* (of Melbourne, Australia), the major German paper *Süddeutsche Zeitung*, *National Catholic Reporter*, and the *Atlantic*.

Loeb has given more than a thousand TV and radio interviews, including nationwide appearances on CNN, PBS, C-SPAN, the NBC Nightly News, Fox News, National Public Radio, and the BBC; the ABC, NBC, and CBS radio networks; American Urban Radio; Voice of America; and the national German, Australian, and Canadian radio networks.

Loeb has also lectured to enthusiastic responses at more than four hundred colleges and universities around the country—including Harvard, Yale, Stanford, Chicago, MIT, Brown, Duke, Wisconsin, and Michigan—and has been a lead speaker at numerous conferences including the Education Commission of the States, National Education Association, American Society on Aging, National Youth Leadership Council, National Association of Student Personnel Administrators, Campus Compact's Presidential Summit, the American Bar Association's Equal Justice Conference, the National Conference on Race and Ethnicity on Campus, the all-company meeting of Patagonia Corporation, the Unitarian General Assembly, and the annual provost's conference of the American Association of State Colleges and Universities. In 2008, he founded the national nonpartisan Campus Election Engagement Project, which worked with 750 colleges and universities in 2012 to engage their students in the presidential election, and continues to help engage students in state and local elections.

Contact Loeb for speaking at *lecture@paulloeb.org* or c/o Paul Rogat Loeb, Campus Election Engagement Project, 3232 41st Ave. SW, Seattle, WA 98116. To receive Loeb's articles regularly (about once a month), or for all other information, visit *www.paulloeb.org*.